Springer Compass International

Series Editors
Steven S. Muchnick
Peter Schnupp

Pankaj Jalote

An Integrated Approach to Software Engineering

With 86 Illustrations

Springer-Verlag
New York   Berlin   Heidelberg   London
Paris   Tokyo   Hong Kong   Barcelona

Pankaj Jalote
Indian Institute of Technology Kanpur
Department of Computer Science
and Engineering Kanpur - 208016
India

(formerly with
Department of Computer Science
University of Maryland
College Park, MD 20742)

Series Editors

Steven S. Muchnick
Sun Microsystems, Inc.
Mountainview, CA 94043

Peter Schnupp
Interface Computer GMbh
D-8000 Munich 81
Federal Republic of Germany

Cover art: Pastel on paper (1984), John Pearson

Library of Congress Cataloging-in-Publication Data
Jalote, P.
An integrated approach to software engineering / Pankaj Jalote.
    p. cm. — (Springer compass international)
    Includes bibliographical references and index.
    ISBN 0-387-97561-6. — ISBN 3-540-97561-6
    1. Software engineering. I. Title. II. Series.
QA76.758.J35   1991
005.1—dc20   91-22054

Printed on acid-free paper.

Typeset by TCSystems, Inc., Shippensburg, PA.
Printed and bound by R.R. Donnelley and Sons, Harrisonburg, VA.
Printed in the United States of America.

9 8 7 6 5 4 3 2

ISBN 0-387-97561-6 Springer-Verlag New York Berlin Heidelberg
ISBN 3-540-97561-6 Springer Verlag Berlin Heidelberg New York

Foreword

I barely found the time to write this Foreword. The reason: currently I spend about 120% of my productive time on my workstation looking at (and sometimes producing) code. In this context, "productive time" should be understood to mean "not used for sleeping, eating, and like luxuries." Because actually I *produce* nothing new at all.

Old software hands will already know what I constantly am working at—program maintenance or, more precisely, the non-productive variety of it. I search for errors and rarely find them. Not because there are none but, quite the opposite, because of their very abundance. And if you now think, "well, there are some awful, oldish assembler programs around," you are wrong in my case. The software product haunting me at the moment is a three-year-old X Windows package, "software engineered" in C under UNIX!

I tell you of my plight not (only) to elicit your empathy, but to show you why I like this book by Pankaj Jalote, *An Integrated Approach to Software Engineering,* you now hold in your hands. The perpetrators of the unpractical program joke mentioned above (that I am trying to transform into an industrial-strength software product) were young programmers with an academic background. You can bet that they heard more than one lecture and read more than one book about software-engineering methods. But evidently nobody told them about *practice:* how to work good theory and perhaps even better ideas into readable, dependable, and faultless running code.

That is the main strength of Jalote's approach. He explains the exercises and the topics using real-life examples and problems. Thanks to this book I can at least hope that in the future fewer computer students will produce software like that I now must delve into again. Wish me luck.

Peter Schnupp
March, 1991

Preface

Development of large software systems is an extremely complex activity full of various opportunities to introduce errors. Software Engineering is the discipline that attempts to provide methods to handle this complexity, enabling us to produce reliable software systems with maximum productivity.

This book offers an integrated approach to software engineering. The "integrated" approach is different from others as the different topics are not covered in isolation. A running case study, used throughout the book, illustrates the different activities of software development on the same project. Most of the major outputs of the project, such as the project plan, design document, code, test plan, and test report, are shown for the case study.

It was felt that it is important, and very instructive, not only to teach the principles of software engineering but also apply them to a software development project so that all aspects of development can be clearly seen on a project. Such an approach, besides explaining the principles, also offers a case study which can be used as a model for a software development project by a student.

Integration is further achieved by combining software metrics with the different development phases, instead of having a separate chapter on the subject. It is recognized that metrics are used for controlling and assessing a software project and are employed throughout the life cycle. In the book, for each phase, relevant metrics and their use is discussed in the chapter for that phase. This conveys the correct idea that metrics is not really a separate topic, complete in itself, but is integrated with the different activities of software development. Similarly, quality assurance activities and the control activities that must be performed simultaneously with each phase are described in the chapter for that particular phase.

The sequence of chapters is essentially the same as the sequence of activities performed during software development. All activities (including quality assurance and control activities) that should be performed during a particular phase are grouped in one chapter. This is particularly useful for a project-based introductory course in software engineering, in which the students and the instructor can follow the chapters in the order given both in the lectures as well as in the project.

This book is for students who have not had any previous training in software engineering, and is suitable for a one semester course. In order to limit the scope of the book and focus it for an introductory course, advanced topics such as software reuse, reverse engineering, and development environments have not been included. It was felt that in an introductory course, rather than trying to give a flavor of all the topics, it is best to introduce the student to the discipline of software engineering and to some of the important topics, thus preparing the student for taking advanced courses in software engineering. The need for this approach is especially clear since in the undergraduate curriculum in computer science of most universities, the students have no exposure to software engineering prior to the introductory course, and often do not have any other follow-up course before they graduate. One of the goals of the book is to include only as much material as can be learned in a semester course, which might be the only software engineering course in a computer science student's education.

I am grateful to my colleagues Victor R. Basili and Dieter Rombach for their valuable inputs during the conceptual stages. I am particularly grateful to students in the software engineering courses that I taught at the University of Maryland and the Indian Institute of Technology Kanpur. Teaching and interacting with the students had great influence on the final form of the book. Students in my course at the Indian Institute of Technology, particularly Sandeep Sharma and Samudrala Sridhar, deserve special thanks for helping with the case study.

Contents

1
Introduction to Software Engineering

The evolution of electronic computers began in the 1940s. Early efforts in the field of computing were focused on designing the hardware, as that was the challenge, and hardware was where most technical difficulties existed. In the early computing systems, there was essentially no operating system, and the programs were fed with paper tapes or by switches. With the evolution of second generation machines in the 1950s, early concepts of operating systems evolved and single user operating systems came into existence. High level languages, particularly Fortran and Cobol, along with their compilers were developed. There was a gradual trend towards isolating the user from the machine internals, so the user could concentrate on solving the problem at hand, rather than getting bogged down with the machine details.

With the coming of the multiprogramming operating systems in the early 1960s, the usability and efficiency of the computing machines took a big leap. Prices of hardware also decreased, and awareness of computers increased substantially since their early days. With the availability of cheaper and more powerful machines, higher level languages, and more user-friendly operating systems, the applications of computers grew rapidly. In addition, the nature of software engineering evolved from simple programming exercises to developing software systems, which were much larger in scope, and required great effort by many people. The techniques for writing simple programs could not be scaled up for developing software systems, and the computing world found itself in the midst of a "software crisis". Two conferences, sponsored by NATO Science Committee, were held in Europe in 1960s to discuss the growing software crisis and the need to focus on software development. The term "software engineering" was coined at these meetings.

Now, with the advancement of technology, the cost of hardware is consistently decreasing. On the other hand, the cost of software is increasing. As a result, the HW/SW ratio for a computer system has shown a reversal from the early years, as is shown in Figure 1.1 [Boe76].

1

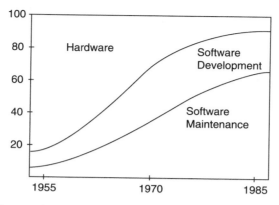

FIGURE 1.1. Hardware-Software cost trends [Boe 76].

The main reason for the high cost of software is that software technology is still labor-intensive. Software projects are often very large, involving many people, and span over many years. The development of these systems is often done in an ad-hoc manner, resulting in frequent schedule slippage and cost overruns in software projects. Some projects are simply abandoned. Hence, there is an urgent need for proper software development methodologies and project management techniques. This is where Software Engineering comes in.

In this chapter we first discuss what we mean by software and software engineering. We then discuss the different phases involved in developing software and the role of project management and software metrics in software development. Finally, we discuss the process models for developing software, with emphasis on the waterfall model.

1.1. Software and Software Engineering

Let us first discuss what we mean by software in the context of software engineering. Software is not merely a collection of computer programs. There is a distinction between a program and a programming systems product. A program is generally complete in itself, and is generally used only by the author of the program. There is usually little documentation or other aids which can help other people use the program. Since the author is the user, the presence of "bugs" is not a major concern; if the program "crashes," the author will "fix" the program and start using it again. These programs are not designed with such issues as portability, reliability, and usability in mind.

A programming system product, on the other hand, is used largely by people other than the developers of the system. The users may be from different backgrounds, so a proper user interface is provided. There is sufficient documentation to help these diverse users use the system. Programs are thoroughly tested before put into operational use, because users do not have the luxury of fixing bugs that may be detected. And since the product may be used in a variety of environments, perhaps on a variety of hardware, portability is a key issue.

Clearly, a program to solve a problem, and a programming systems product to solve the same problem are two entirely different things. Obviously much more effort and resources are required for a programming systems product. Brooks estimates [Bro75] that as a rule of thumb, a programming systems product costs approximately ten times as much as a corresponding program. The software industry is largely interested in developing programming systems products, and most commercial software systems or packages fall in this category. Software engineering is largely concerned with the programming systems product.

Software engineering has to deal with a different set of problems than other engineering disciplines, since the nature of software is different. A software product is an entirely conceptual entity; it has no physical or electrical properties like weight, color, or voltage. Consequently, there are no physical or electrical laws to govern software engineering. In fact, one of the goals of research in software engineering is to form general laws that are applicable to software.

Due to its conceptual nature, there is an "intellectual distance" between the software and the problem the software is solving. This intellectual distance makes it harder for a person who understands the problem to understand the software solving the problem. Due to this intellectual distance, a person responsible for maintaining the software has to spend considerable effort in just trying to understand how the software solves the problem. This makes the task of software maintenance hard and expensive. Clearly, it is desirable to minimize the intellectual distance.

Software failures are also different from failures of, say, mechanical or electrical systems. Products of these other engineering disciplines fail because of the change in physical or electrical properties of the system caused by aging. A software product, on the other hand, never "wears out" due to age. Still we hear about software failing. In software, failures occur due to faults in the conceptual process. In other words, software fails because the design fails. In general, when a design fault is detected in software, changes are usually made to remove that fault so that it causes no failures in the future. Due to this, and other reasons, software must constantly undergo change, which makes maintenance an important issue with software.

With this background we first present the definition of software and software engineering as given in the IEEE glossary on software engineering terminology [Iee87]:

Software is the collection of computer programs, procedures, rules, and associated documentation and data.

Software engineering is the systematic approach to the development, operation, maintenance, and retirement of software.

Another definition from the economic and human perspective is given by Boehm [Boe81] by combining the dictionary's definition of engineering with its definition of software. His definition states:

Software Engineering is the application of science and mathematics by which the capabilities of computer equipment are made useful to man via computer programs, procedures, and associated documentation.

There are a few points worth noting about these definitions. First, software is not just the program, but comprises all of the associated data and documentation as well. This statement is perhaps obvious to someone working in the field, as most practitioners know that a program (particularly object code) is not much use to the user without proper documentation. However, for many students the term software is often synonymous with computer programs. Hence, the undue attention paid to writing of programs in most universities. An implication of the first definition is that the methodologies for software development should also focus on the development of data and documentation, and not simply on the development of computer programs. A good software engineer should learn more than just producing programs.

The use of the terms "systematic approach" or "mathematics and science" for the development of software means that software engineering is to provide methodologies for developing software that are as close to the scientific method as possible. That is, these methodologies are repeatable, and if the methodology is applied by different people similar software will be produced. In essence, the goal of software engineering is to take software development closer to science and away from being an "art".

The phrase "usable to man" emphasizes the needs of the user and the software's interface with the user.This definition implies that user needs should be given due importance in the development of software, and the final program should give importance to the user interface.

The basic **goal of software engineering** is to produce high quality software at low cost. The two basic driving factors are quality and cost. Cost of a completed project can be calculated easily if proper accounting procedures are followed. Quality of software is something not so easy to quantify and measure.

There are a number of factors that determine **software quality.** One can combine these different factors into one "quality metric", but the relative weights of these different factors will depend on the overall objectives of the project. Taking a broad view of software quality we can specify three dimensions of the product whose quality is to be assessed [Cav78]:

Product Operations
Product Transition
Product Revision

The first factor of product operations deals with quality factors such as correctness, reliability, and efficiency. Product transition deals with quality factors like portability and interoperability. The product revision is concerned with those aspects related to modification of programs and include factors like maintainability and testability. These three dimensions and the different factors for each are shown in Figure 1.2.

Correctness is the extent to which a program satisfies its specifications. Reliability is the property which defines how well the software meets its requirements. Efficiency is a factor in all issues relating to the execution of software, and includes such considerations as response time, memory requirement, and throughput. Usability, or the effort required to learn and operate the software properly, is an important property that emphasizes the human aspect of the system. Maintainability is the effort required to locate and fix errors in operating programs. Testability is the effort required to test to ensure that the system or a module performs its intended function. Flexibility is the effort required to modify an operational program (perhaps to enhance its functionality). Portability is the effort required to transfer the software from one hardware configuration to an-

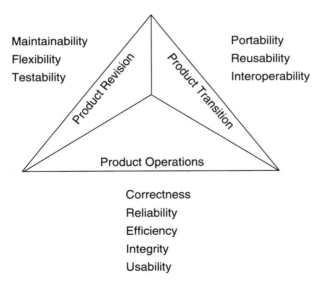

FIGURE 1.2. Software quality factors [Cav 78].

other. Reusability is the extent to which parts of the software can be reused in other related applications. Interoperability is the effort required to couple the system with other systems.

1.2. Phases in Software Development

Whenever we develop a program or build something, there are some activities we perform, either explicitly or implicitly. Suppose that Mr. X, a computer programmer, buys a car, and wants to write a program to verify that his car payments are correct. With this eventual goal, what is the first thing X will do? The first natural thing to do is to try to understand the problem better and more precisely. He will identify that the inputs are the cost of the car, the interest rate, the duration of the loan, and the monthly payment the car dealer has told him. The goal is to determine, given these inputs, if the payment is consistent with the other inputs. Mr. X may do this problem definition implicitly in his mind and without realizing it. However, the problem must always be clearly understood by the programmer, before he starts coding.

The next step that X will take is to decide what course he should follow—should he determine the payments and then compare, or should he use the payments as data and determine the rate and check the rate? What algorithm should he use? In other words, before he starts coding, he has to have a plan in his mind about how to solve the problem. What will he code, if he does not know what he is trying to code? Again, this activity of deciding a plan for a solution may be done implicitly by Mr. X, perhaps while sitting on the terminal and in parallel with coding itself. However, a plan for a solution must be thought of. Once he has coded the plan, he will try to test and debug it.

From this situation we can say that problem solving in software must consist of these activities—understanding the problem, deciding a plan for a solution, coding the planned solution, and finally testing the actual program. For small problems, these activities may not be done explicitly. The start and end boundaries of these activities may not be clearly defined, and no written record of the activities may be kept. However, for large systems where the problem solving activity may last over a few years, and where many people are involved in development, performing these activities implicitly without proper documentation and representation will clearly not work.

For any software system of a non-trivial nature, each of the four activities for problem solving listed above has to be done formally. For large systems, each activity can be extremely complex and methodologies and procedures are needed to perform it efficiently and correctly. Each of these activities is a major task for large software projects. Furthermore, each of the basic activities itself may be so large that it cannot be handled in a single step and must be broken into smaller steps. For example, design of a large software system is almost always broken into multiple, distinct design phases, starting from a very high level design specifying only the components in the system to a detailed design where the logic of the components is specified. The basic activities or phases to be performed for developing a software system are:

Requirements Analysis
Design
Coding
Testing

In addition to the activities performed during software development, some activities are performed after the main development is complete. There is often an Installation (also called Implementation) phase, which is concerned with actually installing the system on the client's computer systems and then testing it. Then, there is software maintenance. *Maintenance* is an activity that commences after the software is developed and deployed. Software needs to be maintained not because some of its components "wear out" and need to be replaced, but because there are often some residual errors remaining in the system which must be removed later as they are discovered. Furthermore, the software often must be upgraded and enhanced to include more "features" and provide more services. This also requires modification of the software. Hence, maintenance is unavoidable for software systems.

In most commercial software developments there are also some activities performed before the requirement analysis takes place. These can be combined into a *feasibility analysis phase*. In this phase the feasibility of the project is analyzed, and a business proposal is put forth, with a very general plan for the project and some cost estimates. For feasibility analysis, some understanding of the major requirements of the system is essential. Once the business proposal is accepted or the contract is awarded, the development activities begin starting with the requirements analysis phase.

In this book we will focus on the activities performed during the development of software. We will only briefly discuss the later phases of installation and maintenance, and will not discuss the feasibility phase. In the remainder of this section, we give an overview of the main phases, and then make some observations about how effort and errors are distributed over these phases.

1.2.1. Requirements Analysis

Requirements analysis is done in order to understand the problem which the software system is to solve. For example, the problem could be automating an existing manual process, or developing a completely new automated system, or a combination of the two. For large systems which have a large number of features, and that need to perform many different tasks, understanding the requirements of the system is a major task. The emphasis in requirements analysis is on identifying *what* is needed from the system, and not *how* the system will achieve its goals. This task is complicated by the fact that there are often at least two parties involved in software development—a client and a developer. The developer has to develop the system to satisfy the client's needs. The developer usually does not understand the client's problem domain, and the client often does not understand the issues involved in software systems. This causes a communication gap, which has to be adequately bridged during requirements analysis.

In most software projects, the requirements phase ends with a document describing all the requirements. In other words, the goal of the requirements specification phase is to produce the **software requirements specification** document (also called the **requirements document**). The person responsible for the requirements analysis is often called the *analyst*.

There are two major activities in this phase—problem understanding or analysis, and requirement specification. In problem analysis, the analyst has to understand the problem and its context. Such analysis typically requires a thorough understanding of the existing system, the parts of which must be automated. A clear understanding is needed of the important data entities in the system, major centers where action is taken, the purpose of the different actions that are performed, and the inputs and outputs. This requires interacting with clients and end users, as well as studying the existing manuals and procedures. With the analysis of the current system, the analyst can understand the reasons for automation and what effects the automated system might have.

Understanding the existing system is usually just the starting activity in problem analysis, and is relatively simple. The goal of this activity is to understand the requirements of the new system that is to be developed. Understanding the properties of a system that does not exist is more difficult, and requires creative thinking. The problem is more complex since a newly automated system offers possibilities that did not exist in the old system, and can affect the way in which the system operates. Consequently, even the client may not really know the needs of the system. The analyst has to make the client aware of the new possibilities, thus helping both client and analyst determine the requirements for the new system.

Once the problem is analyzed and the essentials understood, the requirements must be specified in the requirement specification document. For requirement specification in the form of a document, some specification language has to be selected (e.g. English, regular expressions, tables, or a combination of these). The requirements document must specify all functional and performance requirements, the formats of inputs, outputs, and any required standards, and all design constraints that exist due to political, economic, environmental, and security reasons. For example, the kind of security, recovery or logging requirements that exist should be defined. In other words, besides the functionality required from the system, all the factors that may effect the design and proper functioning of the system should be specified in the requirements document. A preliminary user manual that describes all the major user interfaces frequently forms a part of the requirements document.

The phase ends with validation of the requirements specified in the document. The basic purpose of validation is to make sure that the requirements specified in the document actually reflect the actual requirements or needs, and that all requirements are specified. Validation is often done through *requirement review,* in which a group of people, including representatives of the client, critically review the requirements specification.

1.2.2. Software Design

The purpose of the design phase is to plan a solution of the problem specified by the requirements document. This phase is the first step in moving from the problem domain to the solution domain. In other words, starting with *what* is needed, design takes us towards *how* to satisfy the needs. The design of a system is perhaps the most critical factor affecting the quality of the software, and has a major impact on the later phases, particularly testing and maintenance. The output of this phase is the **design document.** This document is similar to a blue print or plan for the solution, and is used later during implementation, testing and maintenance.

The design activity is often divided into two separate phases—**system design** and **detailed design. System design,** which is sometimes also called **top-level design,** aims to identify the modules that should be in the system, the specifications of these modules, and how they interact with each other to produce the desired results. At the end of system design all the major data structures, file formats, output formats, as well as the major modules in the system and their specifications are decided.

During **detailed design** the internal logic of each of the modules specified in system design is decided. During this phase further details of the data structures and algorithmic design of each of the modules is specified. The logic of a module is usually specified in a high-level design description language, which is independent of the target language in which the software will eventually be implemented.

In system design the focus is on identifying the modules, whereas during detailed design the focus is on designing the logic for each of the modules. In other words, in system design the attention is on *what* components are needed, while in detailed design *how* the components can be implemented in software is the issue.

During the design phase, often two separate documents are produced— one for the system design, and one for the detailed design. Together, these documents completely specify the design of the system. That is, they specify the different modules in the system and the internal logic of each of the modules.

A *design methodology* is a systematic approach to creating a design by application of a set of techniques and guidelines. Most methodologies focus on system design. The two basic principles used in any design methodology are *problem partitioning* and *abstraction*. A large system cannot be handled as a whole, and so for design it is partitioned into smaller systems. This partitioning process can continue further till we reach a stage where the components are small enough to be designed separately. This "divide and conquer" method is essential for handling large projects, and all design methodologies provide methods to partition the problem effectively.

Abstraction is a concept related to problem partitioning. When partitioning is used during design, the design activity focuses on one part of the system at a time. Since the part being designed interacts with other parts of the system, a clear understanding of the interaction is essential for properly designing the part. For this, abstraction is used. An abstraction of a system or a part defines the overall behavior of the system at an abstract level without giving the internal details. While working with a part of the system, a designer needs to understand only the abstractions of the other parts with which the part being designed interacts. The use of abstraction allows the designer to practice the "divide and conquer" technique effectively by focusing on one part at a time, without worrying about the details of other parts.

During system design, the partitioning of the system has to be done in a manner such that the eventual system is modular. A system is modular if it consists of a set of discreet components such that each component supports a well defined abstraction, and a change to one component has minimal impact on other components. Modularity is clearly desirable for implementation and maintenance. Modularity is determined during system design. To provide modularity, a designer has to make sure that the modules specified during system design have minimal interconnections with one another, and that each module is internally cohesive.

Like every other phase, the design phase ends with verification of the design. If the design is not specified in some executable language, the verification has to be done by evaluating the design documents. One way of doing this is through reviews. Typically, at least two design reviews are held—one for the system design and one for the detailed design.

1.2.3. Coding

Once the design is complete, most of the major decisions about the system have been made. However, many of the details about coding the designs, which often depend on the programming language chosen, are not specified during design. The goal of the coding phase is to translate the design of the system into code in a given programming language. For a given design, the aim in this phase is to implement the design in the best possible manner.

The coding phase affects both testing and maintenance profoundly. A well written code can reduce the testing and maintenance effort. Since the testing and maintenance costs of software are much higher than the coding cost, the goal of coding should be to reduce the testing and maintenance effort. Hence, during coding the focus should be on developing programs that are easy to read and understand, and not simply on developing programs that are easy to write. Simplicity and clarity should be strived for during the coding phase.

An important concept that helps the understandability of programs is *structured programming*. The goal of structured programming is to linearize the control flow in the program. That is, the program text should be organized as a sequence of statements, and during execution the statements are executed in the sequence given in the program. For structured programming, a few single-entry-single-exit constructs should be used. These constructs include selection (if-then-else), and iteration (while-do, repeat-until etc.). With these constructs it is possible to construct a program as a sequence of single-entry-single-exit constructs.

There are many methods available for verifying the code. Some methods are static in nature; that is, they do not involve execution of the code. Examples of such methods are data flow analysis, code reading, code reviews. Testing is a method that involves executing the code, and is used very heavily. In the coding phase, the entire system is not tested together. Rather, the different modules are tested separately. This testing of modules is called "unit testing". Consequently, this phase is often referred to as "coding and unit testing".

The output of this phase is the verified and unit tested code of the different modules.

1.2.4. Testing

Testing is the major quality control measure employed during software development. Its basic function is to detect errors in the software. During requirements analysis and design, the output is a document that is usually textual and non-executable. After the coding phase, computer programs are available that can be executed for testing purposes. This implies that testing not only has to uncover errors introduced during coding, but also errors introduced during the previous phases. Thus, the goal of testing is to uncover requirement, design or coding errors in the programs. Consequently, different levels of testing are employed.

The starting point of testing is unit testing. In this a module is tested separately and is often performed by the coder himself simultaneously with the coding of the module. The purpose is to exercise the different parts of the module code to detect coding errors. After this the modules are gradually integrated into subsystems, which are then integrated themselves to eventually form the entire system. During integration of modules, *integration testing* is performed. The goal of this testing is to detect design errors, while focussing on testing the interconnection between modules.

After the system is put together, *system testing* is performed. Here the system is tested against the system requirements to see if all the requirements are met and the system performs as specified by the requirements. Finally, *acceptance testing* is performed to demonstrate to the client, on the real life data of the client, the operation of the system.

For testing to be successful, proper selection of testcases is essential. There are two different approaches to selecting testcases—functional testing and structural testing. In *functional testing* the software or the module to be tested is treated as a black box, and the testcases are decided based on the specifications of the system or the module. For this reason, this form of testing is also called "black box testing". The focus here is on testing the external behavior of the system. In *structural testing* the testcases are decided based on the logic of the module to be tested. A common approach here is to achieve some type of coverage of the statements in the code. One common coverage criterion is statement coverage, which requires that testcases be selected so that together they execute each statement at least once. Structural testing is sometimes called "glass box testing". The two forms of testing are complementary: one tests the external behavior, the other tests the internal structure. Often structural testing is used only for lower levels of testing, while functional testing is used for higher levels.

Testing is an extremely critical and time consuming activity. It requires proper planning of the overall testing process. Frequently the testing process starts with a **test plan.** This plan identifies all the testing related activities that must be performed and specifies the schedule, allocates the resources, and specifies guidelines for testing. The test plan specifies conditions that should be tested, different units to be tested, and the manner in which the modules will be integrated together. Then for different test units, a *testcase specification document* is produced, which lists all the different testcases, together with the expected outputs, that will be used for testing. During the testing of the unit the specified testcases are executed and the actual result compared with the expected output. The final output of the testing phase is the **test report** and the *error report,* or a set of such reports (one for each unit tested). Each test report contains the set of testcases and the result of executing the code with these testcases. The error report describes the errors encountered and the action taken to remove the error.

1.2.5. Maintenance

Maintenance is not a part of software development, but is an extremely important activity in the life of a software product. Maintenance includes all the activities after the installation of software that are performed to keep the system operational. As we have mentioned above, software often has design faults. The two major forms of maintenance activities are *adaptive maintenance,* and *corrective maintenance.*

It is generally agreed that for large systems, removing all the faults before delivery is extremely difficult, and faults will be discovered long after the system is installed. As these faults are detected, they have to be removed. Maintenance activities related to fixing of errors fall under *corrective maintenance.*

Removing errors is one of the activities of maintenance. Maintenance is also needed due to a change in the environment or the requirements of a system. The introduction of a software system affects the work environment. This change in environment often changes what is desired from the system. Furthermore, often after the system is installed and the users have had a chance to work with it for some time, some of the needs that were not uncovered during requirement analysis surface. This occurs since the experience with the software helps the user define the needs more precisely. There might also be changes in the input data, the system environment, and output formats. All these require modification of the software. The maintenance activities related to such modifications fall under *adaptive maintenance.*

Maintenance work is based on existing software, as compared to development work which creates new software. Consequently, maintenance revolves around understanding existing software and maintainers spend most of their time trying to understand the software they have to modify. Understanding the software involves not only understanding the code, but also the related documents. During the modification of the software, the effects of the change have to be clearly understood by the maintainer since introducing undesired side effects in the system during modification is easy. To test whether those aspects of the system that are not supposed to be modified are operating as they were before modification, *regression testing* is done. Regression testing involves executing old testcases to test that no new errors have been introduced.

Thus, maintenance involves understanding the existing software (code and related documents), understanding the effects of change, making the changes—both to the code and to the documents, testing the new parts (changes), and retesting the old parts that were not changed. Since often during development needs of the maintainers are not kept in mind, little support documents are produced during development to aid the maintainer. The complexity of the maintenance task, coupled with the neglect of maintenance concerns during development, makes maintenance the most costly activity in the life of a software product.

1.2.6. Effort Distribution with Phases

A typical software product may take a few months to a few years for development, and is in operation for five to twenty years before it is retired. For software, the cost of development is the cost incurred during requirements analysis, design, coding and testing. Thus the development cost is total cost incurred before the product delivery. The cost of maintenance is the cost of modifying the software due to residual faults in the software, for enhancing or for updating the software. This cost is spread over the operational years of the software. Software engineers generally agree that the total cost of maintenance is *more* than the cost of development of software. The ratio of development to maintenance cost has been variously suggested as 40/60, 30/70 or even lower. However, it is generally accepted that the cost of maintenance is likely to be higher than the development cost. This is significant because in most development projects, the developers are most concerned with reducing the development cost, and are often not at all concerned with the maintenance cost. Since, maintenance depends critically on the software characteristics that are decided during development, maintenance costs can be reduced if maintenance concerns are kept in the forefront during development. One of the reasons why this is often not done is that the development cost is borne by the developers while maintenance is often done by the users. Hence, the developers do not have much incentive for increasing the development effort, in order to reduce the maintenance cost. However, for reduction in overall cost of software, it is imperative that the software be developed so maintenance is easy.

Of the development cost, a typical distribution of effort with the different phases is

Requirements	10%
Design	20%
Coding	20%
Testing	50%

The exact numbers will differ with organization and the type of the project. However, there are some observations we can make. First is that coding consumes only a small percentage of the development effort. This is against the common and naïve notion that developing software is largely concerned with writing programs, and that programming is the major activity. The second important observation is that testing consumes the most resources during development. This is again contrary to the common practice which considers testing as a side activity which is often not properly planned. Underestimating the testing effort often causes the planners to allocate insufficient resources for testing. Insufficient testing in turn results in unreliable software or schedule slippages.

There are some lessons we can derive from the data given above. The first is that the goal of design and coding should not be to reduce the cost of design and coding, but should be to reduce the cost of testing and maintenance, even at the expense of increasing the design and coding cost. Both testing and maintenance depend heavily on the design and coding of software, and these costs can be considerably reduced if the software is designed and coded to make testing and maintenance easier. Hence, during design and implementation the prime issues in our minds should be "can the design be easily tested", and "can it be easily modified". These may require alternate designs, and may increase the cost of design and coding, but this additional cost will pay dividends in the later phases.

1.2.7. Error Distribution

The notion that programming is the central activity during software development is largely because historically programming has been considered to be a difficult task and sometimes an "art". Another consequence of this kind of thinking is the belief that errors largely occur during programming, as it is the hardest activity in software development and offers many opportunities for committing errors. It is now realized that errors can occur at any stage during development. A typical distribution of error occurrences by phase is

Requirements analysis	20%
Design	30%
Coding	50%

As we can see, errors occur throughout the development process. However, the cost of correcting errors of different phases is not the same and depends on when the error is detected and corrected. The cost of correcting errors as a function of where they occur and where they are detected is shown in Figure 1.3 [Dun84].

As one would expect, the greater the delay in detecting an error after it occurs, the more expensive it is to correct it. As the figure shows, an error that occurs during the requirements phase, if corrected after coding is complete, can cost many times more than correcting the error during the requirements phase itself. The reason for this is fairly obvious. If there is an error in the requirements, then the design and the code will be affected by it. To correct the error after the coding is done would require both the design and the code to be changed, thereby increasing the cost of correction.

The main moral of this section is that we should attempt to detect errors that occur in a phase during that phase itself, and should not wait until testing to detect errors. This is not often practiced. In reality, sometimes testing is the sole point where errors are detected. Besides the cost factor, reliance on testing as the primary source for error detection, due to the limitations of testing, will also result in unreliable software. Error detection and correction should be a continuous process that is done throughout software development. In terms of the development phases, what this means is that we should try to validate each phase before starting with the next.

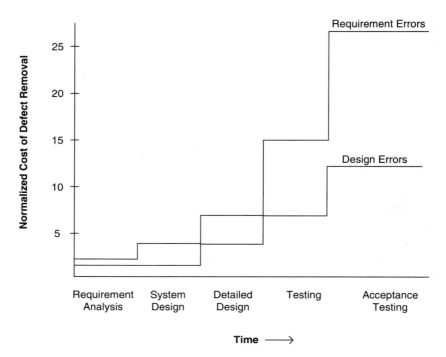

FIGURE 1.3. Cost of correcting errors [Dun 84].

1.3. Software Development Process Models

The goal of any development effort (to develop software or something else) is to produce some **product.** A **development process** is a set of activities, together with an ordering relationship between activities, which if performed in a manner that satisfies the ordering relationship will produce the desired product. A **process model** is an abstract representation of a development process.

In a software development effort the goal is to produce high quality software. The development process is, therefore, the sequence of activities that will produce such software. We have seen that the basic phases are requirements analysis, design, coding and testing, which are usually further broken down into distinct activities. A software development process model specifies how these activities are organized in the entire software development effort.

The purpose of specifying a development process model is to suggest an overall process for developing software. This could be different from the actual process that is employed by a company or a group of people. Existing development processes can also be modeled, and such an exercise is useful for determining the weaknesses in existing practices. The intent of this section is to describe some models which have been proposed for software development.

1.3.1. Waterfall Model

The simplest process model is the *waterfall model,* which states that the phases are organized in a linear order. A project begins with feasibility analysis. On successfully demonstrating the feasibility of the project, the requirements analysis and project planning begins. The design starts after the requirements analysis is complete, and coding begins after the design is complete. Once the programming is completed, the code is integrated and testing is done. On successful completion of testing, the system is installed. After this the regular operation and maintenance of the system takes place. The model is shown in Figure 1.4.

In this book, we will only discuss the activities related to the development of software. That is, we will only discuss phases starting from requirements analysis to testing. The requirements analysis phase is mentioned as "analysis and planning". *Planning* is a critical activity in software development. A good plan is based on the requirements of the system and should be done before later phases begin. However, in practice, detailed requirements are not necessary for planning. Consequently, planning usually overlaps with the requirements analysis, and a plan is ready before the later phases begin. This plan is an additional input to all the later phases.

With the waterfall model, the sequence of activities performed in a software development project is: requirement analysis, project planning, system design, detailed design, coding and unit testing, system integration and testing. This is the order that the different phases will be discussed in this book, keeping the sequence as close as possible to the sequence in which the activities are actually performed.

Linear ordering of activities has some important consequences. First, to clearly identify the end of a phase and beginning of the other, some certification mechanism has to be employed at the end of each phase. This is usually done by some verification and validation means that will ensure that the output of a phase is consistent with its input (which is the output of the previous phase), and that the output of the phase is consistent with overall requirements of the system.

The consequence of the need for certification is that each phase must have some defined output that can be evaluated and certified. Thus, when the activities of a phase are completed, there should be an output product of that phase, and the goal of a phase is to produce this product. The outputs of the earlier phases are often called *intermediate products* and are usually in form of documents like the requirements document or design document. For the coding phase the output is the code. From this point of view, the output of a software project is not just the final program along

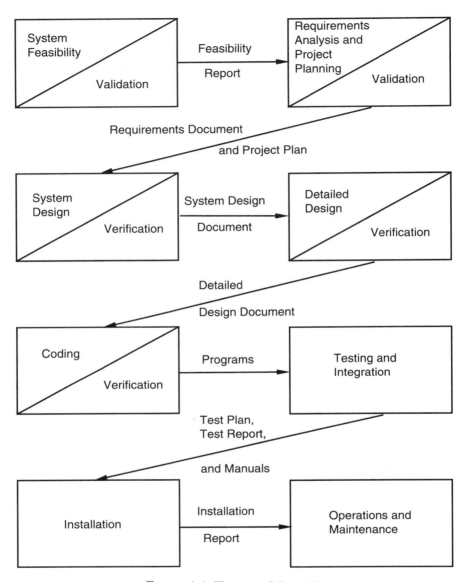

FIGURE 1.4. The waterfall model.

with the user documentation, but also the requirements document, design document, project plan, test plan, and test results.

Another implication of the linear ordering of phases [Boe81] is that after each phase is complete and its outputs certified, these outputs become the inputs to the next phase and should not be changed or modified. However, changing requirements is a reality that must be faced. Since changes performed in the output of one phase affect the later phases that might have been performed, these changes have to be made in a controlled manner, after evaluating the effect of each change on the project. This brings us to the need for **configuration control** or **configuration management.** The certified output of a phase that is released for the next phase is called a **baseline.** The configuration management ensures that any changes to a baseline are made after careful review, keeping in mind the interests of all parties that are affected by it.

Let us now consider the rationale behind the waterfall model. There are two basic assumptions for justifying the linear ordering of phases in the manner proposed by the waterfall model [Boe81].

1. For a successful project resulting in a successful product, all phases listed in the waterfall model must be performed anyway.
2. Any different ordering of the phases will result in a less successful software product.

A successful software product is one that satisfies all the objectives of the development project. These objectives include satisfying the requirements, and performing the development within time and cost constraints. Generally, for any reasonable size project, all the phases listed in the model must be performed explicitly and formally. Informally performing the phases will work only for very small projects.

The second reason is the one that is now under debate. For many projects, the linear ordering of these phases is clearly the optimum way to organize these activities. However, some argue that for many projects this ordering of activities is infeasible or sub-optimum. We will discuss some of these ideas shortly. Still, the waterfall model is conceptually the simplest process model for software development that has been used most often.

PROJECT OUTPUTS IN WATERFALL MODEL

As we have seen, the output of a project employing the waterfall model is not just the final program along with documentation to use it. There are a number of intermediate outputs which must be produced in order to produce a successful product. Though the set of documents that should be produced in a project is somewhat dependent upon the nature of the project, the following is a set of documents that forms the minimum that should be produced in each project.

Requirements document
Project plan
System design document
Detailed design document
Test plan and test report

Final code
Software manuals (e.g. user, installation, etc.)
Review reports

Except for the last one, these are all the outputs of the phases, and have been briefly discussed above. In order to certify an output product of a phase before the next phase begins, reviews are often held. Reviews are necessary especially for the requirements and design phases, since other certification means are frequently not available. Reviews are formal meetings to uncover deficiencies in a product, and will be discussed in more detail later. The review reports are the outcome of these reviews.

LIMITATIONS OF THE WATERFALL MODEL

The waterfall model, although widely used, has received some criticism. Here we list some of these criticisms.

1. The waterfall model assumes that the requirements of a system can be frozen (i.e. baselined) before the design begins. This is possible for systems designed to automate an existing manual system. But for absolutely new systems, determining the requirements is difficult as the user himself does not know the requirements. Hence having unchanging (or changing only a few)requirements is unrealistic for such projects.
2. Freezing the requirements usually requires choosing the hardware (since it forms a part of the requirement specification). A large project might take a few years to complete. If the hardware is selected early, then due to the speed at which hardware technology is changing, it is quite likely that the final software will employ a hardware technology that is on the verge of becoming obsolete. This is clearly not desirable for such expensive software systems.
3. The waterfall model stipulates that the requirements should be completely specified before the rest of the development can proceed. In some situations it might be desirable to first develop a part of the system completely, and then later enhance the system in phases. This is often done for software products that are developed not necessarily for a client (where the client plays an important role in requirement specification), but for general marketing, in which case the requirements are likely to be determined largely by the developers themselves.

Due to these limitations, some alternate models have been proposed for developing software, and work is ongoing for developing alternate models or for providing the technology to make some of the current models feasible. Here we will briefly describe some of these models.

1.3.2. Prototyping

The goal of prototyping based development is to counter the first two limitations of the waterfall model discussed above. The basic idea here is that instead of freezing the requirements before any design or coding can proceed, a throwaway prototype is built to help understand the requirements. This prototype is developed based on the currently known requirements. Development of the prototype obviously undergoes design, coding and testing, but each of these phases is not done very formally or thoroughly. By using this prototype the client can get an "actual feel" of the system, since the interactions with the prototype can enable the client to better understand the requirements of the desired system.

Prototyping is an attractive idea for complicated and large systems for which there is no manual process or existing system to help determine the requirements. In such situations letting the client "play" with the prototype provides invaluable and intangible inputs which help in determining the requirements for the system. It is also an effective method of demonstrating the feasibility of a certain approach. This might be needed for novel systems where it is not clear that constraints can be met or that algorithms can be developed to implement the requirements. The process model of the prototyping approach is shown in Figure 1.5.

The basic reason for little common use of prototyping is the cost involved in this build-it-twice approach. However, some argue that prototyping need not be very costly and can actually reduce the overall development cost. The prototypes are usually not complete systems and many of the details are not built in the prototype. The goal is to provide a system with overall functionality. In addition, the cost of testing and writing detailed documents is reduced. These factors help reduce the cost of developing the prototype. On the other hand, the experience of developing the prototype will be very useful for developers when developing

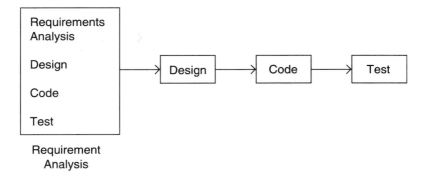

FIGURE 1.5. The prototyping model.

the final system. This experience will help reduce the cost of development of the final system and should result in a more reliable and better designed system.

1.3.3. Iterative Enhancement

The iterative enhancement model [Bas75] counters the third limitation of the waterfall model, and tries to combine the benefits of both prototyping and the waterfall model. The basic idea is that the software should be developed in increments, each increment adding some functional capability to the system, until the full system is implemented. At each step, extensions and design modifications can be made. An advantage of this approach is that it can result in better testing since testing each increment is likely to be easier than testing the entire system, as in the waterfall model. Furthermore, as in prototyping, the increments provide feedback to the client which is useful for determining the final requirements of the system.

In the first step of this model, a simple initial implementation is done for a subset of the overall problem. This subset is one that contains some of the key aspects of the problem which are easy to understand and implement, and which form a useful and usable system. A *project control list* is created that contains, in order, all the tasks that must be performed to obtain the final implementation. This project control list gives an idea of how far the project is at any given step from the final system.

Each step consists of removing the next step from the list, designing the implementation for the selected task, coding and testing the implementation, and performing an analysis of the partial system obtained after this step and updating the list as a result of the analysis. These three phases are called the *design phase, implementation phase,* and *analysis phase.* The process is iterated until the project control list is empty, at which time the final implementation of the system will be available. The iterative enhancement process model is shown in Figure 1.6.

The project control list guides the iteration steps and keeps track of all tasks that must be done. The tasks in the list can include redesign of defective components found during analysis. Each entry in the list is a task that should be performed in one step of the iterative enhancement process, and should be simple enough to be completely understood. Selecting tasks in this manner will minimize the chances of error and reduce the redesign work. The design and implementation phases of each step can be performed in a top-down manner or by using some other technique.

1.3.4. The Spiral Model

This is a recent model that has been proposed by Boehm [Boe88]. As the name suggests, the activities in this model can be organized like a spiral.

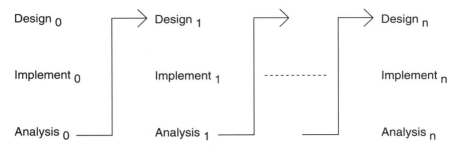

Design $_0$ Design $_1$ Design $_n$

Implement $_0$ Implement $_1$ - - - - - - - - - - -   Implement $_n$

Analysis $_0$ Analysis $_1$ Analysis $_n$

FIGURE 1.6. The iterative enhancement model.

The spiral has many cycles. The radial dimension represents the cumulative cost incurred in accomplishing the steps done so far, and the angular dimension represents the progress made in completing each cycle of the spiral. The model is shown in Figure 1.7.

Each cycle in the spiral begins with the identification of objectives for that cycle, the different alternatives that are possible for achieving the objectives, and the imposed constraints. The next step in the cycle is to evaluate these different alternatives based on the objectives and constraints. This will also involve identifying uncertainties and risks involved. The next step is to develop strategies that resolve the uncertainties and risks. This step may involve activities such as benchmarking, simulation, and prototyping. Next, the software is developed, keeping in mind the risks. Finally the next stage is planned.

The next step is determined by the remaining risks. For example, if performance or user-interface risks are considered more important than the program development risks, the next step may be an evolutionary development that involves developing a more detailed prototype for resolving the risks. On the other hand, if the program development risks dominate and the previous prototypes have resolved all the user-interface and performance risks, the next step will follow the basic waterfall approach.

The risk driven nature of the spiral model allows it to accommodate any mixture of specification-oriented, prototype-oriented, simulation-oriented, or some other approach. An important feature of the model is that each cycle of the spiral is completed by a review which covers all the products developed during that cycle, including plans for the next cycle. The spiral model works for development as well as enhancement projects.

In a typical application of the spiral model, one might start with an extra *round zero,* in which the feasibility of the basic project objectives is studied. These project objectives may or may not lead to a development/enhancement project. Such "high-level" objectives include increasing the

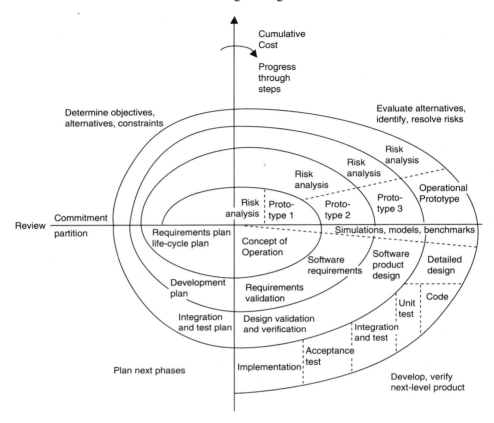

FIGURE 1.7. The spiral model.

efficiency of code generation of a compiler, producing a new full screen text editor, and developing an environment for improving productivity. The alternatives considered in this round are also typically very high-level, such as, should the organization go for in-house development, or should they contract development, or should they buy an existing product. In *round one,* a concept of operation might be developed. The objectives are stated more precisely and quantitatively and the cost and other constraints are defined precisely. The risks here are typically whether or not the goals can be met within the constraints. The plan for the next phase will be developed which will involve defining separate activities for the project. In *round two* the top-level requirements are developed. In *succeeding rounds* the actual development may be done.

This is a relatively new model and can encompass different development strategies. In addition to the development activities, it incorporates some of the management and planning activities into the model. For high risk projects this might be a preferred model.

1.4. Role of Management in Software Development

Proper management is an *integral* part of software development. A large software development project involves many people working for a long period of time. For these people to work efficiently, they have to be organized properly and work must be divided into different parts so that people can work independently. Then progress of these parts must be monitored, and corrective actions taken, if needed, to ensure that the overall project progresses smoothly.

We have seen that the two basic issues for software engineering are software quality and cost. We have also stated that following a properly selected development process model will lead to high quality software at low cost. However, the process model does not specify how to allocate resources for the different activities in the process. Nor does it specify any schedule for the activities. These activities must be specified and performed by the project management. The major issues to be addressed by the project management are:

process management,
resource allocation, and
development schedule.

Process management is concerned with ensuring that the development process is actually followed. The key issue here is, how does one know that the specified process model is being followed correctly? The central issue in resource allocation is how to allocate resources optimally while minimizing the overall resource requirement for the project. The central issue in the project schedule is to determine what is a realistic schedule, and then ensure that the schedule is followed.

The management activities can be divided broadly into two categories—project planning and project monitoring and control. Project planning encompasses those management activities that take place before most of the development phases begin. Project planning is actually a passive activity in that a plan is made, although the activities mentioned in the plan do occur later. The monitoring and control part of project management lasts much longer than the planning part. Monitoring and control takes place throughout the development activities. Executing the plan and modifying and adapting the plan fall under this part.

Project management begins with planning, which is perhaps the single largest responsibility of the project management. The goal is to develop a *plan* for software development such that reliable software is developed most efficiently and economically. Proper planning (and later execution of the plan) is recognized to be a critical ingredient for a successful project. A software plan is usually produced before the development activity begins and is updated as development proceeds and data about progress of the project becomes available. During planning the major activities are cost and resource estimation, schedule and milestone determination, project staffing, quality control plans, and controlling and monitoring plans.

In cost and resource estimation the total cost of the project is estimated. In addition, costs for the different activities of development is also estimated. As people are the major resource in a software development project, these estimations are often in terms of person-months needed for a particular activity of the project. In order to create a realistic schedule, the time required for each of the different activities has to be estimated. Once the schedule and efforts are estimated, then the staffing levels during different phases of the project has to be determined. This specifies the number of people needed at different times during the life of the project.

Controlling and monitoring plans include all the plans for monitoring whether the project is on schedule and within budget. In addition, it includes all monitoring necessary to ensure that quality control measures are being properly employed and the process model selected for development is being properly followed.

1.5. Role of Metrics and Measurement

Software metrics are quantifiable measures that could be used to measure different characteristics of a software system or the software development process. All engineering disciplines have metrics (such as metrics for weight, density, wavelength, and temperature) to quantify various characteristics of their products. Software metrics is an emerging area. Since the software has no physical attributes, conventional metrics are not much help in designing metrics for software. A number of metrics have been proposed to quantify things like the size, complexity, and reliability of a software product.

There are two types of metrics employed for software development—**product metrics** and **process metrics.** Product metrics are used to quantify characteristics of the product being developed, i.e. the software. Process metrics are used to quantify characteristics of the environment or the process being employed to develop the software. Process metrics aim to measure such considerations as productivity, cost and resource requirements, and the effect of development techniques and tools.

Intricately tied to metrics is measurement. Metrics simply provide the scale for quantifying qualities. Actual measurement must be performed on a given software system in order to use metrics for quantifying characteristics of the given software. An analogy in the physical world is that centimeters is the metric of length, but to determine the length of a given rod, one must measure it using some means like a measuring tape. Some characteristics can be directly measured, others might have to be deduced by other measurement (an analogy could be that the distance between two points can be deduced by measuring the speed of a vehicle and measuring the time it takes to traverse the given distance). In either case, measurement is necessary for employing metrics.

If a metric is not measured directly, we call the metric *indirect*. Some factors, like software quality, are not able to be measured directly, either because there are no means to measure the metric directly, or because the final product whose metric is of interest still does not exist. For example, it is desirable to predict the quality of software during the early phases of development, such as, after design. Since the software does not yet exist, the metric will have to be predicted from the factors that can be measured. For predicting, *models* are needed. A model is a relationship of the predicted variable with other variables that can be measured. The model may be determined based on empirical data or may be analytic. We will later see that during project planning different models are used to predict factors such as cost, schedule, and manpower requirement.

Metrics and measurement are necessary aspects of managing a software development project. For effective monitoring, the management needs to get information about the project: how far it has progressed, how much development has taken place, how far behind schedule it is, what is the quality of the development so far, etc. Based on this information, decisions can be made about the project. Without proper metrics to quantify the required information, subjective opinion would have to be used, but this is unreliable and goes against the fundamental goals of engineering.

We will see that there are a number of metrics that have been defined for quantifying properties of the software and the software development process. The most common ones are the Lines of Code (LOC) to specify the size of a software, and Person Months (also called man-months) to specify the effort needed or spent on a project. LOC can also be used to give a more precise characterization to the common notions of "small," "large" or "very large" projects. One such possible characterization is

Size:	Small	Medium	Large	Very Large
LOC:	<2K	2K-8K	8K-32K	>32K

1.6. Summary

Software cost now forms the major component of a computer system's cost. Software is currently extremely expensive to develop and is often unreliable. The goal of Software Engineering is to face this "software crisis." In this chapter, we have introduced some aspects of software engineering. Here we recapitulate some of the major points.

1. Software is not just a set of computer programs but comprises programs, data and documentation necessary for operation and maintenance. Software engineering is the discipline that aims at providing

methodologies or engineering approaches for developing software systems.

2. Software development undergoes different phases. The major phases are requirements analysis, design, coding and testing. The requirements analysis phase is for understanding the goals of the software system; design is a plan for a solution to solve the stated problems; coding is the actual programming of the design in a programming language; and testing is executing the developed programs to determine if they operate correctly or not.

3. Maintenance of software cannot be avoided. Once a software product is delivered, it must be modified either to remove errors that remain in the system or to enhance the software.

4. Coding is only a small part of the software cost. The major cost is in software maintenance. Of the development effort, the costliest phase is software testing. Hence, the goal of design and coding should be to make the job of the tester and maintainer easier.

5. Errors can occur in any phase. The later an error is detected after being introduced, the higher the cost of correction. Hence, methods should be employed to detect errors soon after their occurrence.

6. The waterfall model is conceptually the simplest model of software development, where the requirement, design, coding and testing phases are performed in linear progression. In the waterfall model, the input to a phase is the output of the previous phase. This requires that a defined output be produced after each phase. This output is certified before the next phase begins.

7. The waterfall model is not the only model for software development. It is simple and is widely used, but has limitations. There are other proposed models, like prototyping based development, iterative enhancement, and the spiral model.

8. Project management and software metrics are an integral part of software development projects. Project management concerns planning and control. Project planning is introduced as a separate activity that is performed towards the end of requirements analysis. The project plan is an input to all the later phases. In order to control the project, quantitative data is necessary to evaluate the product and the development process. Metrics and measurement aid in controlling the project, as well as help better understand the process and the product.

1.7. Overview of the Book

This book has a total of seven chapters. Each phase is discussed in a separate chapter. Due to the importance of planning activity, planning is given in a separate chapter and not with the requirements analysis. The order of presentation is the same as the order in which the different phases are performed in a typical development project. **A case study is used in the book,** which is taken through the different phases in the development process. The activity of each phase is performed for the case study and the major outputs are given in the relevant chapters. The following documents of the case study are given in the book: requirements document, project plan, system design document, detailed design document, code, test plan, testcase specification, and test reports.

The structure of most chapters in this book is similar. Most chapters begin by discussing the fundamental concepts for that particular phase. Then the methods for performing the activity for that phase are discussed. This is followed by the verification methods used for that phase. Metrics relevant to the phase are discussed next, followed by the monitoring and control activities to be performed during that phase. Each chapter ends with a discussion of the case study and a description of the case study outputs for that particular phase. Here we give a brief outline of each of the chapters.

Chapter 2 is entitled "software requirement specification" and discusses the different aspects of this phase. The desirable qualities of the requirements document are discussed, along with the different aspects the document should specify. Different methods of representing the requirements are covered, and a brief description of some of the tools available for requirements analysis is included. The metrics of interest in this phase are described, and the monitoring and control activities to be performed are discussed. The chapter ends with the requirements document for the case study.

Chapter 3 is entitled "planning a software project" and discusses the different issues relating to software development project planning. The topics covered are cost estimation, schedule and milestone plan, personnel plan, team structure, software quality assurance plans, configuration management plans, project monitoring plans and risk management. For cost and schedule planning different models are described. In the case study, we follow the COCOMO model. The two basic team structures (democratic and chief programmer) are described. In quality assurance plans, general methods of monitoring, including reviews, are discussed. For risk management, different activities for performing risk management are discussed. A project plan for the case study is then presented, which includes sections on all the major aspects of planning.

Chapter 4 discusses "system design". We consider design as a two-level process combining system design and detailed design (detailed design is discussed in Chapter 5). In Chapter 4 we first discuss the basic principles of design, including problem partitioning, divide and conquer, top-down refinement, modularity and abstraction. We describe two different design techniques, structured design and object oriented design. For the case study we follow the structured design methodology, and give the entire system design. Different methods for verifying a system design, metrics applicable for a system design, and control and monitoring activities performed simultaneously with system design are also discussed.

In Chapter 5 we discuss the issue of detailed design. The first step in designing a module is to specify the module formally and understand it clearly. We discuss some methods of formally specifying modules that support functional or data abstractions. For detailed design we discuss the method of stepwise-refinement, and the program design language (PDL). Different methods for verification, some metrics for complexity, cohesion and coupling, and monitoring and control activities are discussed. The detailed design for the case study is described using the PDL.

Chapter 6 discusses the issues relating to programming. The basic principles for developing programs are discussed. These include structured programming, information hiding, programming style and internal documentation. Many methods for verification exist for programs. In the chapter we discuss code reading, data flow analysis, symbolic execution, program proving, unit testing, code reviews and walkthroughs. Metrics discussed include size metrics and complexity analysis. Different monitoring and control activities for this phase are also discussed.

Chapter 7 is the last chapter which discusses the testing phase. We first clarify the concepts of faults, errors, failures and reliability. Different levels of testing that are usually used and their various purposes are defined. The importance of the psychology of testing is discussed, as well as two basic approaches to testing (functional testing and structural testing). Different heuristics for generating testcases for functional testing are described. Next, given the structural testing approach, we discuss some alternative measures of evaluating test cases, such as statement coverage and branch coverage. The basic metrics we describe are reliability assessment, productivity analysis and error analysis. Two different models for reliability estimation are discussed. Different measures for measuring productivity and defect detection efficiency are also described. The test plan, testcase specifications, testing report, error report for the case study are given. The chapter ends with the analysis of the case study project.

Exercises

1. What are the major phases in the entire life of the software? Which phase consumes the maximum effort? Of the phases performed during development, which phase consumes the maximum effort?
2. What are the major outputs in a development project which follows the waterfall model?
3. Why should a requirement analyst avoid making any design decisions during requirements analysis? Must a good programmer also be a good requirement analyst?

4. Suppose you must build a chair. What are the different activities you will perform? Draw a diagram to model the process you would perform.

5. Draw a process model to represent your current approach to developing software.

6. Suppose a program for solving a problem costs C, and a programming product for solving that problem costs 9C. Where do you think this extra 8C cost is spent? Suggest a possible breakdown of this extra cost.

7. Which of the process models discussed in this chapter will you follow for the following projects? Give justifications.
    1. A simple data processing project.
    2. A data entry system for office staff who have never used computers before. The user interface and user-friendliness are extremely important.
    3. A new system for comparing finger prints. It is not clear if the current algorithms can compare finger prints in the given response time constraints.
    4. A spreadsheet system which has some basic features and many other desirable features that use these basic features.
    5. A new missile tracking system. It is not known if the current hardware/software technology is mature enough to achieve the goals.
    6. An on-line inventory management system for an automobile industry.
    7. A flight control system with extremely high reliability. (There are many potential hazards with such a system.)

8. You and your friend have to deliver a software product in 6 months. Assuming the entire work can be complete within the given time, identify the activities that you and your friend will undertake, and the milestones for completing each of the activities.

9. You have to develop a software product. What exactly will you deliver to the client when the project is complete, if you used good software engineering practices?

10. Why is it desirable to have a detailed design phase as well as a coding phase. Why not go directly from architectural design to coding?

11. If the primary goal is to make software maintainable, list some of the things which you *will* do and some of the things you *will not* do during 1) design, 2) implementation, and 3) testing.

12. Suppose that there are different approaches to developing a software system. In approach 1, the effort distribution among phases is as given in the chapter. In approach 2, the cost of design is higher by 10%, cost of implementation is higher by 10%, but the cost of testing is lower by 15%. Which of the two approaches will you choose?

13. It is reasonable to assume that if a software is easy to test, it will be easy to maintain. Suppose that by putting in extra effort in design and

coding you increase the cost of these phases by 15%, but you reduce the cost of testing and maintenance by 5%. Will you decide to put in the extra effort?

14. If for developing a software product you are given extra time to improve the reliability of the final product, how would you distribute this extra time?

15. List some of the properties the requirements document should satisfy. What kinds of things should it contain and what should it not contain?

16. Suggest some ways to detect software errors in the early phases (when implementation is not yet complete).

17. What are the major management activities in a software project? Why is proper management essential for a successful project?

18. What are software metrics? What is the role of metrics in project management? What are other uses of metrics?

19. Give specific examples of some metrics that can be used for controlling a software project.

20. Define all the metrics you can think of that can characterize a software product (not the process).

21. Define all the metrics you can think of that can characterize a software process.

2
Software Requirements Specification

Software requirements specification (SRS) is the starting point of the software development activity. Little importance was attached to this phase in the early days of software development. The emphasis was first on coding and then shifted to design. The tacit assumption in earlier approaches was that the developers understood the problem clearly when it was explained to them, verbally and informally.

As systems grew more complex it became evident that the goals of the entire system cannot be easily comprehended. Hence the need for the requirements analysis phase arose. Now, for large software systems, requirements analysis is perhaps the most difficult activity and also the most error prone. Many software engineers believe that the software engineering discipline is weakest in this critical area.

Some of the difficulty is due to the scope of this phase. The software project is initiated by the client's needs. In the beginning these needs are in the minds of various people in the client organization. The requirement analyst has to identify the requirements by talking to these people and understanding their needs. In situations where the software is to automate a currently manual process, most of the needs can be understood by observing the current practice. However, even in these situations some of the requirements have to be uncovered through discussion and negotiations. These are the "new features" which the software system will introduce, and which do not exist in the manual process.

Hence, specifying requirements necessarily involves specifying what some people have in their minds. As the information in their minds is by very nature not formally stated or organized, the input to the software requirement specification phase is inherently informal and imprecise, and is likely to be incomplete. When inputs from multiple people are to be gathered, as is most often the case, these inputs are likely to be inconsistent as well.

The SRS is a means of translating the ideas in the minds of the clients (the input), into a formal document (the output of the requirements phase). Thus, the output of the phase is a set of formally specified requirements, which hopefully are complete and consistent, while the input has none of these properties. Clearly, the process of specifying requirements cannot be totally formal. Any formal translation process producing a formal output must have a precise and unambiguous input. A procedure for identifying requirements can therefore be at best a set of guidelines.

The requirement specification phase consists of two basic activities: *problem or requirement analysis,* and *requirement specification.* The first aspect, perhaps the harder and more nebulous of the two, deals with understanding the problem, the goals, and the constraints. In the second, the focus is on clearly specifying what has been found during analysis. Issues such as representation, specification languages and tools, and checking the specification are addressed during this activity. The requirements phase terminates with the production of the validated software requirement specification document. Producing the SRS is the basic goal of this phase. We will discuss both activities of the requirement phase in this chapter.

2.1. Role of SRS

The origin of most software systems is in the need of a client who either wants to automate an existing manual system or desires a new software system. The software system itself is created by the developer. Finally, the completed system will be used by the end-users. Thus, there are three major parties interested in a new system—the client, the users, and the developer. Somehow the requirements for the system that will satisfy the needs of the clients and the concerns of the users have to be communicated to the developer. The problem is that the client usually does not understand software or the software development process, and the developer often does not understand the client's problem and application area. This causes a communication gap between the parties involved in the development project.

The purpose of software requirements specification (SRS) is to bridge this communication gap. SRS is the medium through which the client and user needs are accurately specified; indeed, SRS forms the basis of software development. A good SRS should satisfy all the parties—something very hard to achieve and involving tradeoffs and persuasion.

Often an important purpose of the process of developing an SRS is helping the clients to understand their own needs. The introduction of a software system offers new potential for features such as providing new services, performing activities in a different manner, and collecting data, which were either impossible or unfeasible without a software system. The client has to be made aware of these potentials, and the process of developing SRS can achieve this. This is especially useful if the software system is not for automating an existing manual system, but for creating an entirely new system.

A good SRS provides many benefits. Some of the goals it accomplishes are:

1. Establishing the basis for agreement between client and supplier on what the software product will do.
2. Reducing the development cost. The preparation of the SRS forces rigorous specification of the requirements before the design begins. Careful development of an SRS can reveal omissions, inconsistencies and misunderstandings early in the development cycle, which can considerably reduce cost.
3. Providing a reference for validation of the final product. The SRS assists the client in determining if the software meets the requirements.

2.2. Problem Analysis

The first of the two basic activities performed during the requirement phase is analyzing the problem. Problem analysis is done to obtain a clear understanding of the needs of the clients and the users, and what exactly is desired from the software. Analysis leads to the actual specification. In this section we will focus on the analysis. Specification is discussed in the next section. People performing the analysis (often called *analysts*) are also responsible for specifying the requirements.

Analysis involves interviewing the clients and end users. These people and the existing documents about the current mode of operation are the basic source of information for the analysts. Typically, analysts research a problem by asking questions of the client and the user, and by reading existing documents. The process of obtaining answers to questions that might arise in an analyst's mind continues until the analyst feels that "all" the information has been obtained.

During this process of analysis, a massive amount of information is collected in forms of answers to questions, questionnaires, information from documentation, and so forth. One of the major problems during analysis is how to organize the information obtained so the information can be effectively evaluated for completeness and consistency. The second major problem during analysis is resolving the contradictions that may exist in the information from different parties. The contradictions occur since the perceived goals of the system may be quite different for the end users and the client. The analyst has the thankless job of resolving the contradictions and obtaining a "consensus".

Clearly, during analysis the interpersonal skills of an analyst are just as important, if not more so, as the technical skills. Interviewing the users and clients requires good communication skills. The situation can be more complex if some of the users are reluctant to part with the information they possess. Careful dealing is required to make sure that all that needs to be known is found out. During resolution of conflicts, good communication and interpersonal skills are perhaps the most important tools the analyst needs.

In this section we will discuss some methods for organizing information during analysis, and some methods about how to proceed with the analysis activity. No further discussion on interpersonal skills is provided.

2.2.1. Structuring Information

During analysis, getting information about some aspect of the system is often not very difficult. However, deciding *which* information should be collected is difficult. Determining what questions to ask or what questions to put in a questionnaire is the challenging part of information collection. Properly structuring available information is essential if properly directed questions are to be formed, answers to which will uncover information not known so far.

There are three principles that can be employed for structuring information during problem analysis [Dav90]. These are partitioning, abstraction, and projection. *Partitioning* captures the "whole/part-of" relationship between entities or problems. It is essential to understanding large and complex systems. Most large systems and entities are comprised of different parts. Comprehending the entire system with its complexities is difficult, if not impossible, unless the problem is broken into an understanding of its parts, and how the parts relate to each other. Hence, partitioning is used when it is difficult to describe a system without describing it in terms of its parts. For example, if we have to study an operating system, it is quite difficult to understand the entire system, so we describe it in terms of parts such as the file system, memory management system, process management, and input/output. After partitioning we can analyze the different parts (which themselves may require further partitioning).

Abstraction is another technique fundamental to problem analysis that is employed by all analysts either consciously or by instinct. When using abstraction, we define an entity or a problem in general terms, and the details are provided separately. The abstraction of a system or a problem is devoid of the details and is consequently simpler to specify and comprehend. This technique provides the analyst with the tool to consider a problem at a suitable level of abstraction, where he/she can comprehend the general system, and then analyze the details further. For example, when analyzing the file system of an operating system, we may first want to describe the abstract functions the file system provides. (These abstract functions could include file opening and closing, directory management functions, creating and deleting files, and user interface.) Then the details of the different functions can be studied and specified. With abstraction, whenever one wants to study the details of a particular feature of a system, he does not have to understand the details of other related parts, and can focus on the goal of the study.

Projection is another method that is extremely useful in analysis and is often employed. Projection is defining the system from multiple points of view by taking the projection of the system from different perspectives. Projecting a three dimensional object on the three different two dimensional planes is a similar process. In projection, the problem is studied from different perspectives, and then the different "projections" obtained are combined to form the analysis for the complete system. The advantage of this method is that trying to describe the system from a global view point is difficult and error-prone, and one is more likely to forget some features of the system. Describing the system from the different perspectives is easier, as it limits and focuses the scope of the study. For example, an operating system can be described from the perspective of a general user, a system programmer, or a system administrator (many operating system manuals are divided in this manner). By using the different perspectives it is easy to ensure that the description is indeed complete.

2.2.2. Data Flow Diagrams and Data Dictionary

Data flow diagrams (also called data flow graphs) are commonly used during problem analysis. Data flow diagrams (DFD) are quite general and are not limited to problem analysis for software requirements specification. They have been in use long before the software engineering discipline began. DFDs are very useful in understanding a system and can be effectively used for partitioning during analysis.

A DFD shows the flow of data through a system. The system may be an organization, a manual procedure, a software system, a mechanical system, a hardware system, or any combination of these. A DFD shows the movement of data through the different transformations or processes in the system. The processes are shown by named circles (or "bubbles"), and data flows are represented by named arrows entering or leaving the bubbles. A rectangle represents a source or sink, and is a net originator or consumer of data. A source or a sink is typically outside the main system of study. An example of a DFD for a system that pays workers is shown in Figure 2.1.

In this DFD there is one basic input data flow and that is the weekly timesheet, which originates from the source *worker*. The basic output is the paycheck, the sink for which is also the worker. In this system, first the employee's record is retrieved, using the employee-id, which is contained in the timesheet. From the employee record the rate of payment and overtime rate are obtained. These rates and the regular and overtime hours (from the timesheet) are used to compute the pay. After the total pay is determined, taxes are deducted. To compute the tax deduction, information from the tax-rate file is used. The amount of tax deducted is recorded in the employee and company records. Finally, the paycheck is issued for the net-pay. The amount paid is also recorded in company records.

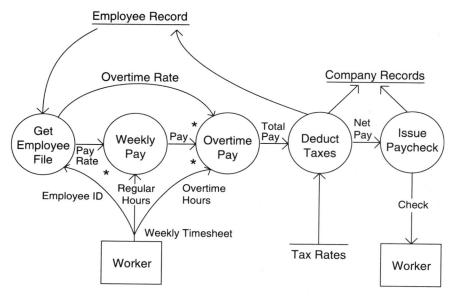

FIGURE 2.1. DFD of a system that pays workers.

Some conventions used in drawing this DFD should be explained. All external files, such as employee record, company record, and tax rates, are shown as a labeled straight line. When multiple data flows are needed by a process, this is represented by a "*" between the data flows. This symbol represents the AND relationship. For example if there is a "*" between the two input data flows A and B for a process, it means that A AND B are needed for the process. In the DFD above, for the process "weekly pay" the data flow "hours" and "pay rate" both are needed, as shown in the DFD. Similarly, the OR relationship is represented by a "+" between the data flows.

This DFD is an abstract description of the system for handling payment. It does not matter if the system is automated or manual. This diagram could very well be for a manual system where the computations are all done with calculators, and the records are physical folders and ledgers. The details and minor data paths are not represented in this DFD. For example, what happens if there are errors in the weekly timesheet is not shown in this DFD. This is done to avoid getting bogged down with details while constructing a DFD for the overall system. If more details are desired, then the DFD can be further refined.

It should be pointed out that a DFD is not a flowchart. A DFD represents the flow of data, while a flowchart shows the flow of control. A DFD does not represent procedural information. So, while drawing a DFD, one *must not* get involved in procedural details, and procedural thinking must be consciously avoided. For example, considerations of loops and decisions must be ignored. In drawing the DFD the designer has to specify *what* are the major transforms in the path of the data flowing from the input to output. *How* those transforms are performed is *not* an issue at all while drawing the data flow graph.

There are no detailed procedures that can be used to draw a DFD for a given problem. Only some directions can be provided. One way to construct a DFD is to start by identifying the major inputs and major outputs. Minor inputs and outputs (like error messages) should be ignored at first. Then starting from the inputs work towards the outputs, identifying the major transforms in the way. An alternative is to work down from the outputs towards the inputs. (Remember that it is important that procedural information like loops and decisions not be shown in the DFD, and the designer should not worry about such issues while drawing the DFD.) Following are some suggestions for constructing a data flow graph [You79, Dem79].

1. Work your way consistently from the inputs to the outputs, or vice versa. If you get stuck, reverse direction. Start with a data flow graph with few major transforms describing the entire transformation from the inputs to outputs, and then refine each transform with more detailed transformations.
2. Never try to show control logic. If you find yourself thinking in terms of loops and decisions, it is time to stop and start again.
3. Label each arrow with proper data elements. Inputs and outputs of each transform should be carefully identified.
4. Make use of * and + operations, and show sufficient detail in the data flow graph.
5. Try drawing alternate data flow graphs before settling on one.

Many systems are too large for a single DFD to describe the data processing clearly. It is necessary that some decomposition and abstraction mechanism be used for such systems. DFDs can be hierarchically organized, which helps in progressively partitioning and analyzing large systems. Such DFDs together are called *leveled DFD set* [Dem79].

A leveled DFD set has a starting DFD, which is a very abstract representation of the system, identifying the major inputs and outputs and the major processes in the system. Then each process is refined and a DFD is drawn for the process. In other words, a bubble in a DFD is expanded into a DFD during refinement. For the hierarchy to be consistent, it is important that the net inputs and outputs of a DFD for a process are the same as the inputs and outputs of the process in the higher-level DFD. This refinement stops if each bubble is considered to be "atomic", in that each bubble can be easily specified or understood. It should be pointed out that during refinement, though the net input and output are preserved, a refinement of the data might also occur. That is, a unit of data may be broken into its components for processing when the detailed DFD for a process is being drawn. So, as the processes are decomposed, data decomposition also occurs.

In a DFD, data flows are identified by giving unique names. These names are chosen so that they convey some "meaning" about what the data is. However, the precise structure of data flows is not specified in a DFD. The *data dictionary* is a repository of various data flows defined in a DFD. The associated data dictionary states precisely the structure of each data flow in the DFD. Components in the structure of a data flow may also be specified in the data dictionary, as well as the structure of files shown in the DFD. To define the structure of a data, different notations are used. These are similar to the notation for regular expressions (discussed later in the chapter). Essentially, besides sequence or composition (represented by +), selection, and iteration are also included. Selection (represented by vertical bar "|") means one OR the other, and repetition (represented by "*") means one or more occurrences. In the DFD shown above, data flows for weekly timesheet are used. The data dictionary for this DFD is shown in Figure 2.2.

Most of the data flows in the DFD above are specified here. Some of the more obvious ones like total pay and net pay are not shown here. The data dictionary entry for weekly_timesheet specifies that this data flow is composed of three basic data entities—the employee name, employee ID, and many occurrences of the two-tuple consisting of regular_hours and overtime_hours. The last entity represents the daily working hours of the worker. The data dictionary also contains entries for specifying the different elements of a data flow.

Once we have constructed a DFD and its associated data dictionary, we have to somehow verify that they are "correct". There can be no formal

weekly timesheet =
        Employee_name +
        Employee_ID +
        [Regular_hours + Overtime_hours]*

pay_rate =
        [Hourly | daily | weekly] +
        Dollar_amount

Employee_name =
        Last + First + Middle_initial

Employee_Id =
        digit + digit + digit + digit

FIGURE 2.2 Data dictionary.

verification of a DFD, since what the DFD is modeling is not formally specified anywhere against which verification can be done. Human processes and rules of thumb must be used for verification. In addition to the walkthrough with the client, the analyst should look for common errors. Some common errors are [Dem79]:

unlabeled data flows,
missing data flows; information required by a process is not available,
extraneous data flows; some information is not being used in the process,
consistency not maintained during refinement,
missing processes, and
contains some control information.

Perhaps the most common error is unlabeled data flow. If an analyst cannot label the data flow, it is quite likely that he does not really understand the purpose and structure of that data flow. A good test for this type of error is to see that entries in the data dictionary are precise for all data flows.

To check if there are any missing data flows, for each process in the DFD the analyst should ask the question ,"Can the process build the outputs shown from the given inputs?". Similarly, to check for redundant data flows, the following question should be asked: "Are all the input data flows required in the computation of the outputs?".

In a leveled set of DFDs it is important that consistency be maintained. Consistency can easily be lost if new data flows are added to the DFD during modification. If such changes are made, appropriate changes should be made in the parent or the child DFD. That is, if a new data flow is added in a lower level DFD, it should also be reflected in the higher level DFDs as well. Similarly, if a data flow is added in a higher level DFD, the DFDs for the processes affected by the change should also be appropriately modified.

The DFDs should be carefully scrutinized to make sure that all the processes in the physical environment are shown in the DFD. It should also be ensured that none of the data flows is actually carrying control information. A data flow without any structure or composition is a potential candidate for control information.

2.2.3 Structured Analysis

One approach in analysis is to consider the functions that must be necessary to solve a particular problem. Such analysis focuses on functions and the data consumed and produced by these functions. This approach is followed in the Structured Analysis technique. The structured analysis method helps an analyst decide what type of information to obtain at different points in analysis, and helps in organizing information so that the analyst is not overwhelmed by the complexity of the problem.

The structured analysis method [Dem79] is a top-down approach which relies heavily on the use of data flow diagrams. It is a technique that analyzes and also produces the specifications. We will limit our attention to the analysis aspect of the approach. The first step in this method is to study the "physical environment". During this, a DFD of the current non-automated (or partially automated) system is drawn, showing the input and output data flows of the system, how the data flows through the system, and what are the processes operating on the data. This DFD might contain specific names for data flows and processes, as used in the physical environment. For example, names of departments, persons, local procedures, and organizational names of files can occur in the DFD for the physical environment. While drawing the DFD for the physical environment, an analyst has to interact with the users to determine the overall process from the point of view of the data. This step is considered to be complete when the entire physical data flow diagram has been described and the user has accepted it as a true representation of the operation of the current system.

The basic purpose of analyzing the current system is to obtain a logical DFD for the system, where each data flow and each process is a logical entity or operation, rather than an actual name. Drawing a DFD for the physical system is only to provide a reasonable starting point for drawing the logical DFD. Hence, the next step in the analysis is to draw the logical equivalents of the DFD for the physical system. During this step, the DFD of the physical environment is taken and all specific physical data flows are represented by their logical equivalents (For example, file 12.3.2 may be replaced by employee salary file). Similarly, the bubbles for physical processes are replaced with logical processes. For example, a bubble named "To-John's-office" in the physical system might be replaced by "issue checks" in the logical equivalent. Bubbles that do not transform the data in any form are deleted from the DFD. This phase also ends when the DFD has been verified by the user.

In the first two steps, the current system is modeled. The next step is to develop a logical model of the new system after the changes have been incorporated, and a DFD is drawn to show how data will flow in the new system. During this step also the analyst works in the logical mode, specifying only what needs to be done, not how it will be accomplished. No separation between the automated and non-automated processes is made.

No general rules are provided for constructing the DFD for the new system. The new system still does not exist, and has to be invented. Consequently, what will be the data flows and major processes in this new system must be determined by the analyst based on his experience and his vision of the new system. No rules can be provided for this decision. However, before this can be done the boundaries of change have to be identified in the logical DFD for the existing system. This DFD models the entire system, and only parts of it may be modified in the new system. Based on the goals of the clients and a clear concept about what the client wants to change, the boundaries of change have to be established in the logical DFD. The DFD for the new system will replace only that part of the existing DFD that is within this boundary. The inputs and outputs of the new DFD should be same as the inputs and outputs for the DFD within the boundary.

The next step is to establish the man-machine boundary by specifying what will be automated and what will remain manual in the DFD for the new system. Note that even though some processes are not automated, they could be quite different from the processes in the original system, as even the manual operations may be performed differently in the new system. Often there is not just a single option for the man-machine boundary. Different possibilities may exist depending on what is automated, and the degree of automation. The analyst should explore and present the different possibilities.

The next two steps are evaluating the different options and then packaging or presenting the specifications.

For drawing a DFD, a top-down approach is suggested in the structured analysis method. In the structured analysis method, a DFD is constructed from scratch when the DFD for the physical system is being drawn, and when the DFD for the new system is being drawn. The second step largely performs transformations on the physical DFD. Drawing a DFD starts with a top-level DFD called the "context diagram", which lists all the major inputs and outputs for the system. This diagram is then refined into a description of the different parts of the DFD showing more details. This results in a leveled set of DFDs. As pointed out earlier, during this refinement, the analyst has to make sure that consistency is maintained, and that net input and output are preserved during refinement.

Clearly, structured analysis provides methods for organizing and representing information about systems. It also provides guidelines for checking the accuracy of the information. Hence, for understanding and analyzing an existing system, this method provides useful tools. However, most of the guidelines given in structured analysis are only applicable in the first two steps, when the DFD for a current system is to be constructed. For analyzing the target system and constructing the DFD or the data dictionary for the new system to be built (done in step three), this technique does not provide much guidance. Of course, the study and understanding of the existing system will help the analyst in this job, but there is no direct help from the method of structured analysis.

AN EXAMPLE

A restaurant owner feels that some amount of automation will help her in making the business more efficient. She also believes that an automated

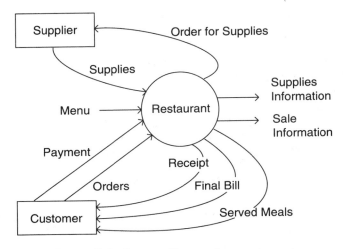

FIGURE 2.3. Context diagram for a restaurant.

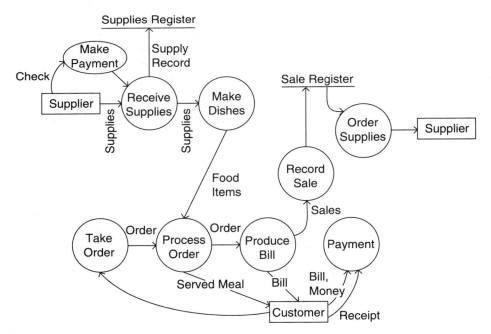

FIGURE 2.4. DFD for an existing restaurant system.

system might be an added attraction for the customers. So she wants to automate as much as possible the operation of her restaurant. Here we will perform the analysis for this problem. Details regarding interviews, questionnaire, or how the information was extracted are not described. First let us identify the different parties involved.

Client: The restaurant owner

Potential Users: Waiters, cash register operator

The context diagram for the restaurant is shown in Figure 2.3.

The inputs and the outputs of the restaurant are shown in this diagram. However, no details about the functioning of the restaurant are given here. Using this as a starting point, a logical DFD of the physical system is given in Figure 2.4 (the physical DFD was avoided for this, as the logical DFD is similar to the physical, and there were no special names for the data or the processes in the physical system). Observing the operation of the restaurant and interviewing with the owner were the basic means of collecting raw information for this DFD.

Now we must draw a DFD that models the new system that will be built. After many meetings and discussions with the restaurant owner, the following goals for the new system were established.

1. Automate much of the order processing and billing.
2. Automate accounting.
3. Make supply ordering more accurate so that left-overs at the end of the day are minimized, and the orders which cannot be satisfied due to non-availability of ingredients are also minimized. Supply ordering was currently being done without a careful analysis of sales.
4. The owner also suspects that the staff might be stealing or eating some supplies. She wants the new system to help in detecting and reducing this.
5. The owner will also like to have statistics about sales of different items.

With these goals, we can define the boundaries for change in the DFD. It is clear that the new system will affect most aspects of the previous system, with the exception of making dishes. So, except for that process, the remaining parts of the old system all fall within our boundary of change. The DFD for the new system is shown in Figure 2.5. Note that although taking orders might remain manual in the new system, the process might change, since the waiter now might need to fill in codes for menu items. That is why it is also within the boundary of change.

The DFD is largely self-explanatory. The major files in the system are: Supplies file, Accounting file, Orders file and the Menu. Some new processes, which did not have equivalents earlier, have been included in the system. These are "Check for Discrepancy," "Accounting Reports," and "Statistics." Note that the processes are consistent in that the inputs given to them are sufficient to produce the outputs. For example,

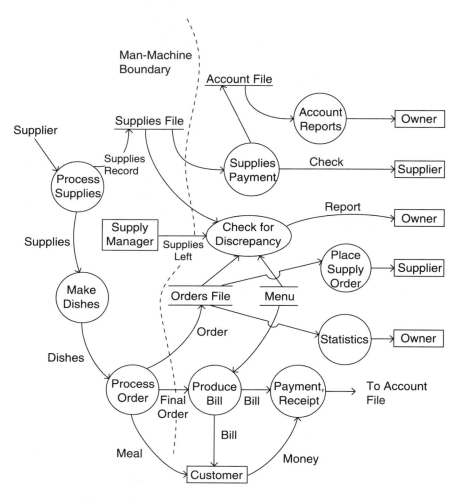

FIGURE 2.5. The DFD for the new restaurant system.

"checking for discrepancy" requires the following information to produce the report: total supplies received (obtained from the Supplies file), supplies left at the end of the day, total orders placed by the customers (from the Orders file), and the consumption rate for each menu item (from the Menu). All these are shown as inputs to the process. Supplies required for the next day are assessed from the total orders placed in the day, and the orders that could not be satisfied due to lack of supplies (both kept in the Order file). To see clearly if the information is sufficient for the different processes, the structure and exact contents of each of the data flows has to be specified. The data dictionary for this is given in Figure 2.6.

The definitions of the different data flows and files are self-explanatory.

Supplies_file =
      [date +
      [item_no + quantity + cost]*]*

Orders_file
      [date +
      [menu_item_no + quantity + status]*]*

status = satisfied | unsatisfied

order =
      [menu_item_no + quantity]*

menu =
      [menu_item_no + name + price + supplies_used]*

supplies_used =
      [supply_item_no + quantity]*

bill =
      [name + quantity + price]* +
      total_price +
      sales_tax +
      service_charge +
      grand_total

discrepancy_report =
      [supply_item_no + amt_ordered + amt_left + amt_consumed + descr]*

FIGURE 2.6. Data dictionary for the restaurant.

Once this DFD and the data dictionary have been approved by the restaurant owner, the phase of understanding the problem is complete. After talking with the restaurant owner the man-machine boundary was also defined (it is shown in the DFD). Now remain such tasks as determining the detailed requirements of each of the bubbles shown in the DFD, determining the non-functional requirements, and deciding codes for the items in the menu and in the supply list. Further refinement for some of the bubbles might be needed. For example, it has to be determined what sort of accounting reports or statistics are needed, and what should be their formats. Once these are done, the analysis is complete, and the requirements can then be compiled in a requirements specification document.

2.2.4. Prototyping

Prototyping is another method that can be used for problem analysis, which is getting a lot of attention these days. In prototyping, a partial system is constructed which is then used by the client, users and the developers to gain a better understanding of the problem and the needs. The idea behind prototyping as an aid to problem understanding and analysis is that the client and the users often do not have a good idea of their needs, particularly if the system is a totally new one, and that clients can assess their needs much better if they can see the working of a system. Prototyping emphasizes that actual practical experience is the best aid for understanding needs, since it is often difficult for us to visualize a system. However, by actually experimenting with a system we can relatively easily make statements like "I don't want this feature", or "I wish it had this feature", or "This is wonderful". Through the actual experience with the prototype, the client's needs can be understood clearly. Once the needs are clear, the specification phase begins, resulting in the requirement specification document, which is then used as the basis of software development.

Since a prototype is a tool which is used for analyzing the problem, it clearly cannot be anywhere close to a final complete system. A prototype is always a *partial system*. There are two approaches to prototyping— throwaway and evolutionary [Dav90]. In the *throwaway* approach the prototype is constructed with the idea that it will be discarded after the analysis is complete, and the final system will be built from scratch. In the evolutionary approach, the prototype is built with the idea that it will eventually be converted into the final system. The first one leads to the prototyping based process model, while the latter leads to the iterative enhancement model.

If a throwaway prototype is to be used for requirements analysis, the common sequence of activities is as follows [Dav90]: (1) develop a preliminary SRS for the system, which is the SRS for the prototype, (2) build the prototype, (3) achieve user and client experience in using the prototype, (4) develop the final SRS for the system, and (5) develop the final system.

Developing the SRS for the prototype requires identifying the areas of the system that should be included in the prototype. This decision is typically application dependent. In general, where the requirements tends to be unclear and vague, or where the clients and users are unsure or keep changing their mind, a prototype would be helpful. User interface, new features to be added (beyond automating what is currently being done), and features that may be infeasible, are some common candidates for prototyping.

Prototype is developed in much the same way as any software is developed, with a basic difference in the development approach. Many of the bookkeeping, documenting, and quality control activities that are usually performed during software product development are kept to a minimum during prototyping. Efficiency concerns also take a back seat, and often very high-level, interpretive languages are used for prototyping.

Experience is gained by putting the system to use with the actual client and users using it. Constant interaction is needed with the client/users during this activity to understand their responses. Questionnaires and interviews might be used for gathering user response.

The final SRS is developed in much the same way as any SRS is developed. The difference here is that the client and the users will be able to answer questions and explain their needs much better because of their experience with the prototype. In addition, some initial analysis is also available.

In order for prototyping for the purposes of requirement analysis to be feasible, its cost must be kept low. Consequently only those features are included in the prototype that will have a valuable return from the user experience. Exception handling, recovery, conformance to some standards, and formats are typically not included in prototypes. Since the prototype is to be thrown away, only minimal development documents need be produced during prototyping; for example, design documents, a test plan, and a test case specification are not needed during the development of the prototype. Another important cost cutting measure is reduced testing, since testing consumes a major part of development expenditure during regular software development. By using cost cutting methods, it is possible to keep the cost of the prototype to less than a few percent of the total development cost.

It should be pointed out that if a prototype costs 8% of the total development cost, it does not mean that the development cost increased by 8%. This cost of the prototype is based on the development cost using the prototyping approach, and not based on the cost which would be incurred if the software were developed without prototyping. Prototyping is often not used as it is feared that development costs may become larger. However, in some situations, the cost of software development without prototyping may be more than with prototyping. There are two major reasons for this. First, the experience of developing the prototype might reduce the cost of the later phases when the actual software development is done. Secondly, in many projects the requirements are constantly changing, particularly when development takes a long time. We have seen earlier that changes in requirements at a late stage during development substantially increase the cost of the project. By elongating the requirements analysis phase (the prototype development does take time), the requirements are "frozen" at a later time, by which time they are likely to be more developed and consequently more stable. In addition, since the client and users get experience with the system, it is more likely that the SRS developed after the prototype will be closer to the actual requirements. This again will lead to fewer changes in the requirements at a later time. Hence, the costs incurred due to changes in the requirements may be reduced substantially by prototyping.

AN EXAMPLE

Let us consider the example of the restaurant automation discussed earlier. An initial structured analysis of the problem was given. During the analysis the restaurant owner was quite apprehensive about the ability and usefulness of the system. She felt that it was risky to automate, as an improper system might cause considerable confusion and might lead to a loss of clientele. Due to the risks involved, it was decided to build a throwaway prototype.

The first step in developing a prototype is to prepare an SRS for the prototype. The SRS need not be formal, but should identify the different system utilities to be included in the prototype. It was decided that the prototype will demonstrate the following features.

1. Customer order processing and billing.
2. Supply ordering and processing.

The first one was included since that is where the maximum risk exists for the restaurant. The second was included because maximum potential benefit can be derived from this feature. Accounting and statistics generation were not to be included in the prototype.

The prototype was developed using a database system, in which good facilities for data entry and form (bill) generation exist. The user interface for the waiters and the restaurant manager was included in the prototype. The prototype system was used, in parallel with the existing system, for a few weeks, and informal surveys with the customers were conducted.

Customers were generally pleased with the accuracy of the bills and the details that it provided. Some gave suggestions about the bill layout. Based on the experience of the waiters, the code for the different menu items was modified to an alphanumeric code. They found that the purely numeric codes used in the prototype were hard to remember. The experience of the restaurant manager, and the feedback from the supplier, were used to determine the final details about supply processing and handling.

2.2.5. Other Tools/Methods for Analysis

Many other languages and related processors have been proposed for requirement analysis and specification. Most of these are not general and cater to some application area. Here we briefly describe some of the major specification languages. These approaches typically are designed for both analysis and specification and provide means for organizing information, as well as producing reports.

Before we describe the languages a word of caution is in order. All these languages provide means for organizing and specifying requirements, but they do not provide much help in determining the requirements. This is not a shortcoming of the languages, but is a feature of the requirement specification problem. Since in the beginning the requirements are in the minds of the people, no language or automated tool can uncover them. Determining the requirements is necessarily a human process. These languages help in writing the requirements in a manner that is useful in later activities. The processors for the languages are often capable of performing cross checking and some amount of consistency checking.

SADT: Structured analysis and design technique (SADT) [Ros77] is designed for information processing systems. It has a graphical language that is based on the concept of blueprints used in civil engineering. A model in SADT is a hierarchy of diagrams supporting a top-down approach for analysis and specification. Embedded in the diagrams are texts in natural language. Hence, the specification language is a combination of a precisely defined graphical language and a natural language.

A diagram in a SADT model is either an activity diagram or a data diagram. Each diagram consists of *boxes* and *arrows*. Boxes represent parts of a whole and arrows represent the interfaces between different parts. Each diagram may be accompanied by some text.

The hierarchy of diagrams starts with the *context diagram,* which is the most abstract description of the problem. The problem is then refined into sub-problems that are shown as another diagram. Each of the sub-problems in this diagram can then be further refined by constructing its diagram. Each diagram represents a limited amount of detail about a well defined sub-problem of a higher level diagram. As the refinement proceeds, our understanding of the problem becomes more detailed and accurate. This method of refinement exposes the details about the problem gradually, which helps the analyst in manage the analysis activity.

Again, the basic components of the SADT diagram are boxes and arrows entering or leaving the boxes. The idea behind the diagrams is similar to that of a DFD, except that the notation is different and there are precise rules for interpretation of arrows, depending on which side of the box they enter. Furthermore, loops might exist in diagrams in SADT, while loops are rare in DFDs.

A box represents a *transformation* (like a bubble does in the DFD). The arrows entering a box from the left represent things that will be transformed. What these are transformed into are shown by arrows leaving from the right. Arrows entering from the top of a box represent some sort of *control,* that affects the transformation of the box. The control arrows are meant to ensure that the transformation is applied only when circumstances are appropriate or the conditions are correct. Arrows entering from the bottom of a box represent *mechanisms* which are needed to perform the transformation. The boxes are labeled by "verbs" representing *happenings,* while the arrows are labeled by "nouns" representing *things.*

When a part of the diagram is refined into another diagram, the overall arrows in the parent diagram should be preserved in the refinement. That is, in general, the arrows going in and coming out of a diagram that is a refinement of a box in a parent diagram should be same as the arrows going

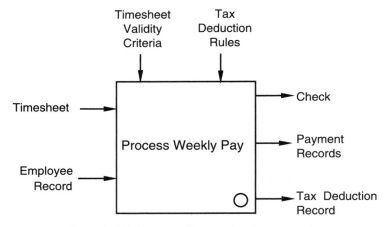

FIGURE 2.7. Context diagram for the pay system.

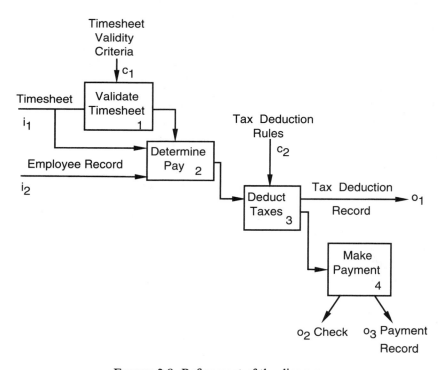

FIGURE 2.8. Refinement of the diagram.

in and coming out of the box in the parent diagram. This is similar to the the consistency requirement imposed on a leveled set of DFDs in the structured analysis approach.

Note that just like in DFD, the refinement does not produce a design. The analysis stays in the problem domain, and during refinement we try to find the different parts of the problem. The solution to the problem is not an issue during analysis.

As an example consider the system that pays workers described earlier by the DFD in Figure 2.1. The context diagram for this is shown in Figure 2.7, and the diagram after one refinement is shown in Figure 2.8.

In the context diagram different inputs and outputs are identified. Note that timesheet validity criteria and tax deduction rules are identified as control inputs. This overall problem is broken into sub-problems during refinement. During the refinement four different boxes are identified. The overall inputs and outputs remain the same (as they should). Note that the output of "validate timesheet is the control input to the "determine pay" box. The boxes, inputs and outputs in the refinement have been given numbers, according to the convention of the SADT diagrams.

PSL/PSA: The Problem Statement Language (PSL) [Tei77] is designed for specifying the requirements of information systems. It is a textual language, as opposed to many other techniques that are a combination of graphical and textual. Problem Statement Analyzer (PSA) is the processor that processes the requirements stated in PSL and produces some useful reports and analyses.

In PSL a system contains a set of objects, each object having properties and defined relationships. The major parts of a system description are system input/output flow, system structure and data structure. The system input/output flow deals with the interaction of the system with the environment and specifies all the inputs received and all the outputs produced. System structure defines the hierarchies among the different objects, and data structure defines the relationships among the data that are used within the system.

PSA operates on the database of information that is collected from the PSL description of the requirements. A number of reports can be produced including the data dictionary, data flow diagrams, a data-base modification report, summary reports, reference reports, and analysis reports. The data-base modification report lists all changes made to the database since the last report. Summary reports produce an overview of all the objects defined and their properties. Analysis reports produce information about inputs and outputs and any consistency problems that have been uncovered.

The PSL method is fundamentally the same as the structured analysis method. The problem description revolves around *process* descriptions. A process is similar to a bubble in a DFD or a box in the SADT diagram. In PSL, a process is described textually. Just like in DFD, the PSL specifica-

PROCESS
>   Pay-processing
DESCRIPTION
>   This process performs actions for paying workers based on
>   their weekly timesheets.
GENERATES   Pay check, payment report, tax deduction report
RECEIVES
>   Weekly timesheet, employee record, tax deduction rules.
SUBPARTS   ARE   validate_timesheet,   determine_pay,   deduct_taxes,
>   make_payment
PART OF
>   Worker management system
DERIVES   total_pay USING timesheet, daily_rate and overtime_rate
>   (from employee_record)
>   tax_deduction USING tax_deduction_rules, total_pay
>   payment_check USING total_pay, tax_deduction
PROCEDURE
>   1. Check validity of timesheet
>   2. Compute total pay
>   3. Deduct taxes
>   4. Generate paycheck
HAPPENS
>   Once every week

FIGURE 2.9. Process description for the top-level process.

tion identifies the different inputs and outputs. In addition, for a hierarchical decomposition, a PSL description of a process specifies its subparts (children), and the process that it is a part of (the parent). A PSL description also specifies the existing procedure used in the process, and the dependencies between an output and different inputs. An example of the process description for the overall procedure of the pay-processing system, whose context diagram is shown in Figure 2.7, is given in Figure 2.9. The specification format used is similar to the one described in [TEI77].

Refinement can proceed by providing process specifications for the subparts identified in the process description. As we can see, the basic information in a PSL description is similar to the information in a DFD or a SADT diagram. The approach of top-down refinement based on refining processes is also similar to other methods.

RSL/REVS: The requirements statement language (RSL) [Alf77] was specifically designed for specifying complex real time control systems. The requirement engineering validation system (REVS) is a set of tools to support the development of requirements in RSL. REVS consists of a translator for the requirements written in RSL, a centralized database in which the translator deposits information, and a set of tools for processing the information in the database.

RSL uses a flow-oriented approach for specifying real time systems. For each flow the stimulus and the final response are specified. In between the major processing steps are specified. Flows can be specified in RSL as requirement networks (R-NETS) which can be represented graphically or textually. REVS contains tools to help in specifying flow paths and for checking completeness and consistency of information, as well as a simulation package. It also has the ability to generate reports and specific analyses.

Unlike other approaches, there is control information specified in RSL. This is because RSL is primarily designed for real-time control systems, where control information is an essential component for completely describing system requirements.

2.3. Requirement Specification

Once the analysis is complete, the requirements must be written or specified. The final output is the software requirements specification document (SRS). For smaller problems or problems that can easily be comprehended, the specification activity might come after the entire analysis is complete. However, it is more likely that problem analysis and specification are done concurrently. An analyst typically will analyze some parts of the problem and then write the requirements for that part. We start this section by discussing the different desirable characteristics of an SRS.

2.3.1. Characteristics of an SRS

To properly satisfy the basic goals, an SRS should have certain properties and should contain different types of requirements. In this section, we discuss some of the desirable characteristics of an SRS, and different components of a SRS. A good SRS is:

1. Understandable
2. Unambiguous
3. Complete
4. Verifiable
5. Consistent
6. Modifiable
7. Traceable

Clearly, an SRS should be understandable, as one of the goals of the requirements phase is to produce a document upon which the client, the users and the developers can agree. Since multiple parties need to understand and approve the SRS, it is of utmost importance that the SRS should be understandable.

An SRS is unambiguous if and only if every requirement stated has one and only one interpretation. Requirements are often written in natural language, which are inherently ambiguous. If the requirements are specified in a natural language, the SRS writer has to be especially careful to ensure that there are no ambiguities. One way to avoid ambiguities is to use some formal requirements specification language. The major disadvantage of using formal languages is the large effort required to write an SRS, and the high cost of doing so.

An SRS is complete if everything the software is supposed to do is in the SRS. A complete SRS defines the responses of the software to all classes of input data. For specifying all the requirements, the requirements relating to functionality, performance, design constraints, attributes and external interfaces must be specified. In addition, the responses to both valid and invalid input values must also be specified.

A requirement is verifiable if there exists some cost-effective process that can check if the final software meets that requirement. An SRS is verifiable if and only if every stated requirement is verifiable. This implies that the requirements should have as little subjectivity as possible because subjective requirements are difficult to verify. Unambiguity is essential for verifiability.

An SRS is consistent if there is no requirement that conflicts with another. Terminology can cause inconsistencies; for example, different requirements may use different terms to refer to the same object. There may be logical or temporal conflict between requirements causing inconsistencies. This occurs if the SRS contains two or more requirements whose logical or temporal characteristics cannot be satisfied together by any software system. For example, suppose a requirement states that an event e is to occur before another event f. But then another set of requirements state (directly or indirectly by transitivity) that event f should occur before event e. Inconsistencies in an SRS can be a reflection of some other major problems.

Writing an SRS is an iterative process. Even when the requirements of a system are specified, they are later modified as the needs of the client change with time. Hence an SRS should be easy to modify. An SRS is modifiable if its structure and style is such that any necessary change can be made easily, while preserving the completeness and consistency. Presence of redundancy is a major hindrance to modifiability, as it can easily lead to errors. For instance, assume that a requirement is stated in two places, and that at a later time the requirement needs to be changed. If only one occurrence of the requirement is modified, the resulting SRS will be inconsistent.

An SRS is traceable if the origin of each of its requirements is clear and if it facilitates the referencing of each requirement in future development [Iee87]. Forward traceability means that each requirement should be traceable to some design and code elements. Backward traceability requires that it should be possible to trace design and code elements to the requirements they support. Traceability aids verification and validation.

Of all these characteristics, completeness is perhaps the most important. The most common problem in requirements specification is when some of the requirements of the client are not specified. This necessitates additions and modifications to the requirements later in the development cycle, which are often expensive to incorporate. Incompleteness is also a major source of disagreement between the client and the supplier. The importance of having complete requirements cannot be over-emphasized.

2.3.2. Components of an SRS

Completeness of specifications is difficult to achieve and even more difficult to verify. Having guidelines about what different things an SRS should specify will help in completely specifying the requirements. Here we describe some of the system properties that an SRS should specify. The basic issues which an SRS must address are:

1. Functionality
2. Performance
3. Design constraints imposed on an implementation
4. External interfaces

The different components of a requirements document are shown in Figure 2.10.

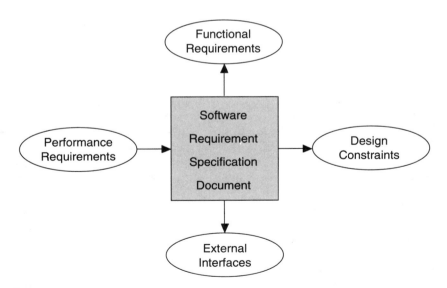

FIGURE 2.10. Major components of an SRS.

FUNCTIONAL REQUIREMENTS

Functional requirements specify which outputs should be produced from the given inputs. They describe the relationship between the input and output of the system. For each functional requirement, a detailed description of all the data inputs and their source, the units of measure, and the range of valid inputs must be specified.

All the operations to be performed on the input data to obtain the output should be specified. This includes specifying the validity checks on the input and output data, parameters affected by the operation, and equations or other logical operations which must be used to transform the inputs into corresponding outputs. For example, if there is a formula for computing the output, it should be specified. Care must be taken not to specify any algorithms that are not part of the system, but which may be needed to implement the system. These decisions should be left for the designer.

An important part of the specification is the system behavior in abnormal situations, like invalid input (which can occur in many ways) or error during computation. The functional requirement must clearly state what the system should do if such situations occur. Specifically, it should specify the behavior of the system for invalid inputs and invalid outputs. Furthermore, behavior for situations where the input is valid but the normal operation cannot be performed should also be specified. An example of this situation is an airline reservation system, where a reservation cannot be made even for valid passengers, if the airplane is fully booked. In short, the system behavior for all foreseen inputs and for all foreseen system states should be specified. These special conditions are often likely to be overlooked, resulting in a system that is not robust.

PERFORMANCE REQUIREMENTS

This part of an SRS specifies the performance constraints on the software system. All the requirements relating to the performance characteristics of the system must be clearly specified. There are two types of performance requirements—static and dynamic.

Static requirements are those that do not impose constraint on the execution characteristics of the system. These include requirements like the number of terminals to be supported, and number of simultaneous users to be supported, number of files and their sizes that the system has to process. These are also called *capacity* requirements of the system.

Dynamic requirements specify constraints on the execution behavior of the system. These typically include response time and throughput constraints on the system. Response time is the expected time for the completion of an operation under specified circumstances. Throughput is the expected number of operations that can be performed in a unit time. For example, the SRS may specify the number of transactions that must be processed per unit time, or what the response time for a particular command should be. Acceptable ranges of the different performance parameters should be specified, as well as acceptable performance for both normal and peak workload conditions.

All of these requirements should be stated in measurable terms. So requirements like "response time should be good", or the system must be able to "process all the transactions quickly", are not desirable as they are imprecise and are not verifiable. Instead, statements like "in 90% of all cases, the response time of command x should be less than one second", or "in 98% of all cases, a transaction should be processed in less than one second" should be used to declare performance specifications.

DESIGN CONSTRAINTS

There are a number of factors present in the client's environment that may restrict the choices of a designer. Such factors include: standards that must be followed, resource limits, operating environment, reliability and security requirements, and policies that may have an impact on the design of the system. An SRS should identify and specify all such constraints.

Standards compliance. This specifies the requirements for the standards that the system must follow. The standards may include the report format and accounting procedures. There may be audit tracing requirements, which require certain kinds of changes or operations that must be recorded in an audit file.

Hardware Limitations: The software may have to operate on some existing or pre-determined hardware, thus imposing restrictions on the design. Hardware limitations can include the type of machines to be used, operating system available on the system, languages supported, and limits on primary and secondary storage.

Reliability and Fault Tolerance: Fault tolerance requirements can place a major constraint on how the system is to be designed. Fault tolerance requirements often make the system more complex and expensive. Requirements about system behavior in the face of certain kinds of faults is specified. Recovery requirements are often an integral part here, detailing what the system should do if some failure occurs in order to ensure certain properties. Reliability requirements are very important for critical applications.

Security: Security requirements are particularly significant in defense systems and many database systems. Security requirements place restrictions on the use of certain commands, control access to data, provide different kinds of access requirements for different people, require the use of passwords, and cryptography techniques, and maintain a log of activities in the system.

EXTERNAL INTERFACE REQUIREMENTS

All the possible interactions of the software with people, hardware, and other software should be clearly specified. For the user interface, the characteristics of each user interface of the software product should be specified. User interface is increasingly becoming more important, and must be given proper attention. A preliminary user manual should be created with all user commands, screen formats, an explanation of how the system will appear to the user, and feedback and error messages. Like other specifications these requirements should be precise and verifiable. So, a statement like "the system should be user friendly", should be avoided in preference to statements like "commands should be no longer than 6 characters", "command names should reflect the function they perform".

For hardware interface requirement, the SRS should specify the logical characteristics of each interface between the software product and the hardware components. If the software is to execute on existing hardware or on pre-determined hardware, all the characteristics of the hardware, including memory restrictions, should be specified. In addition, the current use and load characteristics of the hardware should be given.

The interface requirement should specify the interface with other software which the system will use or which will use the system. This includes the interface with the operating system and other applications. The message content and format of each interface should be specified.

2.3.3. Specification Languages

Requirements specification necessitates the use of some specification language. The language should possess many of the desired qualities (modifiable, understandable, unambiguous, and so forth) of the SRS. In addition, we want the language to be easy to learn and use. As one might expect, many of the above mentioned characteristics conflict in the selection of a specification language. For example, to avoid ambiguity, it is best to use some formal language. But for ease of understanding a natural language might be preferable. Here we describe some of the commonly used languages for requirement specification.

STRUCTURED ENGLISH

Natural languages have been widely used for specifying requirements. The major advantage of using a natural language is that both client and supplier understand the language. Specifying the problem to be solved in a natural language is an expected outcome in the evolution of software engineering. Initially, since software systems were small, requirements were verbally conveyed using the natural language for expression (in fact, much in-house software development is still done in this manner). Later, as software requirements grew more complex, the requirements were specified in a written form, rather than orally, but the means for expression stayed the same.

The use of natural languages has some important drawbacks. By the very nature of a natural language, written requirements will be imprecise and ambiguous. This goes against some of the desirable characteristics that we have stated earlier. Furthermore, efforts to be more precise and complete result in voluminous requirement specification documents, as natural languages are quite verbose.

Due to these drawbacks, there is an effort to move from natural languages to formal languages for requirement specification. However, natural languages are still widely used, and are likely to be in use for the near future. In order to reduce some of the drawbacks, most often natural language is used in a structured fashion. In structured English (choosing English as our natural language), requirements are broken into sections, and paragraphs. Each paragraph is then broken into sub-paragraphs. Many organizations also specify strict uses of some words like "shall", "perhaps", "should" etc., and try to restrict the use of common phrases in order to improve the precision and reduce the verbosity and ambiguity.

REGULAR EXPRESSIONS

Regular expressions can be used to specify the structure of symbol strings formally. String specification is useful for specifying such things as input data, command sequence, and contents of a message. Regular expressions are a useful approach for such cases. Regular expressions can be considered as grammar for specifying the valid sequences in a language, and can be automatically processed. They are routinely used in compiler construction for recognition of symbols and tokens.

There are a few basic constructs allowed in regular expressions.

1. Atoms: The basic symbols or the alphabet of the language.
2. Composition: Formed by concatenating two regular expressions. For regular expressions r1 and r2, concatenation is expressed by (r1 r2), and denotes concatenation of strings represented by r1 and r2.
3. Alternation: Specifies the either/or relationship. For r1 and r2, alternation is specified by (r1 | r2), and denotes the union of the sets of strings specified by r1 and r2.
4. Closure: Specifies repeated occurrence of a regular expression. This is the most powerful of the constructs. For a regular expression r, closure is specified by (r)u*d, which means that strings denoted by r are concatenated zero or more times.

With these basic constructs many data streams can be defined. Hierarchical specifications can also be constructed by using abstract names for specifying the regular expressions, and then giving the regular expression specification for those names. For complex data streams hierarchical specifications can enhance clarity.

Example: Consider a file containing student records. Each student record has the name of the student, followed by the social security number, followed by the sequence of courses the student has taken. This input file can easily be specified as a regular expression.

Record_file = (Name SSN Courses)*
Name = (Last First)
Last, First = (A|B|C| . . . |Z)(a|b|c| . . . |z)*
SSN = digit digit digit digit digit digit digit digit digit
digit = (0|1|2| . . . |9)
Courses = (C_number)*

And C_number can be specified depending on conventions followed
(e.g. "CS" followed by a three digit number). Once the regular expression
is specified, checking that a given input is a valid string in the language (i.e.
has the structure specified by the regular expression) can be done automatically.
Tools exist that will generate the analyzers for a given regular
expression.

DECISION TABLES

Decision tables provide a mechanism for specifying complex decision
logic. It is formal, table based notation which can also be automatically
processed to check for qualities like completeness and lack of ambiguity.

A decision table has two parts. The top part lists the different conditions
and the bottom part specifies different actions. The table essentially specifies
under what combination of conditions what actions are to be performed.
It is best to specify the conditions in a manner such that the
condition can either be true or false, thus taking only two values. In this
case if there are N conditions specified, a complete decision table will have
2^N different combinations listed for which the actions must be specified.
However, not all the combinations of conditions might be feasible.

Example: Consider the part of a banking system that is responsible for
debiting from accounts. For this part the relevant conditions are:

C1: The account number is correct
C2: The signature matches
C3: There is enough money in the account.

The possible actions are:

A1: Give money
A2: Give statement that not enough money is there
A3: Call the vigilance department to check for fraud.

Part of the decision table for this is shown in Figure 2.11. The decision
rules are the different combinations of conditions that are of interest. For
each condition a Y means yes or true, N means no or false, and a dash (—)
means either true or false. If an action is to be taken for a particular
combination of the conditions it is shown by an X for that action. If there is
no mark for an action for a particular combination of conditions, it means
that the action is not to be performed.

	1	2	3	4	5
C_1	N	N	Y	Y	Y
C_2		N	N	Y	Y
C_3			N	Y	N
A_1				X	
A_2			X		X
A_3		X			

FIGURE 2.11. Decision table for the banking example.

FINITE STATE AUTOMATA

Finite state automata (FSA) includes the concept of state as well as input data streams. A FSA has a finite set of states and specifies transitions between the states. The transition from one state to another is based on the input. An FSA can be specified pictorially, formally as grammar and transition rules, or as a transition table.

FSAs are used extensively for specifying communication protocols. They are not used much in data processing type of applications.

Example: Consider a simplified version of the alternating bit protocol for data communication. A node can receive a message numbered 0 or 1. When it receives message 0, it sends an acknowledgment, and waits for the message 1 to arrive. When message 1 arrives, it sends an acknowledgment and then waits for message 0 to arrive. A FSA specifying this required behavior of the node is shown in Figure 2.12.

State s0 is the state where the node is waiting for message 0 to arrive. When this message arrives, a state transition occurs and the state changes from s0 to s1. The output produced during this transition is the ACK message. Similarly, when the system is in state s1, it is waiting for the message 1 to arrive. When the message arrives, it sends the ACK message and changes state to s0.

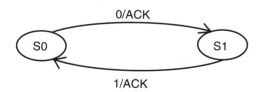

FIGURE 2.12. FSA for the data communication example.

2.3.4. Structure of a Requirements Document

All the requirements for the system have to be included in a document. The requirements document should be clear and concise. For this it may be necessary to organize the requirements document as sections and subsections. There can be many ways to structure a requirements document. Here we present an outline which is derived from the IEEE guide to software requirements specifications [Iee87].

1. Introduction
   1.1 Purpose
   1.2 Scope
   1.3 Definitions, Acronyms and Abbreviations
   1.4 References
   1.5 Overview
2. General Description
   2.1 Product Perspective
   2.2 Product Functions
   2.3 User Characteristics
   2.4 General Constraints
   2.5 Assumptions and Dependencies
3. Functional Requirements
   3.1 Functional Requirement 1
       3.1.1 Introduction
       3.1.2 Inputs
       3.1.3 Processing
       3.1.4 Outputs
   3.2 Functional Requirement 2
4. External Interface Requirements
   4.1 User Interfaces
   4.2 Hardware Interfaces
   4.3 Software Interfaces
5. Performance Requirements
6. Design Constraints
   6.1 Standards Compliance
   6.2 Hardware Limitations
7. Other Requirements

The introduction contains the purpose, scope, and overview of the requirements document. All the references that are cited in the document and any definitions that are used are also listed.

Section 2 describes the general factors that affect the product and its requirements. Specific requirements are not mentioned, but a general overview is presented to make the understanding of the specific requirements easier. Product perspective is essentially the relationship of the product to other products; defining if the product is independent or is a part of a larger product, and what are the principal interfaces of the product. A general high-level description of the functions to be performed by the product is given. Schematic diagrams showing a high-level view of different functions and their relationships with each other can often be useful. Similarly, typical characteristics of the eventual end user and general constraints are also specified.

Sections 3, 4, 5 and 6 specify the particular requirements. All the details the software developer needs to create a design and eventually implement the system are specified. If there are any other requirements that have not been described, they are specified in Section 7. Most products change over time, as the environment in which they operate and the needs of the users change. Modifying existing software can be quite expensive, if software is not properly designed. One of the major goals of design techniques is to develop software that can be easily modified. Towards this end, it is useful if possible future modifications that can be foreseen at the requirements specification time be outlined, so that the system can be designed to ensure that modifications can easily accommodate those changes.

The outline given here is merely a guideline. There are other ways a requirements document can be organized. The key concern is that once requirements have been identified, the requirements document should be organized in such a manner that it aids validation and system design. For different projects many of these sections may not be needed, and can be omitted. Especially for smaller projects, some of the sections and subsections may not be necessary to properly specify the requirements.

2.4. Validation

The development of software starts with the requirements document, which is also used to determine if the software system is acceptable or not. It is therefore important that the requirements specification contain no errors and specify the client's requirements correctly. Furthermore, as we have seen, the longer an error remains undetected, the greater the cost of correcting it. Hence, it is extremely desirable to detect errors in the requirements before the design and development of the software begins.

Due to the nature of the requirement specification phase, there is a lot of room for misunderstanding and committing errors, and it is quite possible that the requirements specification does not accurately represent the client's needs. It has been observed that many errors found later on in the project, are due to the errors in the requirements.

Some techniques have been proposed for verifying the requirements. Requirements verification means checking such factors as completeness, consistency, and testability of the requirements. Since requirements specification is formally specifying something that originally existed informally in peoples' minds, requirements verification often involves interaction with people, particularly the clients. Some automated verification is possible, however, if requirements are stated in a formal language or by using a requirements specification tool.

2.4.1. Reading

The goal in reading [Boe84] is to have someone other than the author of the requirements read the requirements specification document to identify potential problems. By having the requirements read by another person who possibly has a different "interpretation" of requirements, many of the requirements problems caused by misinterpretations or ambiguities can be identified. Furthermore, if the reader is a person who is interested in the project (like a person from the quality assurance group which will eventually test the system), issues that could cause problems later can be brought to surface. For example, if a tester reads the requirements, it is quite likely that the testability of requirements will be well examined.

Reading is effective only if the reader takes the job seriously and reads the requirements carefully. Even with serious readers, reading is limited in scope for catching completeness and consistency errors, particularly for large software systems.

2.4.2. Constructing Scenarios

Scenarios [Boe84] describe different situations of how the system will work once it is operational. The most common area for constructing scenarios is that of system-user interaction. Constructing scenarios is good for clarifying misunderstandings in the human-computer interaction area. They are not of much value for verifying the consistency and completeness of requirements.

2.4.3. Requirement Reviews

Requirements reviews are the most common method employed for validating the requirement specifications. Reviews are used throughout software development for quality assurance and data collection. We will discuss the general procedure of reviews in the next chapter. Here we only discuss some aspects relevant to requirements reviews.

Requirements review is a review by a group of people to find errors and point out other matters of concern in the requirements specifications of a system. The review group should include the author of the requirements document, someone who understands the needs of the client, a person of the design team, and the person(s) responsible for maintaining the requirements document. It is also good practice to include some people not directly involved with product development, like a software quality engineer.

One way to organize the review meeting is to have each participant go over the requirements before the meeting, and mark the items that he has doubts about or that he feels need further clarification. Checklists can be quite useful in identifying such items. In the meeting, each participant goes through the list of potential defects that he has uncovered. As the members ask questions, the requirements analyst (who is the author of the requirements specification document) provides clarifications if there are no errors, or agrees to the presence of errors. Other people may need further clarification or join the discussion at any time. The discussions that take place during the review are likely to uncover errors other than the suspected error that may have started the discussion. These discussions form a very important part of the review process.

Alternatively, the meeting can start with the analyst explaining each of the requirements in the document. The participants ask questions, share doubts or seek clarifications. Errors are uncovered by the participants in the discussion that ensues. Some of the possible errors in the requirements specification are incompleteness, inconsistency, unfeasible requirements, and incorrect translation of requirements [Dun84].

Incompleteness is a common error in requirements, and can occur in different forms. Omitted functions is a frequent problem, in which some of the actual functional requirements of the client may have been omitted during requirements specification. Incomplete specification of the non-functional requirements of the system, or incomplete specification of the properties of the environment that affect the system, will also make the requirements incomplete. Another form of error is incomplete specification of a functional requirement; although a functional requirement may be stated, the behavior may not be completely specified. This often occurs due to failure to specify the behavior for exceptional conditions such as incorrect input.

Another common form of error in requirements is *inconsistency*. Inconsistency can be due to contradictions within the requirements themselves, or due to incompatibility of the stated requirements with the actual requirements of the client or with the environment in which the system will operate. Incompatibility with the environment often occurs due to assumptions or stipulations made about the environment which are not correct. For example, the format of the input data as specified in the requirements document may not be the actual format of the data in the environment. Requirements may be conflicting. For example, response time requirements of different functions may be inconsistent with the response time requirement of the overall system that utilizes those functions.

Other common sources of error are incorrect translation of actual requirements and unfeasible requirements. Incorrect translation can occur during requirements specification due to a communication gap between the client and the team performing the requirements analysis. Infeasibility often occurs because the performance requirements cannot be satisfied with the given hardware, or because the technology is simply not available to develop a system that will satisfy the requirements.

Although the primary goal of the review process is to reveal any errors in the requirements, such as these discussed above, the review process is also utilized to consider factors affecting quality, such as testability and readability. During the review, one of the jobs of the reviewers is to uncover the requirements that are too subjective and are too difficult to define criteria for testing that requirement.

A Sample Checklist: Checklists are frequently used in reviews to focus the review effort and ensure that no major source of errors is overlooked by the reviewers. Based on the common problems that we have discussed above, we present one possible checklist that can be used for reviews [Dun84]. A good checklist will usually depend on the project.

Are all hardware resources defined?
Have the response times of functions been specified?
Have all the hardware, external software and data interfaces been defined?
Have all the functions required by the client been specified?
Is each requirement testable?
Is the initial state of the system defined?
Are the responses to exceptional conditions specified?
Does the requirement contain restrictions, that can be controlled by the designer?
Are possible future modifications specified?

2.4.4. Automated Cross-Referencing

Automated cross-referencing makes use of processors to verify some properties of requirements. Any automated processing of requirements is possible if the requirements are written in a formal specification language, or a language specifically designed for machine processing. We have seen examples of such languages earlier, including PSL/PSA, SSA, and SADT.

If the requirements are in machine processable form, they can be analyzed for internal consistency among different elements of the requirements. Closure properties can also be checked, thus helping to uncover incompleteness of requirements. The language processors can also produce cross-reference information which can then be used in manual analysis.

2.4.5. Prototyping

A prototype can be built to verify requirements. Prototypes can be quite useful in verifying the feasibility of some of the requirements (such as answering the question "is it 'do-able' ") and checking the user interface. As discussed in Chapter 1, prototyping-based development of software offers some advantages. Prototyping can be very helpful for a clear understanding of requirements, removing misconceptions, and aiding clients and developers in requirements analysis. The basic limitation of this approach is the high cost it is likely to incur.

2.5. Metrics

During requirement analysis we are completely in the problem domain. In fact, during requirement analysis, one of the goals is to consciously avoid any decisions regarding the solution. Consequently, the metrics at this stage are unlikely to be useful for predicting quality of the final product. Metrics at this stage can be useful in assessing the quality of the requirements specification itself. In addition, as the requirements are the starting phase of a development project, metrics can also be useful for assessing some aspects of the project.

However, metrics for both these purposes—assessing the quality of the requirements and predicting about the project—are not readily available. Software metrics is in general a neglected area and only recently has it gained importance, but metrics for the early stages of development are, by and large, ignored. This says more about the state-of-the-art of software metrics, rather than the usefulness of such metrics. In this section, we will discuss some of the metrics, and how they can be used. As we will see, these metrics are fairly primitive, and their predictive value is limited and not well established for general use.

2.5.1. Function Points

Function points is a metric that can be applied at the requirements stage, and can be used to predict the size or the cost of the system, as well as assess the project productivity. Using function points for cost, size and productivity estimation is called function point analysis [Inc88]. The idea behind function point analysis is that the size and cost of the final system can be estimated in such terms as the function it implements, the number of inputs, and the number of outputs. These inputs can be easily obtained after requirements analysis. The counts of different parameters are weighted to reflect the value of that particular parameter and are determined by analysis of historical data about similar projects. The formula originally employed for computing the function points, with the weights for different parameters, is as follows:

Function points =
  Number of inputs * 4
  + Number of outputs * 5
  + Number of enquiries * 4
  + Number of master files * 10
  + Number of interfaces * 7

The weights can be adjusted for a particular project, depending on the complexity and importance of the different parameters. Clearly, the data for calculating function points can be easily obtained from the requirements, and the calculation is also easy.

Function points can be the basis of cost estimation. The estimation method is simple. The data about the cost of previous projects is plotted against the function points of those projects. This curve is used to estimate the cost of the current project from the value of its function points. Alternatively, function points can be used to check the cost estimation obtained from different methods. We will discuss cost estimation models in the next chapter.

With historical data about other projects, function points can also be used to assess the project productivity. The data about the productivity of the previous projects is plotted against the function points of those projects. The productivity of the current project is estimated to be the productivity value, as specified by the curve, for the function points of this project. It has been found that productivity decreases as the function points increase. This is consistent with the general experience that productivity decreases as projects become larger.

2.5.2. Number of Errors Found

This metric can be useful for assessing the quality of requirement specifications. The number of errors can be obtained from the requirement review report. The errors can be categorized into different types, and the number of errors for the different types can be observed. Some of the possible types of errors are:

number of missing functional requirements,
number of clarifications/ambiguities,
number of unverifiable requirements, and
number of incorrect requirements.

The effective use of this data will require historical data about errors on other projects. For example, a large number of clarifications/ambiguities can imply that there might be problems during later phases, particularly during acceptance testing. Similarly, other error data can be used to foresee future problems that are likely to arise during the project. Such data can be weighted to produce a single "quality number", but no such effort has been done.

2.5.3. Change Request Frequency

Requirements rarely stay unchanged. Change requests come from the clients (requesting added functionality, a new report, or a report in a different format, for example), or from the developers (infeasibility, difficulty in implementing, etc.). Frequency of such change requests can be used as a metric. Its basic use is to assess the stability of the requirements, and how many changes in requirements to expect during the later stages.

Many organizations have formal methods for requesting and incorporating changes in requirements. Change data can be easily extracted from these formal change approval procedures. The frequency of changes can also be plotted against time. For most projects, the frequency decreases with time. This is to be expected—most of the changes will occur early, when the requirements are being analyzed and understood. Further on, particularly during the later phases, requests for changes should decrease.

For a project, if the change requests are not decreasing with time, it could mean that the requirements analysis has not been done properly. Frequency of change requests can also be used to "freeze" the requirements—when the frequency goes below an acceptable threshold, the requirements can be considered as frozen and the design can proceed. The threshold has to be determined based on experience and historical data.

Change data (such as in requirements, design, and coding) is used throughout the development cycle for project management. No general rules exist regarding how to use this data. The manner in which this data is to be used is likely to depend on the environment and culture of the developer's organization. This metric can be refined by introducing different categories of changes.

2.6. Monitoring and Control

Although the early phases are very important in the overall development process, they typically involve a small number of (usually senior) people, and generally do not last too long. Consequently, stringent monitoring and control mechanisms are not needed.

During analysis, it is important to ensure that different analysis steps are being followed and that user involvement is constant. Comments from users and clients at the different stages of analysis provide useful information about the quality of analysis. Preliminary analysis is also the source for determining how analysis should proceed. In particular, decisions about whether prototyping should be used, and if used, what parts should be included in the prototype, depend upon the initial analysis.

Controlling requirement changes is perhaps the most important control activity in the requirements phase. Controlling these changes is very important for many reasons. The requirements are not entirely under the control of the developers; the clients are also involved. Lack of understanding of the requirements by the clients themselves is a major reason for change requests. Once the requirements have been "frozen" or agreed upon, changing the requirements can change the scope of the system, which can have impact on the overall cost and schedule of the system. Requirement changes that come in later in the cycle can often be quite costly to incorporate. For all these reasons, it is very important that the management closely monitor the requirements and make sure that only limited changes are allowed.

The basic approach is to evaluate the effect of each change request. If a change drastically changes the scope of the project it should either be disallowed or the project should be renegotiated. It is important that any requirement change of any consequence should go through the management and should be permitted only if it is approved. Effectively controlling the changes is the only way to keep the scope of the project in check.

One of the goals of the requirements specification is that the specifications document should be easy to change. This implies that it should be easy to identify where changes must be made, and that a change in requirements should change only one section of the requirement specifications. One way to estimate the "ease of change" is to measure (by having forms filled out, for example) the effort required to make the change, some measure of how much of the document had to be examined to make the change, and how many sections of the document were actually modified to make the change [Bas81]. Comparing this data with past experience will give the project management a good idea of the quality of the requirements, with respect to the ease of change.

Requirement reviews are usually the sole means employed for validating requirements. Consequently, great attention should be given to reviews and the result of the reviews. Firstly, it should be ensured that enough time is allotted for reviews and that reviews are not treated as a routine exercise. The results of the reviews can give a good insight about the quality of the requirements and if there are areas of concern about the project scope. The number of errors found and the nature of the errors can also shed light into possible future changes in the requirements and problems with the clients. It should also be made certain that sufficient evidence has been presented on the completeness and consistency of the SRS.

2.7. Summary

Requirements specification is the starting step for the development activities. It is currently one of the weak areas of software engineering. During requirements specifications the goal is to produce a document of the client's requirements. This document forms the basis of development and software validation. The basic reason for the difficulty in software requirements specification comes from the fact that there are three interested parties—the client, the end users, and the software developer. The requirements document has to be such that the client and users can understand it easily and the developers can use it as a basis for software development. Due to the diverse parties involved in software requirements specification, a communication gap exists. This makes the task of requirements specification difficult.

There are two basic activities in the requirements phase. The first is problem or requirement analysis. The goal of this activity is to understand such different aspects as the requirements of the problem, its context, and how it fits in the client's organization. The second activity is requirements specification, during which the understood problem is specified or written, producing the SRS. The production of the SRS is the goal of the requirement phase.

An SRS, in order to satisfy its goals, should possess certain characteristics. The requirements specification should be complete in that all possible requirements should be specified. It should be consistent, with no conflicting requirements. The requirements should be verifiable, since eventually whether the software satisfies the requirements must be verified. This can only be done if the requirements are verifiable. The requirements specification should also be modifiable and traceable.

In order to specify the requirements completely, a requirements specification should specify certain properties of the software. First, the SRS should specify all the functions the software is supposed to support. Functional requirements essentially are the input/output behavior specification for the software. Secondly, the SRS should have performance requirements. All requirements relating to performance, such as response time, throughput, and number of concurrent users, should be clearly specified. Thirdly, the SRS should specify the design constraints (those factors which are not really features of the software, but constrain the design). Examples of design constraints are standards compliance, operating environment, and hardware limitations. Finally, all the external interfaces of the software should be specified in the SRS. These should include the hardware, software and human interfaces.

It is important that the final requirements be validated before the next phase of software development starts. As far as possible, all errors from the requirements specifications should be removed before design commences. A number of methods exist for requirements validation. The most commonly used method is requirement review. In this technique, a team of persons, including a representative of the client, review the requirements document and ensure that it is complete and consistent.

Exercises

1. What are the central problems in software requirements specification?
2. Is it possible to have a system that can automatically verify completeness of an SRS document? If not, why not?
3. What are the different aspects that should be specified in an SRS?
4. What uses, other than the ones listed in the chapter, can you think of for a good SRS?
5. Construct an example of an inconsistent (incomplete) SRS.
6. How can you specify the "maintainability" of a software system in quantitative terms?

7. How can you specify the "user friendliness" of the software system in quantitative terms?

8. Would you specify that the response time should be always less than T, or that it should be less than T, X% of the times? Why should one be chosen over the other?

9. For a complete and unambiguous response time requirement, the environmental factors on which the response time depends must be specified. Which factors should be considered, and what units should be chosen to specify them?

10. Make a friend of yours as your client. Then sit down with him and write an SRS for the following.
    1. An electronic mail system.
    2. A simple student registration system.
    3. A system to analyze the diet of a person.
    4. A system to manage recipes for a household.
    5. A system to fill tax forms for the current year tax laws.

11. Go to your department office and develop an SRS for automating some of the functions the office performs (such as accounting, purchasing, and mailing letters).

12. In the example for the FSA given in the chapter, assume that a message can get lost during transmission, and a "time out" event occurs at each site to detect the loss of messages. Extend the FSA to model this new system.

13. Write a regular expression for describing the references in the format used in this book.

14. A library data base contains entries which have the name of the book, followed by the author's name, the publisher's name and the year of publication, the ISBN number of the book, and finally the number of copies in the book. Each of the data entries is on a new line. Represent this data base as a regular expression. You should use '0 to represent the new line character.

15. Consider the problem of developing software for controlling a small chemical plant. The plant has a number of emergency situations where specified actions have to be taken. Some of these are: (1) if the temperature exceeds T1, then the water shower is turned on, (2) if the temperature is below T2, then the heat is turned on, (3) if the pressure is above P1, the valve v1 is opened, but if it is above P2 (P2>P1), then both valves v1 and v2 are opened, (4) if the chemical quantity is more than M, and the temperature is more than T3, then the water shower is turned on, and a counter chemical is added, (5) if the pressure is above P2 and temperature is above T1, then the water shower is turned on, valves v1 and v2 are opened and alarm bells are sounded.

   Write the requirements for the control system given above in the form of a decision table.

Case Study

Problem Analysis

The computer science department in a University offers many courses every semester, which are taught by many instructors. These courses are scheduled based on some policy directions of the department. Currently the scheduling is done manually, but the department would like to automate the scheduling. We have to first understand the problem (subject of this section), and then produce a requirements document (described in the next section) based on our understanding of the problem. First we identify the parties involved.

Client: Chairman of the computer science department.

End-users: Department secretary and instructors.

Now we begin to study the current system. After speaking with the instructors, the department chairman, and the secretary, we found that the system operates as follows. Each instructor specifies, on a sheet of paper, the course he is teaching, expected enrollment, and his preferences for lecture times. These preferences must be valid lecture times, which are specified by the department. These sheets are given to the department secretary, who keeps them in the order they are received. After the deadline expires, the secretary does the scheduling. Copies of the final schedule are sent to the instructors. The overall DFD for the system is shown in Figure 2.13.

This DFD was discussed with the chairman and the department secretary and was approved by them. We now focus on the scheduling process, which is our main interest. From the chairman we found that the two major policies regarding scheduling are: (1) the post-graduate (PG) courses are given preference over undergraduate (UG) courses, and (2) no two PG courses can be scheduled at the same time.

The department secretary was interviewed at length to find out the details of the scheduling activity. The schedule of the last few semesters, together with their respective inputs (i.e. the sheets) were also studied. It

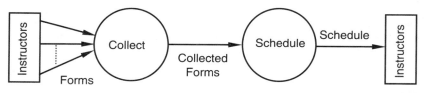

FIGURE 2.13. Top-level DFD for the current scheduling system.

was found that the basic process is as follows. The sheets are separated into three piles—one for PG courses, one for UG courses, and one for courses with no preference. The order of the sheets in the three piles was maintained. First the courses in the PG pile were scheduled and then the courses in the UG pile were scheduled. The courses were scheduled in the order they appeared in the pile. During scheduling no backtracking was done, i.e., once a course is scheduled, the scheduling of later courses has no effect on its schedule. After all the PG and UG courses with preferences were processed, courses without any preferences were scheduled in the available slots. It was also found that information about classrooms and the department-approved lecture times was also tacitly used during the scheduling. The DFD for the schedule process is shown in Figure 2.14.

The secretary was not able to explain the algorithm employed for scheduling. It is likely that some hit-and-miss approach is being followed. However, while scheduling the following was being checked.

1. Classroom capacity is sufficient for the course.
2. A slot for a room is never allotted to more than one course.

The two basic data flows are the sheets containing preferences and the final schedule. The data dictionary entry for these is shown in Figure 2.15.

Now we have to define the DFD for the new or future automated system. Automating scheduling can affect the preference collection method also, so boundaries of change include the entire system. After discussion with the chairman, the instructors, and the secretary, the following decisions were taken regarding what the automated system should do, and what the new environment should be.

1. The preferences will be electronically mailed to the secretary by the instructors. The secretary will put these preferences for different courses in a file in the order in which they are received. The secretary will also make entries for all courses for which no response has been given before the deadline. Entries for these courses will have no preferences.

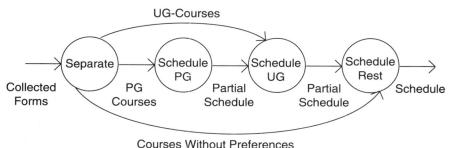

FIGURE 2.14. The DFD for the schedule process.

collected_forms =
  [instructor_name +
  course_number +
  [preferences]*]

schedule =
  [course_number class_room lecture_time]*

FIGURE 2.15. Data dictionary for the scheduling system.

2. The format for each course entry should be similar to the one currently being used.
3. Entries might have errors, so the system should be able to check for errors.
4. The system should make sure that scheduling of UG courses does not make a PG course without any preference unschedulable. This is not being done currently, but is desired.
5. No optimization of the schedule is needed.
6. A reason for unschedulability should be given for the preferences that are not satisfied or for courses that cannot be scheduled.
7. Information about department courses, classrooms, and valid lecture times will be kept in a file.

The DFD for the new logical system (one with automation) is shown in Figure 2.16.

The two important data entities are the two files in the DFD. The data dictionary entry for these is given in Figure 2.17.

It is decided that the scheduling process will be automated. The rest (such as combining preferences) will be done manually. Based on the format currently used in the sheets, a detailed format for the course entries

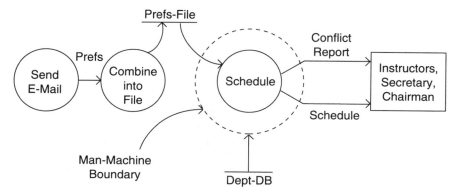

FIGURE 2.16. DFD for the new system.

prefs_file =
  [pref]*

pref =
  course_number + enrollment + [preferences]*

dept_DB =
  [class_rooms]* +
  dept_course_list +
  [valid_lecture_time]*

class_rooms =
  room_no + capacity

FIGURE 2.17. Data dictionary entry for files in the DFD.

was decided upon and approved by the instructors. A detailed format for the dept_DB file was also chosen and approved. The final formats and the requirements are given in the requirements document.

Requirements Specification Document

Abstract: This is the requirements document for the case study that will be used throughout the book. The system to be developed is for scheduling the courses in a computer science department, based on the input about classrooms, lecture times, and time preferences of the different instructors. Different conditions have to be satisfied by the final schedule. This document follows the IEEE standard for a requirements specification document, with some variations.

1. Introduction

1.1. Purpose. The purpose of this document is to describe all external requirements for a course scheduling system. It also describes the interfaces for the system.

1.2. Scope. This document is the only one that describes the requirements of the system. It is meant for use by the developers, and will also be the basis for validating the final delivered system. Any changes made to the requirements in the future will have to go through a formal change approval process. The developer is responsible for asking for clarifications, where necessary, and will not make any alterations without the permission of the client.

1.3. Definitions, Acronyms, Abbreviations. Not applicable.

1.4. References. Not applicable.

1.5. Developer's Responsibilities Overview. The developer is responsible for (a) developing the system, (b) installing the software on the client's hardware, (c) for conducting any user training that might be needed for using the system, and (c) maintaining the system for a period of one year after installation.

2. General Description

2.1. Product Functions Overview. In the computer science department there are a set of classrooms. Every semester the department offers some courses, which are chosen from the set of department courses. A course has an expected enrollment and could be for graduate students or under-graduate students. For each course, the instructor gives time preferences for lectures.

The system is to produce a schedule for the department which specifies the time and room assignments for the different courses. Preference should be given to graduate courses, and no two graduate courses should be scheduled at the same time. If some courses cannot be scheduled, the system should also produce a "conflict report" which lists the courses that cannot be scheduled and the reasons for the inability to schedule them.

2.2. User Characteristics. The main users of this system will be depart-ment secretaries, who are somewhat literate about computers and can use programs such as editors and text processors.

2.3. General Constraints. The system should run on Sun 3/50 work-stations running Unix 4.2 BSD.

2.4. General Assumptions and Dependencies. Not applicable.

3. Functional Requirements

3.1. General Description of Inputs and Outputs. The system has two file inputs, and produces two major outputs. The general description of these is given here. Detailed formats are given later.

Input_file_1: Contains the list of room numbers along with their capacity; list of all the courses in the department catalog; and the list of valid lecture times.

Input_file_2: Contains information about the courses being offered. For each course, it specifies the course number, expected enrollment, and a number of lecture time preferences.

Output_1: Class number and time of all the schedulable courses.

Output_2: List of courses that could not be scheduled and the reason.

3.2. Functional Requirements.

1. Determine the time and room number for the courses such that the following constraints are satisfied.
    1.1. No more than one course should be scheduled at the same time in the same room.
    1.2. The classroom capacity should be more than the expected enrollment of the course.
    1.3. Preference is given to post graduate courses over undergraduate courses for scheduling. Every course with a number greater than 600 is a post graduate course; others are undergraduate courses.
    1.4. The post graduate (undergraduate) courses should be scheduled in the order they appear in the input file, and the highest possible priority of an instructor should be given. If no priority is specified, any class and time can be assigned. If any priority is incorrect, not being a valid lecture time, it is to be discarded.
    1.5. No two post graduate courses should be scheduled at the same time.
2. If no preference is specified for a course, the course should be scheduled in any manner that does not violate the above constraints.
3. Produce a list of all courses that could not be scheduled because some constraint(s) could not be satisfied, and give reasons for unschedulability.
4. The data in the input_file_2 should be checked for validity against the data provided in input_file_1. Where possible, the validity of the data in input_file_1 should also be checked. Messages should be given for improper input data, and the invalid data item should be ignored.

3.3. Detailed Input File formats. File formats are defined in a regular-expression-like manner. Strings within quotation marks in the format specification are constants, while others are variables which are later defined. Limits are also specified for the variables, where applicable.

Input_file_1: The format of the file is

```
"rooms
   room1 ":" cap1
   room2 ":" cap2
   :
   ",",
"courses
   course1 "," course2 "," course3 "," . . . . ";"
"times"
   time1 "," time2 "," time3, ";"
```

Where

room1, room2 are room numbers with three digits.
There are a maximum of 20 rooms in the building.
cap1, cap2 are room capacities and are within the range [10, 300].
course1, course2 are course numbers. They are of the form
   "csddd", where d is a digit. There are no more than 30 courses
   offered by the department.
time1, time2 are valid lecture times. These are of the form
   "MWFd" or "MWFdd" or "TTd" or "TTd:dd" or "TTdd:dd".
   There are no more than 15 such valid lecture times.

An example of this file is:

rooms
   101 : 25
   115 : 50
   200 : 250 ;
courses
   cs101, cs102, cs110, cs120, cs220, cs412, cs430, cs612, cs630 ;
times
   MWF9, MWF10, MWF11, MWF2, TT9, TT10:30, TT2, TT3:30 ;

Input_file_2: The format of the file is

"course	enrollment	Preferences"
c#1	cap1	pre1 "," pre2 "," pre3 . . .
c#2	cap2	pre1 "," pre2 "," pre3 . . .
		:
		:

Where,

c#1, c#2 are valid course numbers
cap1, cap2 are integers in the range [3..250].
pre1, pre2, pre3 are time preferences of the instructor.
   A maximum of 5 preferences are allowed for a course.

An example of this file is

Course Number	Enrollment	Preferences
cs101	180	MWF9, MWF10, MWF11,
cs412	80	TT9 MWF9, TT9, TT10:30
cs612	35	
cs630	40	

3.4. Detailed Output Formats. **Schedule** should be a table of the type

Lecture times

Class   course# s
room
numbers

Unschedulable courses should be listed along with the reasons. For each preference, the reason for inability to schedule should be stated. An example is:
  cs612: Preference 1: Conflict with cs600.
  Preference 2: No room with proper capacity.

4. External Interface Requirements

4.1. User Interface. User Commands: Only one user command is required. The system should prompt for the input file names.

Error Messages

At the minimum, the following error messages are to be given. e1. Input file does not exist.

e2. Input-file-1 has error
    e2.1. The course number has a wrong format
    e2.2. Some lecture time has a wrong format.
    e2.3. Class room number has a wrong format.
    e2.4. Class room capacity is out of range.
e3. Input-file-2 has error e3.1. There is no course of this number.
    e3.2. There is no such lecture time.
e4. There are more than permissible courses in the file.
      The later ones are ignored.
e5. There are more than permissible preferences.
      Later ones are ignored.

5. Performance Constraints

1. For a input_file_2 containing 20 courses, and up to 5 preferences for each course, the reports should be printed in less than 1 minute.

6. Design Constraints

6.1. Software Constraints. The system is to run under the operating system Unix. It has to be written in Pascal.

6.2. Hardware Constraints. The system will run on a Sun workstation. It will have a 8 pages per minute printer attached to it.

7. Acceptance Criteria

Before accepting the system the developer will have to demonstrate that the system works on the data about course for the last 4 semesters. The developer will have to show by suitable testcases that all conditions are satisfied.

3
Planning a Software Project

Software development is a highly labor intensive activity. A large software project may involve hundreds of people, and may span over many years. A project of this dimension can easily turn into chaos if proper management controls are not imposed. To complete the project successfully the large workforce has to be properly organized so that the entire workforce is contributing effectively and efficiently towards the project. Proper management controls and checkpoints are required for effective project monitoring. Controlling the development, ensuring quality, satisfying the constraints of the selected process model (waterfall model in our case) all require careful management of the project.

For a successful project, competent management and competent technical staff are both essential. Lack of any one can cause a project to fail. Traditionally, computer professionals have attached little importance to management and have placed greater emphasis on technical skills. This is one of the reasons why there is a shortage of competent project managers for software projects. Though the actual management skills can only be acquired by actual experience, some of the principles which have proven to be effective can be taught.

Generally, we can divide the management activities over the lifetime of a project into two phases—project planning, and project monitoring and control. Broadly speaking, planning entails all activities that must be performed before starting the development work. Once the project is started, project control begins. In other words, during planning all the activities that the management needs to perform are planned, while during project control the plan is executed and updated. The project monitoring and control activities are spread over the development cycle of the software, and their basic goal is to ensure that the plan is being followed. We will discuss the monitoring and control activities that need to be performed during a development phase in the chapter for that phase. In this chapter we focus on project planning.

Planning is perhaps the most important management activity. Planning is also perhaps the weakest activity in many software projects, and many failures caused by mismanagement can be attributed to lack of proper planning. One of the reasons for improper planning is the old thinking that the major activity in a software project is designing and writing code. Consequently, people who make software tend to rush towards implementation, and do not spend time and effort on planning. No amount of technical effort later can compensate for lack of careful planning. Lack of proper planing is a sure ticket to failure for a large software project. For this reason, we treat project planning as an independent chapter.

The basic goal of planning is to look into the future, identify the activities that need to be done to complete the project successfully, and plan the scheduling and resource allocation for these activities. Ideally, all future activities should be planned. A good plan should be flexible enough to handle unforeseen events that inevitably occur in a large project. Economic, political, and personnel factors all should be taken into account for a realistic plan and thus for a successful project.

The *input* to the planning activity is the requirements specification. A very detailed requirements document is not essential for planning, but for a good plan all the important requirements must be known. The output of this phase is the *project plan,* which is a document describing the different aspects of the plan. The project plan is instrumental in driving the development process through the remaining phases. The major issues which the project plan addresses are:

Cost estimation
Schedule and milestones
Personnel plan
Team structure
Software quality assurance plans
Configuration management plans
Project monitoring plans
Risk management

In the remainder of this chapter we discuss each of these issues, and the techniques that are available for handling the problems in different aspects of project planning.

3.1. Cost Estimation

For a given set of requirements, it is desirable to know how much it will cost to develop the software to satisfy the given requirements, and how much time development will take. These estimates are needed *before* development is initiated. The primary reason for cost estimation is to enable the client or the developer to perform a cost-benefit analysis. A more practical use of cost estimation is in bidding for software projects, where the developers must give cost estimates to a potential client for the development contract.

For the team developing the software, a detailed and accurate cost estimate, for all the different activities, is invaluable for project control, once development begins. Deviations of actual costs from cost estimates are used as a metric for assessing project status. In addition, cost estimates are also required to determine the staffing level for a project during different phases. Due to its importance, cost estimation is considered to be a major planning activity.

Cost in a project is due to the requirements for software, hardware and human resources. Hardware resources are such things as the computer time, terminal time, and memory required for the project, whereas software resources include the tools, and compilers that are needed during development. However, the bulk of the cost of software development is due to the human resources needed, and most cost models focus on this aspect. Most cost estimates are determined in terms of person-months (PM), which can easily be translated into actual dollar cost.

3.1.1. Uncertainties in Cost Estimation

Before we consider some techniques for estimation, let us consider the fundamental limitations of cost estimation. One can provide cost estimates at any point in the software life cycle, and the accuracy of the estimate will depend on the amount of accurate information we have about the final product. Clearly, when the product is delivered, the cost can be accurately determined; all the data about the project and the resources spent on it is fully known by then. This is cost estimation with complete knowledge about the project. On the other extreme is when the project is being initiated, during the feasibility study. At this time, we have only some idea of the classes of data the system will get and produce, and the major functionality of the system. There is large uncertainty about the actual specifications of the system. Specifications with uncertainty represent a range of possible final products, and not one precisely defined product. Hence, the cost estimation cannot be accurate. Estimates at this phase of the project can be off by as much as a factor of four from the actual final cost.

As we specify the system more fully and accurately, the uncertainties are reduced, and more accurate cost estimates can be made. For example, once the requirements are completely specified, more accurate cost estimates can be made as compared to the estimates after the feasibility study. Once the design is complete, the estimates can be made still more accurately. The obtainable accuracy of the estimates as it varies with the different phases is shown in Figure 3.1 [Boe81, Boe84a].

Note that the figure is simply specifying the limitations of cost estimating strategies—the best accuracy which a cost estimating strategy can hope to

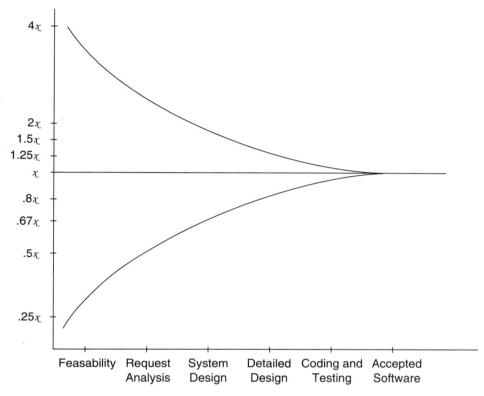

FIGURE 3.1. Accuracy of cost estimation.

achieve. It does not say anything about the existence of strategies that can provide the estimate with that accuracy. For actual cost estimation, cost models have to be developed, which are used for estimation. The accuracy of the actual cost estimates will depend on the effectiveness and accuracy of the cost model employed.

The cost for a project is a function of many parameters. Foremost amongst them is the size of the project. Clearly, more resources are required for a larger project. Other factors that affect the cost are programmer ability, experience of the developers in the area, complexity of the project, and reliability requirements. In some studies it has been found that programmer ability can have productivity variations of up to a factor of ten. Product complexity has an effect on development effort, as more complex projects that are the same size as simpler projects require more effort. Similarly, reliability requirements have considerable impact on cost; the more the reliability need, the higher the development cost. In fact, the cost increase with reliability is not linear, and is often exponential.

The goal of a cost model is to discover relationships between the cost and a set of characteristics that we can measure or estimate. In other words, a model requires some knowledge or estimate of some of the parameters, which are then used to predict the cost. As mentioned above, cost of a project depends on many factors. Many of these factors cannot be easily quantified or measured (such as programmer ability, or past experience), or cannot be accurately estimated in the early phases when cost estimates are made (for example, complexity of the final software).

However, cost estimation models have matured considerably, and generally give fairly accurate estimates. For example, when the COCOMO model was checked with data from some projects, it was found that the estimates were within 20% of the actual cost 68% of the time. In the remainder of this section we discuss some cost models. First we present a simple model for cost estimation. Then we describe the COCOMO model in some detail. For our case study we will use the COCOMO model.

3.1.2. Single-Variable Models

A common approach to estimating effort is to make it a function of a single variable. Often this variable is the *project size*, and the equation of effort is considered as

$$EFFORT = a*SIZE^b$$

where a and b are constants [Bas80]. The constants are usually determined by regression analysis applied to *historical* data, i.e., data about the projects that has been performed in the past. For example, Watson and Felix [Wat77] analyzed the data of IBM Federal Systems Division, and determined the following parameters as a function of the size. If the size estimate is in thousands of delivered lines of code (KDL), the total effort E in person-months (PM) can be given by the equation

$$E = 5.2(KDL)^{.91}$$

The IBM data used to determine the constants was from 60 projects ranging from 4000 to 467,000 lines of delivered source code. A similar study on smaller projects showed that the data fits a straight line quite well, and the equation is of the form

$$EFFORT = a*SIZE + b$$

where a and b are again constants that are obtained by analysis of data of past projects [Bas80]. These equations imply that the project cost increases linearly with the size of the final product for small systems, but has a non-linear growth for larger projects.

3.1.3. COCOMO Model

Instead of having resource estimates as a function of one variable, resource estimates can depend on many different factors, giving rise to multivariable models. A model in this category starts with an initial estimate determined by using the static single variable model equations, and then adjusting the estimates based on other variables. Here we will discuss one such model called the COnstructive COst MOdel (COCOMO) developed by Boehm [Boe81, Boe84a]. This model also estimates the total effort in terms of person-months of the technical project staff. It does not include the cost of the secretarial staff that might be needed. The basic steps in this model are:

1. Obtain an initial estimate of the development effort from the estimate of thousands of delivered lines of source code (KDL).
2. Determine a set of 15 multiplying factors from different attributes of the project.
3. Adjust the effort estimate by multiplying the initial estimate with all the multiplying factors.

The initial estimate (also called nominal estimate) is determined by an equation of the form used in the static, single-variable models, using KDL as the measure of size. To determine the initial effort E_i in person-months the equation used is of the type

$$E_i = a*(KDL)^b$$

The value of the constants a and b depend on the project type. In COCOMO, projects are categorized into three types—organic, semidetached, and embedded. Organic projects are in an area in which the organization has considerable experience, and whose requirements are less stringent. Such systems are usually developed by a small team. Examples of this type of project are simple business systems, simple inventory management systems, and data processing systems. Projects of the embedded type are ambitious and novel, in which the organization has little experience, and have stringent requirements for such aspects as interfacing and reliability. These systems have tight constraints from the environment (software, hardware, and people). Examples are embedded avionics systems and real-time command systems. The semidetached systems fall in between these two types. Examples of semidetached systems include developing a new operating system (OS) or a data base management system (DBMS) and complex inventory management systems. The constants a and b for different systems are given in Table 3.1.

There are 15 different attributes, called cost driver attributes, that determine the multiplying factors. These factors depend on product, computer,

TABLE 3.1. Constants for different project types.

System	a	b
organic	3.2	1.05
semidetached	3.0	1.12
embedded	2.8	1.20

personnel, and technology attributes (called project attributes). The list of these attributes is given below.

Product Attributes
   Required software reliability (RELY)
   Data base size (DATA)
   Product complexity (CPLX)

Computer Attributes
   Execution time constraint (TIME)
   Main storage constraint (STOR)
   Virtual machine volatility (VIRT)
   Computer turnaround time (TURN)

Personnel Attributes
   Analyst capability (ACAP)
   Applications experience (AEXP)
   Programmer capability (PCAP)
   Programming language experience (LEXP)

Project Attributes
   Modern programming practice (MODP)
   Use of software tools (TOOL)
   Required development schedule (SCED)

Each attribute has a rating scale, and for each rating, a multiplying factor is provided. For example, for the product attribute RELY, the rating scale is very low, low, nominal, high, and very high. The multiplying factors for these ratings are .75, .88, 1.00, 1.15 and 1.40, respectively. So, if the reliability requirement for the project is judged to be low then the multiplying factor is .75, while if it is judged to be very high the factor is 1.40. Some of the attributes and their multiplying factors for different ratings are shown in Table 3.2 [Boe81, Boe84a].

The multiplying factors for all 15 factors are multiplied together to get the effort adjustment factor (EAF). The final effort estimate, E, is obtained by multiplying the initial estimate by the EAF.

$$E = EAF*E_i$$

TABLE 3.2. Multipliers for different cost drivers.

	Rating					
Cost Drivers	Very low	Low	Nominal	High	Very high	Extra high
Software reliability req.	.75	.88	1.00	1.15	1.4	
Data base size		.94	1.00	1.08	1.16	
Product complexity	.70	.85	1.00	1.15	1.30	1.65
Execution time constraint			1.00	1.11	1.30	1.66
Main storage constraint			1.00	1.06	1.21	1.56
Virtual machine volatility		.87	1.00	1.15	1.30	
Computer turnaround time		.87	1.00	1.07	1.15	
Analyst capability	1.46	1.19	1.00	.86	.71	
Application experience	1.29	1.13	1.00	.91	.82	
Programmer capability	1.42	1.17	1.00	.86	.70	
Programming language exp.	1.14	1.07	1.00	.95		
Modern prog. practice	1.24	1.10	1.00	.91	.82	
Use of SW tools	1.24	1.10	1.00	.91	.83	
Development schedule	1.23	1.08	1.00	1.04	1.10	

PHASE DISTRIBUTION OF EFFORT

By the above method, the overall cost of the project can be estimated. For planning and monitoring purposes, estimates of the effort required for the different phases is also desirable. In COCOMO, effort for a phase is considered as a defined percentage of the overall effort. The percentage of total effort spent in a phase varies with the type and size of the project. The percentages for an organic software project are given in Table 3.3.

Using this table, the estimate of the effort required for each phase can be determined from the total effort estimate. For example, if the total effort estimate for an organic software system is 20 PM, then the percentage effort for the coding and unit testing phase will be $40 + (38 - 40)/(32 - 8)*20 = 39\%$. The estimate for the effort needed for this phase then is $.39 * 20 = 7.8$ PM. This table does not list the cost of requirements as a percentage of the total cost estimate since the project plan (and cost estimation) is being done after the requirements are complete. In COCOMO the detailed

TABLE 3.3. Phase-wise distribution of effort.

	SIZE			
Phase	Small 2 KDL	Intermediate 8 KDL	Medium 32 KDL	Large 128 KDL
Product Design	16	16	16	16
Detailed design	26	25	24	23
Code and unit test	42	40	38	36
Integration and test	16	19	22	25

design and code and unit testing are sometimes combined into one phase called the programming phase.

For the other two types of software systems, the percentages are slightly different, with the percentage for product design and integration and testing increasing slightly, and the percentage of coding decreasing slightly. An estimate of percentages for project sizes different from the one specified in the table can be obtained by linear interpolation.

COCOMO provides three levels of models of increasing complexity: basic, intermediate and detailed. The model described above is the intermediate COCOMO model. The detailed model is the most complex. It has different multiplying factors for the different phases for a given cost driver. The set of cost drivers applicable to a system or a module is also not the same as the drivers for the system level. However, it might be too detailed for many applications. We will follow the intermediate model described above, even for detailed estimates. COCOMO also provides help in determining the rating of different attributes and performing sensitivity and tradeoff analysis.

3.1.4. On Software Size Estimation

As we can see, one of the key inputs to the cost models is the estimate of the size of the software. If this estimate is inaccurate, the cost estimate produced by the models will also be inaccurate. Hence, it is important that good estimates for the size of the software be obtained.

There is no known method for estimating the size very accurately. Indeed, it might not be possible to do so, as the actual size of the final software depends on many factors, including many human factors like the programming habits of programmers. There are many psychological factors also at play. In the famous experiment done by Weinberg-Schulman [Wei71], it was seen that programmers produce programs that satisfy the goals established. For example, in this experiment the programmers who were to produce the most efficient code, did actually produce the most efficient code, and those who were asked to minimize the memory requirement, produced code that did require less memory than programs of other programmers.

In general, there is often a tendency by people to underestimate the size of the software. There are many reasons for this [Boe81]. First, people are basically optimistic and have a desire to please others. The way to please others and avoid confrontations in this case is to give a low estimate. Most people give estimates based on previous experiences with similar projects. However, people do not tend to remember their experiences completely. Often they tend not to remember the software developed for housekeeping and user interfacing, or the support software developed for a project.

When estimating software size perhaps the best way is to get as much detail as possible about the software to be developed, and be aware of our biases when estimating the size of the various components. With more detail about the system, and the sub-systems and modules that will be required, the estimation should begin with estimating the sizes of the modules and sub-systems, and then add up these estimates to obtain the overall estimates. Estimating the size of smaller units is easier than estimating the size of a large system. By obtaining details and utilizing them for size estimation the estimates are likely to be closer to the actual size of the final software.

3.1.5. An Example

Suppose a system for office automation must be designed. From the requirements it was clear that there will be four major modules in the system: data entry, data update, query, and report generator. It is also clear from the requirements that this project will fall in the organic category. The sizes for the different modules and then the overall system were estimated to be

data entry	0.6 KDL
data update	0.6 KDL
query	0.8 KDL
report generator	1.0 KDL
TOTAL	3.0 KDL.

From the requirements the ratings of the different cost driver attributes was assessed. These ratings, along with their multiplying factors are:

Complexity	high	1.15
Storage	high	1.06
Experience	low	1.13
Programmer capability	low	1.17.

All other factors had nominal rating. From these the effort adjustment factor (EAF) is

$$EAF = 1.15*1.06*1.13*1.17 = 1.61.$$

The initial effort estimate for the project is obtained from the relevant equations. We have

$$E_i = 3.2*3^{1.05} = 10.14PM.$$

Using the EAF, the adjusted effort estimate is

$$E = 1.16 * 10.14 = 16.5 \text{ PM}.$$

PHASE DISTRIBUTION OF EFFORT

Using the table given above, we obtain the percentage of the total effort consumed in different phases. The office automation system's size estimate is 3 KDL, so we will have to use interpolation to get the appropriate percentage (the two end values for interpolation will be the percentages for 2 KDL and 8 KDL). The percentages for the different phases are: design—16%, detailed design—25.83%, code and unit test—41.66%, and integration and testing—16.5%. With these the effort estimates for the different phases are:

System design	.16 * 16.34 = 2.6 PM
Detailed design	.258 * 16.34 = 4.2 PM
Code and unit test	.4166 * 16.34 = 6.8 PM
Integration	.165 * 16.34 = 2.7 PM.

These effort estimates will later be used during personnel planning. Note that in COCOMO, the detailed design and code and unit testing phase are often combined and called the programming phase.

3.2. Project Scheduling

Schedule estimation and staff requirement estimation are perhaps the most important activities after cost estimation. Both are related, if phase-wise cost is available. Here we discuss the schedule estimation. The goal of schedule estimation is to determine the total duration of the project and the duration of the different phases.

First let us see why the schedule is independent of the person-month cost. A schedule cannot be simply obtained from the overall effort estimate by deciding on average staff size and then determining the total time requirement by dividing the total effort by the average staff size. Brooks has pointed out that person and months (time) are not interchangeable. According to Brooks [Bro75], " . . . man and months are interchangeable only for activities that require no communication among men, like sowing wheat or reaping cotton. This is not even approximately true of software . . . ".

Obviously, there is some relationship between the project duration and the staff time (measured in, say, staff-months) required for completing the project. But, this relationship is not linear; to reduce the project duration in half, doubling the staff-months will not work. The basic reason behind this is that if the staff needs to communicate for the completion of a task, then communication time should be accounted for. Communication time increases with the square of the number of staff. For example, if there are n persons, and all need to communicate, then there are $n^2 - 1$ communication paths, and each communication path consumes time. Hence, by increasing the staff for a project we may actually increase the time spent in communication. This is often restated as Brook's Law: "adding man power to a late project may make it later".

From this discussion it is clear that we cannot treat the schedule as a variable totally in the control of the management. Each project will require some time to finish and this time cannot be reduced by putting more people on the project. Hence, project schedule is an independent variable, which must be assessed for planning. Models are used for assessing the project duration.

3.2.1. Average Duration Estimation

Single variable models can be used to determine the overall duration of the project. Again the constants a and b are determined from historical data. The IBM Federal Systems Division found that the total duration, M, in calendar months can be estimated by

$$M = 4.1E^{.36}.$$

In COCOMO, the schedule is determined using the single variable model, like it does the initial effort estimate. However, instead of size, the factor used here is the effort estimate for the project. The equation for an organic type of software is

$$M = 2.5E^{.38}.$$

For the other project types the constants vary only slightly. The duration or schedule of the different phases is obtained in the same manner as in effort distribution. The percentages for the different phases is shown in Table 3.4.

In this COCOMO table, the detailed design, coding and unit testing phases are combined into one "programming phase". This is perhaps done since all these activities are usually done by the programmers, while system design and integration are often done by different people, who may or may not be involved in programming activities of the project.

As we can see these percentages are slightly (but not too much) different from the effort distribution percentages. The percentage of total project duration spent in detailed design, coding and unit testing (together sometimes called the programming activity) is somewhat higher than the percentage of total effort spent in these activities. However, since the per-

TABLE 3.4. Phase-wise distribution of project duration.

| Phase | SIZE | | | |
	Small 2 KDSI	Intermediate 8 KDSI	Medium 32 KDSI	Large 128 KDSI
Product design	19	19	19	19
Programming	63	59	55	51
Integration	18	22	26	30

centages are only slightly different, it means that the average staff sizes computed for the different phases will not be too different from the overall average staff size for the project.

3.2.2. Project Scheduling and Milestones

Once we have the estimates of the effort and time requirement for the different phases, a schedule for the project can be prepared. This schedule will then be used later for monitoring the progress of the project.

A conceptually simple and effective scheduling technique is the Gantt chart, which uses a calendar-oriented chart for representing the project schedule. Each activity is represented as a bar in the calendar starting from the starting date of the activity and ending at the ending date for that activity. The start and end of each activity become a milestones for the project.

Progress can be represented easily in a Gantt chart, by ticking off (or coloring) each of the milestones, when completed. Alternatively, for each activity another bar can be drawn specifying when the activity actually started and when it ended, i.e., when these two milestones were actually achieved.

The main drawback of the Gantt chart is that it does not depict the dependent relations among the different activities. Hence, the effect of slippage in one activity on other activities or on the overall project schedule cannot be determined. However, it is conceptually simple, and easy to understand, and is heavily used. It is sufficient for small and medium-sized projects.

For large projects, the dependencies among activities are important in order to determine which are critical activities, whose completion should not be delayed, and which activities are not critical. To represent the dependencies, PERT charts are often used. A PERT chart is a graph-based chart. It can be used to determine the activities that form the "critical path", which if delayed will cause the overall project to delay. The PERT chart is not conceptually as simple, and the representation is graphically not as clear as are Gantt charts. Its use is well justified in large projects. We will use the Gantt charts for schedule planning.

3.2.3. Example Continued

We continue with the office automation example. Recall that the overall size estimate for the project is 3 KDL, and the final effort estimate obtained was 16.34 PM. As this is an organic system, the overall duration will be determined by the equation $2.5 * E^{0.38}$. Using this we get the project duration D as

$$D = 2.5 * 16.34^{0.38} = 7.23 Months$$

Using the table above which gives the duration of the different phases as a percentage of the total project duration, we can obtain the duration of the different phases. The duration of the different phases is

System design	.19 * 7.23 = 1.37 M
Programming	.623 * 7.23 = 4.5 M
Integration	.1866 * 7.23 = 1.35 M

Assume that the project is to start on Jan 1, 1990. Then according to this, the project will end in the middle of August. The system design phase will terminate in the middle of February, the programming activity will end in late June, and the rest of the time will be spent in integration and testing. Using these estimates an overall schedule for the project can be decided, which can then be represented as a Gantt chart.

3.3. Staffing and Personnel Planning

Once the project schedule is determined, and the effort and schedule of different phases and different tasks are known, staff requirements can be obtained. From the cost and the overall duration of the project, the *average* staff size for the project can be determined by dividing the total effort (in person-months) by the overall project duration (in months).

This average staff size is not detailed enough for proper personnel planning, especially if the variation between the actual staff requirement at different phases is large. Typically the staff requirement for a project is small during the requirement and design, and is the maximum during the implementation and testing, and then again drops during the final phases of integration and testing. Using the COCOMO model, average staff requirement for the different phases can be determined as the effort and schedule for each phase are known. This presents staffing as a step function with time.

For personnel planning and scheduling, it is useful to have effort and schedule estimates for the sub-systems and basic modules in the system. At the planning time, when the system design has not been done, the planner can only expect to know about the major subsystems in the system, and perhaps the major modules in these subsystems. COCOMO can be used to determine the total effort estimate for different subsystems or modules.

Detailed Cost Estimates: An approximate method, suitable for small systems, is to divide the total schedule in terms of the ratio of the sizes of different components. A more accurate method, used in COCOMO, is to start with the sizes of different components (and the total systems). The initial effort for the total system is determined. From this the *nominal productivity* of the project is calculated by dividing the overall size by the initial effort. Using this productivity, the effort required for each of the modules is determined by dividing the size by nominal productivity. This gives an initial effort estimate for the modules. For each module the rating of the different cost driver attributes is determined. From these ratings the effort adjustment factor (EAF) for each module is determined. Using the initial estimates and the EAFs, the final effort estimate of each module is determined. The final effort estimate for the overall system is obtained by adding the final estimates for the different modules.

When component-wise cost estimation is done, the final effort estimate for the overall system must be obtained as a sum of the cost estimates of the different modules. The method described earlier, where the final cost is determined by the initial estimate and EAF for the overall system, does not apply here; that method is applied when only the overall estimates are needed.

It should be kept in mind that these effort estimates for a module are done by treating a module like an independent system, thus including the effort required for design, integration, and testing of the module. When used for personnel planning this should be kept in mind if the effort for the design and integration phases is obtained separately. In that case, the cost of design and integration of a module is included in the design and integration phase effort estimates.

3.3.1. Rayleigh Curve

Staffing in a project, in general, is more a continuous function than a step function with only a few different values. Putnam has proposed a time-dependent, continuous function to estimate the staffing at different times throughout the project duration [Put78]. The basis of the model is the observation that there are regular patterns of manpower build-up and phaseout, independent of the type of work being performed (this was earlier observed in hardware development). It was also observed that the staffing pattern followed the Rayleigh curve. For software development, there is the build-up and phaseout curve for each of the different phases, and each of the curves is a Rayleigh curve. The total staffing pattern, which is determined by summing up the different curves, is also a Rayleigh curve, as shown in Figure 3.2.

If $\hat{y}$ is the staffing rate in PY/year (person-year per year), then this staffing pattern as a function of time t can be represented by the equation,

$$\hat{y} = 2Kate^{-at^2} \text{ PY/yr.}$$

where, K is the total manpower required, or the total area under the curve from t = 0 to infinity. It represents the total person-years used by the project over its entire life cycle. The constant a is the shape parameter, which is determined by the time at which the curve reaches its maximum

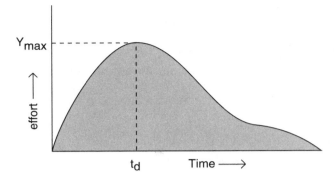

FIGURE 3.2. The Rayleigh curve. t_d = design time (determined empirically by Putnam).

value. The cumulative manpower used up to the time t can be obtained by integrating this equation. Representing the cumulative manpower by y, we have

$$y = K(1 - e^{-at_2}).$$

If $\hat{y}$ peaks at time t_d, the constant a is given by the equation

$$a = 1/2t_d^2.$$

In software projects it has been observed that t_d corresponds closely to the total development time, or the time taken to reach full operational capability. Substituting for "a" we get

$$\hat{y} = (k/t_d^2)te^{-t_2/2t_d^2}.$$

Integrating this equation from t = 0 to t_d we get the total development effort D.

$$D = y(t_d) = K(1 - e^{.5}) = .39K.$$

In other words, the total development cost is approximately 40% of the total life cycle cost.

It was found that the number K/t_d^2 has an interesting property. It represents the difficulty of the system in terms of programming effort required to produce it. When this number is small it corresponds with easy systems; when the number is large it corresponds to difficult systems.

3.3.2. Personnel Plan

Once the schedule for different activities and the average staff level for each activity is known, the overall personnel allocation for the project can be planned. This plan will specify how many people will be needed for the different activities at different times for the duration of the project.

A method of producing the personnel plan is to make it a calendar-based representation, containing all the months in the duration of the project, by listing the months from the starting date to the ending date. Then for each of the different tasks identified, and for which cost and schedule estimates are prepared, list the number of people needed in each of the months. The total effort for each month and the total effort for each activity can easily be computed from this plan. The total for each activity should be the same as (or close to) the overall person-months estimate.

Drawing a personnel plan usually requires a few iterations to ensure that the effort requirement for the different phases and activities (and the duration of the different phases) is consistent with the estimates obtained earlier. The ensuring of consistency is made more difficult by the fact that the effort estimates for individual modules include the design and integration effort for those modules, and this effort is also included in the effort for these phases. It is usually not desirable to state staff requirements in a unit less than 0.5 person in order to make the plan consistent with the estimates. Some difference between the estimates and the totals in the personnel plan is acceptable.

This type of plan, although it has the overall staff requirement, does not distinguish between different types of people. A more detailed plan will list the requirement of people by their speciality; for example, stating how many programmers, analysts, quality assurance people, and so forth are needed at different times.

3.3.3. Example Continued

Now that we have the schedule and the effort estimates, we can obtain the cost estimates of the different components. We will use COCOMO to estimate the effort for different modules. For this project we have the following estimates (repeated here for convenience):

data entry	.6 KDL
data update	.6 KDL
query	.8 KDL
reports	1.0 KDL
TOTAL	3.0 KDL

The initial cost estimate obtained earlier for the total project is 10.14 PM. The nominal productivity for the project is

$$3.0/10.14 = .29 \text{ KDL/PM}.$$

We assume that the cost driver attributes for all the different modules are the same and the EAF for the modules is 1.61 (for a large system, a module should be rated separately, resulting in its own EAF, which might be different from the EAF of others). Using this productivity and EAF, the effort estimate for the different modules can be determined as follows:

Data entry	$0.6/0.184 \times 1.61 = 3.2$ PM
Data update	$0.6/0.184 \times 1.61 = 3.2$ PM
Query	$0.8/0.184 \times 1.61 = 4.3$ PM
Reports	$1.0/0.184 \times 1.61 = 5.4$ PM

The total effort estimate for the project is 16.1 PM, which is close to the total estimate obtained earlier (since the EAF for each module was the same as the system EAF in the example shown before). It should again be pointed out that these estimates include the cost of system design and system testing as well. Using the effort and duration estimates for the different phases obtained earlier, the average staff requirement for the different phases can easily be determined, and we get

System design	$2.6/1.37 = 1.9$ Persons
Programming	$11/4.5 = 2.4$ Persons
Integration	$2.7/1.35 = 2$ Persons.

Using the estimates for the schedule, effort for different phases, and effort for different modules, we can draw a personnel plan. As mentioned earlier, to create a personnel plan that is consistent with the estimates, a few iterations are needed, and the totals in the plan may be somewhat different from the estimates. One plan for this example is shown in Table 3.5.

In this plan we have not included management as a separate activity, as it is a small project and we assume that one of the persons doing the design will be doing the monitoring and control for the duration of the project (and will be spending a fraction of his/her time on such activity). However, in larger projects management requirement should be listed separately. Management for a project will require some personnel throughout the project, and the requirement is not likely to vary. Notice that in the plan the effort requirement for different phases—system design, programming (for which different modules are listed separately) and integration—is close to the

TABLE 3.5. A personnel plan for the example.

	1990								
	Jan	Feb	Mar	Apr	May	Jun	Jul	Aug	Total
Sys Des.	2	2							3.0
D-entry		1	1	1					2.0
Update		1	1	1					2.0
Query				1	1	1			2.5
Report				1	1.5	2			4.0
Integration							2	2	3.0
TOTAL	2	2	2	2	2.5	3	2	1	16.5

estimates obtained earlier. The duration of the different phases is also close to the durations obtained above.

3.4. Team Structure

Often a team of people is assigned to a project. For the team to work as a cohesive group and contribute the most to the project, the people in the team have to be organized in some manner. The structure of the team has a direct impact on the product quality and project productivity.

Two basic philosophies have evolved for organizing a team [Man81]—ego-less teams and chief programmer teams. Ego-less teams consist of ten or fewer programmers. The goals of the group are set by consensus, and input from every member is taken for major decisions. Group leadership rotates among the group members. Due to its nature, ego-less teams are sometimes called democratic teams. The structure results in many communication paths between people, as shown in Figure 3.3.

The structure allows inputs from all members, which can lead to better decisions in difficult problems. This suggests that this structure is well suited for long-term, research type projects which do not have time constraints. On the other hand, it is not suitable for regular tasks that are not too complex, and which have time constraints. For such tasks, the communication in democratic structure is unnecessary and results in inefficiency.

A chief programmer team, in contrast to ego-less teams, has a hierarchy. It consists of a chief programmer, who has a backup programmer, a program librarian, and some programmers. The chief programmer is re-

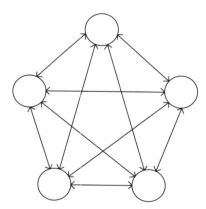

FIGURE 3.3. Communication paths in a democratic team structure.

sponsible for all major technical decisions of the project. He does most of the design, and assigns coding of the different parts of the design to the programmers. The backup programmer helps the chief programmer in making technical decisions, and takes over as the chief programmer if the chief programmer falls sick or leaves. The program librarian is responsible for maintaining the documentation and other communication-related work. This structure considerably reduces interpersonal communication. The communication paths are shown in Figure 3.4. This kind of structure is well suited for projects with simple solutions, with strict deadlines. It is not suitable for difficult tasks where multiple inputs are useful.

A third team structure, called the controlled decentralized team [Man81], tries to combine the strengths of the democratic and chief programmer teams. It consists of a project leader who has a group of senior programmers under him, while under each senior programmer is a group of junior programmers. The group of a senior programmer and his junior programmers behave like a ego-less team, but communication among different groups occurs only through the senior programmers of the groups. The senior programmers also communicate with the project leader. Such a team has fewer communication paths than a democratic team, but has more paths than a chief programmer team. This structure works best for large projects which are reasonably straight-forward. It is not well suited for very simple projects or for research-type projects.

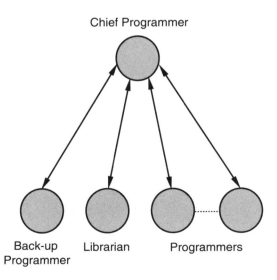

FIGURE 3.4. Communication paths in a chief programmer team.

3.5. Software Configuration Management

Throughout the development, software consists of a collection of items (such as programs, data, and documents) that can easily be changed. During any software development, the design, code and even requirements are often changed. This easily-changeable nature of software and the fact that changes often take place, require that changes be done in a controlled manner. **Software Configuration Management (SCM)** [Bes79, Bes84, Iee87] is the discipline for systematically controlling the changes that take place during development.

The need for configuration management further arises since software can exist in two different forms—executable and non-executable [Bes79]. The executable form consists of the sequences of instructions that can be executed on the computer hardware. The nonexecutable form comprises documentation such as the requirements specifications, design specifications, code listing, and the documents describing the software. As well as maintaining consistency within a form, due to these two forms there is the additional problem of maintaining correspondence between the two forms. Since, in the early stages of development, software may not exist in executable form, SCM is easier towards the start of the development and gets more complex towards the end.

There are four major elements of SCM [Ber79]—configuration identification, control, status accounting, and auditing. These components and their general goals are given in figure 3.5.

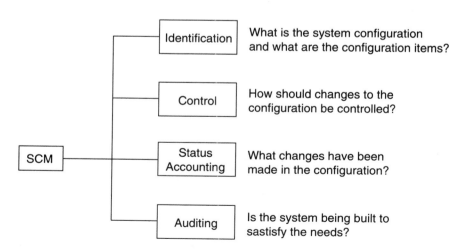

FIGURE 3.5. Elements of Software Configuration Management (SCM).

3.5.1. Configuration Identification

The basic goal of SCM is to manage the configuration of the software as it evolves during development. The configuration of the software is essentially the arrangement or organization of its different functional units or components. An important concept in SCM is that of a "baseline". A baseline forms a reference point in the development of a system, and is formally defined after certain phases in development. A baseline forms the basis for further development and can be changed only through the change procedures specified by the SCM policy. Effective management of the software configuration requires careful definition of the different baselines, and controlling the changes to these baselines.

At the time it is established, a software baseline represents the software in the most recent state. After changes are made (through SCM) to this baseline, the state of the software is defined by the most recent baseline and the changes that were made. Baselines are typically established after the completion of a phase. Some of the common baselines are functional baseline, design baseline, and product baseline. *Functional baseline* is generally the requirements document that specifies the functional requirements for the software. *Design baseline* consists of the different components in the software and their designs. *Product baseline* represents the developed system.

The most elementary entity during configuration identification is the *software configuration item (SCI)*. A SCI is a document or an artifact that is explictly placed under configuration control and that can be regarded as a basic unit for modification. Examples of SCIs are: requirements document, design document, code of a module, test plan. A baseline is essentially a set of SCIs. The first baseline (typically the functional baseline) may consist of only one SCI—the requirements document. As development proceeds the number of SCIs grows and the baseline gets more complex. For example, the design baseline will contain different design objects as the SCIs. The functional and design baselines contain only nonexecutable entities, existing only in the form of documentation.

Since the baseline consists of the SCIs, SCM starts with identification of configuration items. One common practice is to have only coded modules as configuration items since usually in coding a large number of people are involved and the code of one person often depends on the code of another. Hence, changing the code by one person may adversely effect the functioning of the code of some other person. Although this practice may suffice for small or medium-size projects, for a large project, the requirements, design, and code should all come under SCM.

3.5.2. Configuration Control

From the point of view of SCM, the evolution of software is essentially development of baselines and the incorporation of changes in the baselines, where each baseline consists of a set of SCIs. Configuration control focuses on managing changes to the different forms of the SCIs.

The **engineering change proposal** is the basic document that is used for defining and requesting a change to an SCI. This proposal describes the proposed change, the rationale for it, baselines and SCIs that are affected, and cost and schedule impacts.

The engineering change proposals are sent to a **configuration control board (CCB).** The CCB is a group of people responsible for configuration management. The CCB evaluates the request based on its effect on the project, and the benefit due to the change. Based on this analysis the CCB may approve or disapprove the change. If a change is approved then it is the duty of the CCB to inform all parties affected by the change.

The third important factor in configuration control is the procedure for controlling the changes. Once a engineering change proposal has been approved by the CCB, the actual change in the SCI will occur. The procedures for making these changes must be specified. Tools can be used to enforce these procedures. One method for controlling the changes during the coding stages is using program support libraries (PSLs). A PSL is a repository of authoritative and approved versions of the different software components. Some of the facilities typically provided are access control mechanisms (for example, making a component read only), methods for checking in and checking out components from the library, control for software code and change releases, and change tracking.

3.5.3. Status Accounting and Auditing

Incorporating changes, after they have been approved, takes time. So, the changes to a baseline occur over a period of time. Some mechanisms are needed to record how the system evolves and what is its current state. This is the task of status accounting. Its basic function is to record the activities related to the other SCM functions. It is largely administrative in nature, but gets quite complex after the product baseline has been established. This is because both the executable and nonexecutable forms exist at this stage and their correspondence and consistency has to be maintained during changes. Some examples of things that have to be recorded by the accounting procedures are: time of establishment of a baseline, the time when a SCI came into being, information about each SCI, engineering change proposal status, status of the approved changes, and deficiencies uncovered during auditing.

Configuration auditing is concerned with determining how accurately the current software system implements the system defined in the baseline and the requirements document, and with increasing the visibility and traceability of software. Auditing procedures are also responsible for establishing a new baseline. (a baseline is established after it satisfies the auditing procedures). Auditing procedures may be different for different baselines.

3.5.4. Software Configuration Management Plans

From the above discussion, it should be somewhat clear what the SCM plans should contain. The SCM plan, like other plans, has to identify all the activities that must be performed, give guidelines for performing the activities, and allocate resources for them.

The SCM plan needs to specify the type of SCIs that will be selected and the stages during the project where baselines should be established. Note that in the plan only the type of objects that should be selected can be specified; it may not be possible to identify the exact item, as the item may not exist at the planning time. For example, we can specify that code of any module that is independently unit tested will be considered as an SCI. However, we cannot identify the particular modules that will eventually become the SCIs.

For configuration control, the plan has to identify the different members of the configuration control board, the forms to be used for engineering change proposals, and policies, procedures and tools for controlling the changes.

Finally, a SCM plan should include a plan for configuration accounting and auditing. This part of the plan should state how information on the status of configuration items is to be collected, verified, processed, and reported. It should specify all the reports that need to be filed by the people identified as responsible for making the changes. It should also specify the stages at which major audits must be held, the items to be covered during audits, and the procedures to be used for resolving problems that occur during audits.

3.6. Quality Assurance Plans

To ensure that the final product produced is of high quality, some quality control activities must be performed throughout the development. As we have seen in Chapter 1, if this is not done, correcting errors in the final stages can be very expensive, especially if they originated in the early phases. The purpose of the software quality assurance plans (SQAP) is to specify all the documents that need to be produced, activities that need to be performed, and the tools and methods that execute activities to improve the software quality.

The SQAP specifies the tasks that need to be undertaken at different times in the life cycle in order to improve the software quality, and how they are to be managed. These tasks will generally include reviews and audits. Each task should be defined with an entry and exit criterion, or the criteria which should be satisfied to initiate the task, and the criterion that should be satisfied to terminate the task. Both criteria should be stated such that they can be evaluated objectively. The responsibilities for different tasks should also be identified.

The documents that should be produced during software development to enhance software quality should also be specified by the SQAP. It should identify all documents that govern the development, verification, validation, use and maintenance of the software, and how these documents are to be checked for adequacy.

3.6.1. Verification and Validation (V&V)

SQAP has a general and larger view of software quality, and includes different quality criteria. In verification and validation we are most concerned with the correctness of the product. The terms verification and validation are often used interchangeably. However, they have different meanings. *Verification* is the process of determining whether or not the products of a given phase of software development fulfill the specifications established during the previous phase. The verification activities include proving, testing, and reviews. *Validation* is the process of evaluating the software at the end of the software development to ensure compliance with the software requirements. Testing is a common method of validation. Clearly, for high reliability we need to perform both activities. Together they are often called V&V activities.

The major V&V activities for software development are inspection, reviews, and testing. The V&V plan identifies the different V&V tasks for the different phases, and specifies how these tasks contribute to the project V&V goals. The methods to be used for performing these V&V activities, the responsibilities and milestones for each of these activities, inputs and outputs for each V&V task and criteria for evaluating the outputs are also specified. Some of the different V&V activities as proposed in the IEEE standards on verification and validation are shown in Figure 3.6 [Iee87].

3.6.2. Inspections and Reviews

The software inspection process was started by IBM in 1972 [Fag76], for the purposes of improving software quality and increasing productivity. Much of the earlier interest was focused on inspecting code, as coding seemed to be the major hurdle in a software project. However, it was soon discovered that mistakes occur not only during coding but also during design, and this realization led to design reviews. Of course, now we realize that many times defects in the software are caused by not properly understanding the problem, and this has lead to requirement reviews. Today, reviews are widely used and studies have shown that they are an effective method for quality control and tend to enhance productivity.

As the name suggests, the purpose of a review or inspection is to perform a careful scrutiny of the product. In general, a review can be held for any technical product, which may include the requirements specifications, system design document, detailed design, code, and test plan. The

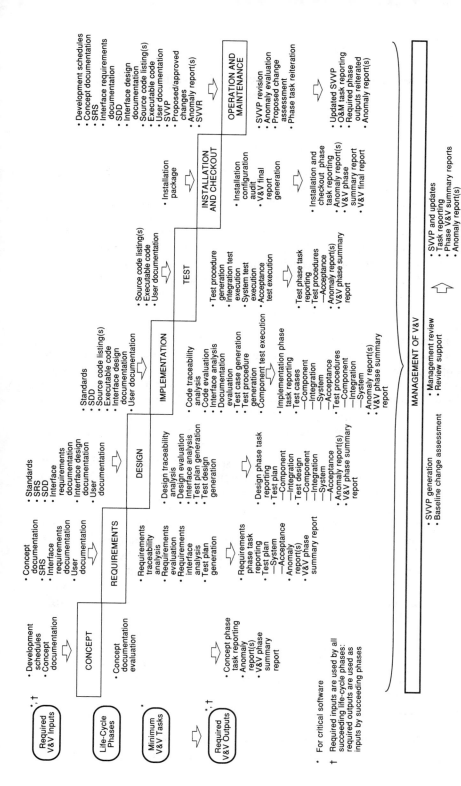

FIGURE 3.6. Software verification and validation plan overview [Iee87].

terms review and inspection are often used interchangeably. There are three basic reasons for having reviews:

Defect removal,
Productivity increase, and
To provide information for project monitoring.

The primary purpose of reviews is to detect defects at different stages during a project. While defects manifest themselves only in the final output, they can be injected at any phase during product development. As we have seen, the cost of detecting and removing a defect that originated during requirements or design, after the system is implemented, can be ten to 100 times the cost if the defect had been removed at the origin. It is for this reason reviews are often held at many different stages during the project. The most common aspects reviewed are the requirements, system design, detailed design, code, and test plan. We will discuss the issues specific to reviews for different phases in later chapters when we discuss those phases.

Increase in productivity and decrease in cost are direct consequences of reviews. Cost is decreased as the defects are detected early in the development, thereby reducing the more expensive corrections that may be needed in the product otherwise. Programmer productivity increases as reviews can substantially decrease the programmer time needed for testing. It should be pointed out that reviews tend to add to the cost of early phases like requirements specification and design, but greatly reduce the cost of later phases.

The reviews, as well as lowering the cost and improving the reliability of systems, have other quality control benefits as well. Reviews also help improve software quality by checking properties like standard compliance, modularity, clarity, and simplicity. Another beneficial side effect is that coders and designers learn from defects found in reviews in their work, which enables them to avoid causing similar defects in future projects, thus improving quality and productivity even further.

For monitoring and control, reliable information about the project is needed, which requires some form of evaluation of the various parts of the project. Evaluation of the people responsible for the technical output cannot be always relied upon. Inspection by a group that includes people not involved with the output can be a means for obtaining reliable evaluation. One of the purposes of reviews is to provide enough information to the management about the project such that management decisions can be made effectively. It should be stressed that review reports should never be used for personnel evaluation, as the reviews produce good results only if the people responsible for products are willing to find defects in their work without fear of jeopardizing their reputation and chances for promotion.

There is another kind of information that can be gathered using reviews that can be useful for setting standards. Which phases have the most defects, the frequency of occurrence of different types of defects, the types of defects caught or that slip by the review process at different stages can all be used for improving the processes and techniques employed. This kind of information can also be used to evaluate new tools and methodologies.

REVIEW PROCESS

The review is done by a group of people. The group usually includes the author of the product under review, a quality control engineer, a person from each phase preceding and the succeeding the phase currently under review. A moderator is appointed or selected for the review. The moderator is the key person, and is not only responsible for ensuring that the review proceed smoothly but also is responsible for the actions that must be performed before and after the review.

There are many steps which must be performed to make the review a success. It starts with the moderator distributing the material to be reviewed. Material to be inspected must meet inspection entry criteria. The participants study the material before the review meeting (sometimes defects can be found by participants while studying the material, although the bulk of the defects are found during the meeting). Checklists can be used to aid in finding potential trouble spots.

The meeting begins with a reader describing the product. Questions about potential defects are raised by the participants and discussion ensues. Discussion is a very important part of reviews, since this is the time when most defects are found. The defects are noted. Effort should *not* be made to suggest methods to remove the defect; that is to be done by the author after the review. Another important factor to be kept in mind about any review process is the psychological frame of mind of a member of the review committee during the review. It is important that the review process should be treated as a constructive engagement, and should not be treated as means of attacking the ability of the author. Such an attitude by the members can force the author to be defensive, which will defeat the purpose of the review.

After the meeting the moderator produces a report of the inspection which lists all issues raised during the meeting that need to be addressed. The authors need to rework to take care of all problems noted in the report and remove all defects. The moderator also has to state in the report whether there should be another review after the rework is complete. If the defects detected and the issues raised are serious, then another meeting should be convened after the rework is done. If no further meeting needs to be convened, then it is the responsibility of the moderator to ensure that the rework has addressed all issues mentioned in the report. This process of review is shown in Figure 3.7.

Proper execution of reviews is critical to their success. Reviews should

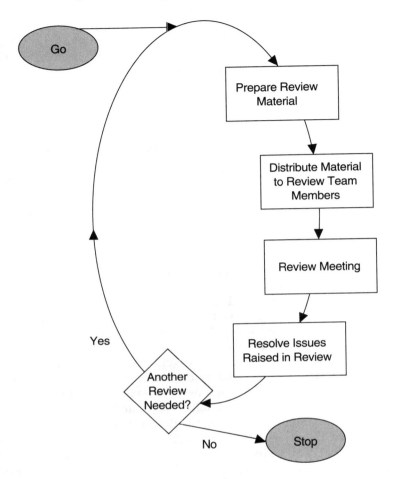

FIGURE 3.7. The review process.

be done at defined points during product development, and time must be allocated in the management plans to accommodate review related activities, particularly the rework. Reviews should not last too long, as the efficiency falls once the participants get tired. A limit of two hours is considered reasonable.

Reviews have been found to be extremely effective for detecting defects, improving productivity, and lowering costs. They provide good checkpoints for the management to study the progress of a particular project. Reviews also are a good tool for ensuring quality control. In short, they have been found to be extremely useful by a diverse set of people, and have found their way into standard management and quality control practices of many institutions. Their use continues to grow.

3.6.3. Outputs of a Software Development Project

As we have discussed earlier, the output of a project employing the water-fall model is not just the final code along with documentation to use it. There are a number of intermediate outputs which must be produced in order to have a successful project that produces a successful product. Although the set of documents that should be produced in a project is somewhat dependent upon the nature of the project, the following is a desired set of documents that should be produced in a project. This list was given in Chapter 1, but is repeated here.

Requirements document
Project plan
System design document
Detailed design document
Test plan
Final code
Software manuals (e.g. user, installation etc.)
Review reports

This is not all the documentation that is produced in a project, but just the major ones. There are other smaller documents that are needed for proper monitoring and control. Examples of these documents are documents and forms related to configuration management, the programmers' notebook which contains all the information about a given unit (and is discussed later in this chapter), time sheets, and weekly/monthly reports.

3.7. Project Monitoring Plans

A good plan is useless unless properly executed. Consequently, the major management activity during the project is to ensure that the plan is properly executed, and when needed, to modify plans appropriately. Project assessment will be straightforward if everything went according to plan and no changes occurred in the requirements. However, on large projects, deviations from the original plan and changes to requirements are both to be expected. In these cases the plan should be modified. Modifications are also needed as more information about the project becomes available, or due to personnel turnover.

The project control phase of the management activity is the longest. For this kind of routine management activity, lasting for a long period of time, proper project monitoring can play a significant role in aiding project management. However, all the methods which the management intends to employ for monitoring the project should be planned before, during the planning phase, so that the management is well prepared to handle the changes and deviations from the plan and can respond quickly. In this section we discuss some methods for monitoring a project.

3.7.1. Timesheets

Once project development commences, the management has to keep track of the progress of the project and the expenditure incurred on the project. Progress can be monitored by using the schedule and milestones that are laid down in the plan. The earned value method, discussed later, can also be used.

The most common method of keeping track of expenditures is by the use of a time sheet. The time sheet records how much time of different project members is being spent on the different sub-systems and modules that have been identified. In addition, information about the nature of the task can also be included (such as design, coding, debugging, and testing).

The time sheet is a common mechanism for collecting raw data. Time sheets could be filled daily or weekly. The data obtained from the time-sheets can be used to obtain information regarding the overall expenditure and its break-up among different tasks and different phases at any given time. For example, the effort distribution with phases (of the type discussed in the first chapter) in a particular organization can be obtained from the time sheets. By assigning codes to projects, tasks within a project, and the nature of the work being done, time sheet processing can easily be automated.

3.7.2. Reviews

We have discussed reviews at some length in an earlier section. We will not go into details of reviews here, but just comment upon a few points regarding the monitoring aspect of reviews. As mentioned above, one of the purposes of reviews is to provide information for project control. Reviews provide a definite and clearly defined milestone. It forces the author of a product to complete the product before the review. Having this goal gives some impetus and motivation to complete the product.

For monitoring, as we have discussed, reviews can provide a wealth of information. First, the review schedules can be used to determine how the project is progressing as compared to its planned schedule. Then the review reports indicate in which parts of the project the programmers/ analysts are having difficulty. With this information, corrective action, such as replacing a junior person by a senior person, can be taken. In addition, review reports provide insight into the quality of the software being produced and the types of errors being detected.

3.7.3. Cost-Schedule-Milestone Graph

A cost-schedule-milestone [Boe81] chart represents the planned cost of different milestones. It also shows the actual cost of achieving the milestones gained so far. By having both the planned cost vs. milestones, and actual cost vs. milestones on the same chart, the progress of the project can be grasped easily.

The x-axis of this chart is time, where the months in the project schedule are marked. The y-axis represents the cost, in dollars or PMs. Two curves are drawn. One curve is the planned cost and planned schedule, in which each important milestone of the project is marked. This curve can be completed after the project plan is made. The second curve represents the actual cost and actual schedule, and the actual achievement of the milestones is marked. Thus, for each milestone the point representing the time when the milestone is actually achieved, and the actual cost of achieving it, is marked. A cost-schedule-milestone chart for the example is shown in Figure 3.8.

The chart shown above is for a hypothetical project whose cost is estimated to be 100K dollars. Different milestones have been identified and a curve is drawn with these milestones. The milestones in this project are PDR (preliminary design review), CDR (critical design review), Module 1 completion, Module 2 completion, integration testing and acceptance testing. For each of these milestones some budget has been allocated based on the estimates. The planned budget is shown by a dotted line. The actual expenditure is shown with a bold line. This chart shows that only

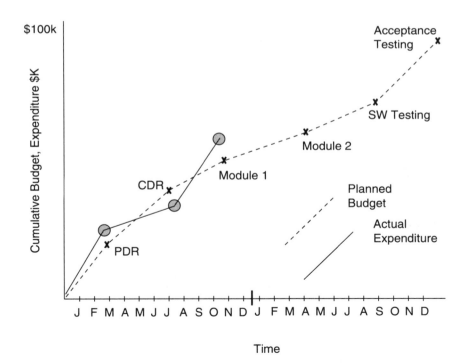

FIGURE 3.8. A cost-schedule-milestone chart.

two milestones have been achieved, PDR and CDR, and though the project was within budget when PDR was complete, it is now slightly over budget.

3.7.4. Earned Value Method

The system design usually involves a small group of (senior) people. Having a large number of people at the system design stage is likely to result in a not very cohesive design. After the system design is complete, a large number of programmers may enter the project whose job is to do the detailed design, coding and testing. During these activities, proper monitoring of people, progress of the different components, and of the overall project is important.

An effective method of monitoring the progress of a project (particularly the phases after system design) is the earned value method. The earned value method employs a **Summary Task Planning Sheet (STPS)** [Boe81]. The STPS is essentially a Gantt chart, with each task (relating to an independently assignable module) having an entry in the chart. Each task has the following milestones marked in STPS: detailed design, coding, testing, and integration.

Each milestone of a task is assigned an *earned value,* which is the value (in dollars or person-months) that will be "earned" on the completion of this milestone. The sum of the assigned values for all the milestones for a task is equal to the total cost assigned to this task (or the total estimated effort requirement for this task).

At any given time, the total effort (or cost) spent on a particular task can be determined from the time sheets. The total value earned can be determined by adding the earned value of all the completed milestones of that task. By comparing the earned value with the total cost spent, the project manager can determine how far the project is deviating from the initial estimates, and then take the necessary actions.

It should be pointed out that, in general, the earned value will be somewhat less than the actual effort spent on a task, since this method only attaches value to the completed milestones. The work in progress does not get adequately represented in the earned value.

The STPS usually has much more detail than needed by project management. The earned value aspect can be summarized in an **earned value summary report.** This report summarizes the earned value for each task, the actual effort spent on that task, and how these compare for a given point in time. The summary report can be produced monthly or biweekly.

3.7.5. Unit Development Folder

The project plan produced after the requirements is a macro-level plan. Even if this plan is prepared meticulously and accurately, if proper control is not exercised at the micro-level (at the level of each programmer and each module), it will be impossible to implement the project plan.

A major problem in tracking micro-level progress is getting accurate information about the status of a module. Often, a manager relies on the person implementing the module to assess the progress. This estimate by individuals about what percentage of work is complete is often not very reliable, and can produce the "90% syndrome" [Boe81].

What happens in the 90% syndrome is that if an individual programmer is asked how much work he has completed, the answer after some time is 90%, and it stays around this percentage for a large period of time. Essentially, an individual programmer's overconfidence results in underestimating the effort needed towards the end.

The unit development folder (UDF) [Ing76] has been used successfully to counter the 90% syndrome. It is sometimes also called the programmers' notebook. The UDF contains the plan, progress and all documentation related to the development of a program unit. A unit of software is one which performs a specific function, is amenable to development by one person, is at a level to which the requirements can be traced, and can be tested independently. A unit could be a module or a procedure or a collection of such modules.

A UDF is typically established after the system design phase, when tasks are distributed among programmers. There is a UDF for each unit, and initially it contains all specifications of that unit, as obtained from the requirements and system design. It is given to the programmer responsible for the development of the unit. All documentation produced for this unit goes in the UDF. This includes the detailed design for the unit, the unit test plan, and the unit test results. The documents from different UDFs are finally merged together to form the system documentation about detailed design, test report, and so forth.

An important element of the UDF is the schedule and progress report of the unit. The overall schedule for the unit is determined from the project plan and is given to the programmer responsible for the unit. The programmer then breaks up the allotted time and produces a detailed schedule for the development of the unit, with intermediate milestones for detailed-design, coding, test plan, unit testing, and the test report. As each of these milestones is achieved, the programmer gets it certified from the manager, and writes the milestone completion date.

The basic idea here is to force the programmer to identify intermediate milestones in the task. The achievement of these milestones is clearly defined and is not subjective. This prevents the programmer from giving the subjective opinion that the work is "90% done".

The advantages of the programmer notebook are that it provides a single place for collecting all the documentation for a unit, provides an orderly and consistent approach for the development of a unit, and provides better management and visibility of the progress in a unit's development.

3.8. Risk Management

Any large project involves certain risks, and that is true of software projects also. Risk management is an emerging area which aims to address the problem of identifying and managing the risks associated with a software project.

Risk in a project is the possibility that the defined goals cannot be met. The basic motivation of having risk management is to avoid disasters or heavy losses. The current interest in risk management is due to the fact that the history of software development projects is full of major and minor failures. A large percentage of projects have run considerably over budget and behind schedule, and many of them have been abandoned mid-way. It is now argued that many of these failures were due to the fact that the risks were not identified and managed properly.

Risk management is an important area, particularly for large projects. Like any management activity, proper planning of that activity is central to success. In this section we discuss some aspects of risk management.

3.8.1. Risk Management Activities

There are a number of activities that have to be performed for effective risk management. The activities can be broadly divided into two groups— those that are geared towards **risk assessment,** and those that are geared towards **risk control.** There are a number of activities that must be performed for both risk assessment and risk control. A breakdown of these activities is given in Figure 3.9 [Boe89].

Risk assessment is an activity that must be undertaken during project planning. This involves identifying the risks, analyzing them and prioritizing them on the basis of the analysis. Once the risks have been assessed, the next step is to control the risks. This involves planning how the risks will be managed, resolving the risks and then monitoring them through the execution.

The major planning activity in risk management is assessment and consequent planning for risk control during the development. Although risk assessment should be done during each phase in the life cycle, it is more important during the early phases. The goal of risk assessment is to prioritize the risks so that risk management can best utilize the given resources for reducing the risks. The activities of risk identification and risk analysis are the steps that must be done in order to prioritize the risks properly. Risk identification is the first step in risk assessment, which identifies all the different risks in a particular project. These risks are project dependent, and their identification is clearly necessary before they can be prioritized. Once the risks have been identified, the next step is to analyze them by assessing the probability of the undesirable event occurring, and the loss that will occur if that event occurs. After this risks can be prioritized based on the expected loss due to different risks.

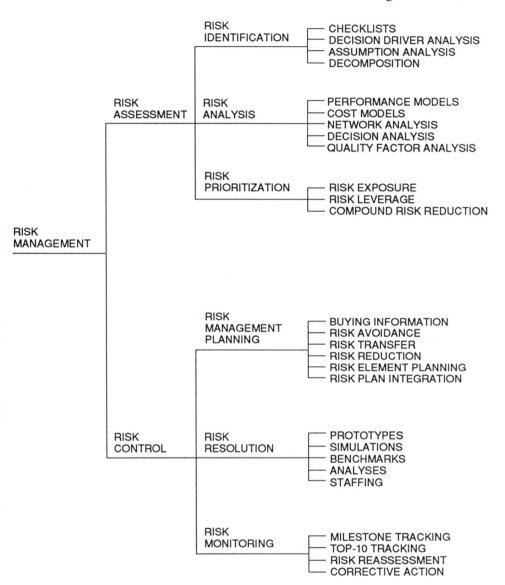

FIGURE 3.9. Risk management activities [Boe 89].

Due to the nature of a software project, most uncertainties are near the beginning of the project (just as for cost estimation). As the project nears its end, risks can be assessed more precisely. Due to this, risk assessment is most needed in the starting phases of the project. In addition, identifying the risks early provides the management with a lot of time to effectively handle the risks.

3.8.2. Risk Identification

At a very high level, the software risks can be broadly divided into three categories. These are:

Cost risk
Performance risk, and
Schedule risk.

Cost risk is the degree of uncertainty associated with budgets and outlays for the project and its impact on the project. Performance risk is the possibility that the system will be unable to deliver all or some of the anticipated benefits, or will not perform according to the requirements. Schedule risk is the degree of uncertainty associated with the project schedule or the ability of the project to achieve the specified milestones.

For practical risk management, a more specific description of risk items is necessary. This is done in risk identification. Based on surveys of experienced project managers, Boehm [Boe89] has produced a list of top-10 risk items which are likely to compromise the success of a software project. Though risks in a project are specific to the project, this list forms a good starting point for identifying such risks. Table 3.6 shows these top-10 items along with the techniques preferred by the management for managing these risks.

The top ranked risk item is personnel shortfalls. This involves just having fewer people than necessary, or not having people with specific skills that a project might require. Some of the ways to manage this risk is to get the top talent possible and to match needs of the project with skills of available personnel. Adequate training along with having some key personnel for critical areas of the project will also reduce this risk.

The second item, unrealistic schedules and budgets, happens very frequently due to business and other reasons. It is very common that the high level management imposes a schedule for a software project that is not based on the characteristics of the project and is unrealistic. This risk applies to all projects. Project-specific risks in cost and schedule occur due to underestimating the value of some of the cost drivers. Recall that cost models like COCOMO estimate the cost and schedule based on some estimates about size and cost drivers. Even if the size estimate is correct, by incorrectly estimating the value of the cost drivers, the project runs the risk of going over budget and falling behind schedule. The cost and schedule risks can be approximated by estimating the maximum value of different cost drivers, along with the probability of occurrence, and then estimating the possible cost and schedule overruns.

The next few items are related to requirements. Projects run the risk of developing the wrong software if the requirements analysis is not done properly and if development begins too early. Similarly, often improper user interface is developed. This requires extensive rework of the user interface later on, or the software benefits are not obtained since the users are reluctant to use it. Gold-plating refers to adding features in the software

TABLE 3.6. Top-10 risk items and techniques for managing them.

RISK ITEM	RISK MANAGEMENT TECHNIQUES
1. PERSONNEL SHORTFALLS	STAFFING WITH TOP TALENT; JOB MATCHING; TEAMBUILDING; KEY-PERSONNEL AGREEMENTS; TRAINING; PRESCHEDULING KEY PEOPLE
2. UNREALISTIC SCHEDULES AND BUDGETS	DETAILED MULTISOURCE COST AND SCHEDULE ESTIMATION; DESIGN TO COST; INCREMENTAL DEVELOPMENT; SOFTWARE REUSE; REQUIREMENTS SCRUBBING
3. DEVELOPING THE WRONG SOFTWARE FUNCTIONS	ORGANIZATION ANALYSIS; MISSION ANALYSIS; OPS-CONCEPT FORMULATION; USER SURVEYS; PROTOTYPING; EARLY USERS' MANUALS
4. DEVELOPING THE WRONG USER INTERFACE	PROTOTYPING; SCENARIOS; TASK ANALYSIS; USER CHARACTERIZATION (FUNCTIONALITY, STYLE, WORKLOAD)
5. GOLD PLATING	REQUIREMENTS SCRUBBING; PROTOTYPING; COST-BENEFIT ANALYSIS; DESIGN TO COST
6. CONTINUING STREAM OF REQUIREMENTS CHANGES	HIGH CHANGE THRESHOLD; INFORMATION HIDING; INCREMENTAL DEVELOPMENT (DEFER CHANGES TO LATER INCREMENTS)
7. SHORTFALLS IN EXTERNALLY FURNISHED COMPONENTS	BENCHMARKING; INSPECTIONS; REFERENCE CHECKING; COMPATIBILITY ANALYSIS
8. SHORTFALLS IN EXTERNALLY PERFORMED TASKS	REFERENCE CHECKING: PREAWARD AUDITS; AWARD-FEE CONTRACTS; COMPETITIVE DESIGN OR PROTOTYPING; TEAMBUILDING
9. REAL-TIME PERFORMANCE SHORTFALLS	SIMULATION; BENCHMARKING; MODELING; PROTOTYPING; INSTRUMENTATION; TUNING
10. STRAINING COMPUTER SCIENCE CAPABILITIES	TECHNICAL ANALYSIS; COST-BENEFIT ANALYSIS; PROTOTYPING; REFERENCE CHECKING

which are only marginally useful. This adds unnecessary risk to the project because gold plating consumes resources and time with little returns. Some requirement changes are to be expected in any project, but sometimes frequent changes are requested, which often is a reflection of the fact that the client has not yet understood or settled on its own requirements. The effect of requirement changes is substantial in terms of cost, especially if the changes occur when the project has progressed to later phases. Performance shortfalls are critical in real-time systems and poor performance can mean the failure of the project.

If a project depends on externally available components—either to be provided by the client or to be procured as an off-the-shelf component—

the project runs some risks. The project might be delayed if the external component is not available on time. The project would also suffer if the quality of the external component is poor, or if the component turns out to be incompatible with the other project components or with the environment in which the software is developed or is to operate. If a project relies on technology that is not well developed, it may fail. This is a risk due to straining the computer science capabilities.

Using the checklist of the top-10 risk items is one way to identify risks. This approach is likely to suffice in many projects. The other methods listed in the figure above are decision driver analysis, assumption analysis and decomposition. Decision driver analysis involves questioning and analyzing all the major decisions taken for the project. If a decision has been driven by factors other than technical and management reasons, then it is likely to be a source of risk in the project. Such decisions may be driven by politics, marketing, or the desire for short-term gain.

Optimistic assumptions made about the project also are a source of risk. Some optimistic assumptions are that nothing will go wrong in the project, no personnel will quit during the project, that people will put in extra hours if required, and that all external components (hardware or software) will be delivered on time. Identifying such assumptions will point out the source of risks. An effective method for identifying these hidden assumptions is comparing them with past experience.

Decomposition implies breaking a large project into clearly defined parts and then analyzing them. Many software systems have the phenomenon that 20 percent of the modules cause 80 percent of the project problems. Decomposition will help identify these modules.

3.8.3. Risk Analysis and Prioritization

Once the risk items are identified, the next step is to analyze the seriousness of different risks and then prioritize them. Not all the items listed above can be analyzed with the use of some models; often subjective analysis needs to be done. However, if cost models are used for cost and schedule estimation, then the same models can be used to assess the cost and schedule risk.

For example, in the COCOMO cost model, the initial estimate of cost is first determined using size as the basic parameter. For the final cost estimate, the value of different cost drivers must be estimated. Examples of these drivers are complexity, reliability, and application familiarity. For average cases, the value of each of these drivers is unity. However, if for example the reliability requirement is high, then the cost driver value is 1.4. By multiplying all the cost drivers we obtain the EAF. The final cost estimate is obtained by multiplying the initial estimate by the EAF.

One possible source of cost risk is in estimating these cost drivers. The other is in estimating the size. Risk analysis can be done by estimating the worst-case value of size and all the cost drivers, and then estimating the project cost from these values. This will give us the worst-case analysis. A more detailed analysis can be done by considering different cases or by considering a distribution of these drivers.

From the worst case effort estimate, the worst case schedule estimate can also be determined. In COCOMO, the schedule of a project is determined from the effort estimate. Using the worst case effort estimate the worst case schedule can easily be obtained.

Other methods can be used for risk analysis, such as decision analysis and network analysis. The reader is referred to [Boe89] for further discussion on these topics.

Once the losses due to different risk items have been analyzed, they have to be prioritized. Risk prioritization is based on the concept of **risk exposure** (RE) [Boe89], which is also sometimes called risk impact. RE is defined by the relationship

$$RE = Prob(UO) * Loss(UO)$$

where Prob(UO) is the probability of an unsatisfactory outcome, or the event whose risks are being analyzed. Loss(UO) is the total loss that is incurred due to the unsatisfactory outcome. The loss is not only the direct financial loss that might be incurred, but also any loss in terms of credibility, future business, and loss of property or life.

The concept of RE is used for risk prioritization. The higher the RE, the higher is the priority of the risk item. This means that a problem that has more likelihood of occurring should not necessarily get more attention. We should also see the loss associated with that problem RE is essentially the expected value of the loss due to the particular risk item.

When using RE for prioritization, the probabilities for the different risk items and the estimate of the loss for each risk item must be assessed. With the probability estimates and the loss estimate, the risk exposure (RE) of different risk items can be determined. The risks can then be prioritized using RE.

It is not always possible to use models and prototypes to assess the probabilities of occurence and of loss associated with particular events. Often subjective methods will have to be used. Risk management is still not advanced enough to have well developed models for risk assessment, as we do for cost estimation. Still, explicitly performing risk management, even though based on subjective evaluation of risks and losses, can be very beneficial to projects and can avoid major problems.

Due to the non-availability of models, assessing risk probabilities is largely subjective. This can be done by the estimate of one person or by using a group consensus technique like the *Delphi* approach. In the Delphi method a group of people discuss the problem of estimation and finally converge on a consensus estimate.

3.8.4. Project Planning and Risk Management

Although risk management is a continuous activity that should be performed throughout the development of the project, it is more important in the early phases. For effective risk management, many of the activities should be performed or planned during project planning.

Risk assessment should be done during project planning (though it should be repeated later during the development as well). This activity is like other assessment or estimation activities. By performing risk assessment (which includes risk identification, analysis and prioritization), during the preparation of the project plan, a properly prioritized list of the project risks will become available. This prioritized list is used for making plans for risk abatement.

Some risk management activities that will need to be performed later during the development (for example, planning for configuration control or having monitoring plans) should be planned for during project planning. A plan to manage the risk should be produced during project planning for each of the risk items that need to be addressed (essentially the top few items in the prioritized risk item list).

The risk management plan for a particular risk item need not be elaborate or extensive. A basic risk management plan has five components [Boe89]. These are: (1) why the risk is important and why it should be managed, (2) what should be delivered regarding risk management and when, (3) who is responsible for performing the different risk management activities, (4) how will the risk be abated, or the approach be taken, and (5) how many resources are needed.

3.9. Summary

Proper project plan is an important ingredient for a successful project. Without proper planning, a large software development project is doomed. Planning is done after the requirements for the project are available. The output of the planning phase is the project plan, which forms an additional input to all later phases. The important planning activities are:

Cost estimation
Schedule and milestones
Staffing and personnel plan
Team structure
Quality assurance plans
Configuration management plans
Project monitoring plans
Risk management.

Cost estimation is the activity where the overall cost requirement for the project as well as the breakup of the cost for different phases is estimated. As human resources are the most important for software development, cost estimates are often given in terms of person-months (PM).

For estimating the cost, cost models are used, that estimate the cost as a function of various parameters. One well known model is the COCOMO model. In this the initial cost estimate is obtained as a function of the size of the final product. Then the cost estimate is refined based on various properties of the project. The cost for different phases is specified as a fixed percentage of the overall cost, and can easily be obtained from the overall cost estimate.

The duration required for the project and for the various activities is an important planning activity. There are models to estimate the duration of a project. In COCOMO, the overall schedule is obtained in a similar manner as the overall cost. The breakup of this duration into duration for different activities is also done in a manner similar to the method for determining cost for different phases.

With the overall cost estimate, and the overall project duration estimate, the average staff requirement for the project can easily be estimated. For planning, a more detailed staff estimate is usually necessary. This can be obtained from the effort and duration estimate for different tasks and phases.

Once the duration and staff requirement is estimated, a personnel plan can be prepared. This plan defines how many people are needed at different times during the life of the project.

Usually a team of people will do the development work. The structure of the team has consequences on productivity and quality. Two team structures have been proposed: the democratic team and the hierarchically structured chief-programmer team. The former results in many communication paths but might produce better decisions. The latter reduces the communication paths and thus reduces communication overhead. It is best suited for projects which are relatively straightforward.

Quality assurance plans are important for ensuring that the final product is of high quality. The quality assurance plan specifies the outputs/reports that will be produced during the development and the criterion for accepting them. It identifies all the V&V activities that have to be performed at different stages in the development. The QAP also schedules these activities.

The configuration management plan is important for large projects that last for a long period of time. In such projects the code, design and even requirements change. Since a change affects many other parts of the system, changes are introduced in a methodical manner by using configuration control. Configuration control planning requires the identification of the configuration items, people who are responsible for configuration control and the criterion used for evaluating change requests.

For a plan to be successfully implemented it is essential that the project be monitored carefully. This requires that project monitoring plans be prepared. There are a number of ways to monitor the progress, cost, schedule or quality of the project. These include timesheets, reviews, a cost-schedule-milestone chart, the earned value method, and the unit development folder. The purpose of all these is to provide accurate and objective information the management. Some of these techniques also help the programmer better assess his own progress.

The last topic we covered in the chapter is risk management. This is a relatively new area which is gaining importance due to the increasing application of computer systems in increasingly complex environments. Risk is the possibility of loss due to inability of the project to meet the goals. Risk management requires that risks be identified, analyzed and then prioritized. Based on the priorities, plans can be devised to minimize the risks.

Exercises

1. What are the major planning activities for a software development project? Out of these, which ones most affect (a) the quality of the product, and (b) the productivity of the project?

2. Suppose that the requirements specification phase is divided into two parts: the initial requirements and feasibility study, and the detailed requirement specification. Suppose that the first part costs about 25% of the total requirement cost. Based on the cost distribution data given in Chapter 1, develop a cost estimation model which can be used to predict the cost *after* (a) the feasibility study and (b) after the detailed requirements. What are the basic parameters for this cost model? How accurate is this cost model? Is the accuracy better for case a or case b?

3. A database system is to be developed. After the requirements, its size is estimated to be 10,000 lines of code. Estimate the overall cost using the Watson and Felix model.

4. Perform the above exercise using the COCOMO model. Assume that the complexity is low, reliability requirement is high, data is high, experience of programmers and the organization in this area is high. The rest of the factors are nominal.

5. In the above example, if the size estimate can be off by 20%, and the reliability and data requirement could have been underestimated by one level, what are the risks in the cost and schedule of the project?

6. Consider a project to develop a full screen editor. The major components identified are (1) screen edit, (2) command language interpretor, (3) file input and output, (4) cursor movement, and (5) screen movement. The sizes for these are estimated to be 4K, 2K, 1K, 2K, and 3K delivered source code lines. Use the COCOMO model to determine (a) overall cost and schedule estimates (assume values for

different cost drives, with at least three of them being different from 1.0), (b) cost and schedule estimates for different phases, and (c) detailed cost and schedule estimates for the different components.

7. For the example above, determine the staff requirement for the different phases. What is the average, maximum, and minimum staff requirement?

8. For the above example, produce a personnel plan, using the schedule and staff estimates obtained in the previous exercise.

9. What are the limitations of the cost estimation models?

10. If you were to choose two variables on which the cost model is to depend, which ones will you choose? Specify the metric of the variables and how you will measure or estimate them in the early phases. Suggest a formula that may be applicable.

11. Consider a variation of the controlled decentralized team structure. A senior programmer and some junior programmers form a team that is structured like a CPT. All the senior programmers and the project leader form a egoless team. Compare the communication paths in this structure with the controlled decentralized structure. What are the advantages and disadvantages of this structure? Under what conditions will you suggest that this structure be used?

12. Suppose each communication path between two people consumes 10% of each person's time. Consider a project that requires six staff-months of technical work, not counting the communication time. What is the difference between the completion times if the team contains five members and (a) if the democratic team structure is used, and (b) if the chief-programmer team structure is used?

13. For the above problem, what is the difference in completion times between the project done by a democratic team of four people and the project done by a democratic team of five people?

14. Suppose each communication path between two people consumes 5% of each person's time. For a project that requires 12 staff-months of programming work, how many people will be needed to finish the project in four months if (a) the democratic team structure is used, and (b) if the chief-programmer team structure is used? If the team consists of four persons, what is the difference in the completion time for a team using the democratic structure and a team using the chief-programmer structure?

15. In the above example, suppose that the company is responsible for maintaining the software for a period of one year after delivery. Assume that the cost of fixing an error after delivery is one staff month. Let the number of errors that are expected to occur in the software produced using the democratic team structure during the maintenance period be two, and the number of errors in software produced using the chief-programmer team structure be four. If four people are used during development, which team structure should be chosen to organize them?

16. What are the major benefits of reviews?
17. Assume that testing (and bug fixing) effort is proportional to the number of errors detected (regardless of the nature of error). Suppose that testing detects 90% of the total errors in the SW (10% remain undetected). By adding design and code reviews, suppose the cost of the design and coding phases increases by 10% each (from the base distribution discussed in Chapter 1), and 10% of the errors are detected in design reviews and 10% in code reviews. (So, testing now detects only 70% errors). What is the overall cost reduction by using reviews?
18. In the example above suppose that the cost of detecting and fixing design errors during testing is five times what it would be if it had been done at the end of the design phase. If 30% of all detected errors are design errors, what is the overall cost reduction by using reviews?
19. You want to monitor the effort spent on different phases in the project as well as the time spent on different components. Design a timesheet or a form to be filled by the programmers which can be used to get this data. The design should be such that automated processing is possible.
20. List the major risks in a software project. What are possible ways to abate the risk of cost and schedule overruns?
21. Suppose that you are the project manager for the full screen editor project described above. Develop a complete plan for this project.

Plan for the Case Study

We present here a plan for the course scheduling project. The plan covers the entire life cycle of the project. For illustration purposes, derivation of the cost and schedule estimates is shown, although in an actual plan these derivations are not needed. Similarly, at many places commentary and explanations have been included for the purpose of explanation and are not usually a part of the plan.

1. COST ESTIMATES

We use the COCOMO model for estimating the cost of the system. As the system is stand-alone and does not interface with other systems, it is regarded as an organic system. In the system for course scheduling, we identify three major modules: input and validate files, schedule, and output. The size estimates for these in lines of code are:

Input	650
Schedule	650
Output	150
TOTAL	1450 = 1.45 KDL

Since this project is somewhat small, COCOMO estimates might be inaccurate (COCOMO is designed for use on systems larger than 2 KDL). The system will be implemented by students, and is not considered very critical. Most cost drivers are considered as nominal, except the following:

Reliability	Low	.88
DB size	Low	.94
Prog. capability	high	.86
Prog. lang. exp.	high	.95
VM volatility	low	.87
Turnaround time	low	.87

From the multipliers for these cost drivers we get the EAF as

$$EAF = .88 * .94 * .86 * .95 * .87 * .87 = 0.51.$$

The initial cost estimate in person–months is

$$E_i = 3.2*(1.4)^{1.05} = 4.7 \text{ PM}.$$

The final cost estimate, after adjustment using the EAF is

$$E = .51 * 4.7 = 2.4 \text{ PM}.$$

To get the phasewise breakup of cost we use the distribution of cost given earlier. The phasewise cost breakup for the project is

Design	2.4 * 0.16 = 0.38 PM
Det. design	.26 * 2.4 = 0.62 PM
Coding and testing	.42 * 2.4 = 1.0 PM
Integration	0.16 * 2.4 = 0.38 PM

2. SCHEDULE ESTIMATES

The estimate for the overall schedule, M, is

$$M = 2.5 * (2.4)^{0.38} = 3.48 \text{ Months}.$$

The distribution of the schedule in different activities is

Design	0.19 * 3.48 = 0.7 Months
Programming	0.63 * 3.48 = 2.2 Months
Testing	0.18 * 3.48 = 0.6 Months

The project will start in the middle of January and end after 3.5 months in the end of April. The proposed schedule for the project is shown in Table 3.7 in the form of a bar-chart.

3. PERSONNEL PLAN AND DETAILED SCHEDULE

The total coding and unit testing effort is one PM. During this the different modules will be coded and tested. We approximate the effort for the different modules in this phase by dividing one PM in the ratio of the sizes

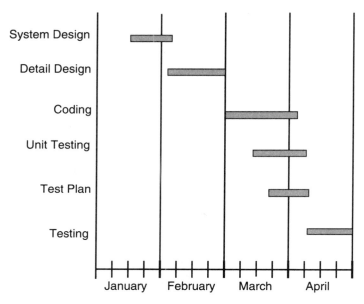

TABLE 3.7. Project schedule.

of the modules. From this we get the estimate for coding and unit testing of different modules as

input	.4
schedule	.4
output	.2.

The team consists of two permanent and one floating member. All these team members are students who will devote about one third of their time to the project. Consequently, the total PM estimate obtained from the personnel plan should be divided by three to obtain the actual person-months cost. The personnel plan is shown in Table 3.8.

From this personnel plan we get the total as 7.25. The total effort in person-months here is 7.25/3 = 2.4 PM, which is the estimate obtained above. The effort sanctioned for each module is also close to the estimates obtained above. For example, for the input or schedule module, 1.0/3 = .33 PM has been allotted, while the estimate is 0.4. The sanctioned effort for system design in this plan is .5 PM, while the estimate above is .7. These minor discrepancies exist because it is not feasible or desirable to plan for a unit less than a week or two weeks.

4. TEAM STRUCTURE

A hierarchical team structure, similar to the chief programmer team, will be used. The group will have a leader, who will allocate tasks to team members. During system and detailed design, only the two permanent

	January	February	March	April	Total
System Design	2 2	2			1.5
Detail Design		2 2 2	2		2.0
Coding Input Sched. Output			1 1 1 1 1 1 1	1 1	1.0 1.0 0.25
Testing				2 2 2	1.5
Total	1.0	2.0	2.25	2.0	7.25

TABLE 3.8. Personnel plan for the project.

members will be involved. During coding and unit testing, the third person might be utilized, if the leader desires. There will be no librarian in the project, as it is a small project, and the programmers themselves will do the documentation and other library tasks. If necessary, the third member of the team will perform the duties of the librarian.

5. CONFIGURATION CONTROL PLAN

In this project, we will only have configuration control for the code. The design will not be under configuration management. The requirements are assumed to be frozen; any change will be negotiated with the management.

The configuration control board (CCB) will consist only of the group leader. A module will be taken for configuration management, only after it has been successfully unit tested and its unit test results have been approved by the group leader. Change requests will be made to the CCB verbally, and the requester will have to justify the request. Requested changes will generally be allowed if the change does not change the interface of the module, and the project is not behind schedule. Changes that will modify the module interface or affect other programmers will, in general, not be approved, unless there are good reasons for doing so. In this case, all the concerned parties will be informed of the change through electronic mail.

6. QUALITY ASSURANCE PLANS

To ensure quality, the following documents (besides this plan and the requirements document) will be produced during the development:

System design document
Detailed design document

Code
Unit test report
System test plan
System test reports.

The following methods will be used for quality control:

Preliminary design review
Detailed design review
Unit testing
System test plan review
System testing.

It is felt that since the system is small, a detailed incremental testing is not needed. A two-level testing is employed: unit testing followed by system testing. The system test plan, however, will be reviewed before the testing is performed. No code-review will be done.

7. MONITORING PLANS

Three basic methods will be used for project monitoring—project logs, biweekly meetings and reviews. Since we do not have a timesheet processing system, each project member will keep a multi-purpose log, in which he will record the different activities he performs and the date and duration of the activity. The failure and error data obtained during testing will also be recorded in the log. Cross checking of the log data can be done by those events in which more than one person of the team participated. The format of the log entries is:

Date	time from	time to	time in mts	activity type	Comments

where activity type is one of the following: requirement understanding, design (system or detailed), coding, testing, report writing, meetings, debugging (including correcting errors), and others. In the comment field, the errors encountered during testing have to be recorded.

Reviews to be held are defined above. In addition to reviews, a biweekly meeting will be held to discuss the progress of the project.

8. RISK MANAGEMENT

The project has no major hazards associated with it. The only risks it has are the cost and schedule risks. Although analysis can easily be done regarding the schedule risks involved, it is felt that since the team has one part-time member (who is largely under-utilized), schedule slippages can be easily handled. Similarly, since the costs are low in this small project, it is felt that an analysis of the cost risk is unnecessary.

4
System Design

The design phase begins when the requirements specification document for the software to be developed is available. While the requirements specification activity is entirely in the problem domain, design is the first step to moving from the problem domain towards the solution domain. Design is essentially the bridge between requirements specification and the final solution for satisfying the requirements.

The term design is used in two ways. Used as a verb, it represents the process of design. Used as a noun, it represents the result of the design process, which is the design for the system. The goal of the design process is to produce a model or a representation of a system which can be used later to build that system. The produced model is called the design of the system.

The design of a system is essentially a blueprint, or a plan for a solution for the system. Here we consider a system to be a set of components with clearly defined behavior, which interact with each other in a fixed, defined manner, to produce some behavior or services to its environment. A component of a system can itself be considered a system, with its own components. In a software system, a component is a software module. We will later define more precisely what we mean by a module.

The design process for software systems often has two levels. At the first level the focus is on deciding which modules are needed for the system, the specifications of these modules, and how the modules should be interconnected. This is what is called the *system design* or *top-level design*. In the second level, the internal design of the modules, or how the specifications of the module can be satisfied is decided upon. This design level is often called *detailed design* or *logic design*. Detailed design essentially expands the system design to contain a more detailed description of the processing logic and data structures such that the design is sufficiently complete for coding.

Since the detailed design is an extension of system design, the system design delineates the major characteristics of the system. The system design has a major impact on the testability and modifiability of a system, and

133

also impacts its efficiency. Much of the design effort for designing software is spent creating the system design. In this chapter we will discuss the different aspects of system design.

A *design methodology* is a systematic approach to creating a design by application of a set of techniques and guidelines. Most design methodologies focus on the system design. In this chapter we will also describe some design methodologies. Most current design methodologies essentially offer a set of guidelines that can be used by the developer to design a system. These techniques are not formalized and do not reduce the design activity to a sequence of steps that can be followed by the designer.

4.1. Design Objectives

The design of a system is *correct* if a system built precisely according to the design satisfies the requirements of that system. Clearly the goal during the design phase is to produce correct designs. However, correctness is not the sole criterion during the design phase. In software engineering, as with any engineering discipline, there can be many correct designs possible. The goal of the design process is not simply to produce a design for the system. Instead the goal is to find the *best* possible design, within the limitations imposed by the requirements and the physical and social environment in which the system will operate.

In order to evaluate a design, we have to specify some properties and criteria that can be used for evaluation. Ideally, these properties should be as quantitative as possible. In that situation we can mathematically evaluate the ''goodness'' of a design and use mathematical techniques to formally determine the best design. However, as with many objects in the real world, criteria for quality of software design is often subjective or non-quantifiable. In such a situation, criteria are essentially ''rules of thumb'' developed to aid the evaluation of a design. We discuss some of the important criteria for evaluating software design in this section. Some desirable properties for a software system design are:

Verifiability
Completeness
Consistency
Efficiency
Traceability
Simplicity/Understandability

Clearly, the first criterion for evaluating a design is that it should be correct. We would like the design to be such that its correctness could be verified. The property of *verifiability* of a design is concerned with how easily the correctness of the design can be argued. *Traceability* is an important property that can aid design verification. It requires that all design elements must be traceable to the requirements.

Completeness requires that all the different components of the design should be specified. That is, all the relevant data structures, modules, external interfaces, and module interconnections are specified.*Consistency* requires that there are no inherent inconsistencies in the design.

Efficiency of any system is concerned with the proper use of scarce resources by the system. The need for efficiency arises due to cost considerations. If some resources are scarce and expensive, then it is desirable that those resources be used efficiently. In computer systems the resources that are most often considered for efficiency are processor time and memory. An efficient system is one that consumes less processor time and requires less memory. In earlier days the efficient use of CPU and memory was important due to the high cost of the hardware. Now that the hardware costs are small compared to the software costs, for many software systems traditional efficiency concerns now take a back seat compared to other considerations. One of the exceptions is real-time systems, where there are strict execution time constraints.

Simplicity and Understandability are perhaps the most important quality criteria for software systems. We have seen that maintenance of software is usually quite expensive. Maintainability of software is one of the goals that we have established. The design of a system is one of the most important factors affecting the maintainability of the system. During maintenance, the first necessary step that a maintainer has to undertake is to understand the system to be maintained. Only after a maintainer has a thorough understanding of the different modules of the system, particularly how they are interconnected and how modifying one will affect the others, should the modification be undertaken. A simple and understandable design will go a long way in making the job of the maintainer easier. Furthermore, a simple design is likely to have a high degree of independence between modules. This will further simplify the task of module modification.

These criterion are not independent, and increasing one may have an unfavorable effect on some other factor. For example, often the "tricks" employed to increase efficiency of a system result in making the system less understandable, and less modifiable. Therefore, in the face of resource restrictions, design decisions involve trade-offs. It is the designers' job to recognize the tradeoffs and achieve the best balance that will satisfy the requirements of quality.

4.2. Design Principles

Producing the design of large systems can be an extremely complex task. Ad-hoc methods for design will not be sufficient, especially since the criteria mentioned above for judging the quality of a design are not quantifiable. In this section we will examine some basic guiding principles that can be employed to produce the design of a system. Some of these design principles are concerned with providing means to effectively handle the complexity of the design process. Effectively handling the complexity will not only reduce the effort needed for design (i.e. reduce the design cost), but can also reduce the scope of introducing errors during design. The principles discussed here form the basis for most of the design methodologies.

4.2.1. Problem Partitioning

When solving a small problem, the entire problem can be tackled at once. The complexity of large problems and the limitations of human minds do not allow large problems to be treated as huge monolithes. For solving larger problems, the basic principle is the time-tested principle of "divide and conquer". Clearly, dividing in such a manner that all the divisions have to be conquered together is not the intent of this wisdom. This principle, if elaborated, would mean "divide into smaller pieces, so that each piece can be conquered separately".

For software design, therefore, the goal is to divide the problem into manageably small pieces that can be solved separately. It is this restriction of being able to solve each part separately that makes dividing a problem into pieces a more complex problem, and which many methodologies for system design aim to address. The basic motivation behind this restriction is the belief that if the pieces of a problem are solvable separately, the cost of solving the entire problem is more than the sum of the cost of solving all the pieces.

However, the different pieces cannot be entirely independent of each other, as they together form the system. The different pieces have to cooperate and communicate in order to solve the larger problem. This communication adds complexity, which arises due to partitioning and which may not have been there in the original problem. As the number of components increases, the cost of partitioning together with the cost of this added complexity may become more than the savings achieved by partitioning. It is at this point that no further partitioning needs to be done. The designer has to make the judgment about when to stop partitioning.

As discussed in the previous section, one of the most important quality criteria for software design is simplicity and understandability. It can be argued that maintenance is minimized if each part in the system can be easily related to the application, and that each piece can be modified separately. If a piece can be modified separately, we call it independent of other pieces. If a module A is independent of a module B, then we can modify A without introducing any unanticipated side effects in B. Total independence of modules of one system is not possible, but the design process should support as much independence between modules as possible. Dependence between modules in a software system is one of the reasons for high maintenance cost. Clearly, proper partitioning will make the system easier to maintain by making the design easier to understand. Problem partitioning also aids design verification.

4.2.2. Abstraction

Abstraction is a very powerful concept that is used in all engineering disciplines. Abstraction is a tool that permits a designer to consider a component at an abstract level, without worrying about the details of the implementation of the component. Any component or system provides some services to its environment. An abstraction of a component describes the external behavior of that component, without bothering about the internal details that produce the behavior. Presumably, the abstract definition of a component is much simpler than the component itself.

Abstraction is an indispensable part of the design process, and is essential for problem partitioning. Partitioning essentially is the exercise in determining the components of a system. However, these components are not isolated from each other, but interact with each other, and the designer has to specify how a component interacts with other components. For deciding how a component interacts with other components, the designer has to know, at the very least, the external behavior of other components. If the designer has to understand the details of the other components to determine their external behavior, then we have defeated the very purpose of partitioning—isolating a component from others. In order to allow the designer to concentrate on one component at a time, abstraction of other components is used.

Abstraction is used for existing components as well as components that are being designed. Abstraction of existing components plays an important role in the maintenance phase. For modifying a system, the first step is understanding what the system does and how it does it. The process of comprehending an existing system involves identifying the abstractions of subsystems and components from the details of their implementations. Using these abstractions, the behavior of the entire system can be understood. This also helps in determining how modifying a component affects the system.

During the design process, abstractions are used in the reverse manner than in the process of understanding a system. During design the components do not exist, and in the design the designer specifies only the abstract specifications of the different components. The basic goal of system design is to specify the modules in a system and their abstractions. Once the different modules are specified, during the detailed design the designer can concentrate on one module at a time. The task in detailed design and implementation is essentially to implement the modules such that the abstract specifications of each module are satisfied.

There are two common abstraction mechanisms for software systems—**functional abstraction** and **data abstraction.** In **functional abstraction,** a module is specified by the function it performs. For example, a module to compute the sine of a value can be abstractly represented by the function sine. Similarly, a module to sort an input array can be represented by the specification of sorting.

The second unit for abstraction is **data abstraction.** Any entity in the real world provides some services to the environment to which it belongs. Often the entities provide some fixed pre-defined services. The case of data entities is similar. There are certain operations that are required from a data object, depending on the object and the environment in which it is used. Data abstraction supports this view. Data is not treated simply as objects, but is treated as objects with some pre-defined operations on them. The operations defined on a data object are the only operations that can be performed on those objects. From outside an object, the internals of the object are hidden and only the operations on the object are visible.

Functional abstraction forms the basis of the structural design methodology, while data abstraction forms the basis of the object-oriented design methodology. We will discuss both of these methodologies later in the chapter.

4.2.3. Top-Down and Bottom-Up Strategies

A system consists of components, which have components of their own; indeed, a system is a hierarchy of components, the highest level component corresponding to the total system. To design such a hierarchy there are two different approaches possible—top-down and bottom-up. The top-down approach starts from the highest level component of the hierarchy and proceeds through to lower levels. By contrast, a bottom-up approach starts with the lowest level component of the hierarchy and proceeds through progressively higher levels to the top-level component.

A top-down design approach starts by identifying the major components of the system, decomposing them into their lower-level components, and iterating until the desired level of detail is achieved. A bottom-up design approach starts with designing the most basic or primitive components and proceeds to higher-level components that use these lower-level components. Top-down design methods often result in some form of *stepwise refinement*. Starting from an abstract design, in each step the design is refined to a more concrete level, until we reach a level where no more refinement is needed and the design can be implemented directly. Bottom-up methods work with *layers of abstraction*. Starting from the very bottom, operations are implemented that provide a layer of abstraction. The operations of this layer are then used to implement more powerful operations and a still higher layer of abstraction, until the stage is reached where the operations supported by the layer are the ones that are desired by the system.

Pure top-down or pure bottom-up approaches are often not practical.

For a bottom-up approach to be successful, we must have a good notion of the top where the design should be heading. Without a good idea about the operations needed at the higher layers, it is difficult to determine what operations the current layer should support. Top-down approaches require some idea about the feasibility of the components specified during design. The components that are specified during design should be implementable, which requires some idea about the feasibility of the lower-level parts of a component. However, this is not a very major drawback, particularly in application areas where the existence of solutions is known (by seeing similar systems, or the nature of the problem, for example). The top-down approach has been promulgated by many researchers and has been found to be extremely useful for design. Many design methodologies are based on the top-down approach.

4.3. Module Level Concepts

Before we discuss some concepts relating to modules, let us define what we mean by a module. A module is a logically separable part of a program. It is a program unit that is discreet and identifiable with respect to compiling and loading. In terms of common programming language constructs, a module can be a macro, a function, a procedure (or subroutine), a process or a package. As mentioned earlier, partitioning a system into modules is useful only if the modules are solvable separately, and modifiable separately. A system is considered **modular** if it consists of discreet components such that each component supports a well-defined abstraction, and if a change to one component has minimal impact on other components. Clearly modularity is a desirable property in a system. A software system cannot be made modular by simply chopping it into a set of modules. Some criteria must be used to select modules so that the modules support well-defined abstractions and are solvable and modifiable separately. Coupling and cohesion are two such modularization criteria, which are often used together.

4.3.1. Coupling

Two modules are considered independent if one can function completely without the presence of other. Obviously if two modules are independent, then they are solvable and modifiable separately. However, all the modules in a system cannot be independent of each other, as they must interact with each other such that together they can produce the desired external behavior of the system. The more the connections between modules, the more dependent they are in the sense that more knowledge about one module is required to understand or solve the other module. Hence, the fewer and simpler the connections between modules, the easier it is to understand one without understanding the other. The notion of coupling [Ste74, You79] attempts to capture this concept of "how strongly" different modules are interconnected with each other.

Coupling between modules is the strength of interconnections between modules, or a measure of interdependence among modules. In general, the more we must know about module A in order to understand module B, the more closely connected is A to B. "Highly coupled" modules are joined by strong interconnections, while "loosely coupled" modules have weak interconnections. Independent modules have no interconnections. For being able to solve and modify a module separately, we would like the module to be loosely coupled with other modules. The choice of modules decides the coupling between modules. Since the modules of the software system are created during the system design, the coupling between modules is largely decided during system design, and cannot be reduced during implementation.

Coupling is an abstract concept and is as yet not quantifiable. So, no formulas can be given to determine the coupling between two modules. However, some major factors can be identified as influencing coupling between modules. Among them the most important are the type of connection between modules, the complexity of the interface, and the type of information flow between modules.

Coupling increases with the complexity and obscurity of the interface between modules. To keep coupling low we would like to minimize the number of interfaces per module, and minimize the complexity of each interface. An interface of a module is used to pass information to and from other modules. Coupling is reduced if only the defined entry interface of a module is used by other modules (for example, passing information to and from a module exclusively through parameters). Coupling would increase if a module is used by other modules via an indirect and obscure interface, like directly using the internals of a module, or utilizing shared variables.

Complexity of the interface is another factor affecting coupling. The more complex each interface is, the higher will be the degree of coupling. For example, complexity of the entry interface of a procedure depends on the number of items being passed as parameters and on the complexity of the items. Some level of complexity of interfaces is required to support the communication needed between modules. However, often more than this minimum is used. For example, if a field of a record is needed by a procedure, often the entire record is passed, rather than just passing that field of the record. By passing the record we are increasing the coupling unnecessarily. Essentially, we should keep the interface of a module as simple and as small as possible.

The type of information flow along the interfaces is the third major factor affecting coupling. There are two kinds of information that can flow along an interface: data or control. Passing or receiving back control information means that the action of the module will depend on this control information, which makes it more difficult to understand the module and provide

TABLE 4.1. Factors affecting coupling [Ste 74].

	Interface complexity	Type of connection	Type of communication
low	simple obvious	to module by name	data
			control
high	complicated obscure	to internal elements	hybrid

its abstraction. Transfer of data information means that a module passes as input some data to another module and gets in return some data as output. This allows a module to be treated as a simple input-output function that performs some transformation on the input data to produce the output data. In general, interfaces with only data communication result in the lowest degree of coupling, followed by interfaces that only transfer control data. Coupling is considered highest if the data is hybrid, that is, some data items and some control items are passed between modules.

The effect of these three factors on coupling is summarized in Table 4.1 [Ste74].

4.3.2. Cohesion

We have seen that coupling is reduced when the relationships among elements in different modules is minimized. That is, coupling reduces when elements that are in different modules have little or no bonds between them. Another way of achieving this effect is to strengthen the bond between elements of the same module, by maximizing the relationship between elements of the same module. Cohesion is the concept that tries to capture this intra-module [Ste74, You79]. With cohesion we are interested in determining how closely the elements of a module are related to each other.

Cohesion of a module represents how tightly bound the internal elements of the module are to one another. Cohesion of a module gives the designer an idea about whether the different elements of a module belong together in the same module. Cohesion and coupling are clearly related. Usually the greater the cohesion of each module in the system, the lower will be the coupling between modules. This correlation is not perfect, but has been observed in practice. There are several levels of cohesion:

Coincidental
Logical
Temporal
Procedural
Communicational
Sequential
Functional

Coincidental is the lowest level and functional is the highest. These levels do not form a linear scale. Functional binding is much stronger than the rest, while the first two are considered to be much weaker than others. Often many levels can be applicable when considering cohesion between two elements of a module. In such situations, the highest level is considered. Cohesion of a module is considered as the highest level of cohesion which is applicable to all elements in the module.

Coincidental cohesion occurs when there is no meaningful relationship among the elements of a module. Coincidental cohesion can occur if an existing program is "modularized" by chopping it into pieces and making different pieces to be modules. If a module is created to save duplicate code by combining some part of code that occurs at many different places, that module is likely to have coincidental cohesion. In this situation, the statements in the module have no relationship among each other, and if one of the modules using the code needs to be modified and this modification includes the common code, it is likely that other modules using the code do not want the code to be modified. Consequently, the modification of this "common module may cause other modules to behave incorrectly. The modules using these modules are therefore not modifiable separately and have strong interconnection between them. We can say that, generally speaking, it is a poor practice to create a module merely to avoid duplicate code (unless the common code happens to perform some identifiable function, in which case the statements will have some relationship between them), or to chop a module into smaller modules to reduce the module size.

A module has logical cohesion if there is some logical relationship between the elements of a module, and the elements perform functions that fall in the same logical class. A typical example of this kind of cohesion is a module that performs all the inputs, or perform all the outputs. In such a situation, if we want to input or output a particular record, we have to somehow convey this to the module. Often this will be done by passing some kind of special status flag, which will be used to determine what statements to execute in the module. Besides resulting in hybrid information flow between modules, which is generally the worst form for coupling between modules, such a module will usually have tricky and clumsy code. In general, logically cohesive modules should be avoided, if possible.

Temporal cohesion is the same as logical cohesion, except that the elements are also related in time, and are executed together. Modules that perform activities like "initialization", "clean-up", and "termination" are usually temporally bound. Even though the elements in a temporally bound module are logically related, temporal cohesion is higher than logical cohesion, since the elements are all executed together. This avoids the problem of passing the flag, and the code is usually simpler.

A procedurally cohesive module contains elements that belong to a common procedural unit. For example, a loop or a sequence of decision statements in a module may be combined to form a separate module.

Procedurally cohesive modules often occur when modular structure is determined from some form of flowchart. Procedural cohesion often cuts across functional lines. A module with only procedural cohesion may contain only part of a complete function, or parts of a several functions.

A module with communicational cohesion has elements that are related by a reference to the same input or output data. That is, in a communicationally bound module, the elements are together because they operate on the same input or output data. An example of this could be a module to "print and punch record". Communicationally cohesive modules may be performing more than one function. However, communicational cohesion is sufficiently high so as to be generally acceptable if alternate structures with higher cohesion cannot be easily identified.

When the elements are together in a module because the output of one forms the input to another, we get sequential cohesion. If we have a sequence of elements in which the output of one forms the input to another, sequential cohesion does not provide any guidelines on how to combine them into modules. Different possibilities exist: combine all in one module, put the first half in one and the second half in another, the first third in one and the rest in the other, and so forth. Consequently, a sequentially bound module may contain several functions or parts of different functions. Sequentially cohesive modules bear a close resemblance to the problem structure. However, they are considered to be far from the ideal, which is functional cohesion.

Functional cohesion is the strongest cohesion. In a functionally bound module, all elements of the module are related to performing a single function. By function, we do not mean simply mathematical functions. Modules accomplishing a single goal are also included. Functions like "compute square root" and "sort the array" are clear examples of functionally cohesive modules.

How does one determine the cohesion level of a module? There is no mathematical formula that can be used. We have to use our judgment for this. A useful technique for determining if a module has functional cohesion is to write a sentence that describes, fully and accurately, the function or purpose of the module. The following tests can then be made [Ste74].

1. If the sentence must be a compound sentence, if it contains a comma, or has more than one verb, the module is probably performing more than one function, and probably has sequential or communicational cohesion.
2. If the sentence contains words relating to time, like "first", "next", "when", "after", etc., then the module probably has sequential or temporal cohesion.
3. If the predicate of the sentence does not contain a single specific object following the verb (such as "edit all data"), the module probably has logical cohesion.
4. Words like "initialize" and "clean-up" imply temporal cohesion.

Modules with functional cohesion can always be described by a simple sentence. However, if a description is a compound sentence it does not mean that the module does not have functional cohesion. Functionally cohesive modules can also be described by compound sentences. If we cannot describe it using a simple sentence, then the module is not likely to have functional cohesion.

To these levels we add another level called *type cohesion,* that was not originally defined. The need for this level is to include the concept of data abstraction. The above levels of cohesion are geared towards modules that support functional abstraction. The reason for this is that when these levels were defined functional abstraction was more prevalent and the concept of data abstraction was not widespread. However, now data abstraction based programming is being promulgated by many.

In languages that support user-defined type, often a module (or a Package) is defined which contains some data representing elements of that type, and a set of operations (procedures/functions) that operate on that data, representing the operations defined on the type. From outside the type module, the data is accessed only through the operations defined on the data. Cohesion of such a module cannot be naturally defined in terms of the seven levels originally defined. We will consider a module as having type cohesion if all the encapsulated data is needed to implement the abstract type (i.e. no extraneous data items), and all the functions/procedures in the module have functional cohesion and directly contribute towards implementing that type.

4.4. Design Methodology—Structured Design

Creating the software system design is the major concern of the design phase. Many design techniques have been proposed over the years to provide some discipline in handling the complexity of designing large systems. The aim of design methodologies is not to reduce the process of design to a sequence of mechanical steps, but to provide guidelines to aid the designer during the design process. Here we describe the structured design methodology [Ste74, You79] for developing system designs.

Structured design methodology (SDM) views every software system as having some inputs which are converted into the desired outputs by the software system. The software is viewed as a transformation function that transforms the given inputs into the desired outputs, and the central problem of designing software systems is considered to be properly designing this transformation function. Due to this view of software, the structured design methodology is primarily functional in nature and relies heavily on functional abstraction and functional decomposition.

The goal is to produce a design for a software system that consists of many modules such that the modules have the least interconnections between them. With such a design, each module can be implemented and changed with minimal consideration of the other modules of the system. In other words, the manner in which SDM attempts to reduce the complexity of the software is by dividing it into functional modules, which have few interconnections between them. In terms of cohesion and coupling we can say that the primary goal of structured design is to divide a problem into modules such that the coupling between different modules is reduced while the cohesion of different modules is enhanced.

4.4.1. Structure Charts

In SDM, the design is represented by structure charts. The structure of a program is made up of the modules of that program together with the interconnections between modules. Every computer program has a structure, and given a program its structure can be determined. The structure chart of a program is a graphic representation of its structure. In a struc-

```
Program addr (infile, output),
(* to determine sum of smallest n numbers *
T : array [1..M] of integer;
var a : T;
procedure read_num (var a : T)
begin
    (read the num. into frame
        file*)
end;
procedure sort (var a : T)
(*do a bubble sort*)
begin
    ⋮
  if a[i] > [it] then
      switch (a[i], a[it1])
    ⋮
end;
function add n (a : T, n : int) : int
(*add first n num of a *)
begin
    ⋮
end;

begin (*main frag*)
    read-num (a);
    sort (a);
    sum: = add_n (a,n):
    print (sum)
end.
```

FIGURE 4.1. A skeleton of a Pascal program and its structure chart.

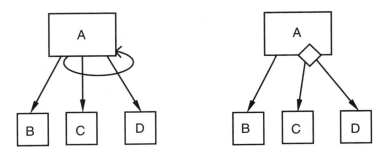

FIGURE 4.2. Iteration and decision representation.

ture chart a module is represented by a box, with the module name written in the box. An arrow from a module A to another module B represents that module A invokes the module B. B is called the *subordinate* of A, and A is called the *superiordinate* of B. The arrow is labeled by the parameters received by B as input, and the parameters returned by B as output, with the direction of flow of the input and output parameters represented by small arrows.

As an example consider the structure of a skeletal Pascal program shown in Figure 4.1. The structure of this program is also shown in Figure 4.1.

In general, procedural information is not represented in a structure chart, and the focus is on representing the hierarchy of modules. However, there are situations where the designer may wish to communicate certain procedural information explicitly, like major loops and decisions. Such information can also be represented in a structure chart. For example, let us consider a situation where a module A has subordinates B, C and D, and A repeatedly calls the modules C and D. This can be represented by a looping arrow around the arrows joining the subordinates C and D to A, as shown in Figure 4.2. All the subordinate modules activated within a common loop are enclosed in the same looping arrow.

Similarly, major decisions can also be represented. For example, if the invocation of modules C and D in the module A depends on the outcome of some decision, then that is represented by a small diamond in the box for A, with the arrows joining C and D coming out of this diamond, as shown in Figure 4.2.

INPUT, OUTPUT, TRANSFORM AND COORDINATE MODULES

Modules in a system can be categorized into various classes. There are some modules that obtain information from their subordinates, and then pass it on to their superiordinate. This kind of module is an *input module*. Similarly, there are output modules. An *output module* takes information from its superiordinate, and passes it on to its subordinates. As the name suggests, the input and output modules are typically used for input and

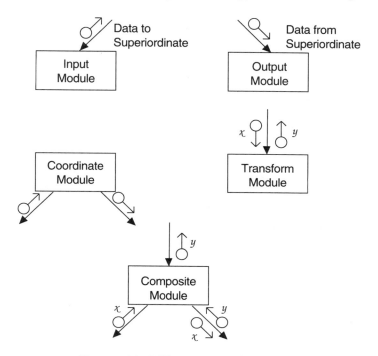

FIGURE 4.3. Different types of modules.

output of data from and to the environment. The input modules get the data from the sources and get it ready to be processed, and the output modules take the output produced, and prepare it for proper presentation to the environment. Then there are modules that exist solely for the sake of transforming data into some other form. Such a module is called a *transform module*. Most of the computational modules typically fall in this category. Finally, there are modules whose primary concern is managing the flow of data to and from different subordinates. Such modules are called *coordinate modules*. The structure chart representation of the different types of modules is shown in Figure 4.3.

A module can perform functions of more than one type of module. For example, the composite module in Figure 4.3 is an input module from the point of view of its superiordinate, as it feeds the data Y to the superiordinate. Internally, A is a co-ordinate module and views its job as getting data X from one subordinate and passing it to another subordinate, which converts it to Y. Modules in actual systems are often composite modules.

STRUCTURED DESIGN AND PROGRAM STRUCTURE

The concept of structure of a program lies at the heart of the structured design method. During design, structured design methodology aims to control and influence the structure of a program. The belief is that the structure of a program is the most significant factor for simplicity and understandability. The aim is to design a system such that programs implementing the design would have a nice hierarchical structure, with as few interconnections between modules as possible.

In properly designed systems it is often the case that a module with subordinates does not actually perform much computation. The bulk of actual computation is performed by its subordinates, and the module itself largely coordinates the data flow between the subordinates to get the computation done. The subordinates in turn can get the bulk of their work done by their subordinates, until the "atomic" modules are reached, which have no subordinates. *Factoring* is the process of decomposing a module so that the bulk of its work is done by its subordinates. A system is said to be completely factored if all of the actual processing is accomplished by bottom level atomic modules, and if non-atomic modules largely perform the jobs of control and coordination. Structured design attempts to achieve a structure that is close to being completely factored.

4.4.2. Design Methodology

We have looked at how to determine the structure of an existing program. But, once the program is written, its structure is fixed, and little can be done about altering the structure. However, for a given set of requirements many different programs can be written to satisfy the requirements, and each different program can have a different structure. That is, although the structure of a given program is fixed, for a given set of requirements, programs with different structures can be obtained. The goal of the structured design is to control the eventual structure of the system by fixing the structure during design.

The overall strategy is to identify the input and output streams and the primary transformations that have to be performed to produce the output. High level modules are then created to perform these major activities, which are later refined. There are four major steps in this strategy:

1. Restate the problem as a data flow graph,
2. Identify the input and output data elements,
3. First-level factoring, and
4. Factoring of input, output, and transform branches.

We will now discuss each of these steps in more detail. The design of the case study using structured design will be given later. For illustrating each of these steps of the methodology as we discuss them, we consider the following problem: there is a text file containing words separated by blanks or new lines. We have to design a software system to determine the number of unique words in the file.

RESTATE THE PROBLEM AS A DATA FLOW GRAPH

In order to employ the SD methodology, the first step is to construct the data flow graph for the problem. We have studied data flow graphs (DFG) earlier in Chapter 2. In the requirements analysis, a DFG is drawn to model the overall system, showing how the data flows. During design activity, we are no longer modeling the overall system, but are developing a model for implementing those parts that are to be automated. In this modeling, the major transforms or functions in the software are decided. Hence, the DFG shows the major transforms that the software will have, and how the data will flow through different transforms. The general rules of drawing a DFG remain the same; we show what transforms are needed in the software and are not concerned with the logic for implementing them. Consider the example of the simple automated teller machine that allows customers to withdraw money. A DFG for this ATM is shown in Figure 4.4.

There are two major streams of input data in this diagram. The first is the account number and the code, and the second is the amount to be debited. The graph is self explanatory. Notice the use of * at different places in the graph. For example, the transform "validate", which verifies if the account number and code are valid, needs not only the account number and code, but also information from the system database to do the validation. And the transform debit account has two outputs, one used for recording the transaction, and the other to update the account.

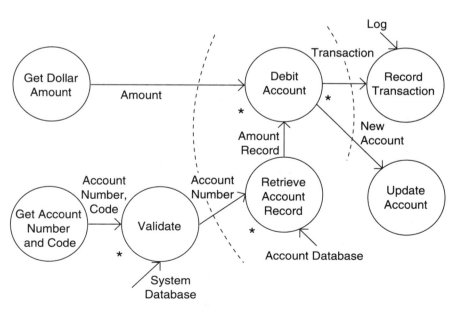

FIGURE 4.4. Data flow graph of an ATM.

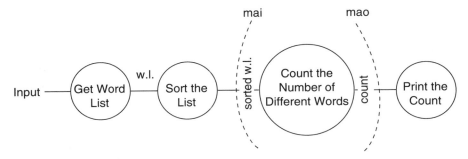

FIGURE 4.5. DFG for "Count-the-number-of-different-words-in-a-file."

As another example, consider the problem of determining the number of different words in an input file. The data flow graph for this problem is shown in Figure 4.5.

This problem has only one input data stream, the input file, while the desired output is the count of different words in the file. In order to transform the input to the desired output, the first thing we do is form a list of all the words in the file. It is best to then sort the list, as this will make identifying different words easier. This sorted list is then used to count the number of different words, and the output of this transform is the desired count, which is then printed. This sequence of data transformation is what we have in the data flow graph.

IDENTIFY THE MOST ABSTRACT INPUT AND OUTPUT DATA ELEMENTS

Most systems have some basic transformations that perform required operations. However, in most cases the transformation cannot be easily applied to the actual physical input and produce the desired physical output. Instead the input is first converted into a form on which the transformation can be applied with ease. Similarly, the main transformation modules often produce outputs that have to be converted into the desired physical output. The goal of this second step is to separate the transforms in the data flow graph that convert the input or output to the desired format from the ones that perform the actual transformations.

For this separation, once the data flow graph is ready, the next step is to identify the highest abstract level of input and output. The *most abstract input data elements* are those data elements in the data flow graph that are furthest removed from the physical inputs, but can still be considered as inputs to the system. The most abstract input data elements often have little resemblance to the actual physical data. These are often the data elements that are obtained after operations like error checking, data validation, proper formatting, and conversion are complete.

Most abstract input (MAI) data elements are recognized by starting from the physical inputs and traveling towards the outputs in the data flow graph, until the data elements are reached that can no longer be considered as incoming. The aim is to go as far as possible from the physical inputs, without loosing the incoming nature of the data element. This process is performed for each of the input streams. Identifying the most abstract data items represents a value judgment on the part of the designer, but often the choice is rather obvious.

Similarly we identify the *most abstract output data elements* (MAO), by starting from the outputs in the data flow graph and traveling towards the inputs. These are the data elements that are most removed from the actual outputs but can still be considered as outgoing. The MAO data elements may also be considered as the logical output data items, and the transforms in the data flow graph after these data items are basically to convert the logical output into a form in which the system is required to produce the output.

There will usually be some transforms left between the most abstract input and output data items. These *central transforms* perform the basic transformation for the system, taking the most abstract input and transforming it into the most abstract output. The purpose of having central transforms deal with the most abstract data items is that the modules implementing these transforms can concentrate on performing the transformation without being concerned with converting the data into proper format, validating the data, and so forth. It is worth noting that if a central transform has two outputs with a + between them, it often indicates the presence of a major decision in the transform (which can be shown in the structure chart).

Let us consider the data flow graph shown in figure 4.5. The arcs in the data flow graph are the most abstract input and most abstract output. The choice of the most abstract input is obvious. We start following the input. First the input file is converted into a word list, which is essentially the input in a different form. The sorted word list is still basically the input, as it is still the same list, in a different order. This appears to be the most abstract input since the next data (i.e. count) is not just another form of the input data. The choice of the most abstract output is even more obvious; count is the natural choice (a data that is a form of input will not usually be a candidate for the most abstract output). Thus we have one central transform, count the number of different words, which has one input and one output data item.

Consider now the data flow graph of the automated teller shown in Figure 4.4. The two most abstract inputs are the dollar amount, and the validated account number. The validated account number is the most abstract input, rather than the account number read in, as it is still the input but with a guarantee that the account number is valid. The two abstract outputs are obvious. The abstract inputs and outputs are marked in the data flow graph.

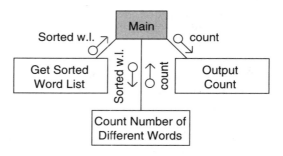

FIGURE 4.6. First-level factoring.

FIRST LEVEL FACTORING

Having identified the central transforms and the most abstract input and output data items, we are ready to identify some modules for the system. We first specify a main module, whose purpose is to invoke the subordinates. The main module is therefore a coordinate module. For each of the most abstract input data items an immediate subordinate module to the main module is specified. Each of these modules is an input module, whose purpose is to deliver to the main module the most abstract data item for which it is created.

Similarly, for each most abstract output data item, a subordinate module which is an output module that accepts data from the main module is specified. Each of the arrows connecting these input and output subordinate modules are labeled with the respective abstract data item, flowing in the proper direction.

Finally, for each central transform, a module subordinate to the main one is specified. These modules will be transform modules, whose purpose is to accept data from the main module, and then return the appropriate data back to the main module. The data items coming to a transform module from the main module are on the incoming arcs of the corresponding transform in the data flow graph. The data items returned are on the outgoing arcs of that transform. Note that here a module is created for a transform, while input/output modules are created for data items. The structure after the first-level factoring of the word counting problem (its data flow graph was given earlier) is shown in Figure 4.6.

In this example, there is one input module which returns the sorted word list to the main module. The output module takes from the main module the value of the count. There is only one central transform in this example, and a module is drawn for that. Note that the data items traveling to and from this transformation module are the same as the data items going in and out of the central transform.

Let us examine the data flow graph of the teller. We have already seen that this has two most abstract inputs, two most abstract outputs, and two

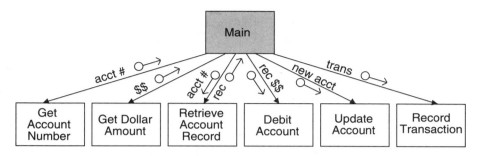

FIGURE 4.7. First-level factoring for ATM.

central transforms. Drawing a module for each of these, we get the structure chart shown in Figure 4.7.

As we can see, the first level factoring is straightforward, after the most abstract input and output data items are identified in the data flow graph. The main module is the overall control module, and will form the main program or procedure in the implementation of the design. It is a coordinate module which invokes the input modules to get the most abstract data items, passes these to the appropriate transform modules, and delivers the results of the transform modules to other transform modules until the most abstract data items are obtained. These are then passed to the output modules.

FACTORING THE INPUT, OUTPUT, AND TRANSFORM BRANCHES

The first-level factoring results in a very high-level structure, where each of the subordinate modules has a lot of processing to do. To simplify these modules, they must be factored into subordinate modules that will distribute the work of a module. Each of the input, output and transformation modules must be considered for factoring. Let us start with the input modules.

The purpose of an input module, as viewed by the main program, is to produce some data. To factor an input module, the transform in the data flow graph that produced the data item is now treated as a central transform. The process performed for the first-level factoring is repeated here with this new central transform, with the input module being factored as the main module. A subordinate input module is created for each input data stream coming into this new central transform, and a subordinate transform module is created for the new central transform. The new input modules now created can then be factored again, until the physical inputs are reached. Factoring of input modules will usually not yield any output subordinate modules. The factoring of the input module get-sorted-list in the first-level structure is shown in Figure 4.8.

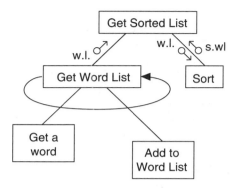

FIGURE 4.8. Factoring the input module.

Factoring of this module is straightforward. The transform producing the input returned by this module (i.e. the sort transform) is treated as a central transform. Its input is the word list. Thus, in the first factoring we have an input module to get the list, and a transform module to sort the list. The input module can be factored further, as the module needs to perform two functions, getting a word and then adding it to the list. Note that the looping arrow is used to show the iteration.

The factoring of the output modules is symmetrical to the factoring of the input modules. For an output module we look at the next transform to be applied to the output to bring it closer to the ultimate desired output. This now becomes the central transform, and an output module is created for each data stream going out of this transform. During the factoring of output modules, there will be usually no input modules. In our example, there is only one transform after the most abstract output, so this factoring need not be done.

If the data flow graph of the problem is sufficiently detailed, factoring of the input and output modules is straightforward. However, there are no such rules for factoring the central transforms. The goal is to determine sub-transforms that will together compose the overall transform, and then repeat the process for the newly found transforms, till we reach the atomic modules. Factoring the central transform is essentially an exercise in functional decomposition, and will depend on the designers' experience and judgment.

One way to factor a transform module is to treat it as a problem in its own right, and start with a data flow graph for it. The inputs to the data flow graph are the data coming into the module and the outputs are the data being returned by the module. Each transform in this data flow graph represents a sub-transform of this transform. The central transform can be factored by creating a subordinate transform module for each of the transforms in this data flow graph. This process can be repeated for the new

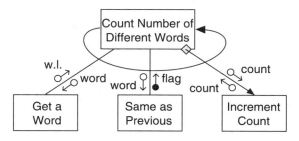

FIGURE 4.9. Factoring the central transform.

transform modules that are created, till we reach atomic modules. The factoring of the central transform count the number of different words is shown in Figure 4.9.

This was a relatively simple transform, and we did not need to draw the data flow graph. To determine the number of words, we have to get a word repeatedly, determine if it is the same as the previous word (for sorted a list, this checking is sufficient to determine if the word is different from other words), and then count the word, if it is different. For each of the three different functions, we have a subordinate module, and we get the structure shown above.

DESIGN HEURISTICS

The design steps mentioned above do not reduce the design process to a series of steps that can be followed blindly. The strategy requires the designer to exercise sound judgment and common sense. The basic objective is to make the program structure reflect the problem as closely as possible. With this in mind the structure obtained by the methodology described earlier should be treated as an initial structure, which may need to be modified. Here we mention some heuristics that can be used to modify the structure, if necessary. It must be kept in mind that these are merely pointers to aid the designer in deciding how the structure can be modified. The designer is still the final judge of whether a particular heuristic is useful for a particular application or not.

Module size is often considered an indication of module complexity. In terms of the structure of the system, modules that are very large may not be implementing a single function and can therefore be broken into many modules, each implementing a different function. On the other hand modules that are too small may not require any additional identity and can be combined with other modules.

However, the decision to split a module or combine different modules should not be based on size alone. Cohesion and coupling of modules should be the primary guiding factors. A module should be split into separate modules only if the cohesion of the original module was low and the resulting modules have a higher degree of cohesion, and the coupling between modules does not increase. Similarly, two or more modules should be combined only if the resulting module has a high degree of cohesion, and the coupling of the resulting module is not greater than the coupling of the sub-modules. Furthermore, a module usually should not be split or combined with another module if it is subordinate to many different modules. As a rule of thumb, the designer should take a hard look at modules that will be larger than about 100 lines of source code, or will be less than a couple of lines.

Another parameter that can be considered during "fine tuning" the structure is the fan-in and fan-out of modules. *Fan-in* of a module is the number of arrows coming in the module, indicating the number of superiordinates of a module. *Fan-out* of a module is the number of arrows going out of that module, indicating the number of subordinates of the module. A very high fan-out is not very desirable, as it means that the module has to control and coordinate too many modules and may therefore be too complex. Fan-out can be reduced by creating a subordinate and making many of the current subordinates, subordinate to the newly created module. In general the fan-out should not be increased above five or six.

Whenever possible, the fan-in should be maximized. Of course, this should not be obtained at the cost of increasing the coupling or decreasing the cohesion of modules. For example, implementing different functions into a single module, simply to increase the fan-in, is not a good idea. Fan-in can be often increased by separating out common functions from different modules and creating a module for implementing that function.

Another important factor that should be considered is the correlation of the scope of effect and scope of control. The scope of effect of a decision (in a module) is the collection of all the modules that contain any processing that is conditional upon that decision or whose invocation is dependent upon the outcome of the decision. The scope of control of a module is the module itself and all of its subordinates (not just the immediate subordinates). The system is usually simpler when the scope of effect of a decision is a subset of the scope of control of the module in which the decision is located. Ideally the scope of effect should be limited to the modules that are immediate subordinates of the module in which the decision is located. Violation of this rule-of-thumb often results in more coupling between modules.

There are some methods that a designer can employ to ensure that the scope of effect of a decision is within the scope of control of the module. The decision can be removed from the module and "moved up" in the structure. Alternatively, modules that are in the scope of effect but are not in the scope of control can be moved down the hierarchy so that they fall within the scope of control.

4.4.3. Transaction Analysis

The structured design technique discussed above is called *transform analysis,* where most of the transforms in the data flow graph have a few inputs and a few outputs. There are situations where a transform splits an input stream into many different substreams, with a different sequence of transforms specified for the different substreams. For example, this is the case with systems where there are many different sets of actions possible, and the actions to be performed depend upon the input command specified. In such situations the transform analysis can be supplemented by *transaction analysis.* In these situations the detailed data flow graph of the transform that is splitting the input may look like the graph shown in Figure 4.10.

The module splitting the input is called the *transaction center.* The transaction center need not be a central transform and may occur on either the input branch or the output branch of the data flow graph of the system. One of the standard ways to convert a data flow graph of the form shown in Figure 4.10 into a structure chart is to have an input module which gets the analyzed transaction and a dispatch module which invokes the modules for the different transactions. This structure is shown in Figure 4.11.

For smaller systems the analysis and the dispatching can be done in the transaction center module itself, giving rise to a more flat structure. For designing systems which require transaction analysis, start with a data flow graph, as in transform analysis, and identify the transform centers. Factor the data flow graph, as is done in transform analysis. For the modules corresponding to the transform centers, draw the detailed data flow graph, which will be of the form shown above. Chose one of the transaction centered organizations, either one with a separate dispatch and input module, or one with all combined in one module. Specify one subordinate module for each transaction. Temptations to combine many similar transactions into one module should be avoided, as it would result in a logically cohesive module. Then each transaction module should be factored, as is done in transform analysis. There are usually many distinct actions which need to be performed for a transaction, and often they are

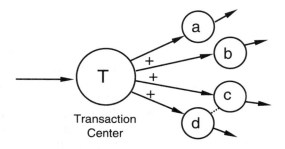

FIGURE 4.10. Data flow graph for transaction analysis.

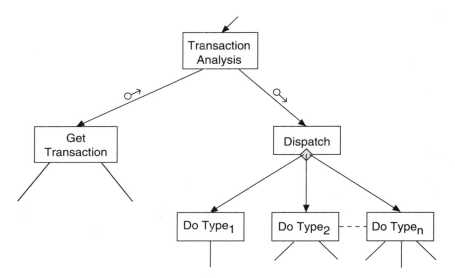

FIGURE 4.11. Factored transaction center.

specified in the requirements for each transaction. In such cases one subordinate module to the transaction module should be created for each action. Further factoring of action modules into many detailed action modules may be needed. In many transaction oriented systems, there is a lot of commonality of actions among the different transactions. This commonality should be exploited by sharing the modules either at the action level or the detailed action level.

4.5. Design Methodology—Object-Oriented Approach

In the last section we discussed the structured design methodology, an approach which concentrates on the functional aspects of the problem, and is based on the concept of functional abstraction. A somewhat different design approach is the object-oriented approach, which is based on the concept of data abstraction.

There is considerable interest in object-oriented systems and object-oriented development. What has come to be known as the object-oriented design in the context of Ada was proposed by Booch [Boo83a, Boo83b, Boo86], and extended in Jalote [Jal89a]. In this section we will discuss the extended object-oriented design methodology proposed in [Jal89a].

Before we discuss the object-oriented approach, let us first define an object. For now, we will consider an object to be a package of information together with the operations that can be performed on that information. In other words, an object supports data abstraction, and can be considered as an entity which encapsulates the *object data,* and provides the user with a set of predefined *operations* to manipulate and access the object data. The object data can only be accessed by the operations defined on the object.

An object has an internal view and an external view. The external view of an object consists of the interface provided by the object, namely, the operations that the object supports. How the operations are implemented, the structure of the object data, and other internals of an object are not visible outside the object. Internally, the object has to consider all these aspects. It has to organize and manipulate data in such a fashion that the external behavior of the operations is maintained. From the outside, an object can only be asked to perform an operation. Internally, the object has to worry about how to actually implement the behavior of different operations.

4.5.1. Functional Approach vs. Object-Oriented Approach

In object-oriented design the decomposition of a system is based upon objects, since during design, objects are considered as the basic units in which a system is decomposed. This is in contrast to functional strategies, like the structured design method discussed earlier, where the basic units for decomposition are functions. In functional methods, each module represents a function or an operation to perform an activity in the system. In the object-oriented approach a module is an object, which is not a functional entity that represents an operation, but is an entity that represents some data items in the system together with the operations that can be performed on the data item during system activity.

Another way of looking at this is that in the functional view a software system consists of data items that represent some information, and a set of procedures that manipulate the data. There is a clear separation of data from procedures in the functional view, even though the procedures operate on data. The functional approaches to design concentrate upon the actions a system has to perform, and data entities upon which the actions are performed, used to represent the state of the system, play a secondary role during the design.

The object-oriented view is that data and procedures should not be treated as independent of each other, and are combined together in the concept of objects. In an object the object data and the operations defined on the object are not independent of each other, and are parts of the same object. Neither the data nor the operations on that data can be separated from the object. Hence, object-oriented development treats data items as integral parts of the system design, unlike the functional approaches.

As an example, let us consider a simple freshman programming exercise of implementing a stack, with push and pop as the desired operations. The functional approach will consider this problem as two sub-problems of defining the data, and designing the two functions. Once the data structure is chosen, the two functions push and pop are defined, operating upon the data structures to provide the required behavior.

In the object-oriented approach, the data and operations are considered together, and are viewed as parts of a single object that has the behavior of a stack. Only the operations are visible outside the object, since the data is hidden from the user of the object. The idea is that the requirements only specified the behavior of the operations, and so only that behavior should be provided. How it is implemented was not specified, and should not be of interest to the user.

In addition to data abstraction, this approach has another property. Suppose that the stack is implemented using an array and a pointer. For the operations push and pop to provide correct behavior, the data structure must possess some correctness properties (such as the pointer should point to the top of the stack and the pointer should never be less than zero). If the correctness properties of the data structure are not satisfied, the behavior of the stack may be incorrect. In a functional implementation, often the data structure can be modified by functions other than push and pop. Hence, though the functions expect some correctness of the data, they do not have exclusive control of that data to ensure the correctness. If the stack is implemented as an object the data is entirely in control of the object, and only actions inside the object can modify the data. In other words, limited data protection can be achieved in the object-oriented approach. This also tends to reduce the overall coupling of the system.

4.5.2. Problem View

Let us now consider the rationale behind the object-oriented approach. The origin of any application which a software system implements usually lies in the real world. The software system usually models entirely or partially some real-world system or problem in software. Systems in real life consist of entities, which have well-defined operations through which they interact with other entities and perform required services to the system or environment that they belong to. An entity in a system may be very complex, but for the system to operate, only the operations required by the system from the entities are of interest. Other details or information about the entities is of no use as far as the operation of the system is concerned. For example, a chair is a very complex entity, if we start looking at the wood, its joints, its construction, how it withholds force, and so forth. However, if a living room is our system, we may only be interested in performing some operations like sitting on the chair or rocking the chair, and are not concerned about the other details. Let us take another example of a notebook. In most situations where the notebook is utilized, the operations which are usually of interest are that we should be able to write on the notebook, and later retrieve what we have written. How the

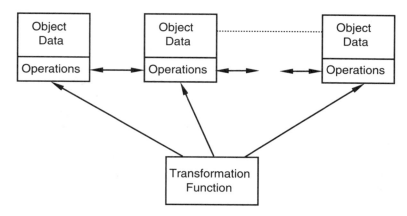

FIGURE 4.12. Model of a system.

notebook is constructed (what kind of paper or binding it has) is of little interest to the user.

With this we can say that a system is essentially a set of entities with operations defined on them, along with a function that operates on the entities through their operations. The function performs the system activity by invoking operations on the entities. For constructing a software system that closely models the real life system and naturally reflects this structure, the concept of objects can be exploited. An entity can be represented as an object with the operations on the object being the same as the operations on the entity being represented. With this approach, a system can be modeled as a set of objects that interact with each other, and as a computer transformation function that operates on the objects to perform the required computation (shown in Figure 4.12). Any interaction with an object is done exclusively through the operations defined on the object.

This approach provides us with a system model which closely represents the real world. The transformation function can be obtained from the function used in a real life system by replacing each operation on an entity with the corresponding operation on the object modeling that entity. A major benefit of this approach is that implementation details of an object can be hidden from the transformation function and other objects, which interact with an object only through the operations defined on the object.

4.5.3. More About Objects

The object-oriented approach is a relatively new concept, and there is no universally acceptable definition of what object-oriented means, although there is some agreement on some requirements for objects for supporting object-oriented development. So, far we have just considered objects as a means for data abstraction. Data abstraction is perhaps the most important feature of objects, but there are two other concepts that often are also considered necessary for object-oriented systems. These are the concepts of class and inheritance.

An object is considered as an instance of a **class,** or an abstract type that describes its behavior. A class describes a set of variables and a set of operations that manipulate those variables, and possibly return some value to the invoker of the operation. A class itself is an abstract entity, which defines a concept, and allows us to define many objects of a particular class. An object is an instantiation of a class, which has its own private memory. Each object belonging to a class has a private copy of the variables defined in the class, on which an operation defined on the class is performed, when the operation is invoked on that object. A class essentially serves to factor out the common properties of all objects belonging to that class, and specifies the behavior of all the objects. It is important to distinguish between a class and an object. The variables are defined in a class, but memory is allocated for those variables in objects. And although the operations are defined in a class, they are performed on, and effect, only the objects of that class.

Another concept that is sometimes considered necessary for objects is that of **inheritance.** Inheritance allows an object to inherit the attributes of another object. Usually inheritance is defined with classes, where a new class may be created by using the definition of other classes. When a class inherits from another class it inherits all the variable and operation declaration. The new class can define its own variables and its own operations. These are besides the variables and operations that the new class inherits. For example if a class A inherits from class B, then objects of class A support all operations supported by objects of class B. In addition an object of class A is guaranteed to contain a part of its internal state that looks like the internal state of an object of type B, since an object of class A contains all the data items defined in class B. B is often called a sub-class, and A a super-class. When an operation is performed on an object of type A, any operation not explicitly defined for A will be obtained from B. In other words, instances of A are also instances of its super-class B, and all operations applicable to B are applicable to A. In case an operation is defined in the new class and also the superclass, some resolution mechanism is defined, depending on the language.

Inheritance can be considered as type of composition that creates a new type from its subtype and its parent type. Inheritance helps to organize similar classes into superclasses, where classes are related to each other by the inheritance relationship. Objects at any level in the hierarchy inherit all the attributes of higher-level objects. Inheritance permits the creation of hierarchical classes, which is considered to be useful for modeling the relationship of different classes of entities that share properties. In the context of object-oriented design we are most interested in the abstraction property of an object, and will not concern ourselves with other issues regarding objects.

4.5.4. Object-Oriented Development with Ada

Though object-oriented development is a philosophy and should not be limited to any programming language, some languages are better suited than others. Clearly, a language that provides support for defining objects is better suited than another language without that feature. Ideally, the language that is used for object-oriented development should support all the features of objects discussed above. Such languages are often referred to as object-oriented languages. But, among those, the facility of data abstraction and the ability to define many objects of a particular class are perhaps the most important. Ada, although generally not considered to be object-oriented, provides support for these two properties, but does not easily lend itself to support inheritance. However, there is considerable interest in object-oriented development using Ada. In this chapter we will use Ada to demonstrate the object-oriented methodology. Here we briefly describe the essential features of the data abstraction facility of Ada.

Data abstraction in Ada is implemented by the use of Packages. A package consists of two parts, the definition and the body. The definition part both defines operations that are defined on the package with the parameters and their types, and also contains type and variable definitions. The body of a package consists of the implementation of all functions and procedures given in the definition. The definition and body of a package can be separately compiled. For specifying the design we will only be concerned with the package definition part. A type can be defined in the package definition part as **private.** The structure of a private type can only be accessed from inside the package, and is not visible from the outside. Variables of the private type can be declared, but these variables can only be manipulated by the application of operations defined in the package where the private type is declared. The private type declaration can be used to define types in Ada. Let us consider the example of the stack with the three operations push, pop, and top defined on it. The package definition is shown in Figure 4.13.

The definition is fairly clear. The three operations are defined as procedures and functions. The actual statements to implement the operations will be defined in the body. In the operation definitions, the **in out** parameters are the ones that take in the value, modify it and return the modified value. These **in out** parameters are passed by reference parameters. The **in** parameters cannot be modified in the body of the procedure of the function, and are passed by value parameters.

We can define as many stacks as we desire by declaring many variables of type STACK.STACK_TYPE. The name of the package is appended before any type, data, or operation that belongs to a package. Only inside

```
package STACK is

    type STACK_TYPE is private;

    procedure push (stk: in out STACK_TYPE; elt: in integer);
    procedure pop (stk: in out STACK_TYPE);
    function top (stk: in STACK_TYPE) return integer;

    private
        type STACK_TYPE record
        end record;

end STACK;
```

FIGURE 4.13. Package definition for stack.

the package the variables and types can be used directly. For example, suppose we have the following declaration outside the package STACK.

$$s1, s2 : STACK.STACK\_TYPE$$

The variables s1 and s2 cannot be manipulated directly. Only the operations defined on the package can be applied to modify them. Suppose we want to push an element i on the stack s1. This can be done by the following statement:

$$STACK.push (s1 , i)$$

In Ada it is not necessary to have a definition like STACK_TYPE in the package definition part. The types and variables needed to implement the package can be defined inside the package body also. In such a case the class of the object is not explicitly defined, and we cannot define many objects of that class. This means there is only object of the class, and that is the package itself.

The separation of package definition and body allows Ada to be used as a design description language also. During the object-oriented design the goal is to generate the package definitions.

4.5.5. Design Methodology

The central problem during the object-oriented design process is identifying the objects and the operations defined on the objects. In addition, the transformation function that performs the system activity utilizing the objects must also be designed. Due to the complexity of large systems we would like this process of identifying objects and operations to be progressive. Here we describe the extended object-oriented design methodology which has a top-down, progressive refinement approach both for designing the transformation function, as well as determining the objects in the system. There are three phases in this approach:

1. Producing the initial design
2. Functional refinement
3. Object refinement.

The idea is to start with an initial high-level design of the system, with high-level objects and the function described in terms of sub-functions and these objects. In later phases the objects and the sub-functions are treated as systems and the process is repeated for them, until we reach a stage where the objects are "atomic objects" that can be implemented directly, and all the functions are completely defined.

PRODUCING THE INITIAL DESIGN

As we have said the central problem in object-oriented design is identifying the objects and their operations as well as defining the transformation function using these objects. One way to identify the objects and operations on the objects is to start with a strategy, and then identify the objects and the operations the strategy employs.

There are three basic steps for doing this: 1. develop a strategy, 2. identify the objects and the operations on the objects, and 3. establish the interface of the objects.

We start with specifying a strategy to solve the problem. Different techniques can be used to specify the strategy. We use English to state the strategy. At any stage the strategy should be kept sufficiently general that it can be stated easily. Such a strategy would contain the operations to be performed and decisions to be taken in order to solve the problem. For any non-trivial problem the operations specified in the strategy will not be operations that are directly supported by the language, but will be operations that must be implemented in order to implement the strategy. For example, a strategy may contain:

Repeatedly *read* an element from the input file, and *add* it to the list until the *list is full*.

The operations specified in this strategy have been italicized. "Read" an element perhaps can be performed by a language statement. The repeat can also be supported by the language construct. But, operations, such as add, have to be implemented in order to implement this strategy.

Hence, a strategy will often contain user-defined operations. With operations come the notion of objects. The operations do not operate in a vacuum; an operation is performed on data entities. Often we can identify the operations being performed on a single abstract entity or object, and the object on which the operation is performed is usually clear. For example, in the above strategy the operations *add* and *list-full* are clearly performed on the object **list,** and the operation *read* is clearly performed on the object input file.

This process of extracting objects and operations from the strategy is central to the object-oriented methodology discussed later. To identify operations, we realize that an operation will always be performing some function, representing action. So, to identify operations we have to identify phrases representing a unit action. Sometimes this may not be very obvious. For example, in the above strategy the phrase "until the list is full", seems to be a statement. But, we know that to satisfy "until the list is full" we have to perform an operation to determine if the list is full. Therefore this phrase actually represents an operation on the object list.

In this initial design phase, when the strategy is stated, we identify the different actions being performed, and the entities upon which those actions are being performed. The phrases that represent some sort of action often represent actions, and the phrases that represent some entities in the system usually represent the objects, upon which some of the identified actions are being performed. Some of the identified actions may not seem to belong to or operate on any of the identified objects. These are identified as functions to be refined during the functional refinement phase. Once the objects, operations on the objects, and functions to be further refined are identified, the strategy can be formalized by defining a function which implements the strategy, using the operations on the objects and the functions marked for refinement. Let us demonstrate this method on the problem of determining the number of different words in a text file.

In the strategy the phrases that represent objects have been $\boxed{\text{boxed}}$, and the operations on the objects have been *italicized*. The operations that are **bold faced** are the ones that have been identified for further refinement. The strategy is shown below.

Get a word from the $\boxed{\text{input file}}$. *Add* the word to the $\boxed{\text{word list}}$, until *no words left* in the input file. *Sort* the word list. **Determine the count** of the numbers of different words in the list. Print count.

The strategy is a natural strategy to solve this problem. We have identified two objects, input-file and word-list in this strategy. Get-a-word and no-word-left are the two operations identified on the object input-file, while add and sort are the two operations on word-list. One function, determine-the-count (of the number of different words) has been specified for refinement. We can consider this operation also as belonging to the object word-list. But, an operation like this is not usually associated with lists, and so we have kept it a separate operation. This is important for software reuse, where the packages can be reused later in other systems. To facilitate reuse it is best to define objects in a manner so that it can be used in many different contexts. For this it is important that if there is a certain functionality associated with an entity, then the object implementing the entity provides that functionality and does not redefine the functionality of the object. The package definitions of the objects with their operations are shown in Figure 4.14.

package WORD_LIST **is**
type LIST_TYPE **is private**
  procedure add (wl: **in** LIST_TYPE; word: **in** WORD_TYPE);
    —operation to add a word
  procedure sort (wl: **in** LIST_TYPE);
    —to sort the list
private
  :
end WORD_LIST;

package IN_FILE **is**
  function get **return** WORD_TYPE;
    —gets a word from the file
  function no_word_left **return** BOOLEAN;
end IN_FILE;

FIGURE 4.14. Package definitions from initial strategy.

We have assumed that a proper type WORD_TYPE is declared (as a string of characters). This is the view of objects which we have after this initial strategy. More operations on objects can be identified during the functional and object refinement steps. Using these operations on the objects and the functions marked for functional refinement, we can specify our main program too. This is easily done by formally writing the strategy, and replacing each action by the corresponding operation on some object or some function specified for refinement. The main program for this strategy is shown in Figure 4.15.

At the end of this phase we would have identified zero or more objects, and zero or more operations for each of the objects identified. In addition

```
declare
    wl: WORD_LSIT.LIST_TYPE;
    word: WORD_TYPE;
    cnt: INTEGER;
begin
    while not IN_FILE.no_word_left loop
        word : = IN_FILE.get;
        WORD_LIST.add (wl, word);
    end loop;
    WORD_LIST.sort (wl);
    cnt : = count (wl);
    —output count
end;
```

FIGURE 4.15. Transformation function specification.

we would have a set of operations that are to be further decomposed. More objects and operations may be identified in later steps. With some practice, we can start writing the strategy directly in an algorithmic form. However, many people may benefit by first stating the strategy in English. We will continue to use this method throughout this chapter.

FUNCTIONAL REFINEMENT

This is an iterative process, with the input to the first refinement coming from the initial design. For each operation marked for functional refinement in the last refinement, we write an informal strategy, identify the objects, operations on them, and operations to be further refined in the next refinement. This refinement process stops when no operations for further refinement are identified.

As the functional refinement proceeds, new objects and operations on them are identified. In addition, during a refinement step, operations may also be identified on objects that were identified in earlier refinement steps. When this refinement process terminates, the transformation function needed to solve the problem would have been decomposed to a required level, with each operation in the algorithm being an operation on some object.

In addition, when the functional refinement process terminates, all the objects in the problem space are identified. The objects that have been identified are the only objects needed to specify the system completely. However, this does not mean that there will be no other objects in the system. More objects (and their functions) may be uncovered when object-refinement takes place in the next phase. But, those objects would be nested within the objects identified by the end of this phase. Thus objects identified in the next phase are exclusively for implementing the objects identified so far, and need not be visible outside.

Let refine of the function **count** that was marked for refinement in the previous phase (and used in the main program). A natural strategy to implement this function is

Initialize the count to 0. Set previous word to nil. *Get a word* from the word list. **If same** as previous word, increment count, else make this word the previous word. Repeat until *list is empty*.

In this strategy we have identified two new operations on the package WORD_LIST, namely get-a-word and is-list-empty. No new objects were uncovered during this refinement, and no operations were uncovered on the package IN_FILE. One function "are-two-words-same" has been identified for further refinement. With the addition of these new functions the package WORD_LIST now has four operations, and the definition of the package is shown in Figure 4.16.

Using these operations and the functions marked for refinement in the

```
package WORD_LIST is
type LIST_TYPE is private
  procedure add (wl: in LIST_TYPE; word: in WORD_TYPE);
    —operation to add a word
  procedure sort (wl: in LIST_TYPE);
    —to sort the list
  function get_word (wl: LIST_TYPE) return WORD_TYPE;
    —returns the first word of the list, and deletes it
  function empty (wl: LIST_TYPE) return BOOLEAN;
    —returns true if all words have been removed
private
  :
end WORD_LIST;
```

FIGURE 4.16. Package definition on functional refinement.

next phase we can now formalize the function **count,** and the code for this function is given in Figure 4.17.

In the next step of functional refinement we have to specify the function strequal. This is a simple function and we leave it as an exercise. It should be pointed out that even though all the objects needed to specify the system completely are identified after functional refinement terminates, the same does not hold for the operations on these objects, since further operations may be identified on the objects in the next phase. This occurs because the implementation of the operations on the objects has not yet been considered. Since the objects interact with each other, services of one object might be required by another object in order to perform its own operations. In this case, the set of operations on each object will be

```
function count (list: in WORD_LIST.LIST_TYPE) return INTEGER is
  prev, word: WORD_TYPE;
  cnt: INTEGER;
begin
  prev : = ' '''';
  cnt : = 0;
  while not WORD_LIST.empty (list) loop
    word : = WORD_LIST.get_word (list);
    if not strequal (word, prev) then
      cnt : = cnt + 1;
      prev : = word;
    end if;
  end loop;
  return cnt;
end;
```

FIGURE 4.17. Functional specification during refinement.

complete only after the design of all the known operations on the objects is completed. This is done in the next phase.

OBJECT REFINEMENT AND NESTED OBJECTS

In this phase we turn our attention to the objects. In our example the two objects are simple objects and will not have any nested objects in them. However, for a large system the objects may be very high-level, with complex operations that may encompass many objects. The aim of this phase is to identify the objects and operations that are required in order to implement the objects.

To refine an object, we write the informal strategy of all the operations defined so far on the object. We then identify any new objects and their operations that are required in order to implement these operations. In addition, we identify any new operations on the objects that have been previously identified. This process is repeated for each object, and we refer to this process as **object refinement.**

The new objects that are identified during refinement of an object are an outcome of the attempt to specify the operations of the object undergoing refinement. Hence, the purpose of these new objects is to provide services that are utilized to implement the operations of the original object undergoing refinement. These new objects should naturally be regarded as nested within the object whose refinement uncovered their existence. In such situations the nested objects are not visible (and need not be) outside the parent object.

Once all the operations on the parent object are identified, refinement of nested objects can begin. The refinement process terminates when the objects are simple enough to be implemented directly. Only for extremely large and complex systems, do we expect the nesting of objects to be very deep.

4.6. Design Specification

With a design methodology like the SDM, a conceptual design can be produced. However, in the case of SDM, this design is in terms of a structure chart, in which each module is represented by a box with a name. The functionality of the module is essentially communicated by the name of the box, and the interface is communicated by the data items labeling the arrows. Relying only on a name to communicate what the module does is clearly not sufficient and can lead to ambiguities later on. To avoid these problems, the design needs to be formally specified. The design specification is then communicated in the **design document,** which is used as the reference for the design phase for later activities like detailed design and implementation.

As the design document is the means by which the design is communicated, it should contain all information relevant to future phases. First let us decide what a document specifying system design should contain. A design specification should contain:

Problem specification,
Major data structures,
Modules and their specifications, and
Design decisions.

The requirements document specifies the problem in the terminology of the problem domain. Often before starting the design, the requirements are translated into a specification of the problem that is more suited for design purposes. In this sense, *problem specification* or restatement is the first step in the design process. In SDM, for example, the data flow graph is a restatement of the requirements of the system. A complete hierarchical data flow graph, with the specification of the data flows that occur in the data flow graph, is the problem specification.

During system design the major data structures for the software are identified—without these the system modules cannot be meaningfully defined during the design. In structure design these are the data elements traveling along the arcs in the structure chart. In the design specification, a formal definition of these data structures should be given.

Module specification is the major part of system design specification. All modules in the system should be identified when the system design is complete, and these modules should be specified in the document. During system design only the module specification is obtained, since the internal details of the modules are defined later. For specifying a module, the design document must specify a) the *interface of the module* (all data items, their types, and whether they are for input and/or output), b) the *abstract behavior* of the module (*what* the module does), by specifying the module's functionality or its input/output behavior, and c) all other modules used by the one being specified. This information is quite useful in maintaining and understanding the design.

In order to aid the understandability of the design, all major *design decisions* that were made by the designers during the design process should be explained explicitly. The choices that were available and the reasons for making a particular choice should be explained. This makes a design more *visible* and will help in understanding the design.

4.7. Verification

The output of the system design phase, like the output of other phases in the development process, should be verified before proceeding with activities of the next phase. Unless the design is specified in a formal, executable language, the design cannot be executed for verification. Other means for verification have to be employed. The most common approach for verification is design reviews or inspections (although sometimes these terms mean different things, we will not distinguish between the two). We will discuss this approach here.

4.7.1. Design Reviews

The purpose of design reviews is to ensure that the design satisfies the requirements, and that the design is of "good quality". If errors are made during the design process, they will ultimately reflect themselves in the code and the final system. As the cost of removing faults caused by errors that occur during design increases with delay in detecting the errors, it is best if the design errors are detected early, before they manifest themselves in the system. Detecting errors in design is the aim of design reviews.

The system design review process is similar to the other reviews, in that a group of people get together to discuss the design with the aim of revealing design errors or undesirable properties. The review group must include a member of both the system design team and the detailed design team, the author of the requirements document, the author responsible for maintaining the design document, and an independent software quality engineer.

The review can be held in the same manner as the requirement review. Each member studies the design before the meeting, and with the aid of a checklist, marks items that the reviewer feels are incorrect or need clarification. The member asks the questions and the chief designer tries to explain the situation. Discussion ensues, and during its course design errors are revealed.

As with any review, it should be kept in mind that the aim of the meeting is to uncover design errors, and not try to fix them. Fixing is done later. Also, the psychological frame of mind should be healthy, and the designer should not be put in a defensive position. The meeting ends with a list of action items, which are later acted upon by the design team. Further reviews may be organized, if needed.

The number of ways in which errors can come in a design is limited only by the creativity of the designer. However, there are some forms of errors that are more often observed. Here we mention some of these [Dun84]. Perhaps the most significant design error is omission or misinterpretation of specified requirements. Clearly, if the system designer has misinterpreted or not accounted for some requirement, this will be reflected later on as faults in the system. Sometimes this design error is caused by ambiguities in the requirements.

There are some other quality factors that are not strictly design errors, but have implications on the reliability and maintainability of the system.

Examples of these are weak modularity (that is, weak cohesion and/or strong coupling), design that is not conducive to modification and expansion, and failure to conform to design standards. For detailed design another possible error is that the detailed design is not consistent with the system design.

A Sample Checklist: The use of checklists can be extremely useful for any review. The checklist can be used by each member during private study of the design and also during the review meeting. For best results the checklist should be tailored to the project at hand, to uncover problem specific errors. Here we list a few general items that can be used to construct a checklist for a design review [Dun84].

Is each of the functional requirements taken into account?
Are there analyses to demonstrate that performance requirements can be met?
Are all assumptions explicitly stated, and are they acceptable?
Are there any limitations and constraints on the design beyond those in the requirments?
Are external specifications of each module completely specified?
Have exceptional conditions been handled?
Are all the data formats consistent with the requirements?
Are the operator and user interfaces properly addressed?
Is the design modular, and does it conform to local standards?
Are the sizes of data structures estimated? Are provisions made to guard against overflow?

4.7.2. Automated Cross-Checking

One of the important issues during system design verification is whether the design is internally consistent. For example, those modules used in a module that is defined in the system design must also be defined in the design. One should also check whether the interface of a module is consistent with the way in which other modules use it. Other internal consistency issues can be consistent use of data structures and whether data usage is consistent with declaration. These consistency issues can be checked during design review, and is usually the place where they are checked if no automated aid is available.

However, if the design is expressed in a language that is designed for machine processing, then most consistency checking can be automated. For example, if a language like PDL (described in the next chapter) is used, then the design can be "compiled" to check for consistency. Similarly, the method used for expressing the system design of the case study later in this chapter can also be formalized to make it suitable for machine processing. The basic requirement is that the data and module definitions be given in a defined format that is suitable for checking.

4.8. Metrics

The goal of having metrics for the system design is to assess the quality of the design, which in turn may predict the quality of the final product. The quality of the intermediate product is of interest in the development process due to the belief that high quality intermediate products lead to a high quality product. We discuss some of the design metrics here.

4.8.1. Total Number of Modules

This metric can be calculated easily once the system design is complete. It specifies the total number of modules that the final system will contain. The basic use of this metric is that by using an average size of a module or size estimates for each module, a size estimate of the final software can be obtained. This estimate can be used to check the initial size estimate, and if the difference is substantial, it will involve a change in plan. Particularly, the allocation of personnel, the schedule and the cost of the project will change and might have to be renegotiated with the client. Such data from many projects can also be used to fine tune the cost and size estimation procedures employed during project planning.

4.8.2. Number of Modules Called

This metric can also be computed easily once the system design is complete. For each module, we can compute how many other module it calls. In addition, we can also determine how many modules call a particular module. These correspond to the *fan-out* and *fan-in* of modules.

The use of this metric is in estimating the complexity of maintaining the software, once it is delivered. A module with high fan-in may mean that the module has functional cohesion and a lot of modules use this function, or it could mean that the module is actually implementing many functions. A high fan-in means that a number of other modules depend on this module. If in the future the specifications of this module change, which is more likely if the high fan-in is due to the latter reason, then other modules will also be have to be modified. This goes against the basic goal of maintainability.

A fan-out of a module means that the module depends on too many modules. This implies that to understand this module a maintainer must first understand the modules on which this module depends. This will clearly make understanding a module harder, and consequently maintaining this module will become more time consuming.

During system design, the designers should carefully evaluate those modules that are called by a large number of modules or that call a large number of modules.

4.8.3. Number of Parameters

The system design specifies modules that will be in the system, as well as their interconnection with other modules. Thus, in addition to specifying the behavior of a module, the system design also specifies the module's interface. The number of parameters of a module can therefore be obtained after the system design is complete.

What constitutes a parameter for the purposes of this metric needs more clarification. Should a complex object in a parameter list be counted as a single parameter or as comprised of many parameters. As an example consider a record which contains many different fields and an instance of this record is passed as a parameter to a module. Should this be considered a single parameter, or multiple parameters, one for each field? If it is considered as a single parameter, the parameter list of all modules can theoretically be reduced to a single parameter (by combining all parameters in a record).

The simplest is to consider each "logical entity" in the parameter list as a parameter. A logical entity can be a record, if the record has a logical reason for its structure and is a natural way of representing a data item. Another way is to consider each basic data item that is used in a module as a parameter. In this case, each of the fields of the record that are used in a module are counted as separate parameters.

This metric is a means to try to capture the "coupling between modules. Although it clearly does not quantify the concept of coupling, it tries to approximate it. A high number of parameters can also mean low cohesion, especially if the parameter list is large since the module is performing too many functions. It is likely that modules with a higher number of parameters will be more tightly coupled with their caller modules, as compared to modules which have a small number of parameters. This means that understanding such modules will require more effort and time, and modifying them is likely to have side effects on other modules. Consequently, the job of the maintainer is made more difficult. Clearly, the modules with a large number of parameters should be carefully scrutinized.

4.9. Monitoring and Control

System design is one of the most important phases affecting testability and maintainability of the system. Hence, it is important to carefully monitor the design process to make sure that the design eases testing and maintenance. We assume that the structured design methodology is being followed for design.

Cost and schedule are obvious candidates for monitoring. The cost and time spent on the design phase should be followed and compared with the cost and schedule estimates of the project plan. It is better to breakdown the schedule for the system design further, as specified in the project plan, into a more detailed schedule with milestones for intermediate stages of design. These milestones could include completion of the data flow graph, completion of the data dictionary, completion and informal review of the top-level structure, and factoring of different components in the top-level structure. Similarly, cost can also be divided between these activities. With a detailed schedule and cost breakup, the design can be monitored closely. Extra resources might be needed to ensure that the design is completed within the schedule.

Software size can be estimated much more accurately after or during system design than during the planning phase. After the design has been done, most of the modules in the system are specified. As discussed above, from the number of modules we can get an estimate of the size of the eventual software by using an average size for each module. Or, a detailed size estimate can be performed by estimating the size of each module. This size estimate will be quite accurate and is likely to be close to the actual size of the eventual software. This size estimate can be compared with the estimates used for developing the project plan. If the estimates are quite different, the project plan will need to be modified. This implies that the cost and schedule estimates will be redone. It should be possible to predict any schedule slippages or cost overruns after the design is complete.

System structure must be carefully monitored during design. As we have discussed, the structure of the software is one of the most important factors affecting the later phases. Even though a formal design review is held towards the end of the design phase, informal reviews and meetings should be held to assess the quality of the structure. It should be seen that as the structure grows, its simplicity is maintained. Often projects have a tendency to start with nice hierarchical structures, but as the design proceeds the structure is modified to handle "special cases", which often complicates the structure. It might be necessary in some cases to stop the design and start afresh with a new design.

Computer time is a useful indicator for estimating if the coding is starting prematurely. Normally, during system design computer time consumption will be low. Only the tools used for producing the design consume computer time. If computer time consumption increases prematurely, it indicates that coding might have begun. This is often not desirable, and actions might be needed to ensure that the design is first completed before the coding begins. The pattern of computer time usage will depend on the organization and the tools used and can be obtained from historical data on similar projects. Major deviations from this pattern should be a source of concern.

Reviews are a prime candidate for monitoring, since they are often the sole means for design verification. Review reports indicate errors found during reviews, how long the reviews lasted, and issues raised. By carefully evaluating the review reports and by talking to review members it should be made sure that the reviews were active and not treated as a mere formality. Further reviews should be scheduled if felt necessary. **Errors** discovered during reviews are a good source of information regarding potential problem areas in design. The frequency of errors can give feedback on which parts of the system design are more error prone. Absence of errors indicated in the review report might signify that the reviews were not done properly.

Requirement tracing is an extremely important activity that should be undertaken before the design is certified and the next phase begins. Before any coding and testing takes place it is best to ensure that all the requirements specified in the requirements document can be met by the design. For this requirements tracing is done. Each requirement is considered and parts of the system that are designed to handle the requirement are evaluated to see if they implement the requirement completely. Besides tracing the functional requirements, performance and other requirements should also be considered. For performance requirements, some analysis should be done during design (and evaluated during requirement tracing) to show that the performance goals can be satisfied. It should also be shown that the design works within the design constraints specified in the requirements document. The interface of the proposed design should be checked to see that it is consistent with the interface requirements.

4.10. Summary

The *design* of a system is a plan for a solution such that if the plan is implemented, the implemented system will satisfy the requirements of the system. The goal of the *design process* is to find the best possible design. The most important criterion to judge a design are *verifiability, reliability,* and *maintainability*. The design activity is a two-level process. The first level produces the *system design,* which defines the components needed for the system, and how the components interact with each other. The *detailed design* refines the system design, by providing more description of the processing logic of components and data structures, so that the design can be easily implemented. A design methodology is a systematic approach to creating a design. Most design methodologies concentrate on system design.

Problem partitioning is a basic principle for guiding the design process. The goal is to effectively handle the complexity of designing large systems by partitioning the problem into separate pieces so each piece can be solved separately. Problem partitioning depends on the effective use of *abstraction*. Abstraction of a component is a view of the component that extracts the essential information relevant to the particular purpose and ignores the rest of the information. It allows a module to be specified by its external behavior only. Abstraction permits a designer to concentrate on one component at a time, by using the abstraction of other components to decide the interaction between components.

Modularity is a means of problem partitioning in software design. A system is considered to be modular if each component has a well-defined abstraction and if change in one component has minimal impact on other components. Two criteria used for deciding the modules during design are *coupling* and *cohesion*. Coupling is a measure of interdependence between modules, while cohesion is a measure of the strength with which the different elements of a module are related. There are different levels of cohesion, functional and type cohesion being the highest levels and incidental being the lowest. In general, other properties being equal, coupling should be minimized and cohesion maximized.

Structured design is one of the best known methods for developing the design of a software system. This method creates a structure chart which can be used to implement the system. The goal is to produce a structure where the modules have minimum dependence on each other (low coupling) and have a high level of cohesion. The basic methodology has four steps: (1) Restate the problem as a data flow graph. (2) Identify the most abstract input and output data elements. (3) Perform first level factoring, which is done by specifying an input module for each of the most abstract inputs, an output module for each of the most abstract outputs, and a transform module for each of the central transforms. (4) Factor each of the input, output, and transform modules.

The methodology does not reduce the problem of design to a series of steps that can be followed blindly. The essential goal is to get a clear hierarchical structure. A number of design heuristics can be used to improve the structure resulting from the application of the basic methodology. The basic guiding principles are simplicity, high cohesion and low coupling.

Object-oriented design is based on the concept of data abstraction. Objects, rather than functional modules, are the basic unit of decomposition. The design methodology that we discussed has three steps: (1) produce the initial design, (2) refine the functional and (3) refine the object. In the first step a high-level strategy for solving the problem is stated in English. From this strategy objects and operations to the objects are identified together with the interfaces of the objects. In addition, functions for refinement are also identified. After functional refinement ends, objects are refined by treating operations on the objects as problems. The objects identified during object refinement are usually nested within the object being refined.

Every phase in the waterfall model must end with verification of the output produced in that phase. In the system design phase the output is the **system design document,** which contains the major data structures and the module definitions. The most common method for verification is *design* *reviews,* in which a team of persons reviews the design. If a design language is used for design specification and if tools are available to process designs expressed in that language, then some amount of consistency checking can be done automatically by these tools.

Exercises

1. Why is design a two level process? Why should the system design be finished before starting the detailed design, rather than starting the detailed design right after the requirements?
2. Consider a program containing many modules. If a global variable x is used to share data between two modules A and B, how can you modify the program to reduce the coupling?
3. What is the difference between functional abstraction and data abstraction?
4. For a large system you want to use a combination of top-down and bottom-up approaches. Device a methodology which supports this.
5. List a set of poor programming practices, based on the criteria of coupling and cohesion.
6. Consider a function which has all data inputs and returns a Boolean. How would you rank its coupling with a module that calls it. Can you reduce it?
7. Suppose a module for supporting files is implemented in a language like Pascal as follows.

```
procedure file (file_ptr, file_name, op_name);
begin
   case op_name of
      "open": perform activities for opening the file.
      "close": perform activities for opening the file.
      "print": print the file
   end case
end
```

   What is the cohesion of this module? How would you change the module to increase cohesion?
8. How are cohesion and coupling related? Give an example where cohesion increases and coupling decreases.
9. Give example modules for the different levels of cohesion.
10. If high independence of modules was your sole criterion for modularization, which would be more important—coupling or cohesion—and why?
11. If some existing modules are to be reused in building a new system, will you use a top-down or bottom-up approach? Why?
12. If a module has logical cohesion, what kind of coupling is this module likely to have with others?

13. What is the difference between a flow chart and the structure chart?
14. Extend the notation for structure charts to represent the structure of programs where modules communicate using global variables.
15. Draw the structure chart for the following program:

```
program xxx (input, output);
var x, y: integer;
procedure a;
begin
  x : = x + y;
  y: = y + 5;
end;
procedure b;
begin
  x : = x + 5;
  y : = y + x;
  a;
end;
begin
  x: = 0; y: = 0;
  a; b;
end.
```

How would you modify this program to improve the structure?
16. Give an example of a procedure that is an input module as well as a transform module.
17. If a '+' is present between two output streams from a transform in a data flow graph, state some specific property about the module for that transform.
18. If a '*' is present between two input streams of a transform in a data flow graph, state some specific property about the module for that transform.
19. Draw the data flow graph for the following.
    1. A system to convert ASCII to EBSDIC.
    2. A system to analyze your diet when given your daily intake (and some data files about different types of food and recommended intakes).
    3. A system to do student registration in the manner it is done at your college.
    4. A system to manage the inventory at a hardware store.
    5. A system for a drug store that will manage inventory, keep track of expiration dates, and allergy records of patients to avoid issuing medicines that might be harmful.
    6. A system that acts as a calculator with only basic arithmetic functions.
20. Use the structured design methodology to produce a design for the systems described in the exercise above.

21. Is this statement true: "If we follow the structured design methodology (without applying any heuristics) the resulting structure will always have one transform module for each bubble in the data flow graph". Explain your answer.

22. In the example in the chapter, what would the structure look like if the word list were not sorted?

23. Suppose we want to determine the ratio of different words to total words in a file. Modify the data flow graph and produce a structure for this problem.

24. Suppose that in a bank teller system we have these inputs: command, account number, amount, and personal code. The possible commands are credit, debit, transfer, and display balance. Draw a data flow graph, and produce a structure for this system.

25. Given a structure with high fan-out, how would you convert it to a structure with a low fan-out?

26. Why must we be very careful when modifying a module with a high fan-in? Is the same care needed for modules with a high fan-out also?

27. What is the effect on modifiability, understandability, coupling and cohesion of modules in a system where the span of effect and span of control rule is violated?

28. What is the fundamental difference between the approaches of structured design and object oriented design?

29. What are the major metrics that can be used to evaluate system design? Which of these can be used to approximate the size of the final system better, and how?

30. What are the major methods for verifying a design? If the design is expressed in a formal language, can an automated tool help in verification, and in what manner?

Case Study

Structured Design

Data Flow Diagram: This is the first step in the structured design method. In our case study, there are two inputs—file1 and file2. Three outputs are required—the time table, the conflict table, and the explanations for the schedule. A high-level data flow diagram of this problem is given in Figure 4.18.

The diagram is fairly clear. First we get from file1 the information about classrooms, lecture times and courses, and validate their format. The validated input from file1 is used for cross validating information in file2. After validating the file2 input, we get an array of valid course records (with preferences, etc.) which must be scheduled. Since PG courses have to be scheduled before UG courses, these course records are separated into different groups—PG courses with preferences, UG courses with

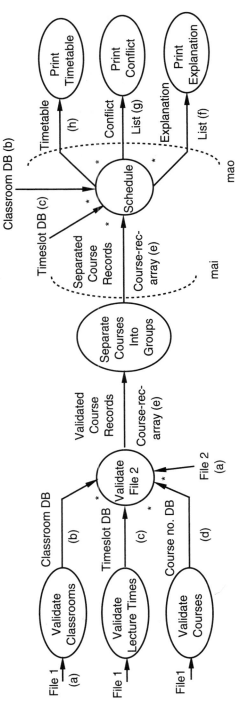

FIGURE 4.18. Data flow diagram for the case study.

preferences, PG courses with no preference, and UG courses with no preference. This separated course list is the input to the schedule transform, the output of which is the three desired outputs.

The most abstract input and most abstract output are fairly obvious here. The "separated course schedule" is the most abstract input and the three outputs of the schedule transform are the most abstract outputs. There is only one central transform—schedule.

First Level Factoring: The first level structure chart can easily be obtained, and is shown in Figure 4.19. In the structure chart, instead of having one output module for each of the three outputs, as is shown in the data flow diagram, we have only one output module, which then invokes three output modules for the different outputs.

Factoring the Input and Output Modules: The output module does not need any factoring. According to the design methodology, the input module "get_validated_input" will have one input module to get the array_of_validated_course_records, and one transform module to "separate into course groups". This input module can then be further factored into three input modules to get different validated inputs from file1, one input module to get data from file2, and one module for validating the file2 data. Since the data from file1 is needed for the central transform also, we modify the structure of the input branch. The structure chart for the input branch is shown in Figure 4.20.

Factoring the Central Transform: Now the central transform has to be factored. According to the requirements, PG courses have to be given preference over the UG courses, and the highest priority of each course must be satisfied. This means that courses with no priority should be scheduled after the courses with priority. Hence, we have four major subordinate modules to the central transform—schedule PG courses with preferences, schedule UG courses with preferences, schedule PG courses

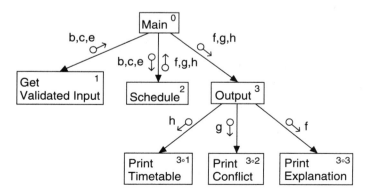

FIGURE 4.19. First level factoring.

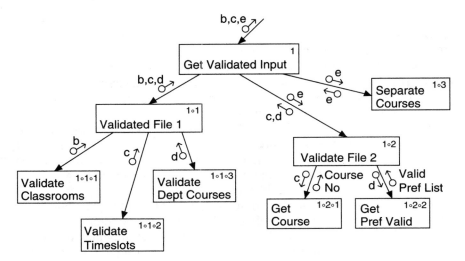

FIGURE 4.20. Factoring of the input branch.

with no preferences, and schedule UG courses with no preferences. The structure of the central transform is shown in figure 4.21.

These can then be combined into a structure chart for the system. This structure chart gives an overall view of the strategy for structuring the programs. Further details about each module will evolve during detailed design and coding.

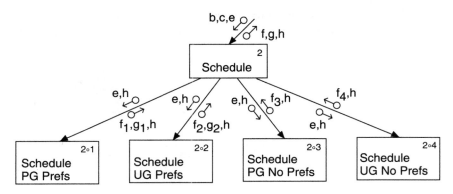

FIGURE 4.21. Factoring the central transform.

Design Document

This document gives the system design for the course scheduling problem, requirements of which were given earlier.

1. PROBLEM SPECIFICATION

The data flow diagram for the system is shown in Figure 4.22.

This specifies the major transform centers in the approach to be followed for producing the software. The structure chart representing the high-level design is shown in Figure 4.23.

2. DATA DEFINITIONS

The major data structures used in the data flow diagram and the structure chart are specified here.

a) File1, File2 : text files
   —The two input files
b) Classroom_DB : array of
   record
       room_no
       capacity
   —database of classrooms sorted in ascending order of capacity
c) Courseno_DB : array of course_no
   —database of department courses
d) Timeslot_DB : array of timeslots
   —database of available timeslots
e) Course_rec_array : array of
   record
       1. course_nos
       2. enrollment
       3. valid_pref_list
   —list of courses to be scheduled
f) Expl_list : array of
   record
       error_code
       room_no
       course_no (* course that conflicted *)
       pref_list (* preferences not honored *)
   —List of courses whose first preferences have not been given
g) Conflict_list : array of
   record
       error_code
       room_no

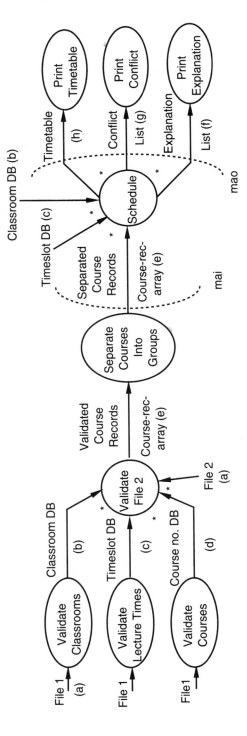

FIGURE 4.22. Data flow diagram for the system.

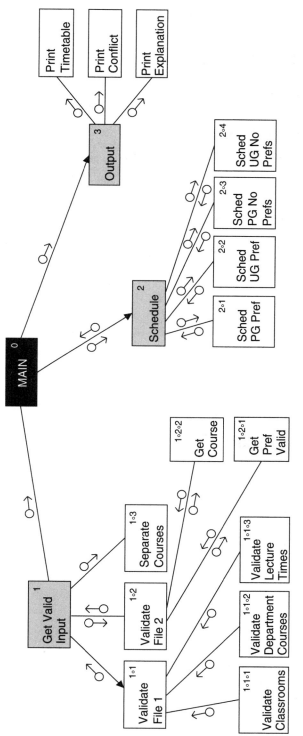

FIGURE 4.23. Structure chart for the system.

course_no (* course that conflicted *)
pref_list (* preferences not honored *)
—List of courses in conflict

h) Time_Table : two dimensional array of integers
   —The rows represent room numbers
   —The columns represent timeslots

3. MODULE SPECIFICATIONS

Precise specifications of the modules shown in the structure chart are given in this section.

0. MAIN_MODULE:-
    Inputs : file names
    Outputs : none
    Subordinates : Get_validated_input
      Schedule
      Output

1. GET_VALIDATED_INPUT:-
    Inputs : file1, file2
    Outputs : course_rec_array
      classroom_DB
      courseno_DB
      timeslot_DB
    Subordinates : Validate_file1
      Validate_file2
      Separate_Courses
    Purpose : Validates the contents of file1 and file2 and produces lists for valid courses, classrooms, timeslots, and courses to be scheduled.

2. SCHEDULE:-
    Inputs : course_rec_array
      classroom_DB
      timeslot_DB
    Outputs : time_table
      expl_list
      conflict_list
    Subordinates : Sched_PG_pref
      Sched_UG_pref
      Sched_PG_no_pref
      Sched_UG_no_pref
    Purpose : Schedule courses, produce a list of courses in conflict, give explanations for courses which could not be scheduled or given first preference.

3. OUTPUT:-
    Inputs : course_rec_array
      time_table
      expl_list
      conflict_list
    Outputs : reports
    Subordinates : Print_Expl
      Print_Conflict
      Print_Timetable
    Purpose : to Produce the three required outputs.

1.1 VALIDATE_FILE1 :-
    Inputs : file1
    Outputs : classroom_DB
      courseno_DB
      timeslot_DB
    Subordinates : validate_classrooms
      validate_dept_courses
      validate_lec_times
    Purpose : Obtain validated data from input file1.

1.2 VALIDATE_FILE2:-
    Inputs : file2
      courseno_DB
      timeslot_DB
    Outputs : course_rec_array
    Subordinates : get_course
      get_pref_valid
    Purpose : Get validated data from file2.

1.3 SEPARATE_COURSES:-
    Inputs : course_rec_array
    Outputs : course_rec_array
    Subordinates :
    Purpose : Rearrange the courses in the following order: PG with prefer-
              ences, UG with preferences, PG without preferences, and UG
              without preferences.

2.1 SCHED_PG_PREF:-
    Inputs : course_rec_array
      timetable
      classroom_DB
    Outputs : timetable
      expl_list-1
      conflict_list-1
    Subordinates :
    Purpose : Schedule the PG courses with preferences. The expl_list and
              conflict_list of modules at this level are collected by the
              SCHEDULE module and combined together.

2.2 SCHED_UG_PREF:-
    Inputs : course_rec_array
      timetable
      classroom_DB
    Outputs : timetable
      expl_list-2
      conflict_list-2
    Subordinates :
    Purpose : Schedule the UG courses with preferences.

2.3 SCHED_PG_NO_PREF:-
    Inputs : course_rec_array
      timetable
      classroom_DB
    Outputs : timetable
      conflict_list-3
    Subordinates :
    Purpose : Schedule the PG courses with no preferences specified.

2.4 SCHED_UG_NO_PREF:-
    Inputs : course_rec_array
      timetable
      classroom_DB
    Outputs : timetable
      conflict_list-4
    Subordinates :
    Purpose : Schedule the UG courses with no preferences.

3.1 PRINT_EXPL:-
    Inputs : time_table
      expl_list
    Outputs : List of explanations
    Subordinates :
    Purpose : Print the reasons why the higher preferences for a course
           could not be honored.

3.2 PRINT_CONFLICT:-
    Inputs : timetable
      conflict_list
    Outputs : List of conflicts
    Subordinates :
    Purpose : Print the list of courses that are not scheduled in the final table,
           and specify the conflicts that prevented their scheduling.

3.3 PRINT_SCHED:-
    Inputs : timetable
    Outputs : Final schedule
    Subordinates :
    Purpose : Print the schedule of courses.

1.1.1 VALIDATE_CLASSROOMS:-
  Inputs : file1
  Outputs : classroom_DB
  Subordinates :
Purpose : Get the list of valid rooms and their capacities.

1.1.2 VALIDATE_DEPT_COURSES:-
  Inputs : file1
  Outputs : courseno_DB
  Subordinates :
  Purpose : Validate courses in input file1.

1.1.3 VALIDATE_TIMESLOTS:-
  Inputs : file1
  Outputs : timeslot_DB
  Subordinates :
  Purpose : Validate timeslots from input file1.

1.2.1 GET_COURSE:-
  Inputs : file2
  Outputs : course_no
  Subordinates :
  Purpose : Get course_no from file2

1.2.2 GET_PREF_VALID:-
  Inputs : file2
      timeslot_DB
  Outputs : valid_pref_list
  Subordinate :
  Purpose : Obtain the valid time preferences for a given course by cross
      verifying with the timeslots in timeslot_DB.

4. ASSUMPTIONS MADE

1. In file 2, data for each course is terminated by a new line character. If the
   data is spread over many lines, all except the last line end with a ",'' (the
   last line ends with a new line character).
2. Within a category (such as PG with preferences and UG with no preferences), the courses are scheduled in the order they appear. No schedule
   optimizations are performed.
3. In file 1, only one room can be listed in a line.

5. REQUIREMENTS TRACING

Here we list each major requirement and then list the modules which
implement that requirement.

  1. No more than one course should be scheduled at the same time in the
     same room:
              SCHED_PG_PREF,   SCHED_UG_PREF,
         SCHED_PG_NO_PREF,   SCHED_UG_NO_PREF

2. The class capacity should be more than the expected enrollment of the course:

    SCHED_PG_PREF,   SCHED_UG_PREF,
    SCHED_PG_NO_PREF,   SCHED_UG_NO_PREF

3. Preference is given to the PG course over UG course for scheduling:

    SCHED_PG_PREF, SCHED_UG_PREF, SCHED_PG_NO_PREF,
    SCHED_UG_NO_PREF

4. The courses should be scheduled such that the highest possible priority of an instructor is given:

    SCHED_PG_PREF,   SCHED_UG_PREF,
    SCHED_PG_NO_PREF,   SCHED_UG_NO_PREF

5. If no priority is specified, any room and time can be assigned:

    SCHED_PG_NO_PREF, SCHED_UG_NO_PREF

6. If any priority is incorrect, it is to be discarded:

    GET_PREF_VALID.

7. No two PG courses should be scheduled at the same time:

    SCHED_PG_PREF, SCHED_PG_NO_PREF.

8. If no preference is specified for a course, the course should be scheduled in any manner than does not violate the above constraints:

    SCHED_PG_NO_PREF, SCHED_UG_NO_PREF

9. The validity of the data in input file1 should be checked where possible:

    VALIDATE_FILE1 and its subordinates.

10. The data in the input file2 should be checked for validity against the data provided in input file1:

    VALIDATE_FILE2

5
Detailed Design

In the last chapter we discussed different issues involved in system design and described two design methodologies. In system design we concentrate on the modules in a system and how they interact with each other. The specifications of a module are often communicated by its name, the English phrase with which we label the module. In previous examples we have used words like "sort" and "assign" to communicate the functionality of the modules. The specifications of a module are conveyed by our understanding of the phrases that label the modules.

When a design of a system is to be converted into an actual implementation, the coder has to use his intuition to determine what activities the module is supposed to perform. This can be dangerous if the coder is a different person than the designer, which is often the case, as then the correct implementation of the module depends on the coder interpreting the names of the modules in precisely the same manner in which the designer intended. Even if the designer and the coder are the same person, problems can occur, as the design can take a long time, and the designer may not remember what precisely the module is supposed to do.

So the first step before the detailed design or code for a module can be developed is that the specification of the module should be given precisely. Once the module is precisely specified, the internal logic for the module that will implement the given specifications can be decided. In our case study a combination of formal and informal methods was used to specify the modules. The interface of the modules was specified formally, but the functionality of the modules was specified in natural language. Use of natural language is the most common means for specifying modules or systems.

In the next section we discuss some formal methods for specifying modules. We consider specification methods for modules supporting functional abstraction and modules supporting data abstraction. Then we discuss methods for specifying the detailed design of a module.

5.1. Module Specifications

Informal means of "specifying" what a module is supposed to do is likely to lead to different interpretations of the specifications, which can lead to incorrect implementations. Formal methods for specification can ensure that the specifications are precise and not open to multiple interpretations.

As discussed in the previous chapter, two types of abstractions are commonly used, functional abstraction and data abstraction. This means that if a system design is modular and modules support a well defined abstraction, most modules will either support functional or data abstraction. In this section we consider a formal specification method for each of the two types of modules.

Let us first discuss what are the desirable properties that module specifications should have. First, the specifications should be **complete.** That is, the given specifications should specify the entire behavior of the module such that only correct implementations satisfy the specifications. A related property is that the specifications should be **unambiguous.** Formal specifications usually are unambiguous while specifications written in natural languages are likely to be ambiguous. The specifications should be easily **understandable** and the specification language should be such that specifications can be easily written. This is required for practical reasons, and is a very desired property if the specification method is to be used in actual software development. It is lack of this feature which makes formal specifications less widely used. Formal specifications are often hard to understand, and equally hard to write.

An important property of specifications is that they should be *implementation independent*. Specifications should be given in an abstract manner independent of the eventual implementation of the module, and not specify or suggest any particular method for implementation of the module. This property specifically rules out algorithmic methods for specification. The specification should only give the external behavior; the internal details of the module should be decided later by the programmer.

Independence of implementation is also a property on which there is no universal agreement. One line of thought is that one can never provide specifications that do not suggest anything about the internals of the module. In this case, it is argued, that it is best to provide **operational specifications,** where the specifications are given in a very high level specification language. The specifications in this case are essentially implementation of the module in this high-level language. If an interpreter or a compiler for the specification language is available, then the added advantage of operational specifications is that a prototype is available once the specifications are provided. This prototype can be used either for testing actual implementations or for building a prototype of the entire system.

5.1.1. Specifying Functional Modules

The most abstract view of a functional module it to treat it as a black box that takes in some inputs and produces some outputs such that the outputs have a specified relationship with the inputs. Most modules are designed to operate only on inputs that satisfy some constraints. The constraints may be on the type of input as well as the range of the inputs. For example, a function that finds the square root of a number may be designed to operate only on real numbers. In addition, it may require that inputs are positive real numbers.

If the inputs satisfy the desired constraints, then the goal of a module is to produce outputs that satisfy some constraints that are often related to the inputs.

Hence, to specify the external behavior of a module supporting functional abstraction, one needs to specify the inputs on which the module operates, the outputs produced by the module, and the relationship of the outputs to the inputs.

One method for specifying modules was proposed by Hoare [Hoa69], based on pre and post conditions. The specification method was chosen more for verification of modules (i.e. verifying that a given implementation of a module satisfies its specifications) rather than specifying modules during design. In this method constraints on the input of a module were specified by a logical assertion on the input state called *pre condition*. The output was specified as a logical assertion on the output state called *post condition*. The post condition is specified as an assertion on the final state of the module. No relationship is explicitly specified between the input and the output. Validity of the output is specified entirely by the post condition assertion. We will discuss this method in more detail in a later chapter when we discuss verification of programs. As an example consider a module SORT to be written to sort a list L of integers in ascending order. The pre and post condition of this module are:

pre condition: non null L
post condition: **forall** i, $1 <= i < size(L)$, $L[i] <= L[i + 1]$

The specification states that if the input state for the module SORT is non-null L, then the output state should be such that the elements of L are in increasing order.

The above specifications are not complete. They only state that the final state of the list L (which is the output of the module SORT) should be such that the elements are in ascending order. It does not state anything about the implicit requirement of the SORT module, that the final state of the list L should contain the same elements as the initial list. In fact, this specification can be satisfied by a module that takes the first element of the list L and copies it on all the other elements.

A variation of this approach is to specify assertions for the input and output states, but the assertions for the output can be stated as a relation between the final state and the initial state. In such methods, while specifying the condition on the output, the final state of an entity E is referred to as E' (the initial state is referred by E itself). Using this notation, a possible specification of the module SORT is

SORT (L: list of integers)
   input: non null L
   output: forall i, $1 <= i < \text{size}(L')$
     $L'[i] \le L'[i + 1]$ **and**
     $L' = \text{permutation}(L)$

This specification, besides the ordering requirement, states that elements of the final list are a permutation of elements of the initial list. This specification will be complete if the module is to be designed only to operate on non-null lists. Often the modules check if the input satisfies the desired constraints. If the constraints are not satisfied, it is treated as an **exception condition,** and some special code is executed. If we want the module to handle exceptions, then we need to specify the **exceptional behavior** of the modules as well. Some work has been done in specifying and verifying modules with exceptions, and the reader is referred to the references [Cri84, Bol89].

5.1.2. Specifying Data Abstractions

Data abstraction is regarded as one of the most important language concepts of recent times. Data abstraction comprises a group of related operations that act upon a particular class of objects, with the constraint that the behavior of the objects can only be observed by application of the operations. Data abstractions when supported as types in a language are also called abstract data types (ADTs). Data abstraction is extremely useful for hiding information and providing high level abstraction. Many languages like Simula, CLU, and Ada support abstract data types.

Various specification techniques have evolved for specifying abstract data types. Here we will describe the axiomatic specification technique [Gut78]. In the axiomatic specification method the operations are not directly specified by specifying the behavior of each operation independently. Instead, axioms are employed that specify the behavior of different interactions of operations. The interactions for which axioms are chosen are such that they completely describe the behavior of the operations.

Before we proceed, let us demonstrate the axiomatic method by writing specifications for a stack of integers. We define a stack that has four operations:

Create: to create a new stack
Push: to push an element on a stack

Pop: to pop the top element from the stack
Top: returns the element on top of the stack

If we were to just specify the stack in the above manner, to convey the semantics of the operations, we have to rely on the meaning of the words like stack, push, and pop. Based on our understanding of stack and these words we may derive proper semantics of operations in this simple case. However, for absolutely new data types, this assumption may not hold. Axiomatic specifications remove this reliance on the meaning of words and intuition by precisely specifying the data type. The specifications of the stack are shown in Figure 5.1.

For axiomatic specifications to be used properly, we must agree on some language to be used for specifications. Here we present the specification language that we will use in this chapter. The specification language we employ has two major components—syntactic specifications and semantic specifications. The syntactic specifications provide the syntactic and type checking information, such as variable names, variable types, and the domain and range of operations. Semantic specifications define the meaning of the operations by stating, in the form of axioms, relationships of the operations among each other.

The syntactic part of the specifications has three components—the header, operation declarations and variable declaration. The header specifies the name of the data type and any parameters it may have. All the operations of the ADT must have a declaration in the operation declaration part. For an operation, the declaration has to specify the type of the input parameters and the result. The type can be either the ADT itself, any of the type parameters of the ADT, or a standard type like Boolean or integer. In

1. stack [integer]
    declare
2.   create ( ) -> stack ;
3.   push (stack , integer) -> stack ;
4.   pop (stack) -> stack ;
5.   top (stack) -> integer U undefined ;
    var
6.   s : stack ; i : integer ;
    forall
7.   top (create ( )) = undefined ;
8.   top (push (s , i)) = i ;
9.   pop (create ( )) = create ( ) ;
10.   pop (push (s , i)) = s ;
    end

FIGURE 5.1. Axiomatic specifications of a stack.

the variable declaration part, variables can be declared only of the types that have appeared before. The variables are declared for use in semantic specifications.

The semantics of the operations in the axiomatic specification technique are specified in the semantic part by enumerating axioms for operations. Axioms attach meaning to operations by specifying the relationship between operations. The following constructs are allowed for writing the axioms:

Free variables,
If-then-else,
Recursion, and
Boolean expressions.

Once we have constructed the specifications for a data type, we have to consider if a sufficient number of consistent axioms have been provided. Consistency means that partial semantics of different operations, specified by the axioms, is not contradictory. Determining consistency is theoretically an undecidable problem, but in practice it is often relatively simple to demonstrate the consistency of a set of axioms. One method of demonstrating consistency is to implement the data type. If the type can be implemented then its consistency is established.

Determining the completeness of a given set of axioms is usually a more difficult problem than determining consistency. For completeness we use use the notion of *sufficient completeness* [Gut78, Gut80]. For defining sufficient completeness we divide the set of operations defined on the ADT into two sets, S and O. The set S contains the operations whose range is ADT, returning a value of the type being specified. The set O contains operations that map values of the type ADT into other types, returning values of types other than the type being specified. The operations in O are often called behavior operations, while we sometimes use the term non-behavior operations to mean operations in the set S. In the example of the stack, the operation "top" is the only behavior operation.

Behavior operations provide a window into the state of instances of the abstract type. Behavior functions allow the actual behavior of an instance to be viewed from the outside. In principle, an abstract type can be defined without having any behavior operations, but for such types there is no way of distinguishing one instance of the abstract type from another, as there are no operations provided to observe the behavior of an instance of the abstract type from the outside. The ability to distinguish two instances depends solely upon the result of behavior operations performed on the instances. Instances of the abstract type, on the other hand, are created and manipulated solely by the non-behavior operations.

A set of axioms specifying an abstract type is considered *sufficiently complete* if and only if for every possible instance (such as an instance that can be created by some sequence of non-behavior operations) of the abstract type, the result of all the behavior operations of the type is defined by the specifications [Gut78]. This notion of sufficient completeness is from the external point of view; external behavior of the ADT should always be specified. The specifications for the type stack given earlier can be shown to be sufficiently complete. However, the general problem of determining if a set of axioms is sufficiently complete is undecidable.

The most obvious reason for incompleteness is that some axioms are not provided. Incompletion results when some of the axioms required to specify a type are omitted. Even though completeness is defined from the point of view of externally observable behavior of the type, incompleteness will result even if the missing axioms are for non-behavior operations, since this could lead to construction of an instance on which the result of some behavior operation is not defined.

A heuristic for generating complete specifications was provided by Guttag. For this we further divide the set S into two categories—constructors and extension operators. Constructors are those operations with which we can construct any instance of the ADT. In other words, any instance of a data type, regardless of what sequence of operations created it, can be created by a sequence of operations consisting solely of constructors. Extension operators are those operations that are not constructors but return a value of type ADT. In the case of the stack the operations "create" and "push" are constructors, while "pop" is an extension operator. Consider the following instance of the type stack

$$push(pop(push(push(create(), 1), 2)), 3)$$

Even though this instance is created by three different operations, the instance can be created by the following expression of constructors:

$$push(push(create(), 1), 3)$$

Identifying constructors cannot be done mechanically. It depends on the data type, and we have to use our judgment for separating constructors from the extension operators. But, for most cases, identifying constructors is relatively easy.

With constructors, another definition can be given for sufficient completeness. When a set of axioms is complete, any expression of the abstract type is reduced to an expression consisting solely of constructors by the application of the axioms. In other words, if axioms are treated as rewrite rules, then in an expression a pattern matching the left hand side of an axiom can be replaced by the expression on the right hand side of the axiom. The set of axioms is complete if by rewriting the expression using the axioms, we eventually reach an irreducible expression that consists solely of constructors.

Once the constructors are identified a sufficiently complete set of axioms can be generated. Consider an expression consisting of a non-constructor applied to a constructor. Form all such different expressions.

These expressions form the left side of the axioms. Such a set of axioms is guaranteed to be sufficiently complete. So, for a data type with n operations, if there are m constructors, the total number of axioms generated by this will be m*(n-m). Thus in the case of the stack we have 2 * 2 = 4 axioms, and the left sides are formed by combining "top" and "pop" with the two constructors "create" and "push".

Note that this method does not specify what the right side of the axiom should be. That we have to determine ourselves. If we do not properly state the right side for each of the cases, we may end up with a set of axioms that is inconsistent, or represents a data type which is different than what we wanted to specify. Clearly, no rules can be given to specify the right side, as it will depend on the type being specified.

Now let us consider a queue. We define the following operations on the type queue:

newq: Creates a new queue.
addq: Adds a new element at the end of the queue.
deleteq: Deletes the element at the front of the queue.
emptyq: Tells if the queue is empty or not.

```
 1.  queue [ Item ]
     declare
 2.      newq ( ) -> queue ;
 3.      addq ( queue , Item ) -> queue ;
 4.      deleteq ( queue ) -> queue ;
 5.      emptyq ( queue ) -> boolean ;
 6.      appendq ( queue , queue ) -> queue ;
 7.      frontq ( queue ) -> Item U undefined ;
     var
 8.      q , r : queue ;
 9.      i : Item ;
     forall
10.      emptyq ( newq ( ) ) = true ;
11.      emptyq ( addq ( q , i ) ) = false ;
12.      frontq ( newq ( ) ) = undefined ;
13.      frontq ( addq ( q , i ) ) = if emptyq ( q ) then i
             else frontq ( q ) ;
14.      deleteq ( newq ( ) ) = newq ( ) ;
15.      deleteq ( addq ( q , i ) ) = if emptyq ( q ) then newq ( )
             else addq ( deleteq ( q ) , i ) ;
16.      appendq ( q , newq ( ) ) = q ;
17.      appendq ( r , addq ( q , i ) ) = addq ( appendq ( r , q ) , i ) ;
     end
```

FIGURE 5.2. Specifications of the type queue.

appendq: Appends another queue at the end of a queue.
frontq: Returns the item at the front of the queue.

The constructors are "newq" and "addq." Any instance, whether created by using "appendq" or "deleteq" can be created by these two operations. Using the technique mentioned above, we will have 4 * 2 = 8 axioms to obtain a sufficiently complete set of axioms. For each of these eight expressions, we have to specify the right side correctly such that they represent the type queue. The axioms are shown in Figure 5.2.

Line 1 of the specification is the header of the ADT that states that this is the specification of a queue of type Items. Lines 2 through 7 specify the different operations defined on the type queue and their domain and range. It should be noted that this type is parameterized with type Item. Lines 8 and 9 declare some variables to be used in the axioms. Lines 1 through 9 form the syntactic specifications. Lines 10 and 11 specify the behavior of the function "emptyq"; if "emptyq" is performed on a "newq" it returns true, and if performed on a queue to which an element has been added it returns false. Lines 12 and 13 specify the behavior of the operation "frontq", lines 14 and 15 the behavior of "deleteq", and lines 16 and 17 the behavior of "appendq". The set of axioms given here can be shown to be complete. It might be pointed out that systems exist that can synthesize implementation from the axiomatic specifications [Jal87], or automatically test the completeness of axioms [Jal88, Jal89a].

5.2. Detailed Design and Progress Design Language

We have seen some techniques for system design. Many design techniques, like structured design, identify the major modules and the major data flow among them. The functionality of the module is communicated by the name of the module, and the interface is expected to be derived from the data flow to and from the module. Although very useful for performing design, structured design is not very precise for communicating or documenting the design. Process design language (PDL) is one way in which the design can be communicated precisely. Furthermore, the graphical representation method for SD can only handle system design, and detailed design cannot be specified. PDL can be used to specify the complete design—system as well as logic design—to whatever degree of detail desired by the designer. PDL is particularly useful in employing top-down refinement techniques to design a system or a module.

5.2.1. PDL

One way to communicate a design is to specify it in a natural language, like English. This approach often leads to misunderstanding, and such imprecise communication is not particularly useful when converting the design into code. The other extreme is to communicate it precisely in a formal language, like a programming language. Such representations often have great detail that is necessary for implementation, but not important for communicating the design. These details are often a hindrance to easy communication of the basic design. Ideally we would like to express the design in a language that is as precise and unambiguous as possible without having too much detail, and that can be easily converted into an implementation. This is what PDL attempts to do.

PDL has an overall outer syntax of a structured programming language, and has a vocabulary of a natural language (English in our case). It can be thought as "structured English". Since the structure of a design expressed in PDL is formal, using the formal language constructs, some amount of automated processing can be done on such designs. As an example consider the problem of finding out the minimum and maximum of a set of numbers in a file, then outputting these numbers in PDL (shown in Figure 5.3).

Notice that in the PDL program we have the entire logic of the procedure, but little about the details of implementation in a particular language. To implement this in a language, each of the PDL statements will have to be converted into programming language statements. Let us consider another example. Text is given in a file with one blank between two words. It is to be formatted into lines of 80 characters, except the last line. A word is not to be divided into two lines, and the numbers of blanks needed to fill the line are added towards the end, with no more than two blanks between words. The PDL program is shown in Figure 5.4. Notice the use of procedure to express the design.

With PDL, a design can be expressed in whatever level of detail that is suitable for the problem. One way to employ PDL is to first generate a

minmax(infile)

ARRAY a

```
DO UNTIL end of input
  READ an item into a
ENDDO
max, min : = first item of a
DO FOR each item in a
  IF max < item THEN set max to item
  IF min > item THEN set min to item
ENDDO
END
```

FIGURE 5.3. PDL description of the minmax program.

```
Initialize buf to empty
DO FOREVER
   DO UNTIL (#chars in buf > = 80 & word boundary is reached)
        OR (end-of-text reached)
      read chars in buf
   ENDDO
   IF #chars > 80 THEN
      remove last word from buf
      PRINT-WITH-FILL (buf)
      set buf to last wordELSEIF #chars = 80 THEN
      print (Buf)
      set buf to empty
   ELSE EXIT the loop
ENDDO


PROCEDURE PRINT-WITH-FILL (buf)

Determine #words and #character in buf
#of blanks needed = 80 − #character
DO FOR each word in the buf
   print (word)
   if #printed words > = (#word − #of blanks needed) THEN
      print (two blanks)
   ELSE print (single blank)
ENDDO
```

FIGURE 5.4. PDL description of text-formatter.

rough outline of the entire solution at a given level of detail. When the design is agreed upon at this level, more detail can be added. This allows a successive refinement approach, and can save considerable cost by detecting the design errors early during the design phase. It also aids design verification by phases, which helps in developing error-free designs. The structured outer syntax of PDL also encourages the use of structured language constructs while implementing the design.

The basic constructs of PDL are similar to that of a structured language. The first is the IF construct. It is similar to the if-then-else construct of Pascal. However, the conditions and the statements to be executed need not be stated in a formal language. For a general selection there is a CASE statement. Some examples of CASE statements are:

CASE OF transaction type

CASE OF operator type.

The DO construct is used to indicate repetition. The construct is indicated by

DO iteration criteria
    one or more statements
ENDDO

The iteration criteria can be chosen to suit the problem, and unlike a formal programming language, they need not be formally stated. Examples of valid uses are

DO WHILE there are characters in input file
DO UNTIL the end of file is reached
DO FOR each item in the list EXCEPT when item is zero.

A variety of data structures can be defined and used in PDL, such as list, tables, scalar, and integers. Variations of PDL, along with some automated support, are used extensively for communicating designs.

5.2.2. Logic/Algorithm Design

The basic goal in detailed design is to specify the logic for the different modules that have been specified during system design. Specifying the logic will require developing an algorithm that will implement the given specifications. Here we consider some principles for designing algorithms or logic that will implement the given specifications.

The term *algorithm* is quite general and is applicable to a wide variety of areas. Essentially, an algorithm is a sequence of steps that need to be performed to solve a given problem. The problem need not be a programming problem. We can, for example, design algorithms for such activities as cooking dishes (the recipes are nothing but algorithms) and building a table. In the software development life cycle we are only interested in algorithms related to software. For this we define an algorithm to be an unambiguous procedure for solving a problem [Goo77]. A *Procedure* is a finite sequence of well-defined steps or operations, each of which requires a finite amount of memory and a finite amount of time to complete. In this definition we assume that termination is an essential property of procedures. From now on we will use procedures, algorithms, and logic interchangeably.

There are a number of steps that one has to perform while developing an algorithm [Goo77]. The starting step in the design of algorithms is *statement of the problem*. The problem for which an algorithm is being devised has to be precisely and clearly stated and properly understood by the person responsible for designing the algorithm. For detailed design, the problem statement comes from the system design. That is, the problem statement is already available when the detailed design of a module commences. The next step is development of a mathematical *model* for the problem. In modeling one has to select the mathematical structures that are best suited for the problem. It can help to look at other similar problems that have been solved. In most cases, models are constructed by taking models of similar problems and then modifying the model to suit the current problem. The next step is the *design of the algorithm*. During this step the data structure and program structure are decided. Once the algorithm is designed, its correctness should be verified.

No clear procedure can be given for designing algorithms. Having such a procedure amounts to automating the problem of algorithm development, which is not possible with the current methods. However, some heuristics or methods can be provided that can help the designer in designing algorithms for modules. The most common method for designing algorithms or the logic for a module is to use the **stepwise refinement technique** [Wir71].

The stepwise refinement technique breaks the logic design problem into a series of steps, such that the development can be done gradually. The process starts by converting the specifications of the module into an abstract description of an algorithm containing a few abstract statements. In each step, one or several statements in the algorithm developed so far are decomposed into more detailed instructions. The successive refinement terminates when all instructions are sufficiently precise that they can easily be converted into programming language statements. During refinement, both data and instructions have to be refined. A guideline for refinement is that in each step the amount of decomposition should be such that it can be easily handled and which represents one or two design decisions.

The stepwise refinement technique is a top-down method for developing detailed design. We have already seen top-down methods for developing system designs. To perform stepwise refinement, a language is needed for expressing the logic of a module at different levels of detail, starting from the specifications of the module. We need a language that has enough flexibility to accommodate different levels of precision. Programming languages typically are not suitable as they do not have this flexibility. For this purpose, PDL is very suitable. Its formal outer syntax ensures that the design being developed is a "computer algorithm whose statements can later be converted into statements of a programming language. Its flexible, natural language based, inner syntax allows for statements to be expressed with varying degrees of precision, and aids the refinement process.

An Example: Let us again consider the problem of counting different words in a text file. Suppose that in the high-level structure chart of a large text processing system a COUNT module is specified whose job is to determine the count of different words. During detailed design we have to determine the logic of this module such that the specifications are met. We will use the stepwise refinement method for this. A simple strategy for the first step is shown in Figure 5.5.

This strategy is simple and easy to understand. This is the strategy that

```
count (in: file) returns integer
var
  wl: word_list;
begin
  read file into wl
  sort (wl);
  count : = different_words (wl);
  print (count);
end;
```

FIGURE 5.5. Strategy for first step in stepwise refinement.

we have proposed in the data flow graph earlier. The "primitive" operations used in this strategy are very high-level which need to be further refined. Specifically, there are three operations that need refinement. These are (1) read file into the word list (wl), whose purpose is to read all the words from the file and create a word list, (2) sort(wl), which sorts the word list in ascending order, and (3) count different words from a sorted word list. So far, only one data structure is defined, and that is the word list. As refinement proceeds, more data structures might be needed.

In the next refinement step, we should select one of the three operations to be refined and further elaborate it. In this step we will refine the reading procedure. One strategy of implementing the read module is to read words and add them to the word list. This is shown in Figure 5.6.

This is a straightforward strategy and is simple enough to be easily handled in one refinement step. Another strategy could be to read large amounts of data from the file in a buffer and then form the word list from this buffer. This might lead to a more efficient implementation. For the next refinement step we select the counting function. A strategy for implementing this function is shown in Figure 5.7.

Similarly, we can refine the sort function. Once these refinements are done, we have a design which is sufficiently detailed and needs no further refinement. For more complex problems many successive refinements

```
read_from_file (in: file, out: wl)
begin
  initialize wl to empty;
  repeat
    get_a_word from file
    add word to wl
  until end_of_file
end;
```

FIGURE 5.6. Refinement of the reading operation.

```
different_words (in: wl) returns integer
var
    last, cur: word;
    cnt: integer;
begin
    last : = first word in wl
    cnt : = 1;
    while not end of list
        cur : = next word from wl
        if (cur ! = last) then begin
            cnt : = cnt + 1;
            last : = cur;
        end;
    end;
    return (cnt);
end;
```

FIGURE 5.7. Refinement of the function different_words.

might be needed for a single operation. Design for such problems can proceed in two ways—depth first or breadth first. In the depth first approach, when an operation is being refined, its refinement is completely finished (which might require many levels of refinement) before refinement of other operations begins. In the breadth first approach, all operations needing refinement are refined once. Then all the operations specified in this refinement are refined once. This is done until no refinement is needed. A combination of the two approaches could also be followed.

It is worth comparing the structure of the PDL programs that are produced by this method as compared to the structure produced using the structured design methodology. The two structures are not the same. The basic difference is that in stepwise refinement the function sort is subordinate to the main module, while in the design produced by using structured design methodology, it is a subordinate module to the input module. This is not just a minor point—it points to a difference in approaches. In stepwise refinement, in each refinement step we specify the operations that are needed (as we do while drawing the data flow diagram). In structured design, the focus in on partitioning the problem into input, output and transform modules, which usually results in a different structure.

5.3. Verification

There are a few techniques available for verifying that the detailed design is consistent with the system design. The focus of verification in the detailed design phase is on showing that the detailed design meets the specifications laid down in the system design. Validating that the system as designed is consistent with the requirements of the system is not stressed during detailed design. The three validation methods we consider are design walkthroughs, critical design review and consistency checkers.

5.3.1. Design Walkthroughs

A design walkthrough is a manual method of verification. The definition and use of walkthroughs changes from organization to organization. Here we describe one walkthrough model. A design walkthrough is done in an informal meeting called by the designer or the leader of the designer's group. The walkthrough group is usually small and contains, along with the designer, the group leader and/or another designer of the group. The designer might just get together with a colleague for the walkthrough or the group leader might require the designer to have the walkthrough with him.

In a walkthrough the designer explains the logic step by step, and the members of the group ask questions, point out possible errors or seek clarification. A beneficial side effect of walkthroughs is that in the process of articulating and explaining the design in detail, the designer himself can uncover some of the errors.

Walkthroughs are essentially a form of peer review. Due to its informal nature, they are usually not as effective as the design review.

5.3.2. Critical Design Review

The purpose of critical design review is to ensure that the detailed design satisfies the specifications laid down during system design. As mentioned earlier, it is very desirable to detect and remove design errors early, as the cost of removing them later can be considerably more than the cost of removing them at design time. Detecting errors in detailed design is the aim of critical design review.

The critical design review process is similar to the other reviews, in that a group of people get together to discuss the design with the aim of revealing design errors or undesirable properties. The review group includes, besides the author of the detailed design, a member of the system design team, the programmer responsible for ultimately coding the module(s) under review, and an independent software quality engineer.

The review can be held in the same manner as the requirement review or system design review. That is, each member studies the design beforehand and with the aid of a checklist, marks out items that the reviewer feels are incorrect or need clarification. The members ask questions and the designer tries to explain the situation. During the course of the discussion design errors are revealed.

As with any review, it should be kept in mind that the aim of the meeting is to uncover design errors, and not try to fix them. Fixing is done later.

Also, the psychological frame of mind should be healthy, and the designer should not be put in a defensive position. The meeting should end with a list of action items, which are later acted upon by the designer.

The use of checklists, as with other reviews, is considered important for the success of the review. The check list is a means of focusing the discussion or the "search" of errors. Checklists can be used by each member during private study of the design and also during the review meeting. For best results the checklist should be tailored to the project at hand, to uncover problem specific errors. Here we list a few general items that can be used to construct a checklist for a design review [Dun84].

A SAMPLE CHECKLIST:

Does each of the modules in the system design exist in detailed design?
Are there analyses to demonstrate that the performance requirements can be met?
Are all the assumptions explicitly stated, and are they acceptable?
Are all relevant aspects of system design reflected in detailed design?
Have the exceptional conditions been handled?
Are all the data formats consistent with the system design?
Is the design structured, and does it conform to local standards?
Are the sizes of data structures estimated? Are provisions made to guard against overflow?
Is each statement specified in natural language easily codable?
Are the loop termination conditions properly specified?
Are the conditions in the loops ok?
Are the conditions in the if statements correct?
Is the nesting proper?
Is the module logic too complex?
Are the modules highly cohesive?

5.3.3. Consistency Checkers

Design reviews and walkthroughs are manual processes. The people involved in the review and walkthrough determine the errors in the design. If the design is specified in PDL or some other formally defined design language, it is possible to detect some design defects by using consistency checkers.

Consistency checkers are essentially compilers that take as input the design specified in a design language (PDL in our case). Clearly, they cannot produce executable code as the inner syntax of PDL allows natural language and many activities are specified in the natural language. However, the module interface specifications (which belongs to outer syntax) is specified formally. A consistency checker can ensure that any modules invoked or used by a given module actually exist in the design, and that the interface used by the caller is consistent with the interface definition of the called module. It can also check if the used global data items are indeed defined globally in the design.

Depending on the precision and syntax of the design language, consistency checkers can produce other information as well. In addition, these tools can also be used to compute the complexity of modules and other metrics, since these metrics are based on alternate and loop constructs, which have a formal syntax in PDL. The tradeoff here is that the more formal the design language, the more checking can be done during design, but the cost is that the design language becomes less flexible and tends towards a programming language.

5.4. Metrics

After the detailed design the logic of the system and the data structures are largely specified. Only the implementation-oriented details, which are often specific to the programming language that is used, need to be further defined. Hence, many of the metrics which are traditionally associated with code can be used effectively after detailed design. During detailed design all the metrics covered during the system design are applicable and useful. So the number of modules (it might change somewhat during detailed design) and the interface complexity of each module are metrics applicable to detailed design. With the logic of modules available after detailed design, it is meaningful to talk about the complexity of a module. Traditionally, complexity metrics are applied to code, but they can easily be applied to detailed design as well. Here we describe some metrics applicable to detailed design.

5.4.1. Complexity Metrics

Based on the capability of the human mind and the experience of people, it is generally recognized that conditions and control statements add complexity to a program. Given two programs with the same size, the program with the larger number of decision statements is likely to be more complex. The simplest measure of complexity then is the number of constructs that represent branches in the control flow of the program, like *if then else, while do, repeat until,* and *go to* statements.

A more refined measure is the *cyclomatic complexity measure* proposed by McCabe, which is based on the control flow graph of the logic of a program. To construct a control flow graph of a program module, break the module into blocks delimited by statements that affect the control flow, like *if, while, repeat, goto.* These blocks form the nodes of the graph. If the control from a block i can branch to a block j, then draw an arc from the node i to node j in the graph. The control flow of a program can be constructed mechanically. An example of the control flow graph is given in Figure 5.8.

For a graph G with n nodes, e edges, and p connected components, the cyclomatic number V(G) is defined as

$$V(G) = e - n + p.$$

The graph of a module will have an entry node and an exit node, corresponding to the first block and the last block of statements. In such graphs there will be a path from the entry node to any node, and a path from any node to the exit node (assuming that the program has no anomalies like unreachable code). If we draw an arc from the exit node to the entry node, the graph will be strongly connected since there is a path between any two nodes. For a strongly connected graph G, the cyclomatic number is equal to the maximum number of linearly independent circuits, or the count of circuits, such that no circuit is totally contained in another circuit or is a combination of other circuits. For calculating the cyclomatic number of a module, we can draw the graph, make it connected by drawing an arc from exit node to the entry node, and then count the number of circuits. In the graph shown above, the cyclomatic complexity is

$$V(G) = 10 - 7 + 1 = 4.$$

The independent circuits are:

ckt 1: b c e b
ckt 2: b c d e b
ckt 3: a b f a
ckt 4: a g a

The cyclomatic number is one quantitative measure of program complexity. It is more suitable at the module level, and McCabe proposed that

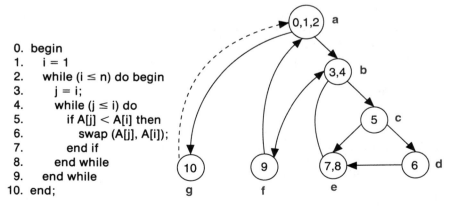

```
 0. begin
 1.    i = 1
 2.    while (i ≤ n) do begin
 3.       j = i;
 4.       while (j ≤ i) do
 5.          if A[j] < A[i] then
 6.             swap (A[j], A[i]);
 7.          end if
 8.          end while
 9.       end while
10. end;
```

FIGURE 5.8. A module with its flow graph.

the cyclomatic complexity of modules should in general be kept below ten. The cyclomatic number can also be used as a number of paths that should be tested during testing. Correlations have been found between the reliability of a module and its cyclomatic complexity.

5.4.2. Data Bindings

We have seen that coupling and cohesion are important concepts for evaluating a design. However, to be truly effective, metrics are needed to "measure the coupling between modules or the cohesion of a module. One metric that attempts to capture the module level concept of coupling is data binding. Data bindings are measures that capture the data interaction across portions of a software system [Hut85]. In other words, data bindings try to specify how strongly coupled different modules are in a software system. Different types of data bindings are possible [Hut85].

A *potential data binding* is defined as a triplet (p, x, q), where p and q are modules and x is a variable within the static scope of both p and q. This reflects the possibility that the modules p and q may communicate with each other through the shared variable x. This binding does not consider the internals of p and q to determine if the variable x is actually accessed in any of the modules. This binding is based on data declaration.

A *used data binding* is a potential binding where both p and q use the variable x for reference or assignment. This is harder to compute than potential data binding and requires more information about the internal logic of a module.

An *actual data binding* is a used data binding with the additional restriction that the module p assigns a value to x and q references x. It is the hardest to compute, and signifies the situation where information may flow from the module p to module q through the shared variable x. Computation of actual data binding requires a detailed logic description of modules p and q.

All of these data bindings attempt to represent the strength of interconnections among modules. The greater the number of bindings between two modules, the higher the interconnection between these modules. For a particular type of binding, a matrix can be computed which contains the number of bindings between different modules. This matrix can be used for further statistical analysis to determine the interconnection strength of the system or a sub-system.

5.4.3. Cohesion Metric

Here we discuss one attempt at quantifying the cohesion of a module [Eme84]. To compute the value of the cohesion metric for a module M, a flow graph G is constructed for M. Each vertex in G is an executable statement in M. For each node, we also record the variable referenced in the statement. An arc exists from a node s1 to another node s2 if the statement s2 can immediately follow the statement s1 in some execution of the module. In addition to these, we add an initial node I from where the execution of the module starts, and a final node T, at which the execution of the module terminates. For termination statements (e.g. RETURN, STOP) we draw an arc from the statement to T.

From G a *reduced* flow graph is constructed by deleting those nodes which do not refer to any variable (such as unconstrained gotos). All the arcs coming in the deleted node are redirected to the node which is the successor of the deleted node (such nodes will have only one successor).

Assume that the variables are sequentially numbered as $1, 2, \ldots, n$. For a variable i, R_i is the reference set, which is the set of all the executable statements which refer to the variable i. The union of all the R_is is the set of all the nodes in the graph (minus the node for T, which is a non-executing node). Let $|G|$ refer to the number of nodes-1 (for T) in the reduced graph.

The cohesion of a set of statements S is defined as

$$C(S) = \frac{|S| \ dim \ S}{|G| \ dim \ G}$$

where dim is the dimension of a set of statements, which is the maximum number of linearly independent paths from I to T which pass through any element of S. Thus, the dimension of a set of statements S is the count of all the independent paths from the start statement to the end statement of a module which includes at least one statement from the set. If S is the set of all the statements in the module, (if S is the same as G), then dim S is the same as the cyclomatic complexity of the module.

The cohesion of a module is defined as the average cohesion of the reference sets of the different statements or nodes in (reduced) G. Hence the cohesion of the module C(M) is

$$C(M) = \frac{\sum\limits_{i=1}^{i=n} C(R_i)}{n}.$$

Essentially, this metric is trying to measure cohesion of a module by seeing how many independent paths of the module go through the different statements. The idea is that if a module has high cohesion, most of the variables will be used by statements in most paths. Hence for a high cohesion module, the cohesion of the reference set of each variable will be high. The highest cohesion number achievable by this is when the dimension of all the reference sets is all the independent paths, thus the same as the cyclomatic complexity. In other words, the highest cohesion is when all the independent paths use all the variables of the module.

5.5. Monitoring and Control

Project monitoring and control activities, although more than in previous phases, still do not need to be as extensive as during coding and testing. As with all phases, the **cost and schedule** needs to be monitored carefully. If the cost and schedule of detailed design is considerably different from the earlier estimates, the estimates should be revised and a careful review of the team's activities should be done to ensure that the team continues to be productive.

One of the means for monitoring the progress of modules is the **Unit Development Folder (UDF),** which we discussed in an earlier chapter. The UDF is started for each unit of the system after the system design is completed. The programmer responsible for that unit prepares a detailed plan for that unit, with identifiable milestones. These milestones and the plan are used for monitoring the progress of the unit. In addition, all information relevant to the unit goes in the notebook. Hence, the notebook contains all information about the state of a unit.

Another factor to be monitored is **module complexity.** After detailed design, complexity of modules can be obtained. If a module is very complex, it is likely to be harder to understand and modify. The goal is to keep the module complexity low. By monitoring the complexity, modules can be identified that are considered "too complex". Alternatives to these modules then need to be devised. An alternative is likely to be in the form of having multiple modules, each being simpler, or having simpler logic for the module. For determining if a module is considered too complex, some metrics and threshold must be selected. The threshold value is likely to depend on the type of application and the culture of the organization. For example, it has been suggested that the cyclomatic complexity of a module should be less than ten. With this criterion, all modules with cyclomatic complexity of more than ten will have to be carefully evaluated and modified.

As in previous phases, review (or any other verification technique employed) provides important data for monitoring the project. Review provides a milestone whose successful completion means that the output of this phase is acceptable for the project.

Number of errors uncovered per module is another metric that should be carefully scrutinized. The number of errors discovered for a module has different interpretations. For example, if the number of errors found is very few, it could mean that the design is of high quality, or it could mean that the review was not done properly. If the number of errors discovered is too high, it could mean that most of the errors of the module have been discovered, or it could mean that many more remain. In general, the number of errors discovered for a module should be within the "expected range". The expected range is determined based on past experience. If the number of errors discovered for a module is too few or too many, those modules should be suspected and the modules and their review proceedings should be scrutinized. If needed, more reviews should be established.

5.6. Summary

Detailed design starts after the system design phase is completed and the system design has been certified through a review. The goal of this phase is to develop the internal logic of each of the modules that have been identified during system design.

Before deciding on the logic of a module, the specifications of the module have to be provided. Many system design methodologies, like the structured design methodology, do not emphasize precise specification of modules. Modules are often specified by their names, and the interfaces are also not defined precisely. Hence, before deciding the internal logic of a module, a precise specification for the module has to be developed.

The specifications should be such that they are complete, unambiguous and precise, and do not suggest any particular implementation. Two module units are frequently chosen for formal specifications—functional modules and data abstraction modules. Both of these formal methods can specify the behavior of the modules without assuming any implementation for the module. We have discussed some such methods. However, most formal methods for specifications tend to be rather cumbersome, not very expressive and hard to understand or write. For this reason, formal specifications are not often used.

For expressing the internal logic of a module, we need a design language. The design language should be such that it is flexible enough to be easily usable, yet precise enough to be easily convertible in code. We have described a language called process design language (PDL) which satisfies the bill. PDL can be used to express the detailed design of systems. It has a formal outer syntax, and a flexible inner syntax and vocabulary, giving it a balance between formalism and ease of expression.

Like any phase, we need some metrics to evaluate the effectiveness of the phase and to evaluate the output of that phase. We have considered a metric for evaluating the complexity of modules from their detailed design. This metric can be used to assess the overall complexity of the system.

A few techniques exist for verifying the detailed design. The most common are design walkthroughs and critical design review. Automated tools can be used for some consistency checking if some well-defined design language, like PDL, is used. Even with automated consistency checkers, reviews and walkthroughs remain the most important methods for verifying the detailed design. We have described the review process and have given a sample checklist that can be used in the review.

Exercises

1. The detailed design of a system can involve many persons, each developing the detailed design of a set of modules. Draw a process diagram for this method of detailed design development.
2. Why are formal specifications of modules desirable? What are the limitations of current formal methods and why have they not come into common use?
3. Formally specify the following modules:
   (a) reverse(L): reverses the input list L.
   (b) insert(S, i): inserts the element i in the set S.
   (c) strcat(s1, s2): concatenates string s2 at the end of s1.
   (d) strlen(s): determines the length of a string s.
   (e) min(S): determines the minimum of the set S.
4. Write the detailed design for these functions.
5. Provide axioms for the data types described below. For each type the name of and operations on that type are given.
   (a) type String
       null () ->
       String isnull (String) -> boolean
       len(String) -> integer
       addchar(String, char) -> String
       index(String, char) -> integer
   (b) type Set
       emptyset() -> Set
       isempty(Set) -> boolean
       insert(Set, item) -> Set
       delete(Set, item) -> Set
       has(set, item) -> boolean
   (c) type Btree a simple binary tree *emptytree() -> Btree
       make(Btree, item, Btree) -> Btree
       isempty(Btree) -> boolean
       left(Btree) -> Btree
       right(Btree) -> Btree
       isin(Btree, item) -> boolean
       insert(Btree, item) -> Btree
   (d) type SymbolTable
       init() -> SymbolTable
       enterblock(SymbolTable) -> SymbolTable
       addid(SymbolTable, identifier, attributelist) -> SymbolTable
       leaveblock(SymbolTable) -> SymbolTable
       isinblock(SymbolTable, identifier) -> boolean
       retrieve(SymbolTable, identifier) -> attributelist
   (e) type Library
       create() -> Library

add(Library, book) -> Library
checkout(Library, book) -> Library
return(Library, book) -> Library
isin(Library, book) -> boolean
isempty(Library) -> boolean

6. Write the detailed design for the data abstractions described above using PDL. You may extend the PDL with constructs to support data encapsulation.
7. What needs to be specified during detailed design? What are the desirable characteristics of a language to express detailed design?
8. What features would you like to add to PDL, if the target source language supports data abstraction?
9. Can you define metrics other than the ones discussed in the chapter which will be applicable to detailed design?
10. Consider an implementation of the type Btree as a set of procedures and functions (without data encapsulation). From the detailed design obtained above, determine the cohesion of different procedures/ functions and coupling between them using the metrics described in the chapter.
11. What is the relation between the cohesion metric and cyclomatic complexity?
12. What are the different methods for verifying a detailed design? Which of these, in your opinion, is likely to be most effective in revealing design errors?

Case Study: Detailed Design Document

This document describes the detailed design for the course scheduling software. The requirements document and the system design document were given earlier, and an understanding of both is needed for understanding the design described here.

1. DESIGN DECISIONS

In refining the system design, some decisions were taken regarding the data structures and the approach to be followed.

1. Room numbers, course numbers and lecture times will be kept in different arrays, and most processing will be done by representing these as indices in their respective arrays.
2. The timetable is kept as a two-dimensional array indexed by the indices for room numbers and indices for lecture times. This representation requires that the print routines have access to the arrays for course numbers, lecture times and classrooms.
3. Rooms are sorted by capacity to simplify room allocation.

4. For each timeslot, the number of PG courses allotted to that timeslot is kept in PG_alloc_array. This simplifies the checking of PG conflict.
5. Conflicts and explanations are represented as records. The error code field represents different errors as a code. There are six different errors. The course index represents the course that has these conflicts and explanations. Room_index represents a room, and is needed only for some errors. Preference list is the preferences for which the conflicts arose.
6. Most major data structures are kept as global for clarity and efficiency reasons. All structures defined in the system design are global.
7. To ensure that a PG course gets preference over a UG course, while scheduling UG courses with preferences, enough slots are saved for PG courses with no prefences. In other words, a UG course with preferences is scheduled only if it does not consume the last possible slot for some PG course without preferences. For this a data structure PG_reserve is used.
8. If an error is detected in the format, where possible, the processing of the data continues to find more errors. In any error is detected, no schedule is generated.

2. Detailed Design

(*————————————— DATA DEFINITIONS ———————————*)

classroom_DB: array of (* classroom info. from file 1 *)
  room_no : string
  capacity : integer

courseno_DB: array of strings (* valid courses from file 1 *)
timeslot_DB: array of strings (* valid lecture times from file 1 *)

course_rec_array : array of (* courses to be scheduled. From file 2*)
  course_index : integer (* index in courseno_DB of the course *)
  enrol : integer
  valid_pref_list : list of integers (* indices in timeslot_DB *)

UGP_start, PGNP_start, UGNP_start: integer (* start of different types of courses in course_rec_array *)

conflict_list, expl_list: array of
  err_code: integer
  course_index: integer (* in courseno_DB *)
  room_index: integer
  pref_list: list of integers

timetable: two dimensional array of integers
(*rows are indices for rooms, columns indices of lecture times *)

PG_alloc_array: array of integers
(* Contains the number of PG courses allotted in different timeslots.
Used for checking conflicts *)

(* Following is used to ensure that a UG allotment does not make a PG
course unschedulable *)
PG_reserve: list of
course_no : integer
list of
timeslot : integer
list of
roomnos

(*——————————— LOGIC DESIGN ——————————*)

MAIN MODULE

1. PROC main()
   BEGIN
       get-validated-input
       schedule
       output
   END.

INPUT MODULE

2. PROC get_validated_input(file1,file2)
   BEGIN
       open(file1)
       If can't open THEN
         print "Input file1 does not exist" and terminate
       ELSE validate_file1
       open(file2)
       If can't open THEN
         print "Input file2 does not exist" and terminate
       ELSE validate_file2
       separate_courses
   END

3. PROC validate_file1(file1)
       (* validates input_file1 and prints appropriate messages for
         improper *)
       (* input data items and ignores invalid data items *)

```
        LOCAL VARS room_no, course_no, timeslot
        OUT classroom_DB, courseno_DB, timeslot_DB

    BEGIN
      get_next_line(file1,buffer)
      IF buffer = "rooms" THEN
        validate_classrooms
      ELSE BEGIN
           print "Format of file1 incorrect : 'rooms' expected
           stop parsing and terminate without scheduling
        END
      get_next_line(file1,buffer)
      IF buffer = "courses" THEN
        validate_dept_courses
      ELSE BEGIN
           print "Format of file1 incorrect : 'courses' expected"
           stop parsing and terminate without scheduling
        END
      get_next_line(file1,buffer)
      IF buffer = "times" THEN
        validate_lecture_times
      ELSE BEGIN
           print "Format of file1 incorrect : 'times' expected"
           stop parsing and terminate without scheduling
      END
    END
```

4. PROC validate_classrooms
   (* Checks if the classroom_number formats and capacities are *)
   (* correct and ignores them if they are invalid. Valid classroom *)
   (* records are kept in the global data structure "classroom_
      B" *)

```
    LOCAL VAR room_no: string
    GLOBAL classroom_DB

    BEGIN
      get_next_line(file1,buffer)
      WHILE (buffer not empty) and (number of classrooms <=
      MAXROOMS) BEGIN
        room_no = get_next_token(buffer)
        IF chk_fmt_room_no(room_no) THEN BEGIN (* room_no
          format ok *)
            token = get_next_token(buffer)
            IF token = ':' THEN BEGIN
```

```
            cap = get_next_token(buffer)
            IF chk_range_cap(cap) THEN BEGIN (* capacity
               within range *)
               BEGIN
                  roomrec.room_no <- room_no
                  roomrec.capacity <- cap
                  add roomrec to classroom_DB
               END
               ELSE BEGIN
                     print room_no: "capacity is out of range
                        [10,300]
               END
            END
         END
         ELSE BEGIN
            print room#: "has wrong format and hence ignored"
         END
         increment number of classrooms
         get_next_line(file1,buffer)
      END
      IF (number of classrooms > MAXROOMS THEN
         print "More than permissible number of rooms: Later ones
            ignored
         Sort classroom_DB by the capacities of the rooms
   END

5. PROC validate_dept_courses
      (* Checks if the course_number formats are correct and
         ignores if *)
      (* they are invalid. If more than MAXCOURSES entries, later
         ones are ignored *)
      (* Valid course numbers are kept as a global data structure
         "courseno_DB" *)

      LOCAL VAR course_no: string
      GLOBAL courseno_DB

      BEGIN
         get_next_line(file1,buffer)
         WHILE (buffer not empty) and (number of courses <=
         MAXCOURSES) DO BEGIN
         course_no = get_next_token(buffer)
         IF chk_fmt_course_no(course_no) THEN (* checks if is in
            format 'csddd' *)
            add course_no to courseno_DB
```

```
            ELSE BEGIN
                print course_no: "has wrong format and hence ignored"
                exit (* from while loop *)
            END
        Increment the number of courses
        END
        IF (number of course > MAXCOURSES) THEN
            print "More than permissible courses; later ones ignored"
    END
```

6. PROC validate_lecture_times
    (* Checks if the lecture_times formats are correct and ignores
    them *)
    (* if they are invalid. If more than MAXTIMES entries, the
    later *)
    (* ones are ignored. Valid lecture times are kept in a global *)
    (* data structure "time_slot_DB" *)

    ```
    LOCAL VAR timeslot: string
    GLOBAL time_slot_DB

    BEGIN
        get_next_line(file1,buffer)
        WHILE (buffer not empty) and (number of timeslots <=
        MAXTIMES) DO BEGIN
        timeslot = get_next_token(buffer)
        IF chk_fmt_timeslot(timeslot) THEN
            (* checks if timeslot is of proper format *)
            add timeslot to time_slot_DB
        ELSE BEGIN
            print timeslot: "has wrong format and hence ignored"
            exit (* from while loop *)
        END
        Increment the number of timeslots
        END
        IF (number of timeslots > MAXTIMES) THEN
            print "There are more than permissible lecture times in
                the file
                The latter ones are ignored"
    END
    ```

7. PROC validate_file2
    (* Checks for validity of input_file2 against the data obtained
    from the *)

(* input_file1 and creates an array of valid course records [global data *)
(* structure "course_rec_array"] *)

LOCAL VAR course_no: string, enrol: integer, pref: string˙
GLOBAL courseno_DB, timeslot_DB, course_rec_array

```
BEGIN
  get_next_line(file2,buffer)
  IF buffer = "COURSE NUMBER ENROLMENT
    PREFERENCES" THEN BEGIN
    get_next_line(file2,buffer)
    WHILE buffer not empty DO BEGIN
        course_no = get_next_token(buffer)
        get_course_index(course_no,course_index) (* gets the
          course index in courseno_DB *)
        IF (course_index = 0) THEN BEGIN
            print "There is no course of this
              number:",course_no
              exit {from while loop}
          END
        enrol = get_next_token(buffer)
      IF duplicate_course (course_index) THEN
          print "Duplicate course; ignored"
      ELSE IF enrol < 3 or enrol>250 THEN
          print "Enrollment outside range"
        ELSE BEGIN
          get_pref_valid(buffer, valid_pref_list)
            form_course_rec(course#, enrol, valid_pref_list)
            get_next_line(buffer)
      END
    END
  END ELSE
    print "Error in title in file 2
END
```

8. PROC get_course_index(course_no,course_index)
   (* Returns the index of course_no in Courseno_DB *)

GLOBAL courseno_DB

```
BEGIN
  IF course_no is present in courseno_DB THEN
    course_index = index of course_no in courseno_DB
```

```
        ELSE BEGIN
            print "There is no course with the number:",course#
            course_index = 0
        END
    END
```

9. PROC get_pref_valid (buffer, valid_pref_list)
    (* Returns a list of indices to the time_slot_DB which
    point to *)
    (* the timeslots present in the pref_list. If the time preference is
    not *)
    (* present in time_slot_DB it prints an error message and ignores
    it. *)

    LOCAL VAR pref, time, #prefs
    GLOBAL time_slot_DB

```
    BEGIN
        WHILE not end of buffer AND #prefs < 5 DO BEGIN
            pref = get_next_preF (pref)
            WHILE lecture_times not empty DO BEGIN
                get_next_lecture_time(time)
                IF pref = time THEN BEGIN (* pref is valid *)
                    add pref to valid_pref_list
                    exit (* from the while loop *)
                END
            END
            IF pref not in lecture_times THEN BEGIN
                print "There is no such lecture time as :",pref
                exit (* from the while loop *)
            END
        END
        if (#prefs > = 5) print "More than 5 prefs; later ones ignored"
    END
```

10. PROC form_course_rec(course_index,enrol,valid_pref_list)
    (* Forms a course record containing the index to the course#, *)
    (* index to the classroom_DB and a list of indices to the *)
    (* time_slot_DB. It also adds the record to the global data *)
    (* structure "course_rec_array"   *)

    LOCAL VAR course_index, enrol, valid_pref_list
    GLOBAL course_rec_array

BEGIN
   course_rec.course_index = course_index
   course_rec.enrol = enrol
   course_rec.valid_pref_list = valid_pref_list
   add course_rec to course_rec_array
END

11. PROC separate_courses
   (* Separates courses into four groups-PG with pref,PG with no
   pref, UG with pref and UG with no pref and store them back in
   that order *)

   LOCAL VARS PGpref , PGnopref , UGpref , UGnopref
   GLOBAL course-rec-array, UGP_start, PGNP_start,
   UGNP_start

   BEGIN
   (* Take the entries in the course-record-array one by one and
   separate them into the local arrays *)

      WHILE (all entries in course-record-array not tried out)
      DO CASE (kind of get-an-entry()) OF BEGIN
        PGpref : place it in PGpref array and increment the
         index
        Pgnopref : place it in PGnopref array and increment the
         index
        UGpref : place it in UGpref array and increment the
         index
        UGnopref : place it in UGnopref array and increment
         the index
      END

    Initialize an index to 0
    WHILE (PGpref array is not empty) DO BEGIN
      Add next entry into course_rec_array
      Increment index by 1
    END

    UGP_start = index
    WHILE (UGpref array is not empty) DO BEGIN
      Add next entry into course_rec_array
      Increment index by 1
    END

PGNP_start = index WHILE (PGnopref array is not empty)
DO BEGIN
   Add next entry into course_rec_array
   Increment index by 1
END

PGNP_start = index
WHILE (PGnopref array is not empty) DO BEGIN
   Add next entry into course_rec_array
   Increment index by 1
END
UGNP_start = index
END.

SCHEDULE MODULE

12. PROC schedule
    (* The schedule module : schedules the courses into the
    timetable *)
    (* It consists of four subordinate modules : sched_PG_pref , *)
    (* sched_UG_pref , sched_PG_no_pref , sched_UG_no_pref *);

    GLOBAL course_rec_array, conflict_list, expl_list,
    PG_alloc_array, time_table

    BEGIN
       sched_PG_pref
       sched_UG_pref
       sched_PG_no_pref
       sched_UG_no_pref
    END.

13. FUNCTION get_room_index(enrol):room_index
    (* Returns an index to the classroom_DB which points to the
    room with the *)
    (* least capacity which satisfies the enrollment. IF no room is
    found then *)
    (* it returns 0. Note that the rooms are sorted by capacity *)

    LOCAL VAR enrol, room_index
    GLOBAL classroom_DB

    BEGIN
       WHILE classroom_DB is not exhausted DO BEGIN

```
        get_room_index = 0
        get_next_classroom(room)
        IF room.capacity > = enrol THEN BEGIN
            get_room_index = index of room exit
        END
    END
END
```

14. PROC sched_PG_pref

    (* The module schedules the PG courses with preference. *)
    (* Each column should contain only one PG course. Allocate
    the *)
    (* smallest room with required capacity   *)

    GLOBAL course_rec_array, conflict_list, expl_list,
    PG_alloc_array, time_table

    ```
    BEGIN
        WHILE there are PG courses with pref DO BEGIN
            get next course;
            WHILE prefs remain DO BEGIN
                IF timeslot column in time_table[] empty THEN BEGIN
                    assign the slot with the smallest room
                    increment number of courses allocated for the timeslot
                        col
                END
            END
            IF course not allocated THEN
                add course to conflict list with error_code as 1.
            ELSE
                IF first pref not honoured THEN
                add course to explanation list with error_code as pref
                honoured.
        END
    END
    ```

15. PROC sched_UG_pref

    (* The module schedules the UG courses with preference. It
    allocates the smallest available room with required capacity
    while keeping enough number of slots for the PG courses
    without any preference which will be allocated later. Note that
    only one PG course can be allocated in one timeslot column. *)

    GLOBAL course_rec_array, conflict_list, expl_list,
    PG_alloc_array, PG_reserve, time_table

```
BEGIN
  initialize_PG_reserve
  WHILE more UG course with pref left DO BEGIN
    get next course;
    WHILE pref for the course not over DO BEGIN
      get next pref;
      IF (some PG course without pref in this slot) THEN
      (* one PG course already allocated, so need not worry *)
        IF a vacant room with capacity available THEN assign
          the room
        ELSE exit(while loop) (* go ahead with next pref *)
      ELSE
        FOR each room_no DO BEGIN
          IF safe_allottment (room, timeslot) THEN BEGIN
            assign the room
            update_PG_reserve (room, pref) (* remove allotted
              room from PG_reserve *)
          END
        END
      IF course not allocated THEN
        add course to conflict list with error_code set to 2.
      ELSE IF first pref not honoured THEN
        add course to explanation list
    END
  END.
```

16. PROC initialize_PG_reserve
    (* Initializes the PG_reserve list for each PG course with no
    pref *)

    GLOBAL course_rec_array, time_table, PG_reserve

```
BEGIN
  FOR each PG course with no pref DO BEGIN
    get course_rec from course_rec_array
    room_index : = get_room_index(course_rec.enrol)
    initialize list of timeslot to nil
    FOR each timeslot with no PG course allocated DO
    BEGIN
      add timeslot to list of timeslots
      initialize list of roomnos to null
      FOR each room > room_index DO
      IF room not assigned a PG course THEN
        put room into roomlist
```

```
              END
           END
        END
```

17. FUNCTION safe_allottment (room, time: integer): boolean

```
        LOCAL VARS course_safe, slot_safe
        GLOBAL course_rec_array, time_table, PG_reserve
        BEGIN
           safe_allottment = True
           FOR each course in PG_reserve DO BEGIN
             course_safe = False
             FOR each timeslot DO BEGIN
               slot_safe = False
               IF timeslot = time THEN
                  IF there is some room with capacity for this slot which
                     is not same as room THEN
                       set course_safe and slot_safe to True
                     exit (for loop)
               ELSE IF some there is some room with capacity THEN
                       set course_safe and slot_safe to True
                     exit (for loop)
             END
             safe_allottment = safe_allottment AND course_safe AND
                slot_safe
           END
        END
```

18. PROC update_PG_reserve(time,room:integer)
    (* This routine removes a room from the PG_reserve, i.e. from
       all the PG_no_pref courses that contain the room in their
       roomlists.. *)

```
        GLOBAL PG_reserve

        BEGIN
           WHILE (PG_reserve is not empty) DO
           BEGIN
             get next courseno along with its list of timeslots and rooms
             WHILE (timeslot list is not empty) DO
             BEGIN
               get next timeslot along with its roomlist
               IF (room is present in roomlist) THEN
                 Remove the room from the roomlist corresponding to
                    the courseno
```

```
            END
          END
        END

19. PROC sched_PG_no_pref
        (* This one schedules the PG courses with no preference. *)
        (* Try the rooms in ascending order of capacity. *)

        GLOBAL course_rec_array, conflict_list, expl_list,
          PG_alloc_array, time_table

      BEGIN
        ncourses_assigned : = 0
        WHILE any more PG course with no preference DO BEGIN
          get next course;
          IF ncourses_assigned > = no of slots having vacancies for
            the PGNP courses THEN BEGIN
            put course in conflict_array with proper error code set
            exit(while loop)
          END
          increment ncourses_assigned
          WHILE course not assigned AND roomlist not over DO
          BEGIN
            get next room#;
            WHILE timeslots for the room# row not over DO BEGIN
              get next timeslot;
              IF time_table[course_rec_array : array
                [1..MAXCOURSES] of course_records BEGIN
                assign the slot;
                increment number of courses allocated for the
                  column;
              END
            END {inner while loop }
          END
          IF course not assigned THEN
            add course to conflict list with error_code set to 3.
        END
      END

20. PROC sched_UG_no_pref
        (* Allocate UG courses with no preference. The job is simple: *)
        (* Try out the rooms in ascending capacity. *)
        (* Allocate the first available slot. *)

        GLOBAL course_rec_array, conflict_list, expl_list,
          PG_alloc_array, time_table
```

```
BEGIN
  WHILE any more UG course with no pref DO BEGIN
    get next course
    WHILE not allocated AND any more rooms with required
      capacity DO BEGIN
      get next room
      IF any timeslot vacant for the room THEN
        assign time_table[room#,timeslot#]
    END
    IF course not allocated THEN
      add course to conflict list with error_code set to 4.
  END
END
```

OUTPUT MODULE

21. PROC output
```
    BEGIN
      print_timetable
      print_explanation
      print_conflict
    END
```

22. PROC print_conflict
```
    GLOBAL conflict_list, error_code, course_index, room_index,
      pref_list
    BEGIN
    {Run down the conflict_list and generate error messages}
      WHILE (conflict_list not empty) DO BEGIN
        conflict_rec = get_next_entry(conflict_list)
        CASE (conflict_rec.error_code) OF
          1 : WHILE (conflict_rec.pref_list not empty) DO BEGIN
                pref = first(conflict_rec.pref_list)
                print "Conflict with course_no : ",course which has
                  been allotted the preference : 'pref'
                remove first entry from the pref_list
              END
          2 : WHILE (conflict_rec.pref_list not empty) DO BEGIN
                pref = first(conflict_rec.pref_list)
                print "No room with proper capacity available
                remove first entry from the pref_list
              END
          3 : print "Excess PG course : no timeslot available
          4 : print "No free room with required capacity available
          5 : print "Enrollment greater than the maximum capacity
                of any room in file1 : course ignored
```

6 : print "Course repeated more than once in file2 :
    ignored"
        END
      END
    END

23. PROC print_explanation
    GLOBAL expl_list, error_code, course_index, room_index,
    pref_list

    BEGIN
    (* Run down the expl-list and generate error messages for each
    entry *)
      WHILE (expl_list not empty) DO BEGIN
        expl_rec = get_next_entry(expl_list)
        WHILE (expl_rec.pref_list not empty) DO BEGIN
          pref = first(expl_rec.pref_list)
          IF (room_index = 0) THEN
            print "Conflict with course_no : ",course which has
              been allotted the preference : 'pref'
          ELSE
            print "No room with proper capacity available
          remove first entry from the pref_list
          END
        END
    END

24. PROC print-timetable
    GLOBAL time_table, classroom-DB, timeslot-DB, courseno-DB

    BEGIN
      print the timetable in the required format
    END.

3. TRACING TO THE SYSTEM DESIGN

All the modules defined in the system design are also present in the
detailed design. No major changes have been made to the structure. The
mapping of modules in the system design to the modules in the detailed
design is given below (the first number indicates the number of the module
in the system design document; the second number is the number of the
corresponding module in the detailed design given above.)

$0 \rightarrow 1, 1 \rightarrow 2, 2 \rightarrow 12, 3 \rightarrow 21, 1.1 \rightarrow 3, 1.2 \rightarrow 7, 1.3 \rightarrow 11, 1.1.1 \rightarrow 4, 1.1.2 \rightarrow 5, 1.1.3 \rightarrow 6, 1.2.1 \rightarrow 8, 1.2.2 \rightarrow 9, 2.1 \rightarrow 14, 2.2 \rightarrow 15, 2.3 \rightarrow 19, 2.4 \rightarrow 20, 3.1 \rightarrow 23, 3.2 \rightarrow 22, 3.3 \rightarrow 24.$

There were a total of 19 modules in the system design, while there are a total of 24 modules in the detailed design. These new modules have been added only at the bottom. That is, some of the lowest level modules in the system design have been further factored during the detailed design. The top level structure of the system remains unchanged. The new modules are:

10. form_course_rec, 13. get_room_index, 16. initialize_PG_reserve, 17. safe_allottment, 18. update_PG_reserve.

6
Coding

The goal of the coding or programming phase is to translate the design of the system produced during the design phase into code in a given programming language which can be executed by a computer, and which performs the computation specified by the design. For a given design, the aim is to implement the design in the best possible manner.

The coding phase affects both testing and maintenance profoundly. As we saw earlier, the time spent in coding is a small percentage of the total software cost, while testing and maintenance consume the major percentage. Thus it should be clear that the goal during coding should *not* be to reduce the implementation cost, but the goal should be to reduce the cost of later phases, even if it means that the cost of this phase has to increase. In other words, the goal during this phase is *not* to simplify the job of the programmer. Rather, the goal should be to simplify the job of the tester and the maintainer.

This distinction is important, as most programmers are individualistic, and are mostly concerned about how to finish their job quickly, without keeping the later phases in mind. During implementation it should be kept in mind that *the programs should not be constructed so that they are easy to write, but that they are easy to read and understand.* A program is read a lot more often, and by a lot more people during the later phases. Often making a program more readable will require extra work by the programmers. For example, sometimes there are "quick fixes" to modify a given code easily, which result in a code which is more difficult to understand. In such cases, in the interest of simplifying the later phases, the easy "quick fixes" should not be adopted.

There are many different criteria for judging a program, including readability, size of the program, execution time, and required memory. In an experiment conducted by Weinberg [Wei71], different programmers were required to implement a program, and were given different goals. It was found that the programs written by different programmers were very different, and each tended to satisfy its goal. For example, the program written by the programmer who was asked to minimize the number of statements indeed had fewer statements than others, but was not easy to understand. This experiment demonstrated that the code produced by a programmer tends to satisfy what the programmer perceives as his goal.

For our purposes ease of understanding and modification should be the basic goals of the programming activity. This means that simplicity and clarity are desirable, while cleverness and complexity are undesirable.

6.1. Programming Practice

As we have said, the primary goal of the coding phase is to translate the given detailed design into source code in a given programming language, such that code is simple, easy to test, and easy to understand and modify. Simplicity and clarity are the properties a programmer should strive for in the programs.

Good programming is a skill that can only be acquired by practice. However, much can be learned from the experience of others, and some general rules and guidelines can be laid for the programmer. Good programming (producing correct and simple programs) is a practice independent of the target programming language, although some well structured languages like Pascal, Ada, and Modula make the job of the programmer simpler. In this section, we will discuss some concepts related to coding in a language-independent manner.

6.1.1. Top-Down and Bottom-Up

The design of a software system consists of a hierarchy of modules. The main program invokes its subordinate modules, which in turn invoke their subordinate modules and so on. Given a design of a system, there are two ways in which the design can be implemented—top-down and bottom-up. In a top-down implementation, the implementation starts from the top of the hierarchy, and then proceeds to the lower levels. First the main module is implemented and then its subordinates are implemented, and then their subordinates, and so on. In a bottom-up implementation, the process is the reverse. The development starts with implementing the modules that are at the bottom of the hierarchy. The implementation proceeds through the higher levels, until it reaches the top.

Top-down and bottom-up implementation should not be confused with top-down and bottom-up design. Here the design is being implemented, and if the design is fairly detailed and complete, its implementation can proceed in either the top-down or the bottom-up manner, even if the design was produced in a top-down manner. Which of the two is used mostly affects testing.

For any large system implementation and testing are done in parts: system components are separately built and tested before they are integrated to form the complete system. Testing can also proceed in a bottom-up or a top-down manner. It is most reasonable to have implementation proceed in a top-down manner if testing is being done in a top-down manner. On the other hand, if bottom-up testing is planned, then bottom-up implementation should be preferred.

For systems where the design is not detailed enough, some of the design decisions have to be made during development. This may be true, for example, when building a prototype. In such cases top-down development may be preferable to aid the design while the implementation is progressing. Many complex systems like operating systems or networking software systems, are organized as layers. In a layered architecture, a layer provides some services to the layers above, which use these services to implement the services that it provides. For a layered architecture, it is generally best for the implementation to proceed in a bottom-up manner.

6.1.2. Structured Programming

Much emphasis is usually placed on structured programming, although the concept and motivation behind structured programming is often not well understood. Structured programming is often regarded as "goto-less programming. Although extensive use of gotos is certainly not desirable, structured programs can be written with the use of gotos as well.

A program has a static structure as well as a dynamic structure. The static structure is the structure of the text of the program which is usually just a linear organization of statements of the program. The dynamic structure of the program is the sequence in which the statements are executed during the program execution. The goal of structured programming is to write a program such that its dynamic structure is the same as its static structure. In other words, the program should be written in a manner such that during execution its control flow is linearized and follows the linear organization of the program text.

Programs in which the statements are executed linearly, as they are organized in the program text, are easier to understand, test, and modify. Since, the program text is organized as a sequence of statements, the close correspondence between execution and text structure makes a program more understandable. However, the main reason why structured programming was promulgated was formal verification of programs. As we will see later in the chapter, during verification a program is considered to be a sequence of executable statements, and verification proceeds step by step, considering one statement in the statement list (the program) at a time. Implied in these verification methods is the assumption that during execution, the statements will be executed in the sequence in which they are organized in the program text. If this assumption is satisfied, the task of verification becomes easier.

Clearly, no meaningful program can be written as a simple sequence of statements without any branching or repetition (which also involves branching). For structured programming, a statement is not a simple assignment statement, but could be a structured statement. The key property is that the statement should have a *single entry and single exit*. That is, during execution, the execution of the statement (or the structured statement) should start from one defined point and the execution should terminate at a single defined point. The most commonly used single entry and single exit statements are:

Selection: if B then S1 else S2
  if B then S1
Iteration: While B do S
  repeat S until B
Sequencing: S1; S2; S3; . . .

It can be shown that these three basic constructs are sufficient to program any conceivable algorithm. Modern languages have other such constructs, like the CASE statement. Often the use of constructs, other than the ones that constitute the theoretically minimal set of constructs to write a program, can simplify the logic of a program (even though they might make formal verification more difficult).

Hence, from a practical point of view, programs should be written such that, as far as possible, single entry, single exit control constructs can be used. The basic goal, as we have tried to emphasize, is to make the logic of the program simple to understand. No hard and fast rule can be formulated that will be applicable under all circumstances. Structured programming practice forms a good basis and guideline for writing programs clearly.

6.1.3. Information Hiding

To reduce coupling between modules of a system it is best that different modules be allowed to access and modify only those data items that are needed by them. The other data items should be "hidden" from such modules and the modules should not be allowed to access these data items. Language and operating system mechanisms should preferably enforce this restriction. Thus modules are given access to data items on a "need to know" basis.

In principle, every module should be allowed to access only some specified data that it requires. This level of information hiding is usually not practical, and most languages do not support this level of access restriction. One form of information hiding that is supported by many modern programming languages is **data abstraction.** We have discussed the concept of data abstraction and abstract data types earlier and have seen that it forms the basis of the object-oriented design approach.

With support for data abstraction, a package or a module is defined which encapsulates the data. Some operations are defined by the module on the encapsulated data. Other modules that are outside this module can only invoke these predefined operations on the encapsulated data. The advantage of this form of data abstraction is that the data is entirely in the control of the module in which the data is encapsulated. Other modules cannot access or modify the data, and the operations that can access and modify are also a part of this module.

Many of the older languages, like Pascal, C, and Fortran do not provide mechanisms to support data abstraction. With such languages data abstraction can be supported only by a disciplined use of the language. That is, the access restrictions will have to be imposed by the programmers; the language does not provide them. For example, to implement a data abstraction of a STACK in Pascal, one method is to define a record containing all the data items needed to implement the STACK, and then define functions and procedures on variables of this type. A possible definition of the record and the interface of the "push" operation is given below.

```
type stk = record
    elts: array [1..100] of integer;
    top: 1..100;
end;
procedure push (var s: stk; i:integer);
```

Note that in implementing information hiding in languages like Pascal, the language does not impose any access restrictions. In the example of the stack above, the structure of a variable s, declared of the type Stk, can be accessed from procedures other than the ones that have been defined for stack. That is why discipline by the programmers is needed to emulate data abstraction. Regardless of whether the language provides constructs for data abstraction or not, it is desirable to support data abstraction in cases where the data and operations on the data are well defined. Data abstraction is one way to increase the clarity of the program, and helps in clean partitioning of the program into pieces that can be separately implemented and understood.

6.1.4. Programming Style

It is impossible to provide an exhaustive list of what to do and what not to do in order to produce a simple and readable code. Being able to do this will amount to providing an algorithm for writing good code. Here we will list some general rules which are usually applicable.

Names: Selecting module and variable names is often not considered of importance by novice programmers. Only when one starts reading programs written by others where the variable names are too cryptic and not representative does one realize the importance of selecting proper names.

Most variables in a program reflect some entity in the problem domain, and the modules reflect some process. Variable names should be closely related to the entity they represent, and module names should reflect their activity. It is bad practice to choose cryptic names (just to avoid typing), or totally unrelated names. It is also bad practice to use the same name for multiple purposes.

Control Constructs: As discussed above, it is desirable that as much as possible single-entry, single-exit constructs should be used. It is also desirable to use a few standard control constructs rather than using a wide variety of constructs, just because they are available in the language.

Gotos: Gotos should be used sparingly and in a disciplined manner (this discussion is not applicable to gotos that are used to support single entry, single exit constructs in languages like Fortran). Only when the alternative to using gotos is more complex should the gotos be used. In any case, alternatives must be thought of before finally using a goto. If a goto must be used, forward transfers (or a jump to a later statement) is more acceptable than a backward jump. Use of gotos for exiting a loop, or for invoking error handlers is quite acceptable (many languages provide separate constructs for these situations, in which case those constructs should be used).

Information Hiding: As discussed above, information hiding should be supported where possible. Only the access functions for the data structures should be made visible, while hiding the data structure behind these functions.

User Defined Types: Modern languages allow the users to define types like the enumerated type. When such facilities are available, they should be exploited where applicable. For example, when working with dates, a type can be defined for the day of the week. In Pascal this is done as follows:

type days = (Mon, Tue, Wed, Thur, Fri, Sat, Sun);
Variables can then be declared of this type. Using such types makes the program much more clear than defining codes for each of the days and then working with codes.

Nesting: The different control constructs, particularly the if-then-else, can be nested. If the nesting becomes too deep, the programs become harder to understand. In case of deeply nested if-then-elses, it is often difficult to determine the if statement to which a particular else clause is associated. Where possible, deep nesting should be avoided, even if it means a little inefficiency. For example, consider the following construct of nested if-then-elses.

```
if C1 then S1
   else if C2 then S2
      else if C3 then S3
         else if C4 then S4;
```

If the different conditions are disjoint (as they often are) then this structure can be converted into the following structure:

    if C1 then S1;
    if C2 then S2;
    if C3 then S3;
    if C4 then S4;

This sequence of statements will produce the same result as the earlier sequence (if the conditions are disjoint), but is much easier to understand. The price is a little inefficiency in that the latter conditions will be evaluated even if a condition evaluates to true, while in the previous case the condition evaluation stops when one evaluates to true. Other such situations can be constructed where alternative program segments can be constructed to avoid a deep level of nesting. In general, if the price is only a little inefficiency, it is more desirable to avoid deep nesting.

Module Size: We have discussed this issue before during system design. A programmer should carefully examine any routine with very few statements (say less than five) or with too many statements (say more than 50). Large modules often will not be functionally cohesive, and too small modules might be incurring unnecessary overhead. There can be no hard and fast rule about module size and the guiding principle should be cohesion and coupling.

Module Interface: A module having a complex interface should be carefully examined. Such modules might not be functionally cohesive and might be implementing multiple functions. As a rule of thumb, any module whose interface has more than five parameters should be carefully examined and broken into multiple modules with a simpler interface, if possible.

Program Layout: How the program is organized and presented can have great effect on the readability of programs. Proper indentation, blank spaces, and parenthesis should be employed to enhance the readability of programs. Automated tools are available to "pretty print" a program, but it is good practice to have a clear layout of programs.

Side Effects: When a module is invoked, it sometimes has side effects of modifying the program state beyond the modification of parameters listed in the module interface definition, for example, modifying global variables. Such side effects should be avoided where possible, and if a module has side effects, they should be properly documented.

Robustness: A program is robust if it does something planned even for exceptional conditions. A program might encounter exceptional conditions in such forms as incorrect input, the incorrect value of some variable, and overflow. A program should try to handle such situations. In general, a program should check for validity of inputs, where possible, and should check for possible overflow of the data structures. If such situations do arise, the program should not just "crash" or "core dump", but should produce some meaningful message and exit gracefully.

6.1.5. Internal Documentation

In the coding phase, the output document is the code itself. However, some amount of internal documentation in the code can be extremely useful in enhancing the understandability of programs. Internal documentation of programs is done by the use of comments. All languages provide means for writing comments in programs. Comments are textual statements that are meant for the program reader and are not executed. Comments, if properly written, and if are kept consistent with the code, can be invaluable during maintenance.

The purpose of comments is not to explain in English the logic of the program—the program itself is the best documentation for the details of the logic. The comments should explain what the code is doing, and not how it is doing it. This means that a comment is not needed for every line of the code, as is often done by novice programmers who are taught the virtues of comments. Comments should be provided for blocks of code, particularly those parts of code which are hard to follow. In most cases only comments for the modules need be provided.

Providing comments for modules is most useful, as modules form the unit of testing, compiling, verification and modification. Comments for a module are often called prologue for the module. It is best to standardize the structure of the prologue of the module. It is desirable if the prologue contains the following information:

1. Module functionality, or what the module is doing.
2. Parameters and their purpose.
3. Assumptions about the inputs, if any.
4. Global variables accessed and/or modified in the module.

An explanation of parameters (whether they are input only, output only or both input and output, why they are needed by the module, and how the parameters are modified) can be quite useful during maintenance. Stating how the global data is affected and what are the side effects of a module is also very useful during maintenance.

In addition to that given above, often other information can be included, depending on the local coding standards. Examples include the name of the author, date of compilation, and the last date of modification.

It should be pointed out that the prologues are useful only if they are kept consistent with the logic of the module. If the module is modified, then the prologue should also be modified, if necessary. A prologue that is inconsistent with the internal logic of the module is probably worse than having no prologue at all.

6.2. Verification

Verification of the output of the coding phase is primarily intended for detecting errors introduced during this phase. That is, the goal of verification of the code produced is to show that the code is consistent with the design it is supposed to implement. It should be pointed out that by verification we do not mean proving correctness of programs, which for our purposes is only *one* method of program verification.

Program verification methods fall into two categories—static and dynamic methods. In dynamic methods the program is executed on some test data, and the outputs of the program are examined to determine if there are any errors present. Hence, dynamic techniques follow the traditional pattern of testing, and the common notion of testing refers to this technique.

Static techniques, on the other hand, do not involve actual program execution on actual numeric data, though it may involve some form of conceptual execution. In static techniques, the program is not compiled and then executed, as is the case in testing. Common forms of static techniques are program verification, code reading, code reviews and walkthroughs, and symbolic execution. In static techniques often the errors are detected directly, unlike dynamic techniques where only the presence of an error is detected. This aspect of static testing makes it quite attractive and economical.

It has been found that the types of errors detected by the two categories of verification techniques are different. The type of errors detected by static techniques are either often not found by testing, or it is more cost effective to detect these errors by static methods. Consequently, testing and static methods are complimentary in nature and both should be employed for reliable software.

6.2.1. Code Reading

Code reading involves careful reading of the code by the programmer to detect any discrepancies between the design specifications and the actual implementation. It involves determining the abstraction of a module and then comparing it with its specifications. The process is just the reverse of design. In design, we start from an abstraction and move towards more details. In code reading we start from the details of a program and move towards an abstract description.

The process of code reading is best done by reading the code inside-out, starting with the inner-most structure of the module. First determine its abstract behavior and specify the abstraction. Then the higher level structure is considered, with the inner structure replaced by its abstraction. This process is continued until we reach the module or the program being read. At that time the abstract behavior of the program/module will be known, which can then be compared to the specifications to determine any discrepancies.

Code reading is very useful and can detect errors often not revealed by testing. Reading in the manner of stepwise-abstraction also forces the programmer to code in a manner conducive to this process, which will lead to well-structured programs. Code reading is sometimes called **desk review.**

6.2.2. Static Analysis

Analysis of programs by methodically analyzing the program text is called static analysis. Static analysis is usually performed mechanically by the aid of software tools. During static analysis the program itself is not executed, but the program text is the input to the tools. The aim of the static analysis tools is to detect errors, potential errors, or generate information about the structure of the program that can be useful for documentation or understanding of the program. Different kinds of static analysis tools can be designed to perform different types of analyses.

Many compilers perform some limited static analysis. More often, tools explicitly for static analysis are used. Static analysis can be very useful for exposing errors that may escape other techniques. As the analysis is performed by the aid of software tools, static analysis is a very cost-effective way of discovering errors. An advantage is that static analysis sometimes detects the errors themselves, not just the presence of errors, as in testing. This saves the effort of tracing the error from the data that reveals the presence of errors. Furthermore, static analysis can also provide "warnings" against potential errors, and can provide insight into the structure of the program. It is also useful for determining violations of local programming standards, which the standard compilers will be unable to detect. Extensive static analysis can considerably reduce the effort later needed during testing.

Data flow analysis [Fos76] is one form of static analysis that concentrates on the use of data by the programs and detects some data flow anomalies. Data flow anomalies are "suspicious" uses of data in a program. In general, data flow anomalies are technically not errors, and can go undetected by the compiler. However, they are often a symptom of some error, caused due to carelessness in typing, or error in coding. At the very least, presence of data flow anomalies implies poor coding. Hence, if a program has data flow anomalies, it is a cause of concern, which should be properly addressed.

An example of the data flow anomaly is the *live variable problem,* in which a variable is assigned some value but then the variable is not used in any later computation. Such a live variable and assignment to the variable are clearly redundant. Another simple example of this is having two assignments to a variable without using the value of the variable between the two assignments. In this case the first assignment is redundant. For example consider the simple case of the code segment shown in Figure 6.1.

Clearly, the first assignment statement is useless. The question is why is that statement in the program? Perhaps the programmer meant to say y : = b in the second statement, and mistyped y as x. In that case, detecting this anomaly and directing the programmer's attention can save considerable amount of effort in testing and debugging.

In addition to revealing anomalies, data flow analysis can provide valuable information for documentation of programs. For example, data flow analysis can provide information about which variables are modified on invoking a procedure in the caller program, and the value of the variables used in the called procedure (this can also be used to make sure that the interface of the procedure is minimum, resulting in lower coupling). This analysis can identify aliasing, which occurs when different variables represent the same data object. This information can be useful during maintenance to ensure that are no undesirable side effects of some modifications being made to a procedure.

Other examples of data flow anomalies are *unreachable code, unused variables,* and *unreferenced labels.* Unreachable code is that part of the code to which there is not a feasible path; there is no possible execution in which it can be executed. Technically this is not an error, and a compiler will at most generate a warning. The program behavior during execution may also be consistent with its specifications. However, often the presence of unreachable code is a sign of lack of proper understanding of the program by the programmer (else why would a programmer leave the unreachable code), which suggests that the presence of error may be likely. Often unreachable code comes into existence when an existing program is modified. In that situation unreachable code may signify undesired or unexpected side effects of the modifications. Unreferenced labels and unused variables are like unreachable code, in that they are technically not errors, but often are symptoms of errors; thus their presence often implies the presence of errors.

Data flow analysis is usually performed by representing a program as a graph, sometimes called the flow graph. The nodes in a flow graph represent statements of a program, while the edges represent control paths from one statement to another. Correspondence between the nodes and

    x : =a;
        :
    x does not appear in the right hand side of any assignment
        :
    x : = b;

FIGURE 6.1. A code segment.

statements is maintained, and the graph is analyzed to determine different relationships between the statements. By use of different algorithms, different kind of anomalies can be detected. Many of the algorithms to detect anomalies can be quite complex and require a lot of processing time. For example, the execution time of algorithms to detect unreachable code increases as the square of the number of nodes in the graph. Consequently, this analysis is often limited to modules, or to a collection of some modules, and is rarely performed on complete systems.

To reduce processing times of algorithms the search of a flow graph has to be carefully organized. Another way to reduce the time for executing algorithms is to reduce the size of the flow graph. Flow graphs can get extremely large for large programs, and transformations are often performed on the flow graph to reduce its size. The most common transformation is to have each node represent a sequence of contiguous statements that have no branches in them, thus representing a block of code that will be executed together. Another transformation often done is to have each node represent a procedure/function. In that case the resulting graph is often called the all graph, in which an edge from one node n to another node m represents the fact that the the execution of the module represented by n directly invokes the module m.

OTHER USES OF STATIC ANALYSIS

We have seen that data flow analysis is a technique for statically analyzing a program to reveal some types of anomalies. Other forms of static analysis to detect different errors/anomalies can also be performed. Here we list some of the other common uses of static analysis tools.

An error often made, especially when different teams are developing different parts of the software, is mismatched parameter lists, where the argument list of a module invocation is different in number or type from the parameters of the invoked module. This can be detected by a compiler if no separate compilation is allowed and the entire program text is available to the compiler (as is the case with standard Pascal). However, if the programs are separately developed and compiled, which is almost always the case with large software developments, this error will not be detected. A static analyzer with access to the different parts of the program can easily detect this error. Such kind of error can also be detected during code reviews, but it is more economical to do it mechanically. An extension of this is to detect calls to nonexistent program modules. Essentially, the interfacing of different modules, developed and compiled separately, can be checked for mutual consistency easily through static analysis. In some limited cases static analysis can also detect infinite loops, or potentially infinite loops, and illegal recursion (e.g., no termination condition for recursion).

There are different kinds of documents that static analyzers can produce, which can be useful for maintenance or for increased understanding of the program. The first is the cross reference of where different variables and constants are used. Often looking at the cross reference one can detect some subtle errors, like many constants defined (with perhaps somewhat different values) to represent the same entity. For example, the value of pi could be defined as constant in different routines with slightly values. A report with cross references can be useful for detecting such errors. To reduce the size of such reports, it is perhaps more useful to limit it to the use of constants and global variables.

Information about the frequency of use of different constructs of the programming language can also be obtained by static analysis. Such information is useful for statistical analyses of programs, such as what types of modules are more prone to defect. Another use is to evaluate the complexity. There are some complexity measures that are a function of the frequency of occurrence of different types of statements. To determine complexity from such measures, this information can be useful.

Static analysis can also produce the structure chart of programs. The actual structure chart of a system is a useful documentation aid. It can also be used to determine the changes made in the design during the coding phase by comparing it to the structure chart produced during system design. A static nesting hierarchy of procedures can also be easily produced by static analysis.

There are some coding restrictions that the programming language imposes. However, different organizations may have further restrictions on the use of different language features for reliability, portability or efficiency reasons. Examples of these include mixed type arithmetic, type conversion, using features that are machine-dependent, and too many gotos. Such restrictions cannot be checked by the compiler, but static analysis can be used to enforce these standards. Such violations can also be checked in code review, but it is more efficient and economical to let a program do this checking.

6.2.3. Symbolic Execution

In the last section we considered techniques in which the program text is scanned to determine possible errors. In this section we consider another approach where the program is not executed with actual data. Instead, the program is "symbolically executed" with symbolic data. Hence the inputs to the program are not numbers but symbols representing the input data, which can take different values. The execution of the program proceeds like normal execution, except that it deals with values that are not numbers but formulas consisting of the symbolic input values. The outputs are symbolic formulas of input values. These formulas can be checked to see if the program will behave as expected. This approach is called by different names like symbolic execution, and symbolic evaluation, and symbolic testing [Che79, Cla76, How77, Kin76].

```
1. function product (x, y, z: integer): integer;
2. var tmp1, tmp2: integer;
3. begin
4.    tmp1 : = x * y;
5.    tmp2 : = y * z;
6.    product : = tmp1*tmp2/y;
7. end;
```

FIGURE 6.2. Function to determine product.

Although the concept is simple and promising for verifying programs, we will see that performing symbolic execution of even modest size programs is very difficult. The problems basically come due to the conditional execution of statements in programs. As conditions of a symbolic expression cannot be usually evaluated to true or false, without substituting actual values to the symbols, a case by case analysis becomes necessary, and all possible cases with a condition have to be considered. In programs with loops this can result in an unmanageably large number of cases.

To introduce the basic concepts of symbolic execution, let us first consider a simple program without any conditional statement. A simple program to compute the product of three positive integers is shown in Figure 6.2.

Let us consider that the symbolic inputs to the function are x_i, y_i, and z_i. We start executing this function with these inputs. The aim is to determine the symbolic values of different variables in the program after "executing" each statement, such that eventually we can determine the result of executing this function. The trace of the symbolic execution of the function is shown in Figure 6.3.

After statement 6 the value of the product is $(x_i * y_i *) * (y_i * z_i)/y_i$. Since this is a symbolic value, we can simplify this formula. Simplification yields product $= x_i * y_i^2 d * z_i/y_i = x_i * y_i * z_i$, the desired result. In this simple example, there is only one path in the function and this symbolic execution is equivalent to checking for all possible values of x, y and z. (Note that the implied assumption is that input values are such that the machine will be able to perform the product and no overflow will occur.) Essentially, with only one path and having an acceptable symbolic result of the path, we can claim that the program is correct.

After statement	x	y	z	Values of the variables		
				tmp1	tmp2	product
1	x_i	y_i	z_i	?	?	?
4	x_i	y_i	z_i	$x_i * y_i$	?	?
5	x_i	y_i	z_i	$x_i * y_i$	$y_i * z_i$	?
6	x_i	y_i	z_i	$x_i * y_i$	$y_i * z_i$	$(x_i * y_i) * (y_i * z_i)/y_i$

FIGURE 6.3. Symbolic execution of the function product.

PATH CONDITIONS

In symbolic execution, when dealing with conditional execution, it is not sufficient to just look at the state of the variables of the program at different statements, as a statement will only be executed if the inputs satisfy certain conditions in which the execution of the program will follow a path which includes the statement. To capture this concept in symbolic execution, we require a notion of "path condition". Path condition at a statement gives the conditions which the inputs must satisfy in order for an execution to follow the path such that the statement will be executed.

Path condition is a Boolean expression over the symbolic inputs, and never contains any program variables. It will be represented in a symbolic execution by pc. Each symbolic execution begins with pc initialized to true. As conditions are encountered, for different cases referring to different paths in the program, the path condition will take different values. For example, symbolic execution of an IF statement of the form

$$\text{if } C \text{ then } S1 \text{ else } S2$$

will require two cases to be considered, corresponding to the two possible paths; one where C evaluates to true and S1 is executed, and the other where C evaluates to false and S2 is executed. For the first case we set the path condition pc to

$$pc \longleftarrow pc \ \& \ C$$

which is the path condition for the statements in S1. For the second case we set the path condition to

$$pc \longleftarrow pc \ \& \ {\sim}C$$

which is the path condition for statements in S2.

On encountering the IF statement, symbolic execution is is said to fork into two executions: one following the then part, the other following the else part. Both these paths are independently executed, with their respective path conditions. However, if at any IF statement we can shown that pc implies C or ${\sim}$C, then we do not need to follow both the paths, and only the relevant path need be executed. Such an IF statement is a nonforking conditional statement, as compared to the former case which is a forking conditional statement.

Let us consider an example involving IF statements. In Figure 6.4, we give a program to determine the maximum of three numbers.

The trace of the symbolic execution of this program is shown in Figure 6.5. As before we assume that the symbolic inputs of the variables x, y, and z are xi, yi and zi, respectively.

Notice how at each IF statement, the symbolic execution forked into two cases, each case having a different path condition. There are a total of four paths in this symbolic execution. We can see that for each path, the

1. **function** max (x, y, x: integer): integer;
2. **begin**
3.   **if** x ≤ y **then**
4.   max : = y
5.   **else**
6.   max : = x;
7.   **if** max < z **then**
8.   max : = z;
9. **end;**

FIGURE 6.4. The code for function max.

value returned is consistent with the specifications of the program. For example, when the inputs satisfy the condition $z_i > x_i > y_i$, the value z_i is the maximum, which is what is returned in symbolic execution. Similarly, we can check other paths as well.

LOOPS AND SYMBOLIC EXECUTION TREES

The different paths followed during symbolic execution can be represented by an "execution tree". A node in this tree represents the execution of a statement, while an arc represents the transition from one statement to another. For each IF statement where both the paths are followed, there are two arcs from the node corresponding to the IF statement, one labeled with T (true) and the other with F (false), for the then and the else paths. At each branching the path condition is also often shown in the tree. Note that the execution tree is different from the flow graph of a program, where nodes represent a statement, while in the execution tree nodes represent

```
Stmt      pc          max
1   true              ?
Case (x > y)
2.  (xi > yi)         ?
3.     –              xi
   case (max < z)
4.  (xi > yi) & (xi < zi)zi
       return this value of max
   case (max ≥ z)
4.  (xi > yi) & (xi ≤ zi)xi
       return this value of max
```
Case (x ≤ y)
    Similar to the above.

FIGURE 6.5. Symbolic execution of the function max.

the execution of a statement. The execution tree of the program discussed above is shown in Figure 6.6.

The execution tree of a program has some interesting properties. Each leaf in the tree represents a path that will be followed for some input values. For each terminal leaf there exists some actual numerical inputs such that the sequence of statements executed with these inputs is the same as the sequence of statements in the path from the root of the tree to the leaf. An additional property of the symbolic execution tree is that path conditions associated with two different leaves are distinct. Thus there is no execution for which both path conditions are true. This is due to the property of sequential programming languages that in one execution we cannot follow two different paths.

If the symbolic output at each leaf in the tree is correct, then it is equivalent to saying that the program is correct. Hence, if we can consider all paths, the correctness of the program can be established by symbolic execution. However, even for modest size programs the tree can be infinite. The infinite trees result from the presence of loops in the programs.

Because of the presence of infinite execution trees, symbolic execution should not be considered as a tool for proving correctness of programs. A program to perform symbolic execution may not stop. For this reason, a more practical approach is to build tools where only some of the paths are symbolically executed, and the user can select the paths to be executed. One must selectively execute some paths, as all cannot be executed.

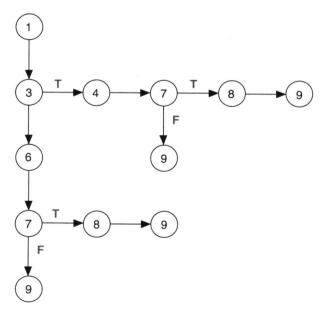

FIGURE 6.6. Execution tree for the function max.

A symbolic execution tool can also be useful in selecting testcases to obtain branch or statement coverage (discussed in the next chapter). Suppose that results of testing reveal that a certain path has not been executed, and it is desired to test that path. In order to execute a particular path, input test data has to be carefully selected to ensure that the given path is indeed executed. Selecting such testcases can often be quite difficult. A symbolic execution tool can be useful here. By symbolically executing that particular path, the path condition for the leaf node for that path can be determined. The input test data can then be selected using this path condition. The testcase data that will execute the path are the ones that satisfy the path condition.

6.2.4. Proving Correctness

Many techniques for verification aim to reveal errors in the programs, since the ultimate goal of making programs correct by removing the errors. In proof of correctness, the aim is to prove a program correct. So, correctness is directly established, unlike the other techniques in which correctness is never really established, but implied (and hoped) by the absence of detection of any errors. Proofs are perhaps more valuable during program construction, rather than an after thought. Proving while developing a program may result in more reliable programs, that of course can be proved more easily. Proving a program not constructed with formal verification in mind can be quite difficult.

Any proof technique must begin with a formal specification of the program. No formal proof can be provided if what we have to prove is not stated or is stated informally in an imprecise manner. So, first we have to state formally what the program is supposed to do. A program will usually not operate on an arbitrary set of input data, and may produce valid results only for some range of inputs. Hence, often it is not sufficient merely to state the goal of the program, but we should also state the input conditions in which the program is to be invoked and for which the program is expected to produce valid results. The assertion about the expected final state of a program is called the *postcondition* of that program, and the assertion about the input condition is called the *precondition* of the program. Often determining the precondition for which the postcondition will be satisfied is the goal of proof. Here we will briefly describe a technique for proving correctness called the axiomatic method, which was proposed by Hoare [Hoa69]. It is often also called Floyd-Hoare proof method, as it is based on Floyd's inductive assertion technique.

In principle, all the properties of a program can be determined statically from the text of the program, without actually executing the program. The first requirement in reasoning about programs is to state formally the properties of the elementary operations and statements that the program employs. In the axiomatic model, the goal is to take the program and construct a sequence of assertions, each of which can be inferred from previously proved assertions and the rules and axioms about the statements and operations in the program. For this we need a mathematical model of a program and all the constructs in the programming language. Using Hoare's notation, the basic assertion about a program segment is of the form

$$P \{S\} Q.$$

The interpretation of this is that if assertion P is true before executing S, then assertion Q will be true after executing S, if the execution of S terminates. Assertion P is the precondition of the program and Q is the postcondition. These assertions are about the values taken by the variables in the program before and after execution of the program. The assertions generally do not specify a particular value for the variables, but specify the general properties of the values and the relationship among them.

To prove a theorem of the form P{S}Q, we need some rules and axioms about the programming language in which the program segment S is written. Here we consider a simple programming language, which deals only with integers and has the following types of statements: 1) assignment, 2) conditional statement, and 3) an iterative statement. A program is considered to be a sequence of statements. We will now discuss the rules and axioms for these statements such that we can combine them to prove the correctness of programs.

Axiom of assignment: Assignments are central to procedural languages. In our language no state change can be accomplished without the assignment statement. The axiom of assignment is also central to the axiomatic approach. In fact, only for the assignment statement do we have an independent axiom; for the rest of the statements we have rules. Consider the assignment statement of the form

$$x : = f$$

where x is an identifier, and f is an expression in the programming language without any side effects. Any assertion which is true about x after the assignment, must be true of the expression f before the assignment. In other words, since after the assignment the variable x contains the value computed by the expression f, if a condition is true after the assignment is made, then the condition obtained by replacing x by f must be true before the assignment. This is the essence of the axiom of assignment. The axiom is stated below.

$$P_f^x \{ x : = f \} P$$

P is the postcondition of the program segment containing only the assignment statement. The precondition is P_f^x, which is an assertion obtained by substituting f for all occurrences of x in the assertion P. In other words if P_f^x is true before the assignment statement, P will be true after the assignment.

This is the only axiom we have in Hoare's axiomatic model, besides the standard axioms about the mathematical operators employed in the language (such as commutativity and associativity of the + operator). The reason that we have only one axiom for the assignment statement is that this is the only statement in our language that has any effect on the state of the system, and we need an axiom to define what the effect of such a statement is. The other language constructs like alternation and iteration are for flow control, to determine which assignment statements will be executed. For such statements rules of inference are provided.

Rule of Composition: Let us first consider the rule for sequential composition, where two statements S1 and S2 are executed in sequence. This rule is called *rule of composition,* and is shown below.

$$\frac{P\{S1\}Q, Q\{S2\}\ R}{P\{S1;S2\}\ R}$$

The explanation of this notation is that if what is stated in the numerator can be proved, then the denominator can be inferred. Using this rule, if we can prove P{S1}Q and Q{S2}R then we can claim that if before execution the precondition P holds, then after execution of the program segment S1;S2 the postcondition R will hold. In other words, to prove P{S1;S2}R, we have to find some Q and prove that P{S1}Q and Q{S2}R.

Rule for Alternate Statement: Let us now consider the rules for an if statement. There are two types of if statement, one with an else clause and one without. The rules for both of them are given below.

$$\frac{P\&B\{S\}Q, P\&\sim B \Rightarrow Q}{P\{\text{if } B \text{ then } S\}\ Q}$$

$$\frac{P\&B\{S1\}\ Q, P\&B\{S2\}\ Q}{P\{\text{if } B \text{ then } S1 \text{ else } S2\}\ Q}$$

Let us consider the if-then-else statement. We want to prove a post condition for this statement. However, depending on the evaluation of B, two different statements can be executed. In both cases the postcondition must be satisfied. Hence if we can show that starting in the state where P&B is true and executing S1, or starting in a state where P&B̃ is true and executing the statement S2, both lead to the post condition Q, then the following can be inferred: if the if-then-else statement is executed with precondition P, the postcondition Q will hold after execution of the statement.

Rules of Consequence: To be able to prove new theorems from the ones we have already proved using the axioms, we require some rules of inference. The simplest inference rule is that if the execution of a program ensures that an assertion Q is true after execution, then it also ensures that every assertion that is logically implied by Q is also true after execution. Similarly, if a precondition ensures that a postcondition is true after execution of a program, then every condition that logically implies the precondition, will also ensure that the postcondition holds after execution of the program. These are called *rules of consequence,* and are formally stated below.

$$\frac{P\{S\}\ R, R \Rightarrow Q}{P\{S\}\ Q} \qquad \frac{P \Rightarrow R, R\{S\}\ Q}{P\{S\}\ Q}$$

Rule of Iteration: Now let us consider iteration. Loops are the trickiest construct when dealing with program proofs. We will consider only the while loop of the form

while B do S.

In executing this loop first the condition B is checked. If B is false S is not executed and the loop terminates. If B is true S is executed and B is tested again. This is repeated until B evaluates to false. We would like to be able to make an assertion that will be true when the loop terminates. Let this assertion be P. As we do not know how many times the loop will be executed, it is easier to have an assertion that will hold true irrespective of how many times the loop body is executed. In that case P will hold true after every execution of statement S, and will be true before every execution of S, since the condition that holds true after an execution of S will be the condition for the next execution of S (if S is executed again). Furthermore, we know that the condition B is false when the loop terminates. These properties have been used in the rule for iteration shown below.

$$\frac{P\&B\{S\}\ P}{P\{while\ B\ do\ S\}\ P\&{\sim}B}$$

As the condition P is unchanging with the execution of the statements in the loop body, it is called the **loop invariant.** Finding loop invariants is the thorniest problem in constructing proofs of correctness. One method for getting the loop invariant which often works is to extract ~B from the postcondition of the loop, and try the remaining assertion as the loop invariant. Another method is to try replacing the variable that binds the loop execution with the loop counter. Thus if the loop has a counter i, which goes from 0 to n, and if the postcondition of the loop contains n, then replace n by i, and try the assertion as a loop invariant.

AN EXAMPLE

Although in a theorem of the form P {S} Q, we say that if P is true at the start and the execution of S terminates, Q will be true after executing S, to prove a theorem of this sort we work backwards. That is, we do not start with the precondition and work our way to the end of the program to

(* Remainder of x/y *)
1. **begin**
2.   q : = 0;
3.   r : = x;
4.   **while** r > = y **do**
5.   **begin**
6.   r : = r − y ;
7.   q : = q + 1 ;
8.   **end;**
9. **end.**

FIGURE 6.7. Program to determine the remainder.

determine the postcondition. Instead we start with the postcondition, and work our way back to the start of the program, and determine the precondition. We use the axiom of assignment and other rules to determine the precondition of a statement, for a given postcondition. If the precondition we obtain by doing this is implied by P, then by rules of consequence we can say that P {S} Q is a theorem. Let us consider a simple example of determining the remainder in integer division, by repeated subtraction. The program is shown in Figure 6.7.

The precondition and postcondition of this program are given as

$$P = \{x \geq 0 \ \& \ y > 0\}$$
$$Q = \{x = qy + r \ \& \ 0 \leq r < y\}$$

We have to prove that P {Program} Q is a theorem. We start with Q. The first statement before the end of the program is the loop. We invent the loop invariant by removing ˜B from the Q, which is also the output assertion of the loop. For this we factor Q into a form like I & B, then choose I as the invariant. For this program we have ˜B = $\{r < y\}$. We have Q = $\{x = qy + r \ \& \ 0 \leq r \ \& \ r < y\}$, hence the invariant I is $\{x = qy + r \ \& \ 0 \leq r\}$.

Proof of the loop:
Starting with I, we use the assignment axiom, and the condition before statement 7 is

$$x = (q + 1)y + r \ \& \ 0 \leq r \ \{q: = q + 1\} \ I$$

Using assignment axiom for statement 6, we get

$$x = (q + 1)y + (r - y) \ \& \ 0 \leq (r - y)$$
$$\{r: = r - y\} \ x = (q + 1)y + r \ \& \ 0 \leq r$$

Using rule of composition we get,

$$x = (q + 1)y +(r - y) \ \& \ 0 \leq (r - y) \ \{r: = r - y; q: = q + 1\} \ I$$
$$x = qy + r \ \& \ 0 \leq r - y \ \{r: = r - y; q: = q + 1\} \ I$$

Since

$$I \ \& \ r \geq y \ x = qy + r \ \& \ 0 \leq r - y$$

by rule of consequence we get

$$I \ \& \ r \leq y \ \{r: \ = r - y; \ q: \ = q + 1\} \ I$$

Using now the rule for the while loop, we have

$$I \ \{\text{while loop in program}\} \ I \ \tilde{\&} \ (r \geq y)$$

where I is

$$x = qy + r \ \& \ 0 \leq r$$

Now let us consider the loop initialization. We can show

$$x = qy + x \ \& \ 0 \leq x \ \{r: \ = x\} \ I$$
$$x = 0y + x \ \& \ 0 \leq x \ \{q: \ = 0\} \ x = qy + x \ \& \ 0 \leq x$$

The precondition is

$$(x = x \ \& \ 0 \leq x) \Rightarrow (0 \leq x)$$

By composition,

$$0 \leq x \ \{q: \ = 0; \ r: \ = x\} \ I$$

Composing the loop with the intialization, we get $0 \leq x$ {the entire program} $I \ \& \ B$. Since $(I \ \& \ B)$ is the postcondition Q of the program, and $0 \leq x$ is the precondition, we have proved the program to be correct.

DISCUSSION

In the axiomatic method, to prove P{S}Q, we assume that S will terminate. So, by proving that the program will produce the desired postcondition using the axiomatic method, we are essentially saying that *if* the program terminates, it will provide the desired postcondition. The axiomatic proof technique cannot prove whether a program terminates or not. For this reason, the proof using the axiomatic technique is called the proof of *partial correctness*.

This is in contrast to the proof of *total correctness,* where termination of a program is also proved. Termination of programs is of considerable interest, for obvious reason of avoiding infinite loops. With the axiomatic method, additional techniques have to be used to prove termination. One common method is to define a well-ordered set which has a smallest member, and then add an expression to the assertions, that produces a value in the set. If after an execution of the loop body, it can be shown that the value of the expression is less than it was on the entry, then the loop must terminate. There are other methods of proving correctness that aim to prove total correctness.

Proofs of correctness have obvious theoretical appeal and a considerable body of literature exists in the area. Despite this, the practical use of these formal methods of verification has been limited. In the software development industry proving correctness is not generally used as a means for verification. If employed, their use is limited to proving correctness of some critical modules.

There are many reasons for the lack of general use of formal verification. Constructing proofs is quite hard and even for relatively modest problems, proofs can be quite large and difficult to comprehend. As much of the work must be done manually (even if theorem provers are available), the techniques are open to clerical errors. In addition, the proof methods are usually limited to proving correctness of single modules. When procedures and functions are employed, constructing proofs of correctness becomes extremely hard. In essence, the technique of proving correctness does not scale up very well to large programs. Despite these shortcomings, proof techniques offer an attractive formal means for verification and hold promise for the future.

6.2.5. Code Reviews and Walkthroughs

The review process was started with the purpose of detecting defects in the code. Though design reviews substantially reduce defects in code, reviews are still very useful and can considerably enhance reliability and reduce effort during testing. Code reviews are designed to detect defects that originate during the coding process, although they can detect defects in detailed design also. However, it is unlikely that code reviews will reveal errors in system design or requirements.

Code reviews are usually held after code has been successfully completed, and other forms of static tools have been applied, but before any testing has been performed. Therefore, activities like code reading, symbolic execution, and static analysis should be performed, and defects found by these techniques corrected, before code reviews are held. The main motivation for this is to save human time and effort which would otherwise be spent in detecting errors that a compiler or a static analyzer can detect. The entry criteria for code review is that the code must compile successfully, and has been "passed" by other static analysis tools.

The documentation to be distributed includes the code to be reviewed and the design document. The review team for code reviews should include the programmer, the designer, and the tester. As with any review, the review starts with the preparation for the review, and ends with a list of action items.

The aim of reviews is to detect defects in the code. An obvious coding defect is that the code fails to implement the design. This can occur in many ways. The function implemented by a module may be different from the function actually defined in the design, or the interface of the modules may not be the same as the interface specified in the design. In addition, the input-output format assumed by a module may be inconsistent with the format specified in the design.

Other code defects can be divided into two broad categories: logic and control, and data operations and computations. Some examples of logic and control defects are infinite loops, unreachable code, incorrect predicate, missing or unreferenced labels, and improper nesting of loops and branches. Example of defects in computation and data operations are missing validity tests for external data, incorrect access of array components, improper initialization, and the misuse of variables.

In addition to defects, there is the quality issue, which the review also addresses. The first is efficiency. A module may be implemented in an obviously inefficient manner, and could be wasteful of memory of the computer time. The code could also be violating the local coding standards. Although non-adherence with coding standards cannot be classified as a defect, it is desirable to maintain the standard. Standards can have restrictions on annotations, internal documentation, use of global variables, use of recursion, naming of variables, maximum nesting of loops, and alternative constructs.

A Sample Checklist: The following are some of the items that can be included in a checklist for code reviews [Dunn84].

Do data definitions exploit the typing capabilities of the language?
Do all the pointers point to some object? (Are there any "dangling pointers"?)
Are the pointers set to NULL, where needed?
Are all the array indexes within bound?
Are indexes properly initialized?
Are all the branch conditions correct (not too weak or too strong)?
Will a loop always terminate (no infinite loops?)
Is the loop termination condition correct?
Is the number of loop executions "off by one"?
Where applicable, are the divisors tested for zero?
Are imported data tested for validity?
Do actual and formal interface parameters match?
Are all variables used? Are all output variables assigned?
Can statements placed in the loop be placed outside the loop?
Are the labels unreferenced?
Will the requirements of execution time be met?
Are the local coding standards met?

6.2.6. Unit Testing

All the methods discussed above are static methods in that the program is not compiled and executed. The program text was the input to these techniques and the text was evaluated and analyzed manually or by the aid of tools. Even symbolic execution is a static method where the program text is "executed". In fact, symbolic execution could be done manually; the use of a symbolic execution tool is essentially to eliminate the potentially cumbersome manual procedure.

In contrast to these methods, unit testing is a dynamic method for verification, where the program is actually compiled and executed. It is one of the most widely used methods, and the coding phase is sometimes called "coding and unit testing phase". As in other forms of testing, unit testing involves executing the code with some testcases and then evaluating the results.

The goal of unit testing is to test modules or "units and not the entire software system. Other levels of testing are used for testing the system. Unit testing is most often done by the programmer himself. The programmer, after finishing the coding of a module, tests it with some test data. The tested module is then delivered for system integration and further testing.

Testing of modules or software systems is a difficult and challenging task. Selection of test cases, and deciding how much testing is enough are two important aspects of testing. Unit testing is dealt with in the next chapter, after the fundamentals of testing and the selection of test cases has been discussed.

6.3. Metrics

Traditionally, the work on metrics has focused on the final product, namely the code. In a sense, all metrics for intermediate products of requirements and design are used basically to ensure that the final product has a high quality and the productivity of the project stays high. That is, the basic goal of metrics for intermediate products is to predict or get some idea about the metrics of the final product.

For the code, the most commonly used metrics are that of size, complexity, and reliability. We will discuss reliability with testing as most reliability models use test data to assess reliability.

6.3.1. Size Measures

Size of a product is a simple measure, which can be easy to calculate. It is a reasonable indicator of the total effort for the project. Size measures are used for cost estimation of future projects, comparison of products, and for determining productivity. Although size is an important measure for determining productivity, complexity and reliability of the product also have a strong impact on productivity.

The most common measure of size is delivered lines of source code, or the number of lines of code (LOC) that is finally delivered. The trouble with LOC is that the lines of code for a project depend heavily on the language employed. For example, a program written in assembly language will show a large size as compared to the same program written in a higher level language, if LOC is used as a size measure. Even for the same language, the size can vary considerably depending on the programmer and other factors. What forms a line in determining the size is also not universally accepted, and depends on the use of the size measure. For example, if we are interested in size for determining the total effort, then it is reasonable to include comment and data lines also. On the other hand, if we are interested in function size, it would be better to include only the executable statements. Despite these deficiencies, LOC remains a handy and reasonable size measure which is used extensively.

Halstead [Hal77] has proposed metrics for length and volume of a program based on the number of operators and operands. In a program we define the following measurable quantities:

n_1 is the number of distinct operators
n_2 is the number of distinct operands
$f_{1,j}$ is the number of occurrences of the jth most frequent operator
$f_{2,j}$ is the number of occurrences of the jth most frequent operand.

Then the vocabulary n of a program is defined as

$$n = n_1 + n_2.$$

With the above measurable parameters, two new parameters are defined:

$$N_1 = \Sigma f_{1,j}, N_2 = \Sigma f_{2,j}.$$

N_1 is the total occurrences of different operators in the program, and N_2 is the total occurrences of different operands. The length of the program is defined as

$$N = N_1 + N_2.$$

From the length and the vocabulary, the volume V of the program is defined as

$$V = N \log_2 n.$$

This definition of the volume of a program represents the minimum number of bits necessary to represent the program. $\log_2 n$ is the number of bits needed to represent every element in the program uniquely, and N is the total occurrences of the different elements. Volume is used as a size metric for a program.

The length of the program can also be approximated by the following expression consisting of only n_1 and n_2.

$$N \approx n_1 \log_2 n_1 + n_2 \log_2 n_2$$

This expression actually represents the number of bits necessary to uniquely represent the different operators and operands that exist in the program at least once.

6.3.2. Complexity Analysis

The productivity, if measured only in terms of lines of code per unit time, can vary a lot depending on the complexity of the system to be developed. Clearly, a programmer will produce a lesser amount of code for highly complex systems programs, as compared to a simple application program. Similarly, complexity has great impact on the cost of maintaining a program. In order to quantify complexity beyond the fuzzy notion of the ease with which a program can be constructed or comprehended, some metrics to measure the complexity of a program are needed.

Some metrics for complexity were discussed in the last chapter. The same metrics that are applicable to detailed design can be applied to code. One such complexity measure discussed in the previous chapter is *cyclomatic complexity*. In cyclomatic complexity, complexity of a module is the number of independent cycles in the flow graph of the module. A number of metrics have been proposed for quantifying the complexity of a program [Har82], and studies have been done to corelate the complexity with maintenance effort. Here we discuss a few more complexity measures. Most of these have been proposed in the context of programs, but can be applied or adapted for detailed design as well.

EXTENSION TO CYCLOMATIC COMPLEXITY

The cyclomatic complexity measure proposed by McCabe considers each decision in the program as a single unit (in the flow graph, one node is created for each condition). With this, the cyclomatic complexity is the same as (under some conditions) the number of decisions plus one. Myers [Mye77] has extended the notion of cyclomatic complexity noting that decisions with multiple conditions (combined together into a predicate by Boolean operators) are typically more complex than decisions with one condition. In this extension, complexity is measured as an interval rather than a single value. The lower bound of the interval is the number of decisions plus one, or the cyclomatic complexity of the program. The upper bound of the interval is the number of individual conditions plus one. Specifying the complexity as an interval accounts for both the decisions and the conditions in a program.

HALSTEAD'S MEASURE

Halstead also proposed a complexity measure (actually an effort measure) based on his software science [Hal77]. Above, a number of variables are defined. These are n1 (number of unique operators), n2 (number of unique operands), N1 (total frequency of operators), and N2 (total frequency of operands). Based on these the effort E is defined as

$$E = \frac{n1 \ N2(N1 + N2) \log_2(n1 + n2)}{2 \ n2}$$

Halstead's complexity measure focused on the internal complexity of a module, as does McCabe's complexity measure. Thus the complexity of the module's connection with its environment is not given much importance. In Halstead's measure, a module's connection with its environment is reflected in terms of operands and operators. A call to another module is considered an operator, and all the parameters are considered as operands of this operator.

LIVE VARIABLES

In a computer program, a typical assignment statement uses and modifies only a few variables. However, in general the statements have a much larger context. That is, in order to construct or understand a statement, a programmer must keep track of a number of variables other than those directly employed in the statement. For a statement such data items are called *live variables*. Intuitively, the more the number of live variables for statements, the harder it will be to understand a program. Hence, the concept of live variables can be used as a metric for program complexity.

First let us define live variables more precisely. A variable is considered live from its first to its last reference within a module, including all statements between the first and the last statement where the variable is referenced. Using this definition, the set of live variables for each statement can be computed easily by analysis of the module's code. The procedure of determining the live variables can easily be automated.

For a statement the number of live variables represents the degree of difficulty of the statement. This notion can be extended to the entire module by defining the average number of live variables. The average number of live variables is the sum of the count of live variables (for all executable statements) divided by the number of executable statements. This is a complexity measure for the module.

Live variables are defined from the point of view of data usage. The logic of a module is not explicitly included. The logic is used only to determine the first and last statement of reference for a variable. Hence, this concept of complexity is quite different from cyclomatic complexity, which is based entirely on logic and considers data as secondary.

KNOT COUNT

A method for quantifying complexity, based on the locations of the control transfers of the program was proposed by Woodward, Hennel and Hedley

[Woo79]. It was designed largely for Fortran programs where explicit transfer of control is shown by the use of goto statements. A programmer, to understand a given program, typically draws arrows from the point of control transfer to its destination, helping create a mental picture of the program and the control transfers in it. According to this metric, the more intertwined these arrows become, the more complex the program. This notion is captured in the concept of a "knot".

A "knot" is essentially the intersection of two such control transfer arrows. If each statement in the program is written on a separate line, this notion can be formalized as follows. A jump from line a to line b is represented by the pair (a , b). Two jumps (a, b) and (p, q) give rise to a knot if either min (a, b) < min (p, q) < max (a, b) and max (p, q) > max (a, b); or min (a, b) < max (p, qa) < max (a, b) and min (p, q) < min (a, b).

Problems can arise while determining the knot count of programs using structured constructs. One method is to convert such a program into one that explicitly shows control transfers, and then compute the knot count. The basic scheme can be generalized to flow graphs, though with flow graphs only bounds can be obtained.

TOPOLOGICAL COMPLEXITY

Chen [Che78] has proposed a complexity measure that is sensitive to the nesting of structures. Like cyclomatic complexity, it is based on the flow graph of a module or a program. The complexity of a program is considered to be its maximal intersect number *min*.

To compute the maximal intersect, a flow graph is converted into a strongly connected graph (by drawing an arrow from the terminal node to the initial node). A strongly connected graph divides the graph into a finite number of regions. The number of regions is (edges − nodes + 2). If we draw a line which enters each region exactly once, then the number of times this line intersects the arcs in the graph is the maximal intersect *min*, which is taken to be the complexity of the program.

6.4. Monitoring and Control

Configuration Control: Coding and testing phases usually involve the maximum number of people. Different programmers are responsible for coding different parts of the design. These parts are supposed to fit together to form the complete software system. In general, the programs being written by a programmer will depend on the programs being written by other programmers. This is one of the reasons why configuration control is needed. Though configuration control is a general concept applicable to earlier phases as well, it is most often applied to the coding phase.

Essentially, configuration control methods aim to ensure that changes in the overall configuration of the software are controlled. This disallows "change-at-will" by programmers, even of the modules they have coded. Once a software is "baselined", changes to it must be reviewed and approved.

The most common method is to have a library of software modules and a configuration control board. Once the programmer has coded and tested its module, he can check it in the library. Once in the library, others can use the module in any manner. Also, once in the library, the programmer cannot modify his own modules without permission. A request to the configuration control board is made if a change to any module in the library is desired. The configuration control board reviews the request and then approves or disapproves it. If a change is approved, appropriate actions are taken to inform other programmers about the change.

Monitoring the *frequency of change requests* by the programmers to the control board and the nature of requests gives valuable information regarding the stability of design and the quality of the programs being written. If frequent change requests are made to change the internal logic of a module, correcting or enhancing the code produced during the coding phase, it might signify the inadequacy of the verification methods (such as unit testing and code review) being employed. In such a situation, actions might be taken to tighten up reviews and testing. If, on the other hand, frequent requests come due to the design, it might mean that the design was not done properly, and it might be appropriate to stop code development and have another review of the design.

Module History: During the coding phase the modules are coded and verified separately. Data about development of each module is useful in identifying potentially troublesome modules. Information about a module is often kept in a *unit development folder (UDF)*. The UDF was discussed earlier as a means of monitoring. The UDF keeps a detailed schedule for the unit, and all the relevant details about the development record of the unit. By entering information regarding effort, schedule, testing and failures, a good snapshot of the state of a module can be obtained from the UDF.

From the UDFs of different units, the overall progress of the coding phase can be judged. It can be determined if the project is behind schedule or not. Similarly, the effort for the coding phase can be determined and can be compared with resources allocated in the plan. If the project is behind schedule or over budget, actions will have to be taken. Some typical actions are to reschedule the project, request more resources, review and reduce the scope of the project, replace junior people with senior people (adding people is not really an option due to Brook's Law).

Unit Testing Review: Review of a module's testing is essential to get an idea about the reliability of a module. Review can be done at different places. A review can be done of the results of testing. In this review, testing results are examined and it is determined if the errors observed during testing need further examination or not. In addition, the coverage obtained during unit testing is also reviewed to ensure that testing has provided acceptable statement or branch coverage.

Review for unit testing can also be done when the testcases for unit testing are selected and specified. This will require that testcases be specified clearly before the testing begins. The review of the testcases can determine if the set of testcases cover all the different conditions that need to be tested. Additional testcases may be specified if the testcases are considered insufficient.

Error Summary Worksheets: The purpose of the error summary worksheet (ESW) is to record errors and change data during coding and unit testing. All errors detected and all changes made for correcting errors are recorded in the ESW. The effort for detecting and correcting errors is also recorded. The ESW can be used to evaluate the effectiveness of unit testing and other methods employed for code verification. It can also be used to determine the efficiency of the verification methods used for detecting errors.

From the error summary the number and severity of errors for different modules can also be determined. Number of errors as a function of modules is useful for identifying modules that need further testing or verification. For example, it is believed that the module for which a lot of errors are detected is likely to be the one in which the most undetected errors remain. This is based on the hypothesis that the number of errors detected is proportional to the number of errors in the module. Since testing has its limitations, a module for which a large number of errors are detected may contain further errors that have not been revealed by testing. Such rules have to be decided based on the history of the organization on similar projects. Data from other projects can be used to "interpret the error data of modules that is obtained.

6.5 Summary

In the coding phase, the design of a system is translated into code that can be compiled and executed. Although the coding phase does not affect the structure of the system, it has great impact on the internal structure of modules, which affects the testability and understandability of the system.

The goal of the coding phase is to produce simple and clear programs. The aim is not to reduce the coding effort, but to program in a manner such that the testing and maintenance costs are reduced. Programs should not be constructed so that they are easy to write; they should be easy to read and understand. Reading programs (mostly by people other than the programmer) is a much more common activity than writing programs. Hence, the goal of the coding phase is to produce simple programs that are clear to understand and modify.

To enhance the readability of programs, structured programming should be used. In structured programs, the program is a sequence of single-entry, single-exit statements, and the control flow during execution is linearized. This makes the dynamic structure of a program similar to the static structure. Such programs are easy to understand and verify.

Information hiding is another principle that can be used to enhance program clarity. In information hiding, the data structures are hidden behind access functions. Different modules are given access to data on a "need to know basis. When supported by language mechanisms, information hiding is a very useful construct that limits coupling between modules by ensuring that the data encapsulated in a module is accessible only to operations defined on that module. From the outside, the data cannot be directly accessed, and only operations on the data can be performed.

Internal documentation is also essential for readable programs. Comments in programs should be written to aid understanding and should provide supplementary information. Usually, comments should be written for blocks of code such as procedures and functions. A prologue for a module should define what the module is doing and the logic of the module. It should also describe the side effects and other information about the module.

Verification of code can be done in a number of ways. These include code reading or desk reviews, data flow analysis, symbolic execution, proving correctness, code reviews and walkthroughs, and unit testing. Of all these, code reviews and unit testing are the most common. In code reviews, a team of persons reviews the code as in a requirement or design review. During testing the program is executed with testcases to determine the presence of errors. Except for testing, all other methods discussed in the chapter are static methods where the program is not executed. Static methods often directly find the error in the program, while testing detects only the presence of errors.

A number of metrics exist for quantifying different qualities of the code. The most commonly used are size metrics, since they are used to assess the productivity of people and are often used in cost estimation. The most common size measure is lines of code (LOC), which is also used in most cost models. There are other measures for size as well.

The goal of complexity metrics is to quantify the complexity of software. Complexity is an important factor affecting the productivity of projects and is a factor in cost estimation. A number of different metrics exist. Perhaps the most common is the cyclomatic complexity, which is based on the internal logic of the program and defines complexity as the number of independent cycles in the flow graph of the program.

Exercises

1. What is structured programming and why is it important?
2. What are the major concepts that help in making a program more readable?
3. Consider the following program which takes in the values A, B and C in sorted order and determines the type of the triangle represented by A, B and C.

```
read(a, b, c);
if (a < b) or (b < c) then
    print("Illegal inputs");
    return;
if (a = b) or (b = c) then
    if (a = b) and (b = c) then print("equilateral triangle")
    else print("isoscles triangle")
else begin
    a : = a * a; b : = b * b; c : = c * c;
    d : = b + c;
    if (a = d) then print("right triangle")
    else if (a < d) then print("acute triangle")
    else print("obtuse triangle");
end;
```

Symbolically execute this program, and show that it is correct. Draw the execution tree.

4. Consider the following program to determine the product of two integers x and y.

```
if (x = 0) or (y = 0) then
    p : = 0
else begin
    p : = x;
    i : = 1;
    while (i ! = y) do begin
        p : = p * x;
        i : = i + 1;
    end;
end;
```

Write formal specifications for a program to compute the product of two numbers. Then using the axiomatic method prove that this program is correct.

5. The two different size measures that are considered are lines of code and Halstead's volume. Define these two. Which of these is a more accurate metric for size? Which of them is more used?
6. Write a sorting module using bubble sort and insertion sort. Determine the McCabe's complexity measure, and compare it with the example. Explain any discrepancies.

7. Perform the live variable complexity analysis for the two modules (and the one given in the chapter). See if this complexity measure is proportional to the cyclomatic complexity measure for these examples.
8. Consider the following two algorithms for searching an element E in a sorted array A, which contains n integers. The first procedure implements a simple linear search algorithm. The second one performs a binary search. Binary search is generally much more efficient in terms of execution time, as compared to the linear search.

```
function lin_search (A, E): boolean
var
    i : integer;
    found: boolean;
begin
    found : = false;
    i : = 1;
    while (not found) and (i ≤ n) do begin
        if (A[i] = E) then found : = true;
        i : = i + 1;
    end;
    lin_search : = found;
end;


function bin_search (A, E): boolean
var
    low, high, mid, i, j : integer;
    found : boolean;
begin
    low : = 1;
    high : = n;
    found : = false;
    while (low ≤ high) and (not found) do begin
        mid : = (low + high)/2;
        if E < A[mid] then high : = mid − 1
            else if E > A[mid] then low : = mid + 1
                else found : = true;
    end;
    bin_search : = found;
end;
```

Determine the cyclomatic complexity, Halstead's measure of complexity, and live variable complexity for these two functions. Is the ratio of two complexity measures similar for the two functions?
9. What is the Halstead's size measure for these two modules? Compare this size with the size measured in LOC.
10. Consider the size measure as the number of bytes needed to store the object code of a program. How useful is this size measure? Is it closer to LOC or the Halstead's metric? Explain.

11. Not all control statements are equally complex. Assign complexity weights (0–10) to different control statements in Pascal, and then determine a formula to calculate the complexity of a program. Can this complexity measure be automatically computed for a program?

12. A combination of conditions in a decision makes a decision more complex. Such decisions should be treated as a combination of different decisions. As compared to the simple measure where each decision is treated as one, how much will be the difference in the cyclomatic complexity of a program with .2 of its conditional statements having two conditions and .2 having three conditions, when evaluated by this new approach?

13. Describe briefly the different methods for code verification. Which of these is best suited for "catching" the maximum number of errors, and which of these is the most cost effective (where cost per error is the lowest)?

14. Suppose multiple methods must be used for verification, as is usually done. Select at least three methods which you want to apply. In what order you will apply these? Justify your answer from the point of view of cost efficiency (where the goal is to reduce the cost), and reliability (where the goal is to detect the maximum number of errors).

Case Study

The programs were written in Pascal on the Sun workstation, as required. The size of the programs is about 1400 lines of executable source code. There were no major schedule slippages during coding. Coding and unit testing were finished within a month, which is consistent with the project plan.

There are a total of 39 modules in the code, while there were 24 modules in the detailed design. The **tracing** of modules specified in the detailed design to the modules in the code is given below. For each module number in the detailed design, the corresponding module number in the code is given. The modules in the code are numbered sequentially in the order in which their declaration statement appears, starting from 0, which is the number for the program (or the main module).

$1 \rightarrow 0, 2 \rightarrow 1, 3 \rightarrow 6, 4 \rightarrow 7, 5 \rightarrow 12, 6 \rightarrow 15, 7 \rightarrow 18, 8 \rightarrow 19, 9 \rightarrow 20, 10 \rightarrow 21, 11 \rightarrow 24, 12 \rightarrow 25, 13 \rightarrow 26, 14 \rightarrow 28, 15 \rightarrow 29, 16 \rightarrow 30, 17 \rightarrow 31, 18 \rightarrow 32, 19 \rightarrow 33, 20 \rightarrow 34, 21 \rightarrow 35, 22 \rightarrow 38, 23 \rightarrow 37, 24 \rightarrow 36.$

The extra modules in the code are:

2. lengthof, 3. get_next_line, 4. get_token, 5. string_to_int, 8. chk_fmt_rm_no, 9. chk_range_cap, 10. sort_rooms, 11. chk_dup (room), 13. chk_fmt_course_no, 14. chk_dup (course), 16. chk_fmt_time_slot,

17. chk_dup (time), 22. form_pref_list, 23. duplicate_course, 24. prep _template.

Most of these extra modules are "service modules", which are used by different modules specified in the design. Some of these modules could have been avoided if some other language, able to provide some of these functions as library functions, had been used.

The complete code for the project is given in Appendix A.

7
Testing

In a software development project, errors can be injected at any stage during the development. For each phase we have discussed different techniques for detecting and eliminating errors that originate in that phase. However, some requirements errors and design errors are likely to remain undetected. Ultimately, these errors will be reflected in the code. Since code is frequently the only product that can be executed and whose actual behavior can be observed, testing is the phase where the errors remaining from the earlier phases also must be detected. Hence, testing performs a very critical role for quality assurance and for ensuring the reliability of software.

During testing, the program to be tested is executed with a set of testcases, and the output of the program for the testcases is evaluated to determine if the program is performing as it is expected to. Due to its approach, dynamic testing can only ascertain the presence of error in the program; the exact nature of the error is not usually decided by testing. Testing forms the first step in determining the errors in a program. Clearly, the success of testing in revealing errors in programs depends critically on the testcases. Much of this chapter is devoted to testcase selection and criteria for selecting testcases, and their effect on testing.

Often when we test our programs, the testcases are treated as "throw away" cases; after testing is complete, testcases and their outcomes are thrown away. However, in software systems the use of testing is not limited to the testing phase. The results of testing are used later on during maintenance also. One of our goals during dynamic testing is to produce a test suite, which contains a set of "interesting" testcases along with their expected output, for future use. Later on when the software is modified, in order to ensure that the modification does not have some undesirable side effect, the test suite is used. This form of testing is sometimes called **regression testing.** For regression testing it is important that proper documentation be available about the testcases and their outcomes.

7.1. Testing Fundamentals

7.1.1. Error, Fault, Failure and Reliability

So far we have used the intuitive meaning of the term error to refer to problems in requirements, design or code. Sometimes error, fault and failures are used interchangeably, and sometimes they refer to somewhat different concepts. Let us start with defining these concepts clearly. We follow the IEEE definitions [Iee87] for these terms.

The term error is used in two different ways. Error refers to the discrepancy between a computed, observed, or measured value and the true, specified, or theoretically correct value. That is, error refers to the difference between the actual output of a software and the correct output. In this interpretation, error essentially is a measure of the difference between the actual and ideal. Error is also used to refer to human action that results in software containing a defect or a fault. This definition is quite general and encompasses all the phases.

Fault is a condition that causes the software to fail to perform its required function. A fault is the basic reason for software malfunction and is synonymous with the commonly used phrase "bug". The term error is also often used to refer to defects (taking a variation of the second definition of error). In this book we will continue to use the terms in the manner commonly used, and no explicit distinction will be made between error and fault, unless necessary.

Failure is the inability of a system or a component to perform a required function according to its specifications. A software failure occurs if the behavior of the software is different from the specified behavior. Failures may be caused due to functional as well as performance reasons. A failure is produced only when there is a fault in the system. However, presence of a fault does not guarantee a failure. In other words, faults have the potential to cause failures and their presence is a necessary but not sufficient condition for failure to occur. Note that the definition does not imply that a failure must be *observed*. It is possible that a failure may occur but not be detected.

We define **software reliability** as the probability that software will not undergo a failure for a specified time under specified conditions. Reliability is essentially the level of confidence one can place in the software, and this level is dependent on time. Simply specifying a reliability number (such as 0.98) is not meaningful until a time period is specified. A proper specification could be that the reliability for a ten hour operation should be 0.98l. Reliability can also be defined in terms of **Mean Time to Failure (MTTF)**, which specifies the average time between the occurrence of two failures. If a reliability function is given, the MTTF can be obtained from the function. We will later look at some models for estimating reliability of software.

The goal of all verification and validation (V&V) activities is to make software more reliable. In software, unreliability is caused by the presence of faults. The fewer the faults in a software, the less likely it is that a failure will occur during execution. This is unlike other engineering disciplines where failures are often caused due to "wear and tear" that occurs with time in a system. With software, there is no wear and tear; faults are the only cause of unreliability. Hence, the major goal of verification and validation techniques is to detect faults in the software. By identifying and removing faults, the software can be made more reliable.

Most of the V&V activities can be classified as *static* or *dynamic*. Static methods are where the behavior of the system is not observed by executing the system. Examples of static methods are reviews, program proving, and code reading. In all these cases the system to be verified is not executed. In *dynamic* methods, the behavior of the system is observed by executing the system. The prime example of this method is testing. That is why testing is sometimes called *dynamic testing*.

These two types of methods take different approaches to improving software reliability. The static methods, by their very nature, do not observe system behavior, and are not looking for system failures. In these methods, faults are directly detected. In testing, by contrast, system behavior is observed. By observing the behavior of a system or a component during testing, we determine if there is a failure or not. By observing failures of the system we can deduce the presence of faults. Hence, testing only reveals the presence of faults. However, if no failure occurs it does not mean that there are no faults in the system. Consequently it is said that testing can reveal the presence of faults but not their absence.

During the testing process only failures are observed, by which the presence of faults is deduced. The actual faults are identified by separate activities, commonly referred to as "debugging". This is one of the reasons why testing is an expensive method for identification and removal of faults, as compared to static methods which directly observe faults. In general, static methods are likely to be more cost effective for identifying and detecting faults.

It should be pointed out that the definition of failure requires that the behavior of the system or component is unambiguously specified and that the specification itself is error-free. The specifications should actually specify the true and correct system behavior. These conditions are hard to satisfy. After all, it is the activity of some earlier phase that determines these specifications, and these activities might be error-prone. Such shortcomings in the specifications are the major cause of situations where the developer claims that a particular condition is not a failure while the client claims that it is a failure. However, there is no easy solution to this problem. Testing does require some specifications against which the given system is tested.

The specifications of a system often specify many properties, although some are considered more important than others. If a failure violates an important property, it is considered more severe than a failure that violates a less important property. To capture this concept of severity of failures, often error-classification is used, in which errors or faults are classified according to the type and severity of failures they cause.

7.1.2. Levels of Testing

We have seen that faults can occur during any phase in the software development cycle. Verification is performed on the output of each phase, but still some faults are likely to remain undetected by these methods. These faults will be eventually reflected in the code. Testing is usually relied upon to detect these faults, in addition to the faults introduced during the coding phase itself. For this, different levels of testing are used, which perform different tasks and aim to test different aspects of the system.

The basic levels are unit testing, integration testing, system and acceptance testing. These different levels of testing attempt to detect different types of faults. The relation of the faults introduced in different phases, and the different levels of testing, are shown in Figure 7.1.

The first level of testing is called **unit testing.** In this, different modules are tested against the specifications produced during design for the modules. Unit testing is essentially for verification of the code produced during the coding phase, and hence the goal is to test the internal logic of the modules.

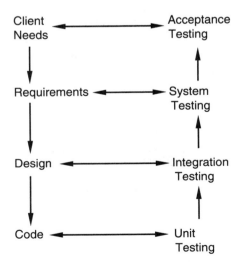

FIGURE 7.1. Levels of testing.

The next level of testing is often called **integration testing.** In this, many tested modules are combined into sub-systems which are then tested. The goal here is to see if the modules can be integrated properly, the emphasis being on testing interfaces between modules. This testing activity can be considered as testing the design, and hence the emphasis on testing module interactions.

The next levels are **system testing** and **acceptance testing.** Here the entire software system is tested. The reference document for this process is the requirements document, and the goal is to see if the software meets its requirements. This is essentially a validation exercise, and in many cases is the only validation activity. Acceptance testing is sometimes performed with realistic data of the client to demonstrate that the software is working satisfactorily. Testing here focuses on the external behavior of the system; the internal logic of the program is not emphasized.

7.1.3. Testcases and Test Criteria

Having proper testcases is central to successful testing. The reason for this is that if there is a fault in a program, the program can still provide expected behavior for many inputs. Only for the set of inputs that exercise the fault in the program will the output of the program deviate from the expected behavior. Hence, it is fair to say that a testing process is as good as its testcases.

Ideally, we would like to determine a set of testcases such that successful execution of all of them implies that there are no errors in the program. This ideal goal cannot usually be achieved due to practical and theoretical constraints. Each testcase costs money, as effort is needed to generate the testcase, machine time is needed to execute the program for that testcase, and more effort is needed to evaluate the results. Therefore, we would also like to minimize the number of testcases needed to detect errors due to the reliability and economic constraints associated with selecting a proper set of testcases

The goal during selecting testcases is to ensure that if there is an error/fault in the program, then it is exercised by one of the testcases. An ideal testcase set is one that succeeds (meaning that its execution reveals no errors) only if there are no errors in the program. One possible ideal set of testcases is one that includes all the possible inputs to the program. This is often called *exhaustive* testing. However, exhaustive testing is impractical and unfeasible, as even for small programs the number of elements in the input domain can be extremely large.

Hence, a realistic goal for testing is to select a set of testcases that is close to ideal. How should we select our testcases? On what basis should we include some element of program domain in the set of testcases and not include others? For this we need some testing criteria. That is, we define a criterion that we believe should be satisfied during testing. The criterion then becomes the basis for testcase selection and a set of testcases is selected that satisfy that criterion. For example, the criterion can be that all statements in the program should be executed at least once. For this testing criterion we have to select a set of testcases that will ensure that each statement of the program is executed by at least one of the testcases.

There are two aspects of testcase selection—specifying a criterion for evaluating a set of testcases, and a procedure for generating a set of testcases that satisfy a given criterion. As we will see, there are many testcase criteria that have been proposed, but there are very few procedures for generating testcases. Often a criterion is specified, and the tester has to generate testcases that satisfy the criterion. In some cases, some guidelines are available for deciding testcases. Overall, the problem of testcase selection is very challenging and the current solutions are limited in scope.

If we choose a criterion that is very weak then testing by that criterion will not be very useful. For example, a criterion that is unsatisfiable will be satisfied by an empty set of testcases, and will be totally useless. There are two desirable properties for a testing criterion: reliability and validity [Goo75]. A criterion is reliable if all the sets (of testcases) that satisfy the criterion detect the same errors. That is, it is insignificant which of the sets satisfying the criterion is chosen; every set will detect exactly the same errors. A criterion is valid if for any error in the program, there is some set satisfying the criterion that will reveal the error. A fundamental theorem of testing is that if a testing criterion is valid and reliable, then if a set satisfying that criterion succeeds (revealing no faults) then the program contains no errors [Goo75]. However, it has been shown that there exists no algorithm that will determine a valid criterion for an arbitrary program.

Getting a criterion that is reliable, valid, and can be satisfied by a small number of testcases is usually not possible. Even devising a criterion itself (other than exhausting testing criteria) is very difficult. So, often criteria are chosen that are not valid or reliable, like "all statements should be executed at once" or "all control flow paths must be executed". Often a criterion is not even clearly specified, as in "all special values in the domain must be included" (what is a "special value"?). In such cases one criterion is often not considered sufficient, and testcases derived from more than one criterion are utilized. On the other hand, generating testcases to satisfy a criterion is not simple either. For example, even for a simple criteria like "each statement of the program should be executed", it is extremely hard to construct a set of testcases that will satisfy this criteria for a large program.

The intent of the above discussion is to illustrate that, generally speaking, all the faults in a program cannot be practically revealed by testing. Due to this limitation, and economic limitations, the goal of testcase selection is to select the testcases such that the maximum possible number of faults are detected by the minimum possible testcases.

7.1.4. Test Oracles

For testing any program we need to have a description of the expected behavior of the program, and a method of determining whether the observed behavior conforms to the expected behavior. For this we need a *test oracle*.

A test oracle is a mechanism, different from the program itself, that can be used to check the correctness of the output of the program for the testcases. Conceptually, we can consider testing as a process in which the testcases are given to the test oracle and the program under testing. The output of the two is then compared to determine if the program behaved correctly for the testcases. This is shown in Figure 7.2.

Test oracles are necessary for testing. Ideally we would like an automated oracle, which always gives a correct answer. However, often the oracles are human beings, who mostly compute by hand what the output of the program should be. As it is often extremely difficult to determine whether the behavior conforms to the expected behavior, our "human oracle" itself may make mistakes. As a result, when there is a discrepancy in the result of the program and the oracle, we have to verify the result produced by the oracle, before declaring that there is a fault in the program. This is one of the reasons why testing is so cumbersome and expensive.

There are some systems where oracles are automatically generated from specifications of programs or modules [Jal87]. With such oracles, we are assured that the output of the oracle is consistent with the specifications. However, even this approach does not solve all our problems, because of the possibility of errors in the specifications. Consequently, an oracle generated from the specifications will only produce correct results if the specifications are correct, and will not be dependable in case of specification errors.

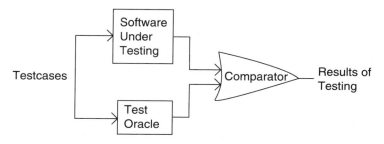

FIGURE 7.2. Testing and test oracles.

7.1.5. Psychology of Testing

As we have seen devising a set of testcases that will guarantee that all errors will be detected is not feasible. Moreover, there are no formal or precise methods for selecting testcases. Even though there are a number of heuristics and rules of thumb for deciding the testcases, selecting testcases is still largely a creative activity, which relies a lot on the ingenuity of the tester. Due to this reason, the psychology of the person performing the testing becomes important.

The aim of testing is often considered to be demonstrating that a program works by showing that it has no errors. This is the *opposite* of what testing should be viewed as. The basic purpose of the testing phase was to ensure some reliability of the software, or detect the errors that may be present in the program. Hence, one should not start testing with the intent of showing that a program works; but the intent should be to show that a program does not work. With this in mind we define testing as [Mye79]. *Testing is the process of executing a program with the intent of finding errors.*

This emphasis on proper intent of testing is not a trivial matter. The reason is that testcases are designed by human beings, and human beings have a tendency to perform actions to achieve the goal they have in mind. So, if the goal is to demonstrate that a program works, then we may consciously or subconsciously select testcases that will try to demonstrate that goal, and that will beat the basic purpose of testing. On the other hand, if the intent is to show that the program does not work, we will challenge our intellect to find testcases towards that end, and we are likely to detect more errors. Testing is essentially a destructive process, where the tester has to treat the program as an adversary who must be beaten by showing the presence of errors. With this in mind a testcase is "good" if it detects an as yet undetected error in the program, and our goal during designing testcases should be design such "good" testcases.

One of the reasons why many organizations require that a product must be tested by people not involved with developing the program before finally delivering it to the customer is this psychological factor. It is hard to be destructive to something we have created ourselves, and we all like to believe that the program we have written "works". So, it is not easy for someone to test his own program with the proper frame of mind for testing. Another reason for independent testing is that sometimes errors occur due to the fact that the programmer did not understand the specifications clearly. Testing of a program by its programmer will not detect such errors, whereas independent testing may succeed in finding these errors.

7.1.6. Top-Down and Bottom-Up Approaches

When testing a large program, it is often necessary to test parts of the program first before testing the entire program. One reason for doing this is that if a testcase detects an error in a large program, it will be extremely difficult to pinpoint the source of the error. In other words, if a huge program does not work, determining which of the modules has errors can be a formidable task. Furthermore, it will be extremely difficult to construct testcases such that different modules are executed in a sufficient number of different conditions so that we can feel fairly confident about them. In many cases, it is even difficult to construct testcases such that all the modules will be executed. This increases the chances of a module's errors going undetected. Hence it is clear that for a large system, we should first test different parts of the system independently, before testing the entire system.

We assume that a system is a hierarchy of modules. For such systems, there are two common ways in which modules can be combined, as they are tested, to form a working program: top-down and bottom-up. In top-down strategy, we start by testing the top of the hierarchy, and incrementally add modules which it calls, and then test the new combined system. This approach of testing requires *stubs* to be written. A stub is a dummy routine that simulates a module. In the top-down approach, a module (or a collection) cannot be tested in isolation as they invoke some other modules. To allow the modules to be tested before their subordinates have actually been coded, stubs simulate the behavior of the subordinates.

The bottom-up approach starts from the bottom of the hierarchy. First the modules at the very bottom, which have no subordinates, are tested. Then these modules are combined further with higher level modules for testing. At any stage of testing all the subordinate modules exist and have been tested beforehand. To perform bottom-up testing *drivers* are needed, to set up the appropriate environment and invoke the module. It is the job of the driver to invoke the module under testing with the different set of testcases.

Notice that both top-down and bottom-up approaches are incremental, starting with testing single modules and then adding untested modules to those that have been tested, until the entire system is tested. In the first case stubs must be written to perform testing, and in the other drivers need to be written. Top-down testing is advantageous if major flaws occur towards the top of the hierarchy, while bottom-up is advantageous if the major flaws occur towards the bottom. Often writing stubs can be more difficult than writing drivers, since one may need to know beforehand the set of inputs for the module being simulated by the stub, and may need to determine proper responses for these inputs. In addition, as the stubs often simulate the behavior of a module over a limited domain, the choice of testcases for the superiordinate module is limited, and deciding testcases is often very difficult.

It is often best to select the testing method to conform with the development method. Thus, if the system is developed in a top-down manner, top-down testing should be used, and if the system is developed in a bottom-up manner, a bottom-up testing strategy should be used. By doing this, as parts of the system are developed, they are tested, and errors are detected as development proceeds. It should be pointed out that we are concerned with the actual program development here, not the design method. The development can be bottom-up even if the design was done in a top-down manner.

7.2. Functional Testing

There are two basic approaches to testing, functional and structural. In functional testing the structure of the program is not considered. Testcases are decided solely on the basis of the requirements or specifications of the program or module, and the internals of the module or the program are not considered for selection of testcases. Due to its nature, functional testing is often called "black box testing". In the structural approach, testcases are generated based on the actual code of the program or module to be tested. This structural approach is sometimes called "glass box testing." In this section we will present some techniques for generating testcases for functional testing. Structural testing is discussed in the next section.

The basis for deciding testcases in functional testing is the requirements or the specifications of the system or the module. For the entire system, the testcases are designed from the requirements specification document for the system. For modules created during design, testcases for functional testing are decided from the module specifications produced during the design.

The most obvious functional testing procedure is exhaustive testing, which, as we have stated, is impractical. One criterion for generating testcases is to generate them randomly. This strategy has little chance for resulting in a set of testcases that is close to optimal (detecting the maximum errors with minimum testcases). Hence, we need some other criterion or rule for selecting testcases. There are no formal rules for designing testcases for functional testing. In fact there are no precise criteria for selecting testcases. However, there are a number of techniques or heuristics that can be used for selecting testcases that have been found to be very successful in detecting errors. Here we mention some of these techniques.

7.2.1. Equivalence Class Partitioning

Since we cannot do exhaustive testing, the next natural approach is to divide the domain of all the inputs into a set of equivalence classes, such that if any test in an equivalence class succeeds, then every test in that class will succeed. That is, we want to identify classes of testcases such that the success of one testcase in a class implies the success of others. If we can indeed identify such classes, and guarantee that each class forms such an equivalence class, then the success of one testcase from each equivalence class is equivalent to successfully completing an exhaustive test of the program.

However, without looking at the internal structure of the program, it is impossible to determine such ideal equivalence classes (even with the internal structure, it usually cannot be done). The equivalence class partitioning method [Mye79] tries to approximate this ideal. Different equivalence classes are formed by putting inputs for which the behavior pattern of the module is specified to be different into similar groups, and then regarding these new classes as forming equivalence classes. The rationale of forming equivalence classes like this is the assumption that if the specifications require exactly the same behavior for each element in a class of values, then the program is likely to be constructed such that either it succeeds or fails for each of the values in that class. For example, the specifications of a module that determines the absolute value for integers specify one behavior for positive integers, and another for negative integers. In this case we will form two equivalence classes, one consisting of positive integers and the other consisting of negative integers.

For robust software, we must also test for incorrect inputs by generating testcases for inputs that do not satisfy the input conditions. With this in mind, for each equivalence class of valid inputs we define equivalence classes for invalid inputs.

Equivalence classes are usually formed by considering each condition specified on an input as specifying a valid equivalence class and one or more invalid equivalence classes. For example, if an input condition specifies a range of values (say 0 < count < Max), then form a valid equivalence class with that range and also two invalid equivalence classes, one with values less than the lower bound of the range (i.e. count < 0) and the other with values higher than the higher bound (count > Max). If the input specifies a set of values, and the requirements specify different behavior for different elements in the set, then a valid equivalence class is formed for each of the elements in the set, and an invalid class for an entity not belonging to the set.

Essentially, if there is reason to believe that the entire range of an input will not be treated in the same manner, then the range should be split into two or more equivalence classes. Also, for each valid equivalence class, one or more invalid equivalence classes should be identified. For example, an input may be specified as a character. However, we may have reason to believe that the program will perform different actions if a character is an alphabet, a number, or a special character. In that case we will split the input into three valid equivalence classes.

It is often useful to consider equivalence classes in the output also. For an output equivalence class, the goal is to generate testcases such that the output for that testcase lies in the output equivalence class. Determining testcases for output classes may be more difficult, but output classes have been found to reveal errors that are not revealed by just considering the input classes.

7.2.2. Boundary Value Analysis

It has been observed that programs that work correctly for a set of values in an equivalence class, fail on some special values. These values often lie on the boundary of the equivalence class. Testcases that have values on the boundaries of equivalence classes are therefore likely to be "high yield" testcases, and selecting such testcases is the aim of the boundary value analysis. In boundary value analysis [Mye79], we choose an input for a testcase from an equivalence class, such that the input lies at the edge of the equivalence classes. Boundary values for each equivalence class, including the equivalence classes of the output, should be covered. Boundary value testcases are also called "extreme cases". Hence, we can say that a boundary value testcase is a set of input data that lies on the edge or boundary of a class of input data or that generates output that lies at the boundary of a class of output data.

In case of ranges, for boundary value analysis it is useful to select the boundary elements of the range, and an invalid value just beyond the two ends (for the two invalid equivalence classes). So, if the range is $0.0 \leq x \leq 1.0$, then the testcases are 0.0, 1.0 (valid inputs), and -0.1, and 1.1 (for invalid inputs). Similarly, if the input is a list, then attention should be focused on the first and the last elements of the list. We should also consider the outputs for boundary value analysis. If an equivalence class can be identified in the output, then we should try to generate testcases that will produce the output that lies at the boundaries of the equivalence classes. Furthermore, we should try to form testcases that will produce an output that does not lie in the equivalence class (If we can produce an input case that produces the output outside the equivalence class, we have detected an error).

7.2.3. Cause-Effect Graphing

One weakness with the equivalence class partitioning and boundary value method is that they consider each input separately. That is, both concentrate on the conditions and classes of one input. They do not consider combinations of input circumstances that may form interesting situations that should be tested. One way to exercise combinations of different input conditions is to consider all valid combinations of the equivalence classes of input conditions. This simple approach will result in an unusually large number of testcases, many of which will not be useful for revealing any new errors. For example, if there are n different input conditions, such that any combination of the input conditions is valid, we will have 2^n testcases.

Cause-effect graphing [Mye79] is a technique that aids in selecting combinations of input conditions in a systematic way, such that the number of testcases does not become unmanageably large. The technique starts with identifying causes and effects of the system under testing. A *cause* is a distinct input condition, and an *effect* is a distinct output condition. Each condition forms a node in the cause-effect graph. The conditions should be stated such that they can be set to either true or false. For example, an input condition can be "file is empty", which can be set to true by having an empty input file, and false by a non-empty file. After identifying the causes and effects, for each effect we identify the causes that can produce that effect, and how the conditions have to be combined to make the effect as true. Conditions are combined using the Boolean operators "and", "or", and "not", which are represented in the graph by &, |, and~. Then for each effect, all combinations of the causes that the effect depends upon which will make the effect to be true are generated (the causes that the effect does not depend upon are essentially "don't care"). By doing this we identify the combinations of conditions which make different effects true. A testcase is then generated for each of the combinations of conditions which make some effect to be true.

Let us illustrate this technique by a small example. Suppose that for a bank database there are two commands allowed.

credit   acct_number transaction_amount
debit   acct_number transaction_amount

The requirements are that if the command is credit, and the acct_number is valid, then the account is credited. If the command is debit, the acct_number is valid, and the transaction_amount is valid (being less than the balance), then the account is debited. If the command is not valid, or the account number is not valid, or the debit amount is not valid, a suitable message is generated. We can identify the following causes and effects from these requirements, shown in Figure 7.3

The cause-effect of this is shown in Figure 7.4.

In the graph, the cause-effect relationship of this example is captured. For all effects, one can easily determine the causes each effect depends

Causes:
  c1. Command is credit
  c2. Command is debit
  c3. Account number is valid
  c4. Transaction_amt is valid

Effects:
  e1. Print "invalid command"
  e2. Print "invalid account_number"
  e3. Print "Debit amount not valid"
  e4. Debit account
  e5. Credit account

FIGURE 7.3. List of causes and effects.

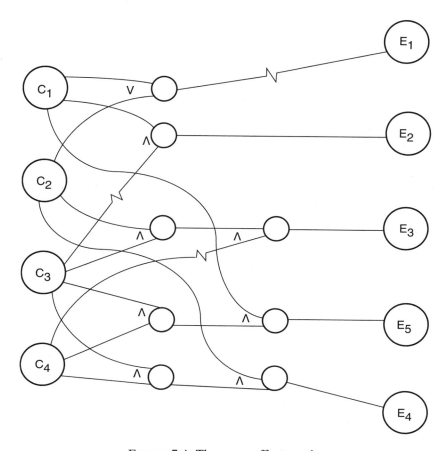

FIGURE 7.4. The cause-effect graph.

upon, and the exact nature of the dependency. For example, according to this graph the effect e5 depends on the causes c2, c3 and c4 in a manner such that the effect e5 is enabled when all c2, c3 and c4 are True. Similarly, the effect e2 is enabled if c3 is False.

From this graph, a list of testcases can be generated. The basic strategy is to set an effect to 1; then set the causes that enable this condition. The condition of causes forms the testcase. A cause may be set to False, True or Don't care (in the case when the effect does not depend at all on the cause). To do this for all the effects, it is convenient to use a decision table. The decision table for this example is shown in Figure 7.5.

This table lists the combinations of conditions to set different effects. A combination of conditions for an effect is a testcase. For example, to test for the effect e3, both c2 and c4 have to be set. That is, to test the effect "Print debit amount not valid", the testcase should be: Command is debit

SNo.	1	2	3	4	5
c1	0	1	x	x	1
c2	0	x	1	1	x
c3	x	0	1	1	1
c4	x	x	0	1	1
e1	1				
e2		1			
e3			1		
e4				1	
e5					1

FIGURE 7.5. Decision table for the cause-effect graph.

(setting c2 to True), the account number is valid (setting c3 to False), and the transaction money is not proper (setting c4 to False).

Cause-effect graphing, beyond generating high yielding testcases, also aids the understanding of the functionality of the system, since the tester must identify the distinct causes and effects. There are methods of reducing the number of testcases generated by proper traversing of the graph. Once the causes and effects are listed and their dependencies specified, much of the remaining work can also be automated.

7.2.4. Special Cases

It has been seen that programs often produce incorrect behavior when inputs form some special cases. The reason is that in programs some combinations of inputs need special treatment, and providing proper handling for these special cases is easily overlooked. For example, in an arithmetic routine, if there is a division and the divisor is zero, some special action has to be taken, which could easily be forgotten by the programmer. These special cases form particularly good testcases, which can reveal errors that will usually not be detected by other testcases.

Special cases will often depend on the data structures and the function of the module. There are no rules to determine special cases, and the tester has to use his intuition and experience to identify such testcases. Consequently, determining special cases is also called *error guessing*.

The psychology is particularly important for error guessing. The tester should play the "devil's advocate", and try to guess the incorrect assumptions the programmer could have made, and the situations which the programmer could have overlooked or handled incorrectly. Essentially, the tester is trying to identify error prone situations. Then testcases are written for these situations. For example, in the problem of finding the number of different words in a file (discussed in earlier chapters) some of the special cases can be: file is empty, only one word in the file, only one word in a line, some empty lines in the input file, presence of more than one blank between words, all words are same, the words are already sorted, and blanks at the start and end of the file.

Incorrect assumptions are usually made because the specifications are not complete, or the writer of specifications may not have stated some properties, assuming them to be obvious. Whenever there is reliance on tacit understanding rather than explicit statement of specifications, there is scope for making wrong assumptions. (These wrong assumptions are often about the environment.) However, it should be pointed out that special cases depend heavily on the problem, and the tester should really try to "get into the shoes" of the designer and the coder to determine these cases.

7.3. Structural Testing

In the previous section we discussed functional testing, which is concerned with the function that the tested program is supposed to perform, and does not deal with the internal structure of the program that is responsible for actually implementing that function. Thus functional testing is concerned with functionality rather than implementation of the program. Structural testing, on the other hand, is concerned with testing the implementation of the program. The intent of the structural testing is not to exercise all the different input or output conditions (although that may be a by product), but to exercise the different programming and data structures used in the program.

For testing the structure of a program, structural testing aims to achieve testcases that will force the desired coverage of different structures. In order to determine if the coverage is sufficient, we have to define what we mean by coverage first, and for that we need some coverage criteria. Thus, structural testing is sometimes also called coverage-based testing. Here we discuss some of the coverage criteria for structural testing. "Note that these criteria are for evaluating a set of testcases, and do not suggest procedures for generating testcases to satisfy a criterion."

7.3.1. Coverage Criteria

Most coverage criteria are based on the number of statements, branches, or paths that are exercised by the testcases. Perhaps the simplest, and weakest, coverage criterion is **statement coverage,** which requires that each statement of the program be executed at least once. This coverage criteria is not very strong, and can leave errors undetected. For example, if there is an if statement in the program without having an else clause, the statement coverage criterion for this statement will be satisfied by a testcase that evaluates the condition to true. No testcase is needed that ensures that the condition in the if statement evaluates to false. This is a serious shortcoming, because decisions in programs are potential sources of errors. As an example consider the following function to compute the absolute value of a number:

function abs (x:integer): integer;
begin
   if x $\geq$ 0 **then** x : = 0 $-$ x;
   abs : = x;
end;

This program is clearly wrong. Suppose we execute the function with the set of testcases {x = 0} (i.e., the set has only one testcase). The statement coverage criteria will be satisfied by testing with this set, but the error will not be revealed.

A little more general coverage criteria is **branch coverage,** which requires that each branch in a program is traversed at least once during testing. In other words, branch coverage requires that each decision in the program be evaluated to true and false values at least once during testing. Testing based on branch coverage is often called *branch testing.* Branch coverage usually implies statement coverage, as each statement is usually a part of some branch, and is usually a better criterion. In the above example, a set of testcases satisfying this criterion will detect the error.

The trouble with branch coverage comes if a decision has many conditions in it (consisting of a Boolean expression with Boolean operators & and |). In such situations, a decision can evaluate to true and false without actually exercising all the conditions. For example consider the following function that checks the validity of a data item. The data item is valid if it lies between 0 and 100.

function check (x: integer): integer;
begin
   if ((x $\geq$ 0) and (x $\leq$ 200))
     then check : = true
     else check : = false;
end;

The module is incorrect as it is checking for x $\leq$ 200 instead of 100 (perhaps a typing error made by the programmer). Suppose the module is tested with the following set of testcases: {x = 5, x = -5}. The branch coverage criterion will be satisfied for this module by this set. However, the error will not be revealed, and the behavior of the module is consistent with its specifications for all testcases in this set. Thus the coverage criterion is satisfied, but the error is not detected. This occurs because the decision is evaluating to true and false because of the condition (x $\geq$ 0). The condition (x $\leq$ 200) never evaluates to false during this testing, hence the error in this condition is not revealed.

This problem can be resolved by requiring that all conditions must evaluate to true and false. However, situations can occur where a decision may not get both true and false values even if each individual condition evaluates to true and false. An obvious solution to this problem is to require decision/condition coverage, where all the decisions and all the conditions in the decisions take both true and false values during the course of testing.

Studies have indicated that there are many errors whose presence is not detected by branch testing. The reason is that some errors are related to some combinations of branches, and their presence is revealed by an execution that follows the path that includes those branches. One possible coverage criteria is that each "logical path" in a program should be tested. A logical path is the sequence of branches that are executed when the program is executed from the start to the end (a complete execution). Testing based on path coverage criteria is often called **path testing.** The difficulty with this criterion is that programs that contain loops can have an infinite number of possible paths. It is, in a sense, the structural testing equivalent of the exhaustive testing approach in functional testing. A method to limit the number of paths is to consider two paths as the same if they differ only in their subpaths that are caused due to the loops. Even with this restriction, the number of paths can be extremely large.

All the above mentioned criteria are not sufficient to detect all kind of errors in programs. If a program is missing some control flow paths, and needs to check for a special value, but fails to do that (like pointer equals nil and divisor equals zero), then even executing all the paths may not detect the error. Hence, even the path coverage criterion, which is the strongest of the criteria we have discussed, is not strong enough to guarantee the detection of all the errors.

7.3.2. Testcase Generation

Once the coverage criteria is decided, testcases have to be generated to satisfy the criteria. This is a particularly difficult task in structural testing. There are no formal methods for choosing testcases. Deciding testcases manually without the aid of any tools is a cumbersome task, as the tester will have to trace each testcase under consideration through the program. Selecting testcases for small modules is feasible to do manually, but generating testcases for large programs can be extremely complex. One method is to randomly select test data until the desired coverage is reached (see the next section for instrumentation to determine the coverage). These methods can result in a lot of redundant testcases, as many the testcases will exercise the same statements or paths.

The most common method of testcase generation is to use some tool to tell the tester what statements, branches, and paths have been covered, and let the tester decide the testcases. Data flow analysis can be used to aid the tester. For example, the analyzer can inform the tester what branches have not been executed. A path can be constructed such that this branch is included in the path. Data flow analysis tools can be used to decide what input values should be chosen such that when the program is executed this particular path is also executed.

Symbolic evaluation tools can be quite useful here for aiding the tester in selecting testcases. Tools can be used to generate paths from a program such that together the paths execute every statement or branch. These paths can be treated as programs in their own right, and symbolically executed. With symbolic execution, the output expression of a path can be obtained in terms of input variables (the output expression will also contain predicates), and then the values for the input variables that will produce the output are selected as testcases. This approach requires a tool to determine paths in a program, and a good symbolical execution tool.

However, selecting testcases is still not a simple mechanical process. Ingenuity and creativity of the tester are still important, despite the availability of the tools to select testcases to ensure coverage. Because of this, often the coverage criteria are weakened, and instead of requiring 100% coverage (of statements and branches), the goal is to achieve some acceptably high percentage (but less than 100%).

7.3.3. Instrumentation for Structural Testing

Tools to determine the actual coverage achieved by the test cases is an integral part of structural testing. (For a given set of testcases we have to determine if the required coverage is achieved, and tools are needed for this.) For example, in branch coverage, a tool is needed that can keep track of which branches are traversed by a set of testcases. Conceivably, the coverage can be computed by hand, but that will require a lot of human effort, and will not be reliable. Keeping track of the coverage can be done effectively and efficiently mechanically by the use of software tools.

These tools must collect information such as which statements or branches have been executed. To achieve this, the execution of the program during testing has be be closely monitored. This requires that the program be instrumented so that required data can be collected. Perhaps the most common method of instrumenting is to insert some statements in the program called *probes*. The sole purpose of the probes is to generate data about program execution during testing that can be used to compute the coverage. With this we can identify three phases in generating coverage data.

1. Instrument the program with probes.
2. Execute the program with testcases.
3. Analyze the results of the probe data.

Probe insertion can be done automatically by a *preprocessor*. The analysis of the probe data can also be done automatically by a *postprocessor*. The first question is where should the probes be inserted. Probes can be inserted after each line of code, but that would be wasteful and inefficient.

We want to identify segments of statements that must be executed together, and insert one probe for the segment. A common technique is to insert probes where a path splits into multiple paths, and where multiple paths merge. A different probe is inserted for each path. Different kinds of probes can be constructed, and one simple method is to insert probes that keep track of the number of times a segment is executed. For example, at some place in the program, the preprocessor can insert a probe of the nature

$$\text{count}[10] : = \text{count}[10] + 1$$

which will tell us how many times the particular segment (which was numbered ten by the preprocessor) was executed.

Note that the preprocessor also inserts proper declarations for the data that is used by the probes, and also has to insert a routine in the end to print the data, or invoke the postprocessor. The postprocessor, in order to determine the statement or branch coverage will need to know where the probes were introduced. Based on the knowledge of counts and the placement of the probes, statistics about the coverage is produced. In addition, useful tools will also point out the statements or branches that have not yet been executed during testing.

7.3.4. Complexity Based Criteria

Based on the cyclomatic complexity, a test criterion has been proposed [Mcc83], for structural testing. This criterion is best suited for unit testing, and like coverage criteria, it can also be used to measure the quality of testing. It does not provide procedures for generating testcases.

We have seen that cyclomatic complexity V of a module is the number of independent paths in the flow graph of a module. As these are independent paths, all other paths can be represented as a combination of these basic paths. These basic paths are finite, whereas the total number of paths in a module having loops may be infinite.

The test criteria is that if the cyclomatic complexity of a module is V, then at least V distinct paths must be executed during testing.

One way to achieve this is to start with a baseline path, which is a good representative of the path in the module (since it is not just an error path). This baseline path (like any other path) represents a sequence of decisions taken in a particular way. Test this path on all functional requirements of the module that are applicable to this path. Then identify the path by changing the outcome of one decision in the path and test this path and its functional requirements. Similarly, determine other paths from the baseline path by changing the outcome of one decision and test all these paths. This method will satisfy the criterion for testing.

7.3.5. Mutation Testing

In the above-mentioned structural approaches to testing, we have seen that testing criteria is in terms of coverage of different structures in the program. However, the program itself is never modified. Mutation testing [DLS78] takes a different approach. Here the program is modified (or the logic of the program is changed) slightly to obtain *mutants* of the original program. The different mutants are then tested along with the original program. The idea is that if a mutant fails on a testcase for which the original program gives a correct answer, then we have more confidence in the testcase. That is, since the mutant program is different from the original program, its behavior should also be different. The testcase that reveals this difference is considered a "good" testcase, as it was able to "catch" the difference. So, for mutation testing we want testcases that produce different behaviors for the original program and a mutant.

Clearly, all testcases will not produce different behaviors between the original program and a mutant. The reason for this is that a testcase may not exercise that part of the code that is different in the mutant and the original program. The goal in mutation testing is to find a testcase that will produce different behaviors for the two programs.

The process of mutation testing is to produce a number of mutations from the original program. Then all the mutants and the program are tested with the set of testcases. Testing is to continue with new testcases until for each mutant an output is found that is different from the original program. Suppose the original program is P, and the set of mutant programs which differ from P in simple ways is MP. Let T be a set of testcases. P and the programs in MP are executed with T. If all mutants give results different from the results obtained from P, then it is highly likely that P is correct (and the mutants are said to "die"). If some mutants give the same results as P (these mutants are said to be "live"), then either the mutants are functionally equivalent to P, or the set T is not adequate. Since we know that the mutant is different from P, the set T should be augmented with more testcases until all mutants "die".

Mutants are formed by making simple changes to the original program. To avoid creating complimentary changes, each mutant is formed by a single change. For producing the mutants, mutation operators have to be defined. Some typical operators are constant replacement, scalar variable replacement, array reference for constant or simple variable replacement, arithmetic operator replacement, relational operator replacement, logical connector replacement, statement deletion, and goto target replacement. For mutation testing to be effective, a large number of mutants must be formed using the mutation operators. This requires that some automated support be available. Once the mutation operators are defined, tools can be developed to produce the mutants.

7.3.6. Combining Functional and Structural Approaches

It is clear that functional and structural approaches are complimentary; one looks at the program from the outside, the other from the inside. The kind of errors they detect are also often different. So, for effective testing of programs, both techniques should be applied. However, the set of testcases for the two approaches may not be disjoint. In other words, testcases chosen for functional testing will undoubtedly execute some statements, branches, and paths, and will provide some coverage. Similarly, the testcases selected for satisfying some coverage criteria will satisfy some of the functional testing criteria. Hence, the first question is how to combine the two approaches, such that the number of testcases is kept to a minimum.

The first thing to realize is that the two approaches are often suited for different kinds of testing. Structural testing is not suitable for testing entire programs, because it is extremely difficult to generate testcases to get the desired coverage. Structural testing is well suited for module testing. In fact one of the goals in design and implementation should be to keep each individual module simple, such that structural testing can be easily performed. So, often structural testing is done only for modules, and only functional testing is done for systems.

To combine functional and structural testing for a module, it is convenient to start with selecting a set of testcases using the different functional criteria. In general, these testcases will provide some coverage but will not satisfy the coverage criterion of structural testing. This set is then augmented with additional testcases such that the coverage criterion is satisfied. This final set of testcases is that used for testing.

7.4. Testing Process

A number of activities must be performed for testing software. In general, testing starts with a *test plan*. The test plan identifies all the testing-related activities that need to be performed along with the schedule and guidelines for testing. The plan also specifies the levels of testing that need to be done, by identifying the different testing units. Based on the plan, the testing commences. For each unit specified in the plan, first the testcases are selected and specified. Then the test unit is executed with the testcases and reports are produced. These reports are analyzed. The testing of units can go on in parallel, and when testing of some units has completed, the tested units can be combined along with some untested modules to form new test units. The flow graph of testing activities is shown in Figure 7.6.

The figure shows that testing commences with a test plan and terminates with acceptance testing. A number of test units are formed during the

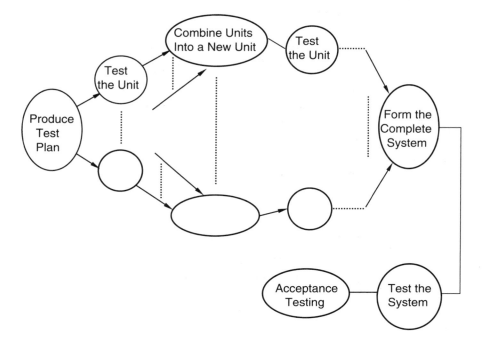

Each "Test the Unit" has the following activities:

FIGURE 7.6. The testing process.

testing, the final unit being the entire system. The testing of many of these units can proceed independently and in parallel. Finally, we have a single unit—the entire system—which is then tested. As shown above, testing of any unit involves three basic activities—specifying the testcases, executing the testcases and then evaluating the results of testing. In the rest of the section, we will discuss the different activities associated with testing in more detail.

7.4.1. Test Plan

A test plan is a general document for the entire project which defines the scope, approach to be taken, and the schedule of testing, as well as identifying the test items for the entire testing process, and the personnel responsible for the different activities of testing. The test planning can be done well before the actual testing commences and can be done in parallel with the coding and design phases. The inputs for forming the test plan are the: (1) project plan, (2) requirements document, and (3) system design document. The project plan is needed to make sure that the test plan is consistent with the overall plan for the project and the testing schedule matches that of the project plan. The requirements document and the design document are the basic documents used for selecting the test units and deciding the approaches to be employed during testing. A test plan should contain the following:

Test unit specification
Features to be tested
Approach for testing
Test deliverables
Schedule
Personnel allocation

A **test unit** is a set of one or more modules together with associated data which are from a single computer program and which are the object of testing [Iee87]. A test unit can occur at any level and can contain from a single module to the entire system. Thus a test unit may be a module, a few modules, or a complete program. Different units are usually specified for unit, integration, and system testing. The identification of test units establishes the different levels of testing that will be performed in the project.

Features to be tested include all software features and combinations of features that should be tested. A software feature is a software characteristic specified or implied by the requirements or design documents. These may include functionality, performance, design constraints, and attributes.

The *approach* for testing specifies the overall approach to be followed in the current project. The techniques that will be used to judge the testing effort should also be specified. This is sometimes called testing criteria, or the criteria for evaluating the set of testcases used in testing. In the previous sections we have discussed many criteria for evaluating and selecting testcases.

Testing deliverables should be specified in the test plan, before the actual testing begins. Deliverables could be a list of testcases that were used, detailed results of testing, test summary report, test log, and data about the code coverage. Selection of testing deliverables will determine what forms must be filled out during testing. In general, a *testcase specification* report, *test summary report* and a *test log* should be specified as deliverables. Testcase specification is discussed below. The test summary report summarizes the results of the testing activities and evaluates the results. It defines the items tested, the environment in which testing was done, and any variances from the specifications that were observed during testing. The test log provides a chronological record of relevant details about the execution of the testcases.

The *schedule* specifies the amount of time and effort to be spent on different activities of testing, and testing of different units that have been identified. *Personnel allocation* identifies the persons responsible for performing the different activities.

7.4.2. Testcase Specifications

Although there is one test plan for the entire project, testcases have to be specified separately for each test unit. Based on the approach specified in the test plan, first the features to be tested for this unit must be determined. The overall approach stated in the plan is refined into specific test techniques that should be followed and into the criteria to be used for evaluation. Based on these, the testcases have to be specified for testing the unit. Testcase specification gives, for each item to be tested, all testcases, inputs to be used in the testcases, and outputs expected for those testcases.

Testcase specification is a major activity in the testing process. Careful selection of testcases that satisfy the criteria and approach specified is essential for proper testing. We have considered many methods for generating testcases and criteria for evaluating testcases. A combination of these need to be used for selecting the testcases. It should be pointed out that testcase specifications contain not only the testcase, but the rationale of selecting a testcase (such as what condition it is testing) and the expected output for the testcase.

7.4.3. Testcase Execution and Analysis

With a specification of testcases to be used, the next step is to execute these testcases. Sometimes, the steps to be performed for executing the testcases are specified in a separate document called *test procedure specification*. This document specifies any special requirements that exist for setting the test environment, and describes the methods and formats for reporting the results of testing. Measurements, if needed, are also specified, along with how to obtain the measurements. Starting, shutdown, and restart procedures are specified.

For evaluation of testing, various outputs of the unit are needed. The two most common are the test log and the test summary report. Sometimes, the events that occur during testing that require further investigations are described in a separate document called *test incident report*.

7.5. Comparison of Different V&V Techniques

After discussing various techniques for verification and validation in the last two chapters, it is natural to ask how these techniques compare with each other. The major technique that we have covered in this chapter and

| | Technique | | | | |
Defect	Code review	Static anal.	Proof	Structural test	Functional test
Computational	Med	Med	High	High	Med
Logic	Med	Med	High	High	Med
I/O	High	Med	Low	Med	High
Data handling	High	High	Med	Low	High
Interface	High	High	Low	High	Med
Data Defn	Med	Med	Med	Low	Med
Data base	High	Low	Low	Med	Med

FIGURE 7.7. Comparison of the different techniques.

the previous chapter are: code reviews, static analysis, proof of correctness, structural testing and functional testing.

It is not easy to compare the effectiveness of the different techniques. The "effectiveness" will, in general, depend on the type of errors that exist in the software. First, in general, static analysis is likely to be the most cost effective, followed by code reviews. That is, from the point of view of cost of detecting errors, these two are likely to be the "best". However, economics is only one aspect of testing, since the major goal is to detect errors. These two techniques are often limited in number and type of errors they can uncover.

In general, no one technique is "best" for all types of errors. Different techniques have different effectiveness for different types of errors. Hence, for comparison it is best to classify the errors into different categories first and then compare the effectiveness of these techniques for these different categories. One such comparison is given in Figure 7.7 [Dun84].

As we can see, according to this comparison, different techniques have different strengths and weaknesses. For example, structural testing, as one would expect, is good for detecting logic errors, but not very good for detecting data handling errors. For the data handling type of error, static analysis is quite good. Thus it is unlikely that one technique will suffice for proper verification and validation. If high reliability is desired for the software, then a combination of these techniques will have to be used. From the table one can see that if code reviews, structural testing and functional testing are all used, then together their strengths are in all the categories described above.

7.6. Metrics

After the complete testing is done and the software delivered, the development is considered over. At this point the entire project can be evaluated and post-mortems can be performed. Metrics can be used for this.

In addition to the evaluation of the project, the most relevant metric relating to testing is reliability. Reliability of software often depends considerably on the quality of testing. Hence, by assessing reliability we can also judge the quality of testing. In this section we will also discuss some methods for reliability assessment. Most of these models are based on the data obtained during testing to predict the reliability of the software during normal operation. Hence, reliability is a particularly pertinent metric that can be assessed after testing is done.

7.6.1. Reliability Assessment

For any product, the user would like to know its reliability. The concept of reliability in software systems is somewhat different from hardware or mechanical systems. In a mechanical or a hardware system, unreliability is caused by the wearing out or aging of the system. By studying how components wear out, we can model the reliability of a system. Software systems are different in this respect. Software has no physical components, and has no "wearing out" process associated with it. Unless changed, a software system does not change with "age." The unreliability in software is caused by faulty design or implementation of the system. With the current level of technology, it is generally thought that it is impossible to detect all the faults in a large software system. Consequently, a software system is expected to have some faults in it. Software reliability is essentially the confidence we place in the design of the system.

We have earlier discussed the concept of faults and failures. Reliability can be defined as the probability that faults do not cause a failure in a specified period of time. It can also be specified as mean time to failure (MTTF). Reliability of a software system tells us how much confidence we can place in the results produced by the system. In addition to this, a measure of reliability is also useful in making design tradeoffs and monitoring a project. Since the reliability of a software system is dependent upon the amount of resources we spend on testing, a reliability measure can be used to determine when to stop testing, or how much testing a system should undergo before delivery.

Many models have been proposed for software reliability assessment [Goe85]. Many of them are based on the history of development and testing of the project. Specifically, the data about failures encountered during system testing is used to predict the reliability of the system. This data about past failures is used in two different ways, giving rise to two different classes of models. In the first, the times between failures is used, and in the second, the number of failures in a specified time interval is used. Here we present a model of each of the two classes.

JELINSKI AND MORANDA (JM) MODEL

The JM model [Jel72] is one of the earliest and one of the most widely used models for assessing software reliability. Software is assumed to have N faults initially. When a failure occurs, the fault that caused the failure is removed. The failure rate of a system at any time is assumed to be proportional to the number of faults present in the system at that time. If the proportionality constant is represented by ϕ, after the first failure, the detection rate drops to $\phi*(N - 1)$, after the second failure to $\phi*(N - 2)$, and so on. So, the failure rate, or the *hazard function*, at a time t_i, between the ith and $(i + 1)$st failures, is given by

$$Z(t_i) = \phi*[N - i].$$

The parameters N and ϕ can be estimated from a sample of actual failure occurrences (by using the maximum likelihood principle). Let $t_1, t_2, \ldots, t_n$ be a sample of time intervals between successive failures (observed during system testing), and the total time for detecting n failures be $T = \sum_{i=1}^{i=n} ki$. Then the estimate of N can be obtained by solving the following equation:

$$\frac{1}{N} + \frac{1}{N - 1} + \ldots + \frac{1}{N - (N - 1)} = \frac{n}{N - \frac{1}{T} \sum_{i=1}^{i=n} (i-1)t_i}.$$

This equation may be satisfied for many values of N. However, only the value $N > n$ is meaningful. From this estimate of N, an estimate of ϕ can be obtained by the following relationship:

$$\phi = \frac{n}{NT - \sum_{i=1}^{i=n} (i - 1)t_i}.$$

With the two constants estimated, the current failure rate can be estimated. The expected time for the next failure at any time is simply 1/current-failure-rate.

GOEL AND OKUMOTO (GO) MODEL

The GO model [Goe79] is based on the number of failures observed in a given time period. The basis is that as failures occur, and the faults are removed, the failures per unit time will decrease. Let $N(t)$ be the cumulative number of failures observed by time t, and $m(t)$ be the expected number of failures observed by time t. The probability that at a given time t, $N(t)$ is y, is given by the following equation.

$$P\{N(t) = y\} = \frac{|m(t)|^y}{y!}e^{-m(t)}, \ y = 0, 1, 2, \ldots$$

where,

$$m(t) = a(1 - e^{-bt}).$$

The failure rate at a time t can be obtained by differentiating $m(t)$, obtaining the hazard function as

$$\dot{Z}(t) = abe^{-bt}.$$

In this model a is the expected number of failures to be observed eventually; $m(t)$ at $t = \infty$ is a. The number of faults to be detected is treated as a random variable, and not a fixed unknown constant, as is done in the JM model. b is the fault detection rate per fault. The expected number of faults remaining in the system at a time t is given by

$$E\{\overline{N}(t)\} = ae^{-bt}.$$

Given that $N(t)$ is y, since y faults have been detected at time t, the expected number of remaining faults can be obtained from the above equation, and evaluates to

$$E\{\overline{N}(t)|N(t) = y\} = a - y.$$

With a given set of data the constants a and b can be estimated. Given that failures are detected at times $T_1, T_2, \ldots, T_n$, a and b can be estimated by numerically solving the following equations:

$$n/a = 1 - e^{-bT_n}$$
$$n/b = \Sigma T_i + aT_n.e^{-bT_n}.$$

It should be pointed out that T_i is the actual time at which the ith error is detected, while t_i, used in the JM model, represents the time between the $(i-i)st$ and the ith failures. If there are n data points, then $\sum_{i=1}^{i=n} t_i = T_n$.

AN EXAMPLE

In this section we will look at the data for an actual development project by the Navy, as reported in [Goe79]. For one of the larger modules, during production, 26 faults were detected over a period of 250 days. In the testing phase an additional five faults were detected in an additional 290 days. In further user operation and testing an additional three faults were detected in another 409 days.

For the JM model, considering the development failures only, we have $n = 26$, and $T = 250$. Substituting these numbers in the equation for solving N, and then solving numerically, we obtain $N = 31.2$. Thus the total number of faults in the module are estimated to be 31.2, which means that the estimated number of faults still present in the module after the development phase is $31.2 - 26 = 5.2$. Using this estimate of N, the value of C is determined to be .0068. With this, the expected time for the next failure to occur is

$$\frac{1}{.0068*(31.2 - 26)} = 23.5 \text{ days.}$$

For the GO model, n is 26, and T_n, the time at which the last fault is detected, is 250. Using these values in the equations for estimating a and b, and solving those numerically we get $a = 34$ and $b = .0058$. This means that the expected number of total faults in the module is 34, and the expected number of faults remaining is $34 - 26 = 8$.

ASSUMPTIONS AND LIMITATIONS OF SOFTWARE RELIABILITY MODELS

Many models have been proposed to predict software reliability. An excellent survey of different models is given in [Goe85]. All the models make many assumptions about the software development process, in order to develop a mathematically tractable model. The results produced by such models will only be valid if the assumptions made are a good approximation of the actual situation. Here we mention some of the assumptions made by different models and comment upon their validity.

It is generally assumed that the times between failures are independent. This will be true if the input data used for failure detection is randomly chosen. During program testing often the testcases are not randomly chosen. Once a fault is detected, test data is often selected to execute program statements where the fault was detected. However, if there is some degree of independence between the testcases, this is a reasonable assumption. It is also assumed that the failure rate is proportional to the number of remaining faults, which implies that each fault has the same chance of causing failure. This will hold if the input data is such that there is equal probability of executing all portions of the code. Although, not strictly valid, it is a reasonable assumption.

It is often assumed that the detected fault is immediately corrected, and that new faults are not introduced during the fault removal process. Sometimes, testing proceeds even after a failure is detected without removing the fault. The assumption will still be valid in such situations if future failures are not caused by the fault that would have been removed earlier, if fault removal had been done. The assumption that no new faults are introduced during the fault removal process is also not always valid, as faults are sometimes introduced by the fault removal process itself. Some models have been proposed which do not assume a perfect fault removal process. However, the assumption will hold if the failures caused by the faults introduced during fault removal are not considered in the data and their effect is properly removed from the data.

7.6.2. Programmer Productivity

Once the project is finished, one can look at the overall productivity achieved by the programmers during the project. Productivity data can be used for managing the resources and reducing cost by increasing productivity, establishing "baselines" in productivity from the history of different projects to help in productivity and cost estimation of future projects, and developing cost and productivity models. Perhaps the first reason is the major factor why productivity analysis is used in companies.

To measure productivity, first we need some metrics for productivity that are applicable for a wide variety of projects. One common method for measuring productivity is **lines of code written per programmer-month**. This measure can be obtained easily from the data about the total programmer-months spent on the project, and the total number of source code lines written during the project.

There are many flaws with this metric. A fundamental problem with this metric is having a precise definition of what constitutes "lines of code" [Jon78], since programs consist of more than executable statements, such as declaration lines and comments. Between the two extremes of counting all lines and counting only the executable lines there could be more than a two-to-one variation. Even with the same counting procedure, the lines of code for the same program are different for different programming languages. However, this problem can be countered by precisely defining what should be counted and keeping the counting method in mind when interpreting the productivity figures.

It should also be kept in mind that productivity by this measure depends considerably on the source language. For higher level language we can expect fewer source code lines for a problem, as compared to assembly language. This leads to an anomaly that the productivity of projects using a higher level language is *less than* the productivity of projects using assembly language. This is clearly counterintuitive and wrong. Comparing the two productivity figures here is like comparing apples and oranges. Two productivity figures can be compared only if their line counting procedures are the same, and if the source code was written in the same programming language.

There are other minor problems with counting lines of code. Even if we agree on counting only executable lines, do we count lines or statements? In many languages it is possible to write multiple statements in one line. How should this be accounted for? Similarly, for developing software, usually support software is built (test drivers and stubs, for example) which is not a part of the final system and is not delivered, but consumes effort nonetheless. Some method has to be used to account for the support software properly. In many software systems, different parts of the system may be written in different languages. In such a situation, there is no easy way to count the lines. Another problem comes when some parts of existing systems are reused to build a new system. How should the reused parts be counted? They cannot be discarded, as effort is required in identifying these modules and modifying them to make them suitable for the current system. They cannot be counted entirely, since the effort required for these lines is less than writing them from scratch (that is the fundamental reason for reusing). This problem can be handled by giving a different weightage to the reused lines of code for calculating the productivity.

There are other metrics of productivity. Some of these are number of pages of documentation written per programmer-month and CPU hours/ connect hours per programmer-month. These have problems of their own and have not gained in popularity.

Another way of measuring productivity is in terms of cost per unit of work (e.g. per thousand lines, per thousand bytes). This approach is different from the previous approaches where productivity is measured in terms of work-units, whereas in this case it is measured in terms of cost-units. Often the measure in cost-units is better suited for measuring productivity. A typical unit could be programmer-months per thousand lines of code.

7.6.3. Error Removal Efficiency

Although software quality comprises many different attributes, reliability is perhaps the most important. As reliability depends on the number of faults in the software, it is important to assess the effectiveness of the different methods employed for defect removal. Furthermore, as considerable effort is employed in the form of different techniques for detection and removal of errors from the software, it is essential that these error removal processes be efficient. Due to cost constraints in any project, by using more effective methods more errors can be removed before the software is delivered. For measuring the efficiency of these methods some metrics are needed. Here we will discuss some of these metrics briefly.

The efficiency of a defect removal process can be defined if the total number of errors in the software is known. This data is not known but is approximated by counting all defects detected before and after delivery. The *defect removal efficiency* [Jon78] of a defect removing process is defined as the percentage reduction of the defects that are present before the initiation of the process. The *cumulative defect removal efficiency* of a series of defect removal processes is the percentage of defects that have been removed by this series, based on the number of defects that are present at the beginning of the series.

For example, suppose a total of ten defects are detected during development and during field operation. We can estimate the total number of errors present in the software before the defect removal operations began to be ten. Suppose that during reviews four defects were removed. The defect removal efficiency of reviews in this example is 40%. Suppose that during testing another four defects are removed. The defect removal efficiency of testing then is 66% (as it removed four out of six remaining defects). The cumulative defect removal efficiency of reviews followed by testing is 80%.

These measures require the total number of defects in the software to be known. This information can be estimated by carefully recording all the defects removed. This includes the defects detected during development as well as the defects removed during field operation. This data will therefore be collected over a few years. The total number of defects detected can be used as an estimate of the total number of defects in the software. If we use this method (and the metrics above), it will not provide us with the efficiency at any time of the development. These measures are therefore useful to obtain historical data and observe trends in error detection, which can then be used for a given project. Thus the error data about a project is not directly used to control that project. However, data from many similar projects can be used to establish trends. These trends and data from a project can then be used to assess the project.

Another metric that is used is *defects per thousand lines of source code,* where source lines are defined according to local conventions. This is a cruder measure than the one before and measures only the overall defect rate. It is not useful for assessing the effectiveness of a particular defect removal process. In this measure, all defects regardless of where they are removed are combined together to get this metric.

Another metric used for assessing the effectiveness of defect removal mechanisms is *cost per defect.* Costs of defects are important since about half the total development costs go towards removing defects. This measure can also be viewed as defect removal cost per thousand lines of code. There are some problems with this measure of efficiency, since it tends to penalize high quality programs. High quality programs often have fewer defects, and these defects are not likely to be the ones that are straightforward to identify. The cost of detecting errors for such programs is likely to be much higher than programs that have more defects in them. Hence, cost per defect as a measure of a defect removal processes' efficiency is not a reliable measure.

7.7. Monitoring and Control

Testing and coding are the two phases that require careful monitoring, as these phases involve the maximum number of people. The first thing that has to be ensured by proper monitoring is that the test plan is being followed. For example, if it has been decided (and stated in the test plans) that unit, integration and system testing will be performed, then it must be ascertained that these different levels of testing were indeed performed. Additionally, it has to be ensured that the criteria specified in the plans are being met.

For example, a test plan might require 100% statement coverage for unit testing, and for system testing might require that there be at least two different test cases to test each condition listed in the requirement. Monitoring has to ensure that this is indeed the case.

One means of monitoring is **test case review,** and review of the test results. In the testcase specifications, all the conditions that need to be tested are listed, along with the test cases that will test the condition. In addition, expected output for the testcases is given. In the test plan review, it can be determined if the conditions that are being tested are sufficient for the project, if the testcase selected is indeed testing the condition, and if the testcases together satisfy the specified testcase criteria. A test plan review forces the tester to think and write down all the testcases, thus reducing the on-the-fly testing, which is often done and is usually unreliable.

Test log and test summary reports provide information for monitoring the testing activities. A **test log** provides a chronological record of relevant details about testing, while the **test summary report** summarizes the results of testing. Entries in a test log are made during testing, and describe the activities and events that occur. Study of the test log can reveal how testing is being performed and whether proper procedures are being followed. The test log is also supposed to contain descriptions of any anomalous events that occur during testing. The frequency of such occurrences can be used to assess the quality of the software. The test summary report specifies the test items, the environment under which testing was done, the variances observed in the behavior as compared to the requirements or specifications, and an assessment of whether testing has evaluated relevant features sufficiently (and which ones it has not). This gives an overview of testing, and is useful in evaluating the quality of testing and deciding if further testing is necessary.

Coverage is a metric that should be monitored. As we have seen, there are a few different coverage metrics. For monitoring, both statement and branch coverage should be monitored. If only functional testing is being done, the coverage achieved during testing can be an indicator of how extensive is the testing. From past experience it can be determined what coverage is achieved when functional testing is performed.

Testing time is the total time or effort spent by the project team in testing activities. This is an excellent indicator of whether testing is sufficient or not. In particular, if inadequate testing is done, it will be reflected in a reduced testing effort. From past experience we know that the total testing effort should be about 40% of the total effort for developing the software. This percentage can easily be converted into a percentage relative to coding or design effort, and a proper figure for an organization can be obtained from past projects. Monitoring the testing effort will catch the "miracle finish" cases, where the project "finishes" suddenly, soon after the coding is done. Such "finishes" occur for reasons such as unreasonable schedules, personnel shortages, and slippage of schedule. However, such a finish usually implies that in order to finish the project the testing phase has been compressed too much, which is likely to mean that the software has not been evaluated properly.

Computer time consumed during testing is another measure that can give valuable information to the project management. In general, in a software development project, the computer time consumption is low at the start, increases as time progresses, and reaches a peak. Thereafter it reduces, as the project reaches its completion. Maximum computer time is consumed during the latter part of coding and testing. By monitoring the computer time consumed, one can get an idea about how thorough the testing has been. Again, by comparing the previous build-ups in the computer time consumption, computer time consumption of the current project can provide valuable information about whether the testing is adequate or not.

Error Tracing is an activity which does not directly affect the testing of the current project, but has many long term quality control benefits. By error tracing we mean that when a fault is detected after testing, it should be studied and traced back in the development cycle to determine where it was introduced. This exercise has many benefits. First, it gives quantitative data about how many errors slip by the earlier quality control measures, which phases are more error prone. If some particular phase is found to be more error prone, the verification activity of that phase then should be strengthened in the future, and proper standards and procedures need to be developed to reduce the occurrence of errors in the future. By seeing how many and what type of faults are slipping by the earlier quality assurance measures provide valuable input for evaluation of the quality control strategies. This evaluation can be used to determine which quality control measures should be strengthened and what sort of techniques should be added. Another benefit of error tracing is productivity improvement in the future. Error tracing is a feedback mechanism which is invaluable for learning. A designer/programmer, by seeing the mistakes that occurred during his activities, will learn from the information and is less likely to make similar mistakes in the future, thereby increasing his productivity. If this feedback is not provided, no such learning is possible.

7.8. Summary

Testing plays a critical role in quality assurance for software. Due to the limitations of the verification methods for the previous phases, design and requirement faults also appear in the code. Testing is used for detecting these errors, in addition to detecting the errors introduced during the coding phase.

Testing is a dynamic method for verification and validation, where the system to be tested is actually executed and the behavior of the system is observed. Due to this, testing observes the failures of the system, from which the presence of faults can be deduced. However, separate activities have to be performed to identify the faults (and then remove them).

Different levels of testing are often employed. Unit testing is used for testing a module or a small collection of modules. Its goal is to detect coding errors in modules. During integration testing, modules are combined into sub-systems, which are then tested. The goal here is to test the system design. In system testing and acceptance testing, the entire system is tested. The goal here is to test the system against the requirements, and to test the requirements themselves.

There are two approaches to testing, functional and structural. In functional testing, the internal logic of the system under testing is not considered and the testcases are decided from the specifications or the requirements. It is often called "black box testing". Equivalence class partitioning, boundary value analysis, and cause-effect graphing are examples of methods for selecting testcases for functional testing. In structural testing, the testcases are decided entirely on the internal logic of the program/module under testing. The external specifications are not considered. Often a structural criterion is specified, but the procedure for selecting testcases is left to the tester. The most common structural criteria are statement coverage and branch coverage.

Testing usually commences with a test plan, which is the basic document guiding the entire testing of the software. It specifies the levels of testing and the units to be tested. For testing different units, first the testcases are specified, which are then executed. In testcase specification, different methods for selecting testcases can be used. A number of different methods have been discussed in the chapter.

The main metric of interest during testing is the reliability of the software under testing. Reliability of software depends on the faults in the software. To assess the reliability of software, reliability models are needed. To use a model for a given software system, data is needed about the software that can be used in the model to estimate the reliability of the software. Most reliability models are based on the data obtained during the system and acceptance testing. Data about time between failures observed during testing are used by these models to estimate the reliability of the software. We have discussed two such reliability models in the chapter and have discussed the limitations of reliability models.

Exercises

1. Define error, fault and failure. What is the difference between a fault and a failure? Does testing observe faults or failures?

2. What are the different levels of testing and the goals of the different levels? For each level, specify which of the testing approaches (functional, structural or some other) is most suitable.

3. What is the goal of testing? Why is the psychology of the tester important?

4. Testing often consumes more resources than any other phase in software development. Describe three major factors that make testing so expensive.

5. What is the difference between functional and structural testing? Is determining testcases easier in functional or structural testing (for branch coverage)? Is it correct to claim that if functional testing is done properly, it will achieve close to 100% branch coverage?

6. What are the different structural testing criteria? These criteria do not specify any method for testcase selection. Define an approach that you can use for selecting testcases for satisfying the different criteria.

7. Consider a simple text formatter problem. Given a text consisting of words separated by blanks (BL) or newline (NL) characters, the text formatter has to covert it into lines, such that no line has more than MAXPOS characters, breaks between lines occurs at BL or NL, and the maximum possible number of words are in each line. The following program has been written for this text formatter [Goo75].

```
alarm := false;
bufpos := 0;
fill := 0;
repeat
  inchar(c);
  if (c = BL) or (c = NL) or (c = EOF)
  then
    if bufpos ! = 0
    then begin
      if (fill + bufpos < MAXPOS) and (fill ! = 0)
      then begin
        outchar(BL);
        fill : = fill + 1; end
      else begin
        outchar(NL);
        fill : = 0; end;
      for k: = 1 to bufpos do
        outchar(buffer[k]);
      fill : = fill + bufpos;
      bufpos : = 0; end
  else
    if bufpos = MAXPOS
    then alarm : = true
```

  else begin
   bufpos : = bufpos + 1;
   buffer[bufpos] : = c; **end**
until alarm or (c = EOF);

For this program, do the following:

 a. Select a set of testcases using the functional testing approach. Use as many techniques as possible, and also select testcases for special cases using the "error guessing" method.

 b. Select a set of testcases that will provide a 100% statement coverage. Then select a set of testcases that will provide a 100% branch coverage. Notice the difference between the two sets of testcases, if any.

 c. Suppose that this program is written as a procedure. Write a driver for testing this procedure with the testcases selected in (a) and (b). Clearly specify the format of the testcases and how they are used by the driver.

8. Suppose three numbers A, B, and C are given in ascending order representing the lengths of the sides of a triangle. The problem is to determine the type of the triangle (whether it is isosceles, equilateral, right, obtuse or acute). Consider the following program written for this problem.

```
read(a, b, c);
if (a < b) or (b < c) then
    print("Illegal inputs");
    return;
if (a = b) or (b = c) then
    if (a = b) and (b = c) then print("equilateral triangle")
    else print("isoscles triangle")
else begin
    a : = a * a; b : = b * b; c : = c * c;
    d : = b + c;
    if (a = d) then print("right triangle")
    else if (a<d) then print("acute triangle")
    else print("obtuse triangle");
end;
```

For this program, do the following:

 a. Select a set of testcases using the functional testing approach. Use as many techniques as possible, and also select testcases for special cases using the "error guessing" method.

 b. Select a set of testcases that will provide a 100% statement coverage. Does this set provide a 100% branch coverage also?

c. Suppose that this program is written as a procedure. Write a driver for testing this procedure with the testcases selected in (a) and (b). Clearly specify the format of the testcases and how they are used by the driver.

d. Suppose that this module is called by another module M, to which this module returns different codes for different types of triangles. Depending on the triangle type, M performs different activities. You have to test M without the code for this module being available. Write a stub for this module such that testing of M can proceed.

9. Why does software fail after it has passed acceptance testing? Remember, software does not deteriorate with time.

10. Do the reliability models actually measure reliability or estimate it from some other measurements?

11. What are the assumptions and limitations of the current reliability models?

12. Another method for evaluating software reliability is to use the Mill's seeding approach. In this method some faults are seeded in the program, and reliability is assessed based on how many of these seeded faults are detected during testing. Develop a simple reliability model based on this approach. Define your parameters, and give a formula for estimating the reliability and the number of faults remaining in the system.
What are the drawbacks and limitations of this seeding model? What are the assumptions about the seeded faults?

13. If you were to evaluate the reliability of software later by using the JM or GO model, what data do you need to collect during development? Design a form that should be filled out by the programmer to provide the necessary information.

14. You want to find if there is a correlation between complexity and reliability, and size and reliability. What data will you collect during and after termination of a project? How can this data be obtained? How many projects do you feel are necessary to get some confidence in the co-relation numbers obtained by this study?

Case Study Testing

Test Plan

This document describes the plan for testing the course scheduling software. All major testing activities are specified here; additional testing may be scheduled later if necessary.

1. TEST UNITS

In this project we will perform two levels of testing—unit testing and system testing. Since the system is small, it is felt that there is no need for elaborate integration testing. The basic units to be tested are:

Modules to input file-1
Modules to input file-2
Modules for scheduling

In addition, some other units may be chosen for testing. The testing for these different units will be done independently.

2. FEATURES TO BE TESTED

All the functional features specified in the requirements document will be tested. No testing will be done for the performance, as the response time requirement is quite weak.

3. APPROACH FOR TESTING

For unit testing, structural testing based on branch coverage criteria will be used. The goal is to achieve a branch coverage of more than 95%. System testing will be largely functional in nature. The focus is on invalid and valid cases, boundary values, and special cases.

4. TEST DELIVERABLES

The following documents are required (besides this test plan):

Unit test report for each unit
Testcase specification for system testing
Test report for system testing
Error report.

The testcase specification for system testing has to be submitted for review before the system testing commences.

5. SCHEDULE AND PERSONNEL ALLOCATION

The entire testing—unit and system—will be finished within the month of April. Much of the unit testing will be done in the first two weeks of April. Testcase specifications for the system testing will be produced while unit testing is going on. This schedule is consistent with the overall schedule of the project. The schedule for testing is shown below.

```
Unit testing        | ******     Person-1
Unit testing        | ******     Person-2
Testcase specs      | *****      Person-3
System testing      |      ********** 2 Persons
                    |_____|
                              April
```

```
PROGRAM test_driver(input,output,file1,file2);

Data and type decls from the program

PROCEDURE validate_classrooms(var num_of_rooms : integer);
(* This is the module to be unit tested    *)
(* It Validates the classrooms and capacity in input file1 *)
(* Other modules in the test unit are also included *)

BEGIN (* Driver *)
   open(file1,'test'); (* File test contains the input test data *)
   reset(file1);
   validate_classrooms(num_of_rooms);
   IF not error THEN
      FOR i: = 1 to num_of_rooms DO BEGIN
              writeln('classroom no ',classroom_DB[i].room_no);
              writeln('room capacity ',classroom_DB[i].capacity);
      END
   ELSE BEGIN
       writeln('Fatal error(s) encountered in parsing the input file1');
       writeln('Scheduling aborted');
   END;
   close(file1);
END.
```

FIGURE 7.8. Code for test driver.

Unit Test Report

Here we present the unit testing report for one unit. Some details are shown here for the purposes of illustration, and are usually not included in unit test reports. The goal of unit testing is to achieve over 95% branch coverage.

The unit chosen is *validate_classrooms,* which is the module to validate the class and capacity data given in input file-1. This unit testing includes testing of get_next_line, get_token, and lengthof modules also, which are used by the validate_classrooms module.

1. DRIVERS AND STUBS

Since all procedures and functions that the validate_classrooms calls are included in testing, no stubs need to be written. The testcases are kept in a file and a driver is written to read the testcases and invoke the test unit with the different testcases. For illustration, the basic code employed during testing is shown in Figure 7.8.

2. TEST SUMMARY

a. Name of Module   : VALIDATE_CLASSROOMS
b. Description of Module : This module validates the classrooms and their corresponding capacities in the input file1 and, if there is any error, it completes the parsing of the file, but does not generate any schedule.
c. Other modules included in this testing :
   GET_NEXT_LINE, GET_TOKEN, STRING_TO_INT, LENGTHOF
   d. Size of the unit   : About 200 Lines of code.
   e. Approach used   : Branch coverage
   f. Testcase selection   : Test cases are generated until each branch is covered. Three different input data files were used for testing.
   g. Coverage   : 100% Branch coverage was achieved during testing.
   h. Test routines   : A test driver was written to read data from the input test file and execute the unit.
   i. Errors   : A total of four errors were detected and removed.

3. ERROR REPORT

Seq.	Error	Action taken
1	Abnormal exit on encountering a non-digit capacity	Fixed
2	Rooms not getting sorted by room capacity	Fixed
3	Input limits not being recognized	Fixed
4	Abnormal exit on end of file1	Fixed

Testcase Specifications for System Testing

Here we specify all testcases that are used for system testing. First, the different conditions that need to be tested, along with the testcases used for testing those conditions and the expected output are given. Then the data files used for testing are given. The testcases are specified with respect to these data files. The testcases have been selected using the functional approach. The goal is to test the different functional requirements, as specified in the requirements document. Testcases have been selected for both valid and invalid inputs.

SEQ NO.	TEST_CASE [File]	CONDITION BEING CHECKED	EXPECTED OUTPUT
1	Empty_file	Empty F1	Print message and stop
2	Empty_file	Empty F2	Print message and stop
3	No file	F1 does not exist	Print message and stop
4	No file	F2 does not exist	Print message and stop

SEQ NO.	TEST_CASE [File]	CONDITION BEING CHECKED	EXPECTED OUTPUT
For checking FILE1 format error			
5	[F1.1]	Incorrect course no. format	Print course no. and error message
6	[F1.7]	More than allowed(30) courses	Error message and skip to lecture times
7	[F1.4]	Course list empty to lecture times	Error message and skip
8	[F1.5]	Spelling of header	Error message and stop
9	[F1.1]	Lecture time format	Print time, error mesage and continue
10	[F1.2]	More than allowed no. of lecture times(15).	Error message, discard extra and skip to room no.s
11	[F1.4]	lecture times list empty	Print "No lecture times" and parse rooms.
12	[F1.1]	Incorrect room no format	Print room no. and message
13	[F1.1]	No colon (:) between room# and capacity.	Continue
14	[F1.1]	Capacity format	Print message with room no., capacity and continue
15	[F1.1]	Capacity more than limit(300).	Error message, continue
16	[F1.1]	Capacity less than 10	Error message, continue
17	[F1.7]	More than 20 room#,cap entries	Error message, stop
18	[F1.4]	Room list empty	Error message, stop
19	[F1.1]	No correct room entries	Error message, no scheduling, continue parsing
20	[F1.3]	Same course_no entered more than once	Print message and discard the entry.
21	[F1.3]	Duplicate lecture time	Print message, discard it and continue
22	[F1.3]	Duplicate room entry	Print message, ignore it and continue
FILE2 format (for FILE1, F1.8 is used)			
23	[F2.1]	Enrollment ≤ 2	Print message, ignore it, continue
24	[F2.1]	Enrollment in range [3-250]	Executes normally
25	[F2.1]	Enrollment exceeds 250	Print message, continue
26	[F2.2]	No preference specified	Scheduled
27	[F2.1]	More than allowed number of preferences(5).	Print message, and discard the rest
28	[F2.1]	Duplicate course entry	Print message and ignore duplicate
Consistency of FILE2 with FILE1. File F1.8 used for file 1.			
29	[F2.1]	Course not present in the list of offered courses	Print message, ignore it, continue

SEQ NO.	TEST_CASE [File]	CONDITION BEING CHECKED	EXPECTED OUTPUT
30	[F2.1]	Preference not found in lecture time list.	Print message and ignore the preference
31	[F2.1]	Enrollment > max. room capacity available	Error message
32	[F2.4]	Missing enrollment field	Ignore the course

SCHEDULING cases. File F1.8 used for file 1.

33	[F2.4]	No valid courses in F2	Print message and stop
34	[F2.2]	No PG course with pref.s	Schedule
35	[F2.4]	No UG course with pref.s	Schedule
36	[F2.4]	No PG courses with no pref.	Schedule
37	[F2.2]	No two courses allotted at the same time and in the same room	The first course is given the first preference
38	[F2.2]	Room capacity is more than the classroom	Course scheduled in a room with capacity more than enrollment
39	[F2.2]	PG courses given priority over UG courses even if UG course appears before the PG course in input	PG course is scheduled; UG course faces conflict
40	[F2.2]	Courses scheduled in the order they appear in the input file	The first course is given best pref., second the next pref. and so on
41	[F2.2]	Highest possible preference of a course is honored	The nth pref. honored with explanation for all the earlier n-1 preferences
42	[F2.3]	No two PG courses scheduled in the same slot even if same pref. given	The first one scheduled and conflict shown for the second course
43	[F2.3]	PG course with pref. given priority over PG courses with no preference	Courses with pref.s are scheduled before
44	[F2.2]	PG courses with no pref.s are guaranteed room even if some UG course has to be "unscheduled	PG course scheduled and conflict generated for the UG course
45	[F2.2]	No room with required capacity available for UG course with no preference	Error message

Data Files for Testcases

Note: To present these files compactly, all the new line characters are not included. Some formatting has been done to enhance readability.

File F1.1

rooms
   F-101 30 105 : 40 1052 : 25 F30:50 301 :9 311: 325 320 200
   310 : 211 312 2a 313 : 34 201 :00 678 ;
courses
   XC539 x29 53ABc cs5394 csa59 cs250 CS 245 CS665 ;
times
   TT TW10 TT10:30 MWF10:30 MWF9 MWF09 MWF789 10253 TTL2
   TT11 TT10-30 ;

File F1.2

rooms
   100 20 200 39 201 45 202 50 203 50 204 60 205 200 206 299
   207 10 208 300 209 100 301 11 302 25 303 15 304 56 305 77
   306 30 307 40 308 60 309 90 400 95 404 44 405 67 ;
courses
   cs444 cs_233 CS555,cs3423 cs665 ;
times
   TT8 TT9 MWF8 MWF9 MWF10 MWF11 MWF12 MWF2 MWF3
   MWF4 TT1:30 TT11:30 TT1 TT3 TT5 TT12:30 TT3:30 ;

File F1.3

rooms
   101 :250 303 49 401 40 101 30 303 45 202 50 ;
courses
   cs320 cs741 cs201 cs320 cs622 ;
times
   TT9 MWF12 TT10:30 MWF12 TT10:30 ;

File F1.4

rooms
   ;
courses
   ;

times
  ;

File F1.5

rooms
  202 34 100 10 ;
corse
  cs330 ;
timeslot
  TT1 MWF12 ;

File F1.6

rooms
  202:39 300 56 ;
courses
  ;
times
  TT3 ;

File F1.7

rooms
  101:25 456:78 345 90 346 90 347 90 348 90 349 90
  355 90 365 90 375 90 385 90 395 90 305 90 335 90
  495 90 545 90 645 90 745 90 945 90 946 90 155 90 ;
courses
  cs301, cs302, cs303, cs304 ,cs305, cs306 cs307 cs308
  cs309 cs201 cs601 cs602 cs603 cs604 cs605 cs606 cs607
  cs608 cs609 cs611 cs641 cs751 cs752 cs753 cs754 cs755
  cs756 cs757 cs758 cs759 cs123 ;
times
  MWF1, MWF2, MWF3, MWF4 MWF5 MWF6 MWF7 MWF8 MWF9
  MWF91 MWF92 MWF93 MWF94 MWF98 MWF99 MWF56

File F1.8

rooms
    201:50 202 75 203 30 204 150 ;
courses
    cs310, cs320, cs330, cs340 cs350 cs315 cs335 cs365 cs325 cs345,
    cs355 cs305 cs360 cs370 cs380 cs375, cs610 cs620 cs605 cs615,
    cs630, cs625, cs635 cs640 cs650 cs645 cs660, cs655 cs665 cs670 ;
times
    MWF9, MWF11, MWF2 TT8:30 TT1 TT11:30 ;

File F2.1

course
    cs305 25 TT8 TT6 TT9 MWF8
    cs344 45 TT1
    cd456 56 Tw56
    cs365 200 TT1 MWF9
    cs3a0 301 TT1
    cs345 0 TT11:30
    cs601 267 TT4
    cs665 140 TT1
    cs305 45 TT1
    cs335 df TT1
    cs645 45 TT1 TT11:30 TT8:30 MWF2 MWF11 MWF9
    cs330 100 TT1 MWF9,
        MWF2 MWF11

File F2.2

course enrollment preferences
    cs355 35 TT1
    cs660 70
    cs310 79 MWF11
    cs640 100
    cs315 50 TT11:30
    cs320 100 MWF9
    cs305 50 TT1
    cs325 70 TT1

     cs345 35
     cs365 70

File F2.3

course enrollment preferences
     cs605 70 TT1
     cs310 50 TT11:30, TT1
     cs625 35 TT11:30
     cs615 70
     cs325 35 MWF9
     cs330 55 MWF9
     cs610 100 TT1 TT11:30, MWF9
     cs335 50 MWF9, TT11:30, TT1
     cs650 150 MWF2 MWF9
     cs635 50
     cs660 150
     cs655 30 TT1, MWF2 MWF9
     cs315 52
     cs320 75
     cs305 70 MWF11
     cs340 150 TT8:30
     cs345 70 TT8:30 MWF11
     cs350 50 TT8:30 MWF11
     cs355 50 TT8:30 MWF11, MWF2
     cs360 50 MWF9 MWF11
     cs365 30
     cs370 50
     cs375 50
     cs620 155

File F2.4

course enrollment preferences

cs635	45	MWF11,TT11:30
cs620	36	TT1
cs330		
cs320	26	

System Test Report

A total of about 12 errors were detected during system testing. These were all minor and most of them were resolved within an hour. All these errors were removed and after their removal no error was uncovered during testing. The detailed output of all the test runs is not shown here. Output of one sample run in which the input file 1 was F1.8 and file 2 was F2.3 is given below.

OUTPUT OF THE TEST RUN: (WITH FILES F1.8 AND F2.3)

TIME TABLE

RM	MWF9	MWF11	MWF2	TT8:30	TT1	TT11:30
203	cs365					
201	cs325	cs350	cs355	cs635	cs370	cs625
202	cs330	cs305	cs315	cs345	cs605	cs310
204	cs610	cs615	cs650	cs340	cs320	cs335

Explanation Report
cs610 :
  TT1 : Conflict with course_no cs605
  TT11:30: Conflict with course_no cs625
cs335 :
  MWF9 : No room with proper capacity available
  TT11:30 :
    room#201: Conflict with course_no cs625
    room#202: Conflict with course_no cs310
cs350 :
  TT8:30 : No room with proper capacity available
cs355 :
  TT8:30 : No room with proper capacity available
  MWF11 : No room with proper capacity available

Conflict Report
cs620 :
  Ignored : Enrollment greater than the greatest capacity of any room in
    FILE1
cs655 :
  TT1   : Conflict with course_no cs605
  MWF2   : Conflict with course_no cs650
  MWF9   : Conflict with course_no cs610
cs360 :
  MWF9   : No room with proper capacity available
  MWF11 : No room with proper capacity available
cs660 :

Excess PG course : no time_slot available
cs375 :
No free room with required capacity available

Error Report

The main errors detected during system testing are given below.

Seq#	Error	Action taken
1	Accepting MAXCOURSES + 1	Fixed
2	If more than permissible rooms given, it does not skip to courses section after the message that remaining courses are being discarded.	Fixed / A routine was written
3	Same UG course scheduled more than once.	Fixed
4	Check for at least one room for each course not done in safe_allotment routine.	Fixed
5	Boundary error: last timeslot not tried in scheduling PG_no_pref courses.	Fixed
6	Wrong course numbers printed in conflict report—typing mistake in sched_module	Fixed
7	Boundary error: last course in UG_no_pref not scheduled.	Fixed
8	First conflict not printed. Initialization error in expl_index and conflict_index.	Fixed
9	Absence of capacity in last room entry is not detected.	Fixed
10	Not skipping over misspelt header in file.	Fixed
11	Empty time table produced if no valid entry.	Fixed

Case Study: Project Analysis

From the data collected about the project we can do some analysis of the development process and the project plan used for this project. In the project, the basic source of data (as specified in the monitoring plans) was the log book kept by each member of the project. The log entries were very detailed and the effort and schedule for different activities was easily obtained from it.

FINAL COST

The total effort spent on different activities relating to developing software was 283 person-hours. In a typical month there are about 22 working days, and if we assume that in each day a person works for about six hours on the project (the rest of the time goes for personal work), one person-month contains 132 hours. With this, the total effort on the project is about 2.1 person-months, which is somewhat lower than our estimate of 2.4 PM.

FINAL SCHEDULE

Overall about three calendar months were assigned for the project, and it was completed within this time. This is about 0.5 month less than the estimated schedule.

EFFORT DISTRIBUTION

The distribution of effort in this project for the different activities is given below.

Requirement	2%
System Design	16%
Detailed Design	20%
Coding and debugging	24%
Testing	37%

The requirements were specified before the project began. The only effort spent was on understanding the requirements. Coding includes debugging effort also.

PROJECT PRODUCTIVITY

After 2.1 person-months 1400 lines of Pascal source code was delivered. The productivity of the project is 660 LOC/PM.

ERRORS AND ERROR DETECTION

Most of the errors were detected during testing. In system and detailed design reviews, the design was modified to enhance the system, but no specific errors were detected. The errors detected during system testing were all coding errors, since they were introduced during the coding phase.

During system testing 11 errors were detected. Hence, after unit testing, the system contains 8.5 defects/KLOC.

From the logs we determine that the total time spent on detecting and correcting these errors was about six hours. Hence the cost per defect is about 0.5 person-hours, which is fairly small.

Appendix A:
Code for the Case Study

(* ──

This software is for scheduling a set of courses offered by the Computer Science Department. It takes two file inputs. File1 contains information about the courses in the department catalog, rooms in the building and the valid lecture times. The second file contains, for each course offered in a given semester, the course number, its enrollment and a set of time preferences given by the instructor of the course. The goal is to schedule these courses in the rooms such that the constraints given in the requirements document are satisfied.

VERSION: 1.0 , DATE OF RELEASE: April, 1990

DEVELOPED BY: IIT Kanpur

SECURITY: Unrestricted

── *)

PROGRAM schedule(input, output, file1, file2);

```
CONST
    MAXROOMS = 20;      (* Maximum no. of rooms *)
    MAXCOURSES = 30;      (* Maximum no. of courses *)
    MAXTIMES = 15;      (* Maximum no. of timeslots *)
    MAXCAP = 300;        (* Maximum capacity of a room *)
    MINCAP = 10;        (* Minimum capacity of a room *)
    MAXLINELENGTH = 50;   (* Maximum line length in either of input
        files *)
    FIL1 = 1;          (* File-descriptor FOR file1 *)
    FIL2 = 2;          (* File-descriptor FOR file2 *)
```

```
TYPE
  string3 = packed array [1..3] of char;
  string5 = packed array [1..5] of char;
  string7 = packed array [1..7] of char;
  line    = packed array [1..MAXLINELENGTH] of char;

  p_list_str = ^ p_node_str; (* List of actual preferences *)
  p_node_str =
  RECORD
    p_index: string7;
    p_ptr: p_list_str
  END;

  p_list_i = ^ p_node_i; (* List of preferences as indices in timeslot-DB *)
  p_node_i =
  RECORD
    p_index: integer;
    p_ptr: p_list_i
  END;

  course_rec =          (* Information about a course being offered *)
  RECORD
    course_i: integer;
    enrol: integer;
    valid_pref_list: p_list_i
  END;

  room_rec =
  RECORD
    room_no: string3;
    capacity: integer
  END;

  course_array = array [0..MAXCOURSES] of string5;
  room_array = array [1..MAXROOMS] of room_rec;
  time_array = array [1..MAXTIMES] of string7;

  ig_set = set of char; (* for skipping characters while reading a token *)

  confl_rec =           (* TYPE of conflict list and explaination list *)
  RECORD
    err_code: integer;
    course_index: integer; (* Index into courseno_DB *)
    room_index: integer;   (* Index into classroom_DB *)
    pref_list: p_list_i
  END;
```

(* Following are for reserving slots FOR PG_no_prefs courses *)

r_list = ^ r_node;   (* List of indices into classroom_DB; Contains *)

r_node =   (* rooms with capacity > enrol of PG_no_pref *)
RECORD
   r_index: integer;
   r_ptr: r_list
END;

t_slot_list = ^ t_slot_node; (* List of possible timeslots FOR PG_no
   _prefs *)
t_slot_node =   (* i.e. ones with no conflict *)
RECORD
   timeslot: integer;
   roomlist: r_list;
   t_ptr: t_slot_list
END;

pg_res_list = ^ pg_res_node; (* List of PG_no_pref courses *)
pg_res_node =
RECORD
   course: integer;
   timeslots: t_slot_list;
   res_next: pg_res_list
END;

VAR
   time_table: array [1..MAXROOMS, 1..MAXTIMES] of integer;
      (* The rows are indices into classroom_DB, columns are indices into
         timeslot_DB *)
   pg_alloc_array: array [1..MAXTIMES] of integer;
      (* Keeps track of PG courses occupying different timeslots. Used for
         checking PG conflicts *)
   conflict_list, expl_list: array [1..MAXCOURSES] of confl_rec;
      (* Contain conflicts encountered during scheduling *)

   conflict_index, (* Represents last entry in conflict_list *)
   expl_index,   (* Represents last entry in expl_list *)
   ugpstart,   (* Start of UG_prefs courses in course_rec array *)
   pgnpstart,   (* Start of PG_no_prefs in course_rec array *)
   ugnpstart,   (* Start of UG_no_prefs in course_rec array *)
   tot_courses   (* total course in file 2 *)
               : integer;

```
file1, file2: text;

classroom_DB: room_array;
course_no_db: course_array;
time_slot_db: time_array;

num_of_rooms,   (* Total number of rooms *)
num_of_times,   (* Total number of possible lecture times *)
num_of_courses, (* Total courses in file 1 *)
num_of_lines    (* For printing line numbers in error messages *)
          : integer;

error: boolean; (* Set if error in syntax of input file *)

course_rec_array: array [1..MAXCOURSES] of course_rec; (* Courses
  to be scheduled *)
```

(*||||||||||||||||||||||||||||||||||||||||||||||||||||||||||||||||||||||||||||||||||||||||||||||||||||||||||||||||||||||||||||||||||||||||||||*)
(*||||||||||||||||||||||||||||||||||||||||||||||||||||||||||||||||||||||||||||||||||||||||||||||||||||||||||||||||||||||||||||||||||||||||||||*)

```
PROCEDURE get_validated_input;

(* This module gets validated input from file1 and file2 *)

VAR
line_no: integer;
msgbuf: line;
  filename : packed array [1..20] of char;
```

(*——————— GENERAL UTILITIES FOR INPUT ———————*)

```
FUNCTION lengthoF (buffer: line): integer;

(* Returns the length of the buffer *)

VAR
  i, j: integer;

BEGIN
  IF length(buffer) = 0 THEN
  lengthof : = 0
  ELSE BEGIN
  i : = 1;
  WHILE buffer[i] = ' ' DO
      i : = i + 1;
```

```
    j : = 0;
    WHILE (i ≤ MAXLINELENGTH) and (buffer[i] <> ' ') DO
      BEGIN
        j : =j + 1;
        i : = i + 1
      END;
      lengthof : = j
    END
  END; { lengthof }
```

(* ——————————————————————————————————— *)

```
PROCEDURE get_next_line(file_no: integer; VAR buffer: line);

    (* Returns a non_empty line read from a file IF it is not empty *)
    (* Keeps on skipping empty lines UNTIL end of file is
       encountered      *)

BEGIN
  IF file_no = 1 THEN BEGIN
  IF eoF (file1) THEN
    buffer : = 'eof'
  ELSE
    readln(file1, buffer)
  END ELSE IF file_no = 2 THEN BEGIN
  IF eoF (file2) THEN
    buffer : = 'eof'
  ELSE
    readln(file2, buffer)
  END ELSE
  writeln('Error in file no ');
  IF buffer = ' ' THEN BEGIN
  get_next_line(file_no, buffer);
  line_no : = line_no + 1
  END
END; { get_next_line }
```

(* ——————————————————————————————————— *)

```
FUNCTION get_token(ignore_set: ig_set; VAR buffer: line): line;

    (* Returns the first token in the buffer    *)
    (* The token is delimited by ig_set *)

VAR
  i, j: integer;
  local_buf: line;
```

```
BEGIN
  IF buffer = ' ' THEN
  get_token : = 'eob'
  ELSE BEGIN
  i : = 1;
  WHILE (i ≤ MAXLINELENGTH) and (buffer[i] = ' ') DO
    i : = i + 1;
  CASE buffer[i] in ignore_set of
    true:
    BEGIN
      local_buF [1] : = buffer[i];
      FOR j : = 2 to MAXLINELENGTH DO
      local_buF [j] : = ' ';
      get_token : = local_buf;
      buffer[i] : = ' '
    END;
    OTHERWISE
    BEGIN
      j : = 1;
      WHILE (i < = MAXLINELENGTH) and not (buffer[i] in ['
        '] + ignore_set) DO BEGIN
      local_buF [j] : = buffer[i];
      buffer[i] : = ' ';
      i : = i + 1;
      j : = j + 1
      END;
      FOR i : = j to MAXLINELENGTH DO
      local_buF [i] : = ' ';
      get_token : = local_buf
    END
  END
  END
END; { get_token }
```

(* ———————————————————————————————— *)

```
FUNCTION string_to_int(token: line): integer;

  (* Converts a given string into an integer *)

VAR
  i, value: integer;

BEGIN
  IF token = ' ' THEN
  string_to_int : = 0
```

```
ELSE BEGIN
i : = 1;
value : = 0;
WHILE (i ≤ MAXLINELENGTH) and (token[i] = ' ') DO
  i : = i + 1;
WHILE (i ≤ MAXLINELENGTH) and (token[i] <> ' ') and
  (token[i] in ['0'..'9']) DO BEGIN
    value : = value * 10 + (ord(token[i]) − ord('0'));
    i : = i + 1
END;
IF (token[i] = ' ') or (i > MAXLINELENGTH) THEN
  string_to_int : = value
ELSE IF not (token[i] in ['0'..'9']) THEN
  string_to_int : = 0
END
END; { string_to_int }
```

(***)
(***)

```
PROCEDURE validate_file1;

VAR
  buffer, local_buf: line;
```

(* ——————————————————————————————————— *)

```
PROCEDURE validate_classrooms;
```

```
(* Validates the classrooms along with the capacity obtained  *)
(* from the i/p file1. If any error is encountered it continues *)
(* parsing the rest of the file, but scheduling is aborted.   *)
(* If no error is encountered, the room_nos are stored in     *)
(* increasing order of capacity in a global data structure    *)
(* 'CLASSROOM_DB'                                             *)
```

```
CONST
str_length = 3;

VAR
room_no: string3;
buffer, msgbuf, token: line;
i, cap: integer;
flag: boolean;
```

(* ——————————————————————————————————— *)

```
FUNCTION chk_fmt_rm_no(rm_no: line): boolean;

    (* Returns true if the Format of room_no is correct *)

VAR
  i: integer;
  noerror: boolean;

BEGIN

  IF lengthoF (rm_no) > str_length THEN
  noerror : = false
  ELSE BEGIN
  i : = 1;
  noerror : = true;
  WHILE (i ≤ str_length) and noerror DO BEGIN
    IF not (rm_no[i] in ['0'..'9']) THEN
    noerror : = false;
    i : =i + 1
  END
  END;
  IF not noerror THEN BEGIN
  writeln('Line # ', line_no: 3, ' ** ', msgbuf);
  writeln('        Error in format of room no : ', rm_no)
  END;
  chk_fmt_rm_no : = noerror
END; { chk_fmt_rm_no }
```

(* —————————————————————————————————— *)

```
FUNCTION chk_range_cap(cap: integer): boolean;

    (* Returns true IF capacity is within the range [10..300] *)

BEGIN
  IF (cap ≥ MINCAP) and (cap ≤ MAXCAP) THEN
    BEGIN
  chk_range_cap : = true
  END ELSE BEGIN
  writeln('Line # ', line_no: 3, ' ** ', msgbuf);
  writeln('        Error in range of capacity :', cap: 3);
  chk_range_cap : = false
  END
END; { chk_range_cap }
```

(* —————————————————————————————————— *)

```pascal
PROCEDURE sort_rooms(no_of_rms: integer; VAR rm_arr:
  room_array);

    (* Sorts the room RECORD in increasing order of capacity
       using *)
    (* Bubble sort                                    *)

VAR
  i, j: integer;
  temp_rm: room_rec;
BEGIN
  FOR i : = 1 to no_of_rms − 1 DO
  FOR j : = 1 to no_of_rms − i DO
    IF rm_arr[j].capacity > rm_arr[j + 1].capacity THEN
      BEGIN
    temp_rm.room_no : = rm_arr[j].room_no;
    temp_rm.capacity : = rm_arr[j].capacity;
    rm_arr[j].room_no : = rm_arr[j + 1].room_no;
    rm_arr[j].capacity : = rm_arr[j + 1].capacity;
    rm_arr[j + 1].room_no : = temp_rm.room_no;
    rm_arr[j + 1].capacity : = temp_rm.capacity
      END
END; { sort_rooms }
```

(* _____ *)

```pascal
FUNCTION chk_dup(room_no: string3): boolean;
    (* Checks if the room_no given already exists in the
       classroom_DB *)

VAR
  i: integer;
  flag: boolean;
BEGIN
  chk_dup : = false;
  flag : = false;
  i : = 1;
  WHILE (i < = num_of_rooms) and not flag DO
    BEGIN           (* I ModIF *)
  IF room_no = classroom_DB[i].room_no THEN BEGIN
    chk_dup : = true;
    flag : = true
  END;
  i : = i + 1
  END
END; { chk_dup }
```

(* —————————————————————————————— *)

```
BEGIN (* validate_classrooms *)

error : = false;
num_of_rooms : = 0;
get_next_line(1, buffer);
line_no : = line_no + 1;
msgbuf : = buffer;
flag : = false;

WHILE (buffer <> 'eof') and (num_of_rooms < MAXROOMS)
  and not flag DO BEGIN
  token : = get_token([';', ':'], buffer);
  IF token = '; ' THEN BEGIN
  flag : = true
  END;
  IF not flag THEN BEGIN
  IF not chk_fmt_rm_no(token) THEN BEGIN
    error : = true
  END;
  FOR i : = 1 to str_length DO
    room_no[i] : = token[i];
  token : = get_token([';', ':'], buffer);
  IF token = ': ' THEN
    token : = get_token([';', ':'], buffer);
  cap : = string_to_int(token);
  IF not chk_range_cap(cap) THEN
    error : = true;
  IF not error THEN
    IF not chk_dup(room_no) THEN BEGIN
    num_of_rooms : = num_of_rooms + 1;
    classroom_DB[num_of_rooms].room_no : = room_no;
    classroom_DB[num_of_rooms].capacity : = cap
    END ELSE BEGIN
    writeln('Line # ', line_no: 3, ' ** ', msgbuf);
    writeln('         Classroom entry specified more than once :',
      room_no, ' ** ignored **')
    END;
  token : = get_token([';', ':'], buffer);
  IF token = '; ' THEN
    flag : = true
  ELSE IF num_of_rooms <> MAXROOMS THEN BEGIN
    get_next_line(1, buffer);
    line_no : = line_no + 1;
    msgbuf : = buffer
```

```
            END
            END
         END;
         IF num_of_rooms = 0 THEN BEGIN (* Empty File *)
            writeln('There are no correct entries of rooms in the input file1 ');
            error : = true
         END ELSE IF (num_of_rooms = MAXROOMS) and not
            (token = '; ') THEN BEGIN
            get_next_line(FIL1, buffer);
            line_no : = line_no + 1;
            token : = get_token([';', ':'], buffer);
            IF token <> '; ' THEN BEGIN
            writeln('More rooms in FILE1 than are permissible ==>
               Later ones are ignored');
            WHILE (token <> '; ') and (token <> 'eof') DO
               IF token = 'eob' THEN BEGIN
               get_next_line(FIL1, buffer);
               line_no : = line_no + 1;
               token : = get_token([';', ':'], buffer)
               END ELSE
               token : = get_token([';', ':'], buffer)
            END
      END;
      IF token = 'eof' THEN BEGIN
         writeln('Skipped over to eof on account of ";' '');
         error : = true
      END;
      sort_rooms(num_of_rooms, classroom_DB)
   END; (* validate_classroom *)

      (* _____ *)

   PROCEDURE validate_dept_courses;

   VAR
   i: integer;
   course_no, buffer: line;
   local_course_no: string5;
   flag, flag1: boolean;

      (* _____ *)

   FUNCTION chk_fmt_course_no(course_no: line): boolean;
   VAR
      noerror: boolean;
      i: integer;
```

```
BEGIN
  noerror : = true;
  IF lengthoF (course_no) < = 5 THEN
  IF (course_no[1] in ['C', 'c']) and (course_no[2] in ['s', 'S'])
    THEN BEGIN
    FOR i : = 3 to 5 DO
    IF not (course_no[i] in ['0'..'9']) THEN
      noerror : = false
  END ELSE
    noerror : = false
  ELSE
  noerror : = false;
  IF not noerror THEN BEGIN
  writeln('Line # ', line_no: 3, ' ** ', msgbuf);
  writeln('        Error in FORmat of course no : ', course_no)
  END;
  chk_fmt_course_no : = noerror
END; { chk_fmt_course_no }
```

(* ———————————————————————————— *)

```
FUNCTION chk_dup(course_no: string5): boolean;
        (* See if the course is a duplicate *)

VAR
  i: integer;
  flag: boolean;

BEGIN
  chk_dup : = false;
  flag : = false;
  i : = 1;
  WHILE (i < = num_of_courses) and not flag DO BEGIN
  IF course_no = course_no_db[i] THEN BEGIN
    chk_dup : = true;
    flag : = true
  END;
  i : = i + 1
  END
END; { chk_dup }
```

(* ———————————————————————————— *)

```
BEGIN (* validate courses *)
```

```
get_next_line(FIL1, buffer);
msgbuf : = buffer;
line_no : = line_no + 1;
num_of_courses : = 0;
flag1 : = false;

WHILE (buffer <> 'eof') and (num_of_courses < MAXCOURSES)
    and not flag1 DO BEGIN
    flag : = false;
    WHILE    (buffer    <>    ' ')    and    (num_of_courses    <
        MAXCOURSES) and not flag DO BEGIN
    course_no : = get_token([',', ';'], buffer);
    IF course_no = ', ' THEN BEGIN
        course_no : = get_token([',', ';'], buffer);
        IF course_no = 'eob' THEN
        flag : = true
    END ELSE IF course_no[1] = ';' THEN
        flag : = true;
    IF not flag THEN BEGIN
        IF chk_fmt_course_no(course_no) THEN BEGIN
        FOR i : = 1 to 5 DO
            local_course_no[i] : = course_no[i];
        IF not chk_dup(local_course_no) THEN BEGIN
            num_of_courses : = num_of_courses + 1;
            course_no_db[num_of_courses] : = local_course_no
        END ELSE BEGIN
            writeln('Line # ', line_no: 3, ' ** ', msgbuf);
            writeln('        Course_no entry specified more than once :',
                local_course_no, ' ** ignored **')
        END
        END ELSE
        error : = true
    END
    END;
    IF course_no = '; ' THEN
    flag1 : = true
    ELSE IF num_of_courses <> MAXCOURSES THEN BEGIN
    get_next_line(FIL1, buffer);
    msgbuf : = buffer;
    line_no : = line_no + 1
    END
END;
IF num_of_courses = 0 THEN BEGIN
    error : = true;
    writeln('There are no correct entries of courses in the input file 1 ')
```

```
END ELSE IF (num_of_courses = MAXCOURSES) and not (get
  _token([',', ';'], buffer) = '; ') THEN BEGIN
  get_next_line(FIL1, buffer);
  msgbuf : = buffer;
  line_no : = line_no + 1;
  course_no : = get_token([',', ';'], buffer);
  IF course_no <> '; ' THEN BEGIN
  writeln('More courses in FILE1 than are permissible ==> Later
    ones are ignored');
  WHILE (course_no <> '; ') and (course_no <> 'eof') DO
    IF course_no = 'eob' THEN BEGIN
    get_next_line(FIL1, buffer);
    msgbuf : = buffer;
    line_no : = line_no + 1;
    course_no : = get_token([',', ';'], buffer)
    END ELSE
    course_no : = get_token([',', ';'], buffer)
  END

END;
IF course_no = 'eof' THEN BEGIN
  writeln('Skipped over to eof on account of ";' ");
  error : = true
END
END; (* validate courses *)
```

(* _____ *)

```
PROCEDURE validate_lec_times;
VAR
i: integer;
time_slot, buffer: line;
local_time_slot: string7;
flag, flag1: boolean;
```

(* _____ *)

```
FUNCTION chk_fmt_time_slot(time_slot: line): boolean;
VAR

  noerror: boolean;
  len: integer;

BEGIN
  noerror : = false;
```

```
len : = lengthoF (time_slot);
IF (len > 2) and (len < 8) THEN
CASE len of
   3:
   IF (time_slot[1] in ['t', 'T']) and (time_slot[2] in ['t', 'T']) and
      (time_slot[3] in ['1'..'9']) THEN
      noerror : = true;
   4:
   IF (time_slot[1] in ['m', 'M']) and (time_slot[2] in ['w', 'W'])
      and (time_slot[3] in ['f', 'F']) and (time_slot[4] in ['1'..'9'])
      THEN
      noerror : = true;
   5:
   IF (time_slot[1] in ['m', 'M']) and (time_slot[2] in ['w', 'W'])
      and (time_slot[3] in ['f', 'F'])
   and (time_slot[4] in ['0'..'2']) and (time_slot[5] in ['0'..'9'])
      THEN
      noerror : = true;
   6:
   IF (time_slot[1] in ['t', 'T']) and (time_slot[2] in ['t', 'T']) and
      (time_slot[3] in ['1'..'9'])
   and (time_slot[4] = ':') and (time_slot[5] in ['0'..'6']) and
      (time_slot[6] in ['0'..'9']) THEN
      noerror : = true;
   7:
   IF (time_slot[1] in ['t', 'T']) and (time_slot[2] in ['t', 'T']) and
      (time_slot[3] in ['0'..'2'])
   and (time_slot[4] in ['0'..'9']) and (time_slot[5] = ':') and
      (time_slot[6] in ['0'..'6']) and (time_slot[7] in ['0'..'9']) THEN
      noerror := = true
END;
IF not noerror THEN BEGIN
writeln('Line # ', line_no: 3, ' ** ', msgbuf);
writeln('        Error in FORmat of timeslot : ', time_slot)
END;
chk_fmt_time_slot : = noerror
END; { chk_fmt_time_slot }

   (* _____ *)

FUNCTION chk_dup(time_slot: string7): boolean;
   (*check if a duplicate*)
VAR
   i: integer;
   flag: boolean;
```

```
BEGIN
  chk_dup : = false;
  flag : = false;
  i : = 1;
  WHILE (i < = num_of_times) and not flag DO BEGIN
  IF time_slot = time_slot_db[i] THEN BEGIN
    chk_dup : = true;
    flag : = true
  END;
  i : = i + 1
  END
END; { chk_dup }
```

        (* ——————————————————————————————— *)

```
BEGIN (* validate_lec_times *)
get_next_line(FIL1, buffer);
msgbuf : = buffer;
line_no : = line_no + 1;
num_of_times : = 0;
flag1 : = false;
WHILE (buffer <> 'eof') and (num_of_times < MAXTIMES) and
  not flag1 DO BEGIN
  flag : = false;
  WHILE (buffer <> ' ') and (num_of_times < MAXTIMES)
    and not flag DO BEGIN
  time_slot : = '    ';
  time_slot : = get_token([',', ';'], buffer);
  IF time_slot = ', ' THEN BEGIN
    time_slot : = get_token([',', ';'], buffer);
    IF time_slot = 'eob' THEN
    flag : = true
  END ELSE IF time_slot = '; ' THEN
    flag : = true;
  IF not flag THEN BEGIN
    IF chk_fmt_time_slot(time_slot) THEN BEGIN
    local_time_slot : = '    ';
    FOR i : = 1 to lengthoF (time_slot) DO
      local_time_slot[i] : = time_slot[i];
    IF not chk_dup(local_time_slot) THEN BEGIN
      num_of_times : = num_of_times + 1;
      time_slot_db[num_of_times] : = local_time_slot
    END ELSE BEGIN
      writeln('Line no ', line_no: 3, ' ** ', msgbuf );
```

```
      writeln('        Time_slot entry specIFied more than once :
        ', local_time_slot, ' ** ignored **')
    END
    END ELSE
    error : = true
  END
  END;
  IF (time_slot = '; ') or (time_slot = 'eof') THEN
  flag1 : = true
  ELSE IF num_of_times <> MAXTIMES THEN BEGIN
  get_next_line(FIL1, buffer);
  msgbuf : = buffer;
  line_no : = line_no + 1
  END ELSE
  time_slot : = get_token([',', ';'], buffer)
  END;

  IF num_of_times = MAXTIMES THEN
    IF time_slot = 'eob' THEN BEGIN
    get_next_line(FIL1, buffer);
    msgbuf : = buffer;
    line_no : = line_no + 1;
    IF get_token([',', ';'], buffer) <> '; ' THEN
      writeln('More timeslots in FIL1 than are permissible ==>
        Later ones are ignored')
  END;
  IF num_of_times = 0 THEN BEGIN
    error : = true;
    writeln('There are no correct entries of timeslots in the input file
      1 ')
  END
  END; (* validate_lec_times *)
```

(* ——————————————————————————————— *)

```
  BEGIN (* validate_file1 *)
    line_no : = 0;
    get_next_line(FIL1, buffer);
    line_no : = line_no + 1;
    msgbuf : = buffer;
    local_buf : = get_token([], buffer);
    IF (local_buf = 'rooms') or (local_buf = 'ROOMS') THEN BEGIN
    validate_classrooms;
    get_next_line(FIL1, buffer);
    line_no : = line_no + 1;
```

```
msgbuf : = buffer;
local_buf : = get_token([], buffer);
IF (local_buf = 'courses') or (local_buf;tn;= 'COURSES') THEN
  BEGIN

      validate_dept_courses;

      get_next_line(FIL1, buffer);
      line_no : = line_no + 1;
      msgbuf : = buffer;
      local_buf : = get_token([], buffer);
      IF (local_buf = 'times') or (local_buf = 'TIMES') THEN
      validate_lec_times

      ELSE BEGIN
      error : = true;
      writeln('Line # ', line_no, ' ** ', msgbuf);
      writeln('          Cannot recover ==> times expected ')
      END
  END ELSE BEGIN
      error : = true;
      writeln('Line # ', line_no, ' ** ', msgbuf);
      writeln('          Cannot recover ==> courses expected ')
  END
  END ELSE BEGIN
  error : = true;
  writeln('Line # ', line_no, ' ** ', msgbuf);
  writeln('          Cannot recover ==> rooms expected ')
  END
  END; (* validate_file1 *)


(*************************************************************)
(*************************************************************)


PROCEDURE validate_file2;
    (* Validate the file2 , looking up the DB's maintained earlier ,
      and , if an entry is not found or misspelt , it is ignored *)

VAR
    buffer: line;
    course_no: string5;
    enrollment: integer;
    i, course_index: integer;
    pref_list: p_list_str;
    valid_pref_list: p_list_i;
```

```
local_error: boolean;
local_buf: line;
```

(* —————————————————————————————— *)

```
PROCEDURE get_course_index(course_no: string5; VAR course_i:
    integer);

(* look up the database of course_no 's and return the index in the
    array *)

VAR
i: integer;
flag: boolean;

BEGIN

i : = 1;
course_i : = 0;
flag : = false;
WHILE (i < = num_of_courses) and not flag DO
    IF course_no = course_no_db[i] THEN BEGIN
    course_i : = i;
    flag : = true
    END ELSE
    i : = i + 1
END; { get_course_index }
```

(* —————————————————————————————— *)

```
PROCEDURE  get_pref_valid(pref_list:  p_list_str;  VAR  valid_
    pref_list: p_list_i);

(* Validate the preferences against the database ,
    Return a validated list of preferences *)

VAR
i: integer;
temp_list: p_list_i;
num_of_pref: integer;
flag: boolean;
BEGIN
num_of_pref : = 0;
valid_pref_list : = nil;
WHILE pref_list <> nil DO BEGIN
```

```
num_of_pref : = num_of_pref + 1;
i : = 1;
flag : = false;
WHILE (i < = num_of_times) and not flag DO BEGIN
IF pref_list^.p_index = time_slot_db[i] THEN BEGIN
   new(temp_list);
   temp_list^.p_index : = i;
   IF num_of_pref = 1 THEN
   temp_list^.p_ptr : = nil
   ELSE
   temp_list^.p_ptr : = valid_pref_list;
   valid_pref_list : = temp_list;
   flag : = true
END ELSE
   i : = i + 1
END;
IF i > num_of_times THEN BEGIN
writeln('Line # ', line_no: 3, ' ** ', msgbuf);
writeln('      No  such  preference  in  the  DB  :  ', pref_list^.
   p_index);
num_of_pref : = num_of_pref - 1
END;
   pref_list : = pref_list^.p_ptr
END
END; { get_pref_valid }
```

(*———————————————————————— *)

```
PROCEDURE  form_course_rec(course_i,  enrol:  integer;  valid
   _pref_list: p_list_i);
```

   (* Form the course record *)

```
BEGIN
course_rec_array[tot_courses].course_i : = course_i;
course_rec_array[tot_courses].enrol : = enrol;
course_rec_array[tot_courses].valid_pref_list : = valid_pref_list
END; { form_course_rec }
```

(*———————————————————————— *)

```
PROCEDURE form_pref_list(VAR pref_list: p_list_str);
```

   (* Forms a list of preferences in the reverse order. When validated
   after a call to get_pref_valid, original order is restored, with
   invalid courses deleted   *)

```
VAR
num_of_pref, i: integer;
pref: line;
temp_pref_list: p_list_str;
local_error: boolean;
BEGIN
local_error : = false;
num_of_pref : = 0;
IF buffer = ' ' THEN
  pref_list : = nil
ELSE BEGIN
  WHILE (buffer <> ' ') and (num_of_pref < 5) DO BEGIN
  num_of_pref : = num_of_pref + 1;
  pref : = get_token([','], buffer);
  IF pref = ', ' THEN BEGIN
    pref : = get_token([','], buffer);
    IF pref = 'eob' THEN BEGIN
    get_next_line(FIL2, buffer);
    pref : = get_token([','], buffer);
    END
  END;
  IF lengthoF (pref) > 7 THEN
    local_error : = true;
  IF not local_error THEN BEGIN
    new(temp_pref_list);
    temp_pref_list^.p_index : = '      ';
    FOR i : = 1 to lengthoF (pref) DO
    temp_pref_list^.p_index[i] : = preF [i];
    IF num_of_pref = 1 THEN
    temp_pref_list^.p_ptr : = nil
    ELSE
      temp_pref_list^.p_ptr : = pref_list;
      pref_list : = temp_pref_list
    END
    END;
    IF get_token([','], buffer) <> 'eob' THEN BEGIN
    writeln('Line # ', line_no: 3, ' ** ', msgbuf);
    writeln('      More than 5 prefs specIFied and later ones
      ignored ')
    END
END;
END; { form_pref_list }
```

(* _____ *)

FUNCTION duplicate_course(c_index: integer): boolean;

```
        (* Checks if a course is a duplicate *)

VAR
i: integer;
flag: boolean;
BEGIN
i : = 1;
flag : = false;
duplicate_course : = false;
WHILE (i < = tot_courses) and not flag DO BEGIN
   IF c_index = course_rec_array[i].course_i THEN BEGIN
   duplicate_course : = true;
   flag : = true
   END ELSE
   i : = i + 1
END
END; { duplicate_course }
```

(* —————————————————————————————————————— *)

```
BEGIN (* validate_file2 *)
   tot_courses : = 0;
   line_no : = 0;
   get_next_line(FIL2, buffer);
   line_no : = line_no + 1;
   msgbuf : = buffer;
   local_buf : = get_token([], buffer);
   IF  (local_buf = 'course')  or  (local_buf = 'COURSE')  THEN
      BEGIN
   get_next_line(FIL2, buffer);
   line_no : = line_no + 1;
   msgbuf : = buffer;
   WHILE buffer <> 'eof' DO BEGIN
      local_error : = false;
      local_buf : = get_token([], buffer);
      IF lengthoF (local_buf) > 5 THEN BEGIN
      writeln('Line # ', line_no: 3, ' ** ', msgbuf);
      writeln('        error in FORmat of course_no : ', local_buf);
      local_error : = true
      END ELSE
      FOR i : = 1 to lengthoF (local_buf) DO
         course_no[i] : = local_buF [i];
      get_course_index(course_no, course_index);
      IF course_index = 0 THEN BEGIN
      writeln('Line # ', line_no: 3, ' ** ', msgbuf);
```

```
        writeln('        No Such course in the DB : ', course_no);
        local_error : = true
        END ELSE IF duplicate_course(course_index) THEN BEGIN
        writeln('More than one occurence of the course : ', course_no);
        conflict_list[conflict_index].course_index : = course_index;
        conflict_list[conflict_index].err_code : = 6;
        conflict_index : = conflict_index + 1;
        local_error : = true
        END;
     local_buf : = get_token([], buffer);
     enrollment : = string_to_int(local_buf);
     IF lengthoF (local_buf) > 3 THEN BEGIN
     writeln('Line # ', line_no: 3, ' ** ', msgbuf);
     writeln('        Error in FORmat of enrollment :', local_buf);
     writeln('        Course ignored :', course_no);
     local_error : = true
     END ELSE IF (enrollment < 3) or (enrollment > 250) THEN
        BEGIN
     writeln('Line # ', line_no: 3, ' ** ', msgbuf);
     writeln('        Error in range of enrollment :', local_buf);
     writeln('        Course ignored :', course_no);
     local_error : = true
     END;
     FORm_pref_list(pref_list);
     IF pref_list <> nil THEN
     get_pref_valid(pref_list, valid_pref_list)
     ELSE
     valid_pref_list : = nil;
     IF not local_error THEN BEGIN
     tot_courses : = tot_courses + 1;
     FORm_course_rec(course_index, enrollment, valid_pref_list)
     END;
     get_next_line(FIL2, buffer);
     line_no : = line_no + 1;
     msgbuf : = buffer
  END
  END ELSE BEGIN
  writeln('Incorrect Format in File2 : FATAL ERROR ==> Cannot
     read input file2 , anymore', buffer);
  error : = true
  END
END; (* validate_file2 *)


(**************************************************************)
(**************************************************************)
```

```
PROCEDURE separate_courses;

  (* This module separates the courses into PG with pref, PG without
    pref etc.*)

VAR
  pg_array, ug_array, pgn_array, ugn_array:  array  [1..MAX-
    COURSES] of course_rec;
  i, a, b, c, d: integer;
  temp: string5;
BEGIN
  i : = 0;
  a : = 0;
  b : = 0;
  c : = 0;
  d : = 0;
  WHILE i < = tot_courses DO BEGIN
  i : = i + 1;
  with course_rec_array[i] DO BEGIN
    temp : = course_no_db[course_i];
    IF temp[3] > = '6' THEN
    IF valid_pref_list <> nil THEN BEGIN
      a : = a + 1;
      pg_array[a] : = course_rec_array[i]
    END ELSE BEGIN
      b : = b + 1;
      pgn_array[b] : = course_rec_array[i]
    END
    ELSE IF valid_pref_list <> nil THEN BEGIN
    c : = c + 1;
    ug_array[c] : = course_rec_array[i]
    END ELSE BEGIN
    d : = d + 1;
    ugn_array[d] : = course_rec_array[i]
    END
  END
  END;
  ugpstart : = a + 1;
  pgnpstart : = ugpstart + c;
  ugnpstart : = pgnpstart + b;
  i : = 0;
  WHILE a > = 1 DO BEGIN
  i : = i + 1;
  course_rec_array[i] : = pg_array[i];
  a : = a - 1
```

```
    END;
    WHILE c > = 1 DO BEGIN
    i : = i + 1;
    course_rec_array[i] : = ug_array[i − ugpstart + 1];
    c : = c − 1
    END;
    WHILE b > = 1 DO BEGIN
    i : = i + 1;
    course_rec_array[i] : = pgn_array[i − pgnpstart + 1];
    b : = b − 1
    END;
    WHILE d > = 1 DO BEGIN
    i : = i + 1;
    course_rec_array[i] : = ugn_array[i − ugnpstart + 1];
    d : = d − 1
    END
  END; { separate_courses }
```

```
(*************************************************************)
(*************************************************************)
```

```
  BEGIN (* get_validated_input *)
  expl_index : = 1;
  conflict_index : = 1;
    writeln;
    write('Pl. enter filename 1 : ');
    readln(filename);
    writeln;
  reset(file1,filename);
  validate_file1;
  IF error THEN BEGIN
    writeln('Fatal error(s) encountered in parsing the input file1');
    writeln('Stopped')
  END ELSE BEGIN
    writeln;
    write('Pl. enter filename 2 : ');
    readln(filename);
    writeln;
    reset(file2,filename);
    validate_file2;
    separate_courses
  END
  END; (* get_validated_input *)
```

```
(*|||||||||||||||||||||||||||||||||||||||||||||||||||||||||||||||||||||||||||||||||||||||||||||||||||||||||||*)
(*|||||||||||||||||||||||||||||||||||||||||||||||||||||||||||||||||||||||||||||||||||||||||||||||||||||||||||*)
```

```
PROCEDURE schedule;


(***********************************************************)
(***********************************************************)


FUNCTION get_rooom_index(enrol: integer): integer;

   (*Returns the index of the smallest room that can accommodate the
   course. Note that course_no 's are sorted on capacity *)

VAR
   i: integer;
   flag: boolean;

BEGIN
   i : = 1;
   get_rooom_index : = 0;
   flag : = false;
   WHILE not flag and (i ≤ num_of_rooms) DO
   IF enrol ≤ classroom_DB[i].capacity THEN BEGIN
      get_rooom_index : = i;
      flag : = true
   END ELSE
      i : = i + 1
END; { get_rooom_index }


(***********************************************************)
(***********************************************************)


PROCEDURE prep_template;
   (* To prepare an empty time_table FOR schedule. *)
   (* PG_alloc_array indicates FOR each timeslot, the PG course alloted
      in it *)
   (* The purpose is to avoid search in the slot FOR a PG course every
      time we try to *)
   (* allot a course in the slot in sched_PG_pref,sched_UG_pref and
      sched_PG_no_pref *)

VAR
   i, j: integer;

BEGIN

   { Initialize the time_table   }
   FOR i : = 1 to MAXROOMS DO
```

```
   FOR j : = 1 to MAXTIMES DO
      time_table[i, j] : = 0;
   { Initialize the PG_alloc_array }
   FOR i : = 1 to MAXTIMES DO
   pg_alloc_array[i] : = 0;
   course_no_db[0] : = '  '    (* this is just to make printing of time
      _table easy *)
END; { prep_template }
```

(***)
(***)

```
PROCEDURE sched_pg_pref;
```

   (* This routine schedules the PG courses with preferences Allots best
   possible preference FOR a course, alloting the courses in the order
   they appear in the input. PG_alloc_array is used FOR checking
   conflicts. *)

```
VAR
   pref_honored,    (* index of preference finally given to the course *)
      first_pref,        (* Index for first preference *)
      cur_course_index, (* index for the loop *)
      cur_pref,          (* preference being handled *)
      cur_course_no,   (* current course being handled *)
      cur_course_enrol, (* enrollment of current course *)
      cur_room_index   (* index of current room *)

               : integer;

   done: boolean;       (* Set if the course is scheduled *)
   local_error: boolean; (* set if no room of proper capacity *)

   cur_p_list_i: p_list_i; (* List of pref.s for the current course *)
   cur_course_rec: course_rec;
   temp_p_list_i,    (* List of preferences that had conflicts *)

      temp,                (* temp node for adding to the above list *)
      tail                 (* this list is FIFO, so need a tail ptr also *)
               : p_list_i;
BEGIN
   cur_course_index : = 1;
   WHILE cur_course_index < ugpstart DO BEGIN
   local_error : = false;
```

```
cur_course_rec : = course_rec_array[cur_course_index];
cur_p_list_i : = cur_course_rec.valid_pref_list;
first_pref : = cur_p_list_i^.p_index;
cur_course_no : = cur_course_rec.course_i;
cur_course_enrol : = cur_course_rec.enrol;
cur_room_index : = get_rooom_index(cur_course_enrol);
IF cur_room_index = 0 THEN BEGIN
  local_error : = true;
  conflict_list[conflict_index].course_index : = cur_course_no;
  conflict_list[conflict_index].err_code : =  = 5;
  conflict_index : = conflict_index + 1
END;

done : = false;
tail : = nil;
WHILE (cur_p_list_i <> nil) and not DOne and not local_error DO
  BEGIN
  cur_pref : = cur_p_list_i^.p_index;
  IF pg_alloc_array[cur_pref] = 0 THEN BEGIN
  pref_honored : = cur_pref;
  pg_alloc_array[cur_pref] : = cur_course_no;
  time_table[cur_room_index, cur_pref] : = cur_course_no;
  DOne : = true
  END ELSE BEGIN (* conflict at the pref; pref is added to the list *)
  new(temp);
  temp^.p_index : = cur_pref;
  temp^.p_ptr : = nil;
  IF tail = nil THEN BEGIN
    tail : = temp;
    temp_p_list_i : = tail
  END ELSE BEGIN
    tail^.p_ptr : = temp;
    tail : = temp
  END
  END;
  cur_p_list_i : = cur_p_list_i^.p_ptr
END;

IF not done and not local_error THEN BEGIN (* course not
  scheduled. Make entry in conflict list *)
  conflict_list[conflict_index].err_code : = 1;
  conflict_list[conflict_index].course_index : = cur_course_no;
  (* The list
  of prefs is also added. Reason is printed after looking at
  the timtetable *)
```

```
          conflict_list[conflict_index].pref_list : = temp_p_list_i;
          conflict_index : = conflict_index + 1
      END ELSE IF (pref_honored <> first_pref) and not local_error
      THEN BEGIN
          (* scheduled but not at the first pref. Make entries FOR earlierprefs
            in expl_list *)
          expl_list[expl_index].err_code : = pref_honored;
          expl_list[expl_index].pref_list : = temp_p_list_i;
          expl_list[expl_index].course_index : = cur_course_no;
          expl_list[expl_index].room_index : = 0;
          expl_index : = expl_index + 1
      END;
      cur_course_index : = cur_course_index + 1
      END
    END; { sched_PG_pref }


(*************************************************************)
(*************************************************************)


  PROCEDURE sched_ug_pref;

  (* Schedules the UG courses with preferences. For each PG course with
    no preference,it keeps track of the possible rooms FOR each timeslot
    with no PG course already alloted in the data structure PG_reserve.
    This is used to guarantee allotment of the PG no pref courses. Update
    _PG_reserve removes one room from all the PG_no_pref courses and
    all timeslots. Safe_allotment checks IF alloting a room to a UG course
    results in unschedulability of any room for a PG_no_pref course.
    Initialize_PG_reserve puts all the possible rooms for a PG_no_pref
    course in PG_reserve *)

  VAR
    npgnp,              (* Num of pg courses with no pref *)
      pref_honored,
      cur_room,
      first_pref,
      cur_course_index, (* these VARs are same as in previous proc *)
      cur_pref,
      cur_course_no,
      cur_course_enrol   : integer;

    slots_available: integer;
    DOne, local_error: boolean;
    cur_pref_list: p_list_i;
    cur_course_rec: course_rec;
```

```
temp_p_list_i, temp, tail: p_list_i;
pg_reserve: pg_res_list; (* List of PG courses with no prefs *)
```

(* ——————————————————————————————————————— *)

```
PROCEDURE initialize_pg_reserve;
```

(* First determines how many pgnp courses have to be scheduled. For
each of these it sets up all the timeslots they can be scheduled in,
and FOR each timeslot the rooms where the course can go. This
2-dimensional linked-list is tmp_PG_reserve *)

```
VAR
index, tobescheduled, i, j, k, cur_room_index: integer;
tail_pg_res, temp_pg_res: pg_res_list;
temp_timeslots, temp_slot: t_slot_list;
temp_roomlist, temp_room: r_list;

BEGIN
(* Determine the number of pgnp courses that have to be scheduled *)
index : = pgnpstart;
npgnp : = ugnpstart - pgnpstart;
slots_available : = 0;
FOR i : = 1 to num_of_times DO
  IF pg_alloc_array[i] = 0 THEN
  slots_available : = slots_available + 1;
IF slots_available < npgnp THEN
  tobescheduled : = slots_available
ELSE
  tobescheduled : = npgnp;

tail_pg_res : = nil;
FOR i : = 1 to tobescheduled DO BEGIN
  new(temp_pg_res);
  temp_pg_res^.course : = course_rec_array[index].course_i;
  cur_room_index                    : = get_rooom_index(course_rec_
    array[index].enrol);
  IF cur_room_index <> 0 THEN BEGIN
  temp_timeslots : = nil;
  (* add each slot where this course
    can be scheduled, to the list *)
  FOR j : = num_of_times DOwnto 1 DO BEGIN
    IF pg_alloc_array[j] = 0 THEN BEGIN
    new(temp_slot);
    temp_slot^.timeslot : = j;
```

```
temp_roomlist : = nil;
(* add each room to
   the list where the course can be scheduled FOR this slot*)
FOR k : = num_of_rooms DOwnto cur_room_index DO BEGIN
   new(temp_room);
   temp_room^.r_index : = k;
   temp_room^.r_ptr : = temp_roomlist;
   temp_roomlist : = temp_room
END;
temp_slot^.roomlist : = temp_roomlist;
temp_slot^.t_ptr : = temp_timeslots;
temp_timeslots : = temp_slot
END
END;

(* adding this new course at the tail of the tmp_PG_res *)
temp_pg_res^.timeslots : = temp_timeslots;
temp_pg_res^.res_next : = nil;
IF tail_pg_res = nil THEN BEGIN
   tail_pg_res : = temp_pg_res;
   pg_reserve : = tail_pg_res
END ELSE BEGIN
   tail_pg_res^.res_next : = temp_pg_res;
   tail_pg_res : = temp_pg_res
END;
index : = index + 1
END
END
END; { initialize_PG_reserve }
```

(* ——————————————————————————————————— *)

FUNCTION safe_allotment(time_slot, roomno: integer): boolean;

(* Checks IF an allotment FOR a UG course with preference is
'safe' i.e. it DOesnot exhaust all slots FOR all rooms reserved
FOR a PG course with no preference. It is called only when the
number of PG_free slots with possible rooms vacant equals the
PG courses with no pref. If all the rooms reserved FOR a PG
course except the currently considered room are exhausted the
flag all_courses_safe is set to false. If all rooms except the
considered room of the time slot for all courses are exhausted
THEN the flag time_slot_safe is set to false. If either flag is
false, allotment is not safe. *)

```
VAR
  temp_pg_res: pg_res_list;
  slot_safe,        (* even IF the roomno is allotted, is the slot safe? *)
    course_safe,    (* can the current PG course from PG_res be allotted *)
    all_course_safe : boolean;

  temp_t_slots: t_slot_list;


BEGIN
  slot_safe : = false;
  all_course_safe : = true;
  temp_pg_res : = pg_reserve;
  WHILE temp_pg_res <> nil DO BEGIN
    temp_t_slots : = temp_pg_res^.timeslots;
    course_safe : = false;
    WHILE temp_t_slots <> nil DO BEGIN
            (* look at all timeslots FOR this course*)
    IF temp_t_slots^.timeslot = time_slot THEN BEGIN
            (* IF same as parm timeslot *)
      IF temp_t_slots^.roomlist <> nil THEN
      IF   (temp_t_slots^.roomlist^r_index   <>   roomno)   THEN
        BEGIN
        (*IF there are two rooms FOR this slot, or there is one room
            which is different than roomno, THEN both course and slot
            are safe *)
          course_safe : = true;
          slot_safe : = true
        END
      END ELSE IF temp_t_slots^.roomlist <> nil THEN
        (* IF one room but is dIFf
        from roomno, THEN the course is safe *)
        course_safe : = true;
      temp_t_slots : = temp_t_slots^.t_ptr
      END;
      all_course_safe : = all_course_safe and course_safe;
      temp_pg_res : = temp_pg_res^.res_next
  END;
  safe_allotment : = slot_safe and all_course_safe
END; { safe_allotment }
```

(* _____ *)


```
PROCEDURE update_pg_reserve(time, room: integer);
```

(* This routine removes a room from the PG_reserve and thus from all the PG_no_pref courses. This also checks IF the particular timeslot has become empty FOR all the PG_no_pref courses. If so, THEN the slots_available FOR PG_no_pref courses is reduced by one. It is called after allotting a UG course to (time, room) *)

```
VAR
slot_full: boolean;
temp_pg_res: pg_res_list;
temp_timeslots: t_slot_list;
temp_room_list: r_list;
flag: boolean;


BEGIN
slot_full : = true;
temp_pg_res : = pg_reserve;
WHILE temp_pg_res <> nil DO BEGIN
  temp_timeslots : = temp_pg_res^.timeslots;
  WHILE (temp_timeslots <> nil) and (temp_timeslots^.timeslot <>
    time) DO
  temp_timeslots : = temp_timeslots^.t_ptr;
  IF temp_timeslots <> nil THEN BEGIN
  temp_room_list : = temp_timeslots^.roomlist;
  IF (temp_room_list <> nil) and (temp_room_list^.r_index = room)
    THEN BEGIN
    temp_timeslots^.roomlist : = temp_timeslots^.roomlist^.r_ptr;
    IF temp_timeslots^.roomlist <> nil THEN
    slot_full : = false
  END ELSE BEGIN
    slot_full : = false;
    IF temp_room_list <> nil THEN BEGIN
    flag : = false;
    WHILE not flag and (temp_room_list^.r_ptr <> nil) DO
      IF temp_room_list^.r_ptr^.r_index <> room THEN BEGIN
      temp_room_list : = temp_room_list^.r_ptr
      END ELSE
      flag : = true;
    IF temp_room_list^.r_ptr <> nil THEN
      temp_room_list^.r_ptr : = temp_room_list^.r_ptr^.r_ptr;
    END
  END
  END;
  temp_pg_res : = temp_pg_res^.res_next
END;
```

```
IF slot_full THEN
   slots_available : = slots_available - 1
END; { update_PG_reserve }
```

(* ——————————————————————————————— *)

```
BEGIN (* sched_UG_pref *)

   initialize_pg_reserve;
   cur_course_index : = ugpstart;
   npgnp : = ugnpstart − pgnpstart;
   WHILE cur_course_index < pgnpstart DO BEGIN
      (* FOR each UG course DO *)
   local_error : = false;
   cur_course_rec : = course_rec_array[cur_course_index];
   cur_course_no : = cur_course_rec.course_i;
   cur_course_enrol : = cur_course_rec.enrol;
   cur_pref_list : = cur_course_rec.valid_pref_list;
   first_pref : = cur_pref_list^.p_index;
   DOne : = false;
   tail : = nil;
   WHILE (cur_pref_list <> nil) and not DOne and not local_error DO
      BEGIN
      cur_pref : = cur_pref_list^.p_index;

      cur_room : = get_rooom_index(cur_course_enrol);
      IF cur_room = 0 THEN BEGIN
         (* unschedulable course *)
      local_error : = true;
      conflict_list[conflict_index].course_index : = cur_course_no;
      conflict_list[conflict_index].err_code : = 5;
      conflict_index : = conflict_index + 1
         END;

         (* Already a PG course
         allotted, hence cannot be reserved FOR a PG course, hence
            safe *)
         IF (npgnp = 0) or (pg_alloc_array[cur_pref] > 0) THEN BEGIN
         WHILE not DOne and (cur_room ≤ num_of_rooms) and not
            local_error DO BEGIN
         IF time_table[cur_room, cur_pref];tn;= 0 THEN BEGI
         time_table[cur_room, cur_pref] : = cur_course_no;
         pref_honored : = cur_pref;
         DOne : = true
         END;
```

```
        cur_room : = cur_room + 1
      END;
      END ELSE BEGIN (* No PG course allotted, have to check
        safety *)
      WHILE not DOne and (cur_room ≤ num_of_rooms) and not
        local_error DO BEGIN
        IF (time_table[cur_room, cur_pref] = 0) and ((slots_available
          > npgnp) or safe_allotment(cur_pref, cur_room)) THEN
          BEGIN
        time_table[cur_room, cur_pref] : = cur_course_no;
        pref_honored : = cur_pref;
        update_pg_reserve(cur_pref, cur_room);
        DOne : = true
        END;
        cur_room : = cur_room + 1
      END;
      END;

      (* DIFferent CASEs handled as beFORe in PG with prefs *)
      IF not DOne THEN BEGIN
      new(temp);
      temp^.p_index : = cur_pref;
      temp^.p_ptr : = nil;
      IF tail = nil THEN BEGIN
        tail : = temp;
        temp_p_list_i : = tail
      END ELSE BEGIN
        tail^.p_ptr : = temp;
        tail : = temp
      END
      END;
      cur_pref_list : = cur_pref_list^.p_ptr
    END;
    IF not DOne and not local_error THEN BEGIN
      conflict_list[conflict_index].err_code : = 2;
      conflict_list[conflict_index].course_index : = cur_course_no;
      conflict_list[conflict_index].pref_list : = temp_p_list_i;
      conflict_index : = conflict_index + 1
    END ELSE IF (pref_honored <> first_pref) and not local_error
      THEN BEGIN
      expl_list[expl_index].err_code : = pref_honored;
      expl_list[expl_index].pref_list : = temp_p_list_i;
      expl_list[expl_index].course_index : = cur_course_no;
      expl_list[expl_index].room_index            : = get_rooom_
        index(cur_course_rec.enrol)
```

```
      expl_index : = expl_index + 1
   END;
   cur_course_index : = cur_course_index + 1
   END
END; (* sched_UG_pref *)
```

(**)
(**)

```
PROCEDURE sched_pg_no_pref;

(* This module schedules the PG courses with no preference. It assumes
   that enough timeslots are available FOR the courses. If a course
   DOes not find a room it must be a superfluous course and put in the
   conflict list. It starts with the smallest room
   and goes towards bigger rooms. *)

VAR
   cur_course_index,    cur_slot,    cur_room_index,    cur_course_no,
      cur_course_enrol: integer;
   DOne: boolean;
   cur_course_rec: course_rec;
   local_error: boolean;
BEGIN
   cur_course_index : = pgnpstart;
   WHILE cur_course_index < ugnpstart DO BEGIN
   local_error : = false;
   cur_course_rec : = course_rec_array[cur_course_index];
   cur_course_no : = cur_course_rec.course_i;
   cur_course_enrol : = cur_course_rec.enrol;

   cur_room_index : = get_rooom_index(cur_course_enrol);
   IF cur_room_index = 0 THEN BEGIN
      local_error : = true;
      conflict_list[conflict_index].course_index : = cur_course_no;
      conflict_list[conflict_index].err_code : = 5;
      conflict_index : = conflict_index + 1
   END;

   DOne : = false;
   WHILE not DOne and (cur_room_index ≤ num_of_rooms) and not
      local_error DO BEGIN
      cur_slot : = 1;
      WHILE not DOne and (cur_slot ≤ num_of_times) DO BEGIN
      IF   (pg_alloc_array[cur_slot] = 0)   and   (time_table[cur_room_
```

```
          index, cur_slot] = 0) THEN BEGIN
          time_table[cur_room_index, cur_slot] : = cur_course_no;
          pg_alloc_array[cur_slot] : = cur_course_no;
          DOne : = true
        END;
        cur_slot : = cur_slot + 1
      END;
      cur_room_index : = cur_room_index + 1
    END;
    IF not DOne and not local_error THEN BEGIN
      conflict_list[conflict_index].err_code : = 3;
      conflict_list[conflict_index].course_index : = cur_course_no;
      conflict_index : = conflict_index + 1
    END;
    cur_course_index : = cur_course_index + 1
    END
  END; { sched_PG_no_pref }


(****************************************************************)
(****************************************************************)


PROCEDURE sched_ug_no_pref;

  (* This module schedules the UG courses with no preference
    assuming that all others are already scheduled. It starts with the
    smallest room and goes towards bigger ones until it is scheduled or
    no slot is left. If not allotted,it is put in conflict_list *)

VAR
    cur_course_index,   cur_slot,   cur_room_index,   cur_course_no,
      cur_course_enrol: integer;
    DOne, local_error: boolean;
    cur_course_rec: course_rec;
BEGIN
    cur_course_index : = ugnpstart;
    WHILE cur_course_index ≤ tot_courses DO BEGIN
    local_error : = false;
    cur_course_rec : = course_rec_array[cur_course_index];
    cur_course_no : = cur_course_rec.course_i;
    cur_course_enrol : = cur_course_rec.enrol;

    cur_room_index : = get_rooom_index(cur_course_enrol);
    IF cur_room_index = 0 THEN BEGIN
      local_error : = true;
      conflict_list[conflict_index].course_index : = cur_course_no;
```

```
      conflict_list[conflict_index].err_code : = 5;
      conflict_index : = conflict_index + 1
    END;

    DOne : = false;
    WHILE not DOne and (cur_room_index ≤ num_of_rooms) and not
      local_error DO BEGIN
      cur_slot : = 1;
      WHILE not DOne and (cur_slot ≤ num_of_times) DO BEGIN
      IF time_table[cur_room_index, cur_slot] = 0 THEN BEGIN
        time_table[cur_room_index, cur_slot] : = cur_course_no;
        DOne : = true
      END;
      cur_slot : = cur_slot + 1
      END;
      cur_room_index : = cur_room_index + 1
    END;
    IF not DOne and not local_error THEN BEGIN
      conflict_list[conflict_index].err_code : = 4;
      conflict_list[conflict_index].course_index : = cur_course_no;
      conflict_index : = conflict_index + 1
    END;
    cur_course_index : = cur_course_index + 1
    END
END; { sched_UG_no_pref }


(*************************************************************)
(*************************************************************)


  BEGIN   (* SCHEDULE *)
  prep_template;
  sched_pg_pref;
  sched_ug_pref;
  sched_pg_no_pref;
  sched_ug_no_pref;
  END; { schedule }


(* |||||||||||||||||||||||||||||||||||||||||||||||||||||||||||||||||||||||||||||||||||| *)
(* |||||||||||||||||||||||||||||||||||||||||||||||||||||||||||||||||||||||||||||||||||| *)


  PROCEDURE print_output;


(*************************************************************)
(*************************************************************)
```

```
PROCEDURE print_time_table;
VAR
  i, j: integer;

BEGIN
  writeln;
  FOR i : = 1 to num_of_times div 2 * 10 DO
  write(' ');
  writeln('T I M E    T A B L E');
  FOR i : = 1 to num_of_times div 2 * 10 DO
  write(' ');
  writeln('————    ————');
  writeln;
  FOR i : = 1 to num_of_times * 13 + 6 DO
  write('-');
    writeln;
  write('ROOM | ');
  FOR i : = 1 to num_of_times DO
  write(' ', time_slot_db[i], '   | ');
  writeln;
  FOR i : = 1 to num_of_times * 13 + 6 DO
  write('-');
  writeln;
  FOR i : = 1 to num_of_rooms DO BEGIN
  write(' ', classroom_DB[i].room_no, ' | ');
  FOR j : = 1 to num_of_times DO
    write(' ', course_no_db[time_table[i, j]], '    ');
  writeln;
  FOR j : = 1 to num_of_times * 13 + 6 DO
    write('-');
  writeln;
  END
END; { print_time_table }
```

(***)
(***)

```
PROCEDURE print_explanation;

VAR
  i, room_index, honoured_pref: integer;
  temp: p_list_i;

BEGIN
  IF expl_index > 1 THEN BEGIN
    writeln;
```

```
writeln('  E X P L A N A T I O N    R E P O R T ');
writeln('      ————    ———');
writeln;
i : = 1;
WHILE i < expl_index DO BEGIN
  writeln(course_no_db[expl_list[i].course_index], ' :');
  temp : = expl_list[i].pref_list;
  room_index : = expl_list[i].room_index;
  honoured_pref : = expl_list[i].err_code;
  WHILE temp <> nil DO BEGIN
  write('      ', time_slot_db[temp^.p_index], ': ');
  IF room_index = 0 THEN
    writeln('Conflict    with    course_no    ',    course_no_db[pg_
      alloc_array[temp^.p_index]])
  ELSE
    writeln('No room with proper capacity available');
  temp : = temp^.p_ptr
  END;
  IF (room_index <> 0) and (time_table[room_index, honoured
    _pref] <> expl_list[i].course_index) THEN BEGIN
  writeln('      ', time_slot_db[honoured_pref], ' :');
  WHILE    time_table[room_index,    honoured_pref]    <>    expl_
    list[i].course_index DO BEGIN
    write('          room#',                  classroom_DB[room_in
      dex].room_no, ': ');
    writeln('Conflict with course_no ', course_no_db[time_table
      [room_index, honoured_pref]]);
    room_index : = room_index + 1
  END
  END;
  i : = i + 1
END;
writeln
END
END; { print_explanation }


(*************************************************************)
(*************************************************************)


PROCEDURE print_conflict;

VAR
  i: integer;
  temp: p_list_i;
```

```
BEGIN
  IF conflict_index > 1 THEN BEGIN
    writeln;
    writeln('      C O N F L I C T   R E P O R T  ');
    writeln('         ————— ————  ');
    writeln;
    i : = 1;
    WHILE i < conflict_index DO BEGIN
      writeln(course_no_db[conflict_list[i].course_index], ' :');
      CASE conflict_list[i].err_code of

      1:
        BEGIN
        temp : = conflict_list[i].pref_list;
        WHILE temp <> nil DO BEGIN
          write('     ', time_slot_db[temp^.p_index], ': ');
          writeln('Conflict   with   course_no  ',   course_no_db[pg_
            alloc_array[temp^.p_index]]);
          temp : = temp^.p_ptr
        END
        END;
      2:
        BEGIN
        temp : = conflict_list[i].pref_list;
        WHILE temp <> nil DO BEGIN
          write('     ', time_slot_db[temp^.p_index], ': ');
          writeln('No room with proper capacity available');
          temp : = temp^.p_ptr
        END
        END;
      3:
        writeln('     Excess PG course : no time_slot available');
      4:
        writeln('     No free room with required capacity available');
      5:
        writeln('     Ignored : Enrollment greater than the greatest
          capacity of any room in FILE1');
      6:
        writeln('     Ignored : Course REPEATed more than once in
          FILE2')
      END;
      i : = i + 1
    END;
    writeln
  END
END; { print_conflict }
```

```
BEGIN
  print_time_table;
  print_explanation;
  print_conflict
END; { print_output }
(****   END OF OUTPUT MODULE   *****)
```

(*||||||||||||||||||||||||||||||||||||||||||||||||||||||||||||||||||||||||||||||||||||||||||||||||||||||||||||||*)
(*||||||||||||||||||||||||||||||||||||||||||||||||||||||||||||||||||||||||||||||||||||||||||||||||||||||||||||||*)

```
BEGIN     (* MAIN PROGRAM *)
  get_validated_input;
  IF error THEN
  writeln('Scheduling aborted')
  ELSE IF tot_courses > 0 THEN BEGIN
  schedule;
  print_output
  END ELSE BEGIN
  writeln('No course is correctly recognized from file2 !');
  writeln('Scheduling aborted')
  END
END.
```

References

General Book References:

[Boe81] B. Boehm, "Software Engineering Economics", *Prentice-Hall,* Englewood Cliffs, NJ 1981.

[Boe89] B. Boehm, ed, "Tutorial: software risk management", *IEEE Computer Society,* Washington D.C., 1989.

[Bro75] F. Brooks, "The mythical man month", *Addison-Wesley,* Reading, MA 1975.

[Cho85] T. S. Chow, ed., "Tutorial: software quality assurance—a practical approach", *IEEE Computer Society,* 1985.

[Con86] S. D. Conte, H. E. Dunsmore and V. Y. Shen, "Software engineering metrics and models", *Benjamin/Cumminghams Publishing Company, Inc.,* 1986.

[Dav90] A. M. Davis, "Software requirements—analysis and specification", *Prentice Hall,* 1990.

[Dem79] T. DeMarco, "Structured analysis and system specification", *Yourdon Press,* 1979.

[Dun84] R. H. Dunn, "Software defect removal", *McGraw-Hill, Inc.,* 1984.

[Fai85] R. E. Fairley, "Software engineering concepts", *McGraw Hill, Inc.,* 1985.

[Goo77] S. E. Goodman and S. T. Hedetniemi, "Introduction to the design and analysis of algorithms", *McGraw-Hill Inc.,* 1977.

[Iee87] "Software Engineering Standards", *IEEE Press,* 1987.

[May90] A. v. Mayrhauser, "Software engineering, methods and management", *Academic Press,* 1990.

[Mye79] G. Myers, "The art of software testing", *Wiley-Interscience,* New York, 1979.

[Pre87] R. S. Pressman, "Software engineering", Second Edition, *McGraw Hill, Inc.,* 1987.

[Som85] I. Somerville, "Software engineering", Second Edition, *Addison-Wesley Publishing Company, Ltd.,* 1985.

Specific References:

[Alf77] M. Alford, "A requirement engineering methodology for real-time processing requirements", *IEEE Transactions on Software Engineering,* Vol. SE-3, no. 1, pp. 60-69, Jan 1977.

[Bas75] V. R. Basili and A. Turner, "Iterative enhancement, a practical technique for software development", *IEEE Transactions on Software Engineering*, vol SE-1, no. 4, Dec. 1975.

[Bas80] V. R. Basili, "Tutorial on models and metrics for software management and engineering", *IEEE Press*, 1980.

[Bas81] V. R. Basili and D. M. Weiss, "Evaluation of a software requirements document by analysis of change data", *Proc. 5th Int. Conf. on Software Engg.*, 1981, pp. 314–323.

[Bel86] B. Belkhouche and J. E. Urban, "Direct implementation of abstract data types from abstract specifications", *IEEE Tran. on Software Eng.*, Vol SE-12, no. 5, 1986, pp. 649–461.

[Ber79] E. H. Bersoff, V. D. Henderson, and S. G. Siegel, "Software configuration management: a tutorial", *IEEE Computer*, Jan 1979, pp. 6–14.

[Ber84] E. H. Bersoff, "Elements of software configuration management", *IEEE Trans. of Software Eng.*, Jan. 1984, pp. 79–87.

[Boe76] B. Boehm, "Software Engineering", *IEEE Transactions on Computers*, vol. C-25, no. 12, Dec. 1976.

[Boe81] B. Boehm, "Software Engineering Economics", *Prentice-Hall*, Englewood Cliffs, NJ 1981.

[Boe84] B. Boehm, "Verifying and validating software requirements and design specifications", *IEEE Software*, Jan 1984, pp. 75–88.

[Boe84a] B. Boehm, "Software engineering economics", *IEEE Tran. on Software Engg.*, Vol. SE-10, no. 1, Jan 1984, pp. 4–21.

[Boe88] B. Boehm, "A spiral model of software development and enhancement", *IEEE Computer*, May 1988, pp. 61–72.

[Boe89] B. Boehm, "Tutorial: software risk management", *IEEE Computer Society*, Washington D.C., 1989.

[Bol89] J. C. Bolot and P. Jalote, "Formal verification of programs with exceptions", *Proc. 19th Fault Tolerant Computing Symposium, FTCS-19*, Chicago, 1989, pp. 283–290.

[Boo83a] G. Booch, "Software engineering with Ada", *Benjamin/Cumminghams Publishing Company, Inc.*, 1983.

[Boo83b] G. Booch, "Object-oriented design", in *Tutorial in Software Design Techniques*, P. Freeman and A. I. Wasserman, eds, IEEE Press, 1983.

[Boo86] G. Booch, "Object-oriented development", *IEEE Tran. on Software Engg.*, Vol. SE-12, no. 2, Feb. 1986, pp. 211–222.

[Bro75] F. Brooks, "The mythical man month", *Addison-Wesley*, Reading, MA 1975.

[Cav78] J. P. Cavano and J. A. McCall, "A framework for the measurement of software quality", *Proc., ACM Software Quality Assurance Workshop*, Nov. 1978, pp. 133–139.

[Che78] E. Chen, "Program complexity and programmer productivity", *IEEE Tran. on Software Engg.*, Vol. SE-4, May 1978, pp. 187–194.

[Che79] T. E. Cheatham, G. H. Holloway and J. A. Townley, "Symbolic evaluation and the analysis of programs", *IEEE Tran. on Software Engg.*, Vol. SE-5, no. 4, July 1979.

[Cla76] L. A. Clarke, "A system to generate test data and symbolically execute programs" *IEEE Tran. on Software Engg.*, Vol. SE-2, no. 3, July 1976.

[Cri84] F. Cristian, "Correct and robust programs", *IEEE Tran. on Software Engineering*, Vol. SE-10, no. 2, March 1984.

[Dav90] A. M. Davis, "Software requirements—analysis and specification", *Prentice Hall*, 1990.

[Dem79] T. DeMarco, "Structured analysis and system specification", *Yourdon Press*, New York, 1978.

[DLS78] R. A. DeMillo, R. A. Lipton and F. G. Sayward, "Hints on test data selection: help for the practicing programmer", *IEEE Computer*, Apr. 1978, pp. 34–41.

[Dun84] R. H. Dunn, "Software defect removal", *McGraw-Hill, Inc.*, 1984.

[Eme84] T. J. Emerson, "A discriminant metric for module cohesion", *Proc. of the 7th Int. Conf. on Software Engg.*, 1984, pp. 294–303.

[Fag76] M. E. Fagan, "Design and code inspections to reduce errors in program development", *IBM System Journal*, 1976, pp. 182–211.

[Fos76] L. D. Fosdick and L. J. Osterweil, "Data flow analysis is software reliability", *ACM Computing Surveys*, vol 8, no. 3, Sep. 1978.

[Goe79] A. L. Goel and K. Okumoto, "A time dependent error detection rate model for software reliability and other performance measures", *IEEE Tran. on Reliability*, Bol. R-28, 1979, pp. 769–774.

[Goe85] A. L. Goel, "Software reliability models: assumptions, limitations, and applicability", *IEEE Tran. on Software Engg.*, Vol. SE-11, Dec. 1985, pp. 1411–1423.

[Goo75] J. Goodenough and S. L. Gerhart, "Towards a theory of test data selection", *IEEE Tran. on Software Engg.*, Vol. SE-1, 1975, pp. 156–173.

[Goo77] S. E. Goodman and S. T. Hedetniemi, "Introduction to the design and analysis of algorithms", *McGraw-Hill Inc.*, 1977.

[Gut78] J. V. Guttag and J. J. Horning, "The algebraic specifications of abstract data types", *Acta Informatica*, vol 10, 1978, pp. 27–62.

[Gut80] J. V. Guttag, "Notes on type abstraction (version 2)", *IEEE Tran. on Software Engineering*, Vol Se-6, no. 1, Jan 1980, pp. 13–23.

[Har82] W. Harrison, K. Magel, R. Kluczny, and A. DeKock, "Applying software complexity metrics to program maintenance", *IEEE Computer*, Sept. 1982, pp. 65–79.

[Hal77] M. Halstead, "Elements of software science", *Eslevier North-Holland*, New York, 1977.

[Hoa69] C. A. R. Hoare, "An axiomatic basis for computer programming", *Communications of the ACM*, vol.12, no. 3, 335–355.

[How77] W. E. Howden, "Symbolic testing and the DISSECT symbolic evaluation system", *IEEE Tran. on Software Engineering*, Vol SE-3, no. 4, July 1977. Jan 1980, pp. 13–23.

[Hut85] D. H. Hutchens and V. R. Basili, "System structure analysis: clustering with data bindings", *IEEE Transactions on Software Engineering*, Vol. SE-11, no. 8, Aug. 1985, pp. 749–757.

[Iee87] "Software Engineering Standards", *IEEE Press*, 1987.

[Inc88] D. Ince, "Software Metrics", In *Measurement for Software Control and Assurance*, eds: B. A. Kitchenham and B. Littlewood, Eslevier Applied Science, 1989.

[Ing76] F. S. Ingrass, "The unit development folder (UDF): an effective management tool for software development", In *Tutorial: Software Management*, 3rd Edition, D. J. Reifer, ed., IEEE Computer society, 1986.

[Jal87] P. Jalote, "Synthesizing implementations of abstract data types from axiomatic specifications", *Software Practice and Experience,* vol 17, no. 11, Nov. 1987, pp. 847–858.

[Jal88] P. Jalote and M. Caballero, "Automated testcase generation of abstract data types from axiomatic specifications", *Proc. COMPSAC 88,* Chicago, Oct. 1988, pp. 205–210.

[Jal89a] P. Jalote, "Functional refinement and nested objects for object-oriented design", *IEEE Transactions on Software Engineering,* Vol 15, no. 3, March 1989, pp. 264–270.

[Jal89b] P. Jalote, "Testing the completeness of specifications", *IEEE Transactions on Software Engineering,* Vol 15, no. 5, May 1989, pp. 526–531.

[Jel72] Z. Jelinski and P. Moranda, "Software reliability research", In *Statistical Computer Performance Evaluation,* W. Freiberger, Ed., New York: Academic, 1972, pp. 465–484.

[Jon78] T. C. Jones, "Measuring programming quality and productivity", *IBM Systems Journal,* vol 17, no. 1, 1978.

[Kin76] J. C. King, "Symbolic execution and program testing", *Communications of the ACM,* Vol 19, no. 7, July 1976.

[Man81] M. Mantei, "The effect of programming team structure on programming tasks", *Communications of the ACM,* Vol 24, no. 3, March 1981.

[Mcc76] T. J. McCabe, "A complexity measure", *IEEE Transactions on Software Engineering,* Vol. SE-2, no.4, Dec 76, pp. 308–320.

[Mus80] D. R. Musser, "Abstract data type specification in the AFFIRM system", *IEEE Tran. on Software Engg.,* Vol. SE-6, no. 1, Jan 1980, pp. 24–32.

[Mye77] G. Myers, "An extension to the cyclomatic measure of program complexity", *ACM SIGPLAN Notices,* Oct. 1977, pp. 61–64.

[Mye79] G. Myers, "The art of software testing", *Wiley-Interscience,* New York, 1979.

[Put78] L. H. Putnam, "A general empirical solution to the macro software sizing and estimation problem", *IEEE Tran. on Software Engg.,* July 1978, pp. 345–361.

[Ros77] D. Ross, "Structured analysis (SA): a language for communicating ideas", *IEEE Tran. on Software Engineering,* Vol SE-3, no. 1, Jan 1977.

[Rei77] D. Reichrow and E. Hershey, "PSL/PSA: A computer aided technique for structured documentation and analysis of information processing systems", *IEEE Transactions on Software Engineering,* Vol SE-3, no. 1, Jan 1977.

[Ste74] W. P. Stevens, G. J. Myers and L. Constantine, "Structured design", *IBM System Journal,* Vol. 13, no. 2, 1974.

[Wat77] C. Watson and C. Felix, "A method of programming measurement and estimation", *IBM Systems Journal,* Vol 16, no. 1, Jan. 1977.

[Wei71] G. Weinberg, "The psychology of computer programming", *Van Nostrand Reinhold,* New York, 1971.

[Woo79] M. Woodward, M. Hennell, and D. Hedley, "A measure of control flow complexity in program text", *IEEE Trans. on Software Engg.,* Vol. SE-5, Jan. 1979, pp. 45–50.

[Wir71] N. Wirth, "Program development by stepwise refinement", *Comm. of the ACM,* Vol. 14, no. 4, Apr. 1971, pp. 221–227.

[You79] E. Yourdon and L. Constantine, "Structured Design" *Prentice Hall,* Englewood Cliffs, NY, 1979.

Index